M.M.Jocelyne Fernandez-Vest, Robert D. Van Valin, Jr.
Information Structuring of Spoken Language from a Cross-linguistic Perspective

Trends in Linguistics
Studies and Monographs

Editor
Volker Gast

Editorial Board
Walter Bisang
Jan Terje Faarlund
Hans Henrich Hock
Natalia Levshina
Heiko Narrog
Matthias Schlesewsky
Amir Zeldes
Niina Ning Zhang

Editor responsible for this volume
Volker Gast

Volume 283

Information Structuring of Spoken Language from a Cross-linguistic Perspective

—

Edited by
M.M.Jocelyne Fernandez-Vest
Robert D. Van Valin, Jr.

DE GRUYTER
MOUTON

ISBN 978-3-11-057786-0
e-ISBN (PDF) 978-3-11-036875-8
e-ISBN (EPUB) 978-3-11-039335-4
ISSN 1861-4302

Library of Congress Cataloging-in-Publication Data
A CIP catalog record for this book has been applied for at the Library of Congress.

Bibliographic information published by the Deutsche Nationalbibliothek
The Deutsche Nationalbibliothek lists this publication in the Deutsche Nationalbibliografie; detailed bibliographic data are available on the Internet at http://dnb.dnb.de.

© 2016 Walter de Gruyter GmbH, Berlin/Boston
This volume is text- and page- identical with the hardback published in 2016.
Typesetting: RoyalStandard, Hong Kong
Printing and binding: CPI books GmbH, Leck
♾ Printed on acid-free paper
Printed in Germany

www.degruyter.com

Table of contents

M.M.Jocelyne Fernandez-Vest and Robert D. Van Valin, Jr.
Introduction —— 1

I Theoretical Approaches to IS

M.M.Jocelyne Fernandez-Vest
1 Detachment Linguistics and Information Grammar of Oral Languages —— 7

Jeanette K. Gundel and Nancy Hedberg
2 Reference and Cognitive Status: Scalar Inferences and Typology —— 33

Mitsuaki Shimojo
3 Saliency in Discourse and Sentence Form: Zero Anaphora and Topicalization in Japanese —— 55

Robert D. Van Valin, Jr.
4 An Overview of Information Structure in three Amazonian Languages —— 77

II IS and Spoken language

Delia Bentley, Francesco Maria Ciconte, Silvio Cruschina, Michael Ramsammy
5 Micro-variation in Information Structure: Existential Constructions in Italo-Romance —— 95

Ricardo Etxepare
6 How does Adjacency arise? Grammatical Conditions on Focus-verb Adjacency in Basque —— 121

Ritva Laury and Marja-Liisa Helasvuo
7 Detached NPs with Relative Clauses in Finnish Conversations —— 149

Dejan Matić
8 Tag Questions and Focus Markers: Evidence from Even —— 167

Victor Pan
9 Syntactic and Prosodic Marking of Contrastiveness in Oral Mandarin —— 191

Heete Sahkai
10 Demonstratives and IS in Spoken Estonian —— 211

III IS and Discourse Particles

Oleg Belyaev and Diana Forker
11 Word Order and Focus Particles in Nakh-Daghestanian Languages —— 239

Annie Montaut
12 The Discourse Particle to and Word Ordering in Hindi: from Grammar to Discourse —— 263

IV IS and Language Contacts

Fida Bizri
13 Information Structuring Strategies in Pidgin Madam —— 285

Peter Slomanson
14 New Information Structuring Processes and Morphosyntactic Change —— 305

Name index —— 327
Language index —— 332

M.M.Jocelyne Fernandez-Vest and Robert D. Van Valin, Jr.
Introduction

This book has gathered around a common project researchers who are both involved in language theories and in field linguistics. The book thus combines theory and description, and steers nevertheless a steady course: the analysis of Information Structuring (IS) of oral and spoken language corpora – with some marginal incursions into written language. Intending at bringing a fresh contribution to current debate in linguistics, the collection takes up principally two challenges. On the one hand, the perspective should not be restricted to a single theory or a single language. Several books have been published during the last decade about Information Structuring; their theoretical frame is generally limited – often the functional-generativist (e.g. Erteschik-Shir 2007, Féry, Fanselow & Krifka [eds.] 2007, López 2009); the analysis is concentrated on a single language or a pair of languages (Gómez-González 2009, Lambrecht 1994), or, when comparative, on genetically related languages (Mereu [ed.] 2009, Fiedler & Schwartz [eds.] 2010). A second challenge was precisely to investigate the Information Structuring of *spoken language*. Apart from a few already well-described languages, spoken languages have been scarcely studied from the perspective of IS, for lack of reliable corpora requiring a native speaker's knowledge of lesser-known languages. Our objective was here twofold: to engage into some exploring, innovative though tentative studies of languages little described from the point of view of syntax, prosody and IS without neglecting what we have learnt from already well-established theories on widespread languages. The explicit ambition of the book remains therefore, although it could not concern more than a sample of the world's languages, to present examples from different language families, specially non Indo-European and little described, and under varied theoretical and methodological angles, mainly: the Functional-Enunciative approach, which hypothesizes a double tripartite organization of information for both sentences and discourses; the Role and Reference Grammar approach, which investigates the role played by Information Structuring in explaining cross-linguistic differences in grammatical systems; the formal semantic approach, which gives a central role to syntax (e.g. configurational languages and their relation to truth-conditional ambiguity).

The starting point of this collection of papers was an international program coordinated 2009–2013 by M.M.Jocelyne Fernandez-Vest, *Information Structuring and Typology (ISTY): Detachment Constructions in Languages and Discourses* (CNRS – Fédération de Typologie et Universaux Linguistiques). An International

Workshop was organized in collaboration with Robert D. Van Valin Jr, coordinator of the Research group *Syntax, typology and information structure* (Max Planck Institute for Psycholinguistics, Nijmegen, 2008–2014) at the 2011 LSA Linguistic Institute, Boulder, Colorado: *Information Structure and Spoken Language: Cross-Linguistic Comparative Studies*. The goal of this workshop was to analyze and compare some of the main processes involved in Information Structuring in several typologically different languages (Indo-European, Finno-Ugric and Uralic, Amerindian, Austronesian, Indonesian, Semitic languages; Basque, Thai, Vietnamese) and with distinct theoretical and methodological approaches. A second International Workshop, arranged in 2012 at the MPI Nijmegen (*Categories of Information Structure across Languages*) also gathered participants from the two teams.

The book presently edited results from a first selection of papers, achieved in 2012 by an international scientific committee, including the editors and two members of the initial team: 40% of the LSA Workshop papers have been completed by contributions from specialists of Information Structure in other languages (Chinese, Even, Italo-Romance, Japanese, Nakh-Daghestanian...), fourteen chapters in all. Four main topics, distributed into four separate Sections, have been distinguished: Theoretical Approaches to IS; IS and Spoken Language; IS and Discourse Particles; IS and Language Contacts.

Section I, **Theoretical approaches to Information Structure**, includes four contributions. Centered on the role of *Detachment Constructions* for IS and sentence combining, M.M. Jocelyne Fernandez-Vest's chapter extends to spoken French a functional-enunciative model based on oral Uralic languages and synthetizes research paths opened by the author's previous publications (2015 *et passim*). Jeanette Gundel and Nancy Hedberg, continuing a discussion raised by their preceding publications on the *Givenness Hierarchy* (Gundel, Hedberg and Zacharski 1993, 2012), update the theory and discuss some of its typological predictions. Mitsuaki Shimojo's chapter combines Centering Theory with Role and Reference Grammar (Van Valin 2005) for an empirical study of *topicalization in Japanese narrative discourse*. Robert Van Valin's chapter applies the Role and Reference Grammar approach to the analysis of information structure to three unrelated and typologically distinct Amazonian languages.

Section II contains six papers dealing with the central topic of the book, **Information Structure of Spoken language**, in typologically different languages. Delia Bentley, Francesco Maria Ciconte, Silvio Cruschina and Michael Ramsammy analyze *the encoding of IS in twenty Italo-Romance dialects* and identify three principal patterns of micro-variation. Ricardo Etxepare studies the *Grammatical conditions on focus-verb adjacency in Basque*: he argues against the traditional view that the adjency relation between the focus and the finite verbal complex reflects a configurational relation and shows that the adjacency requirement is not an obligatory condition. Ritva Laury and Marja-Liisa Helasvuo's chapter shows with a methodology of conversation analysis that *Finnish Detached NPs and relative clauses* are responsive to local contingencies: the direction of continuation of reference is relevant for their form and function and how they are treated in the interaction. Dejan Matić investigates in Tompo Even corpora how *Question tags* can be the source of morphological focus markers; he hypothesizes that this grammaticalization path might be common to other languages. Victor Pan discusses the labor division between *Syntactic and prosodic marking of IS in oral Mandarin Chinese* and claims that prosody is activated as "repair strategy" when syntax fails to mark a contrastive element. Heete Sahkai's study of *Demonstratives and IS in spoken Estonian* insists on adnominal demonstratives functioning as focus- and topic-markers and the cross-linguistic tendency of spoken language to recruit for focus-marking particle-like elements.

The two chapters of Section III concentrate on **Discourse Particles** as essential devices of Information Structuring in spoken discourse. Oleg Belyaev and Diana Forker present a novel analysis of *Focus Particles in Nakh-Daghestanian Languages*, based on their field work in Daghestan: they reject the usual partition into "topic" vs. "focus" particles and claim that most of the functions of these particles are equally compatible with topical and focal interpretations of their hosts. Annie Montaut explains *The Discourse Particle* **to** *in Hindi*, previously described as covering two different units (conjunction and emphatic particle), as the result of a common enunciative operation with two distinct scopes: restrictive scope as a Theme marker, and wider scope as an argumentative Discourse Particle.

Section IV tackles with two chapters dedicated to two different multilingual situations the still scarcely investigated topic of **Information Structuring and Language contacts**. Fida Bizri studies *IS strategies in Pidgin Madam discourse*, that is in the conversational and narrative corpora of a new pidgin based on Arabic: the correlation between intonational patterns, word order and grammaticalized lexemes as assertive markers shed an interesting light on IS within exolingual communication. Peter Slomanson's chapter on *New Information Structuring processes and morphosyntactic change* in Sri Lankan Malay, a contact language spoken by an historically bilingual population, analyzes the transfer of information-structuring conventions involving "detachment", used as a cover term for movement to the sentence periphery.

References

Erteschik-Shir, Nomi. 2007. *Information structure. The syntax-discourse interface* (Oxford Surveys in syntax and morphology). Oxford: Oxford University Press.

Fernandez-Vest, M.M.Jocelyne. 1987 [1984]. *La Finlande trilingue. 1. Le discours des Sames. Oralité, contrastes, énonciation.* Préface de Claude Hagège. Paris: Didier Erudition.

Fernandez-Vest, M.M.Jocelyne. 2015. *Detachments for Cohesion – Toward an Information Grammar of Oral Languages* (Empirical Approaches to Language Typology, EALT 56). Berlin & Boston: De Gruyter Mouton, XVI–290 p.

Féry, Caroline, Gisbert Fanselow and Manfred Krifka (eds.). 2007. *The Notions of Information Structure. Interdisciplinary Studies on Information Structure* (Working Papers of the SFB 632, 6). Potsdam: Universitätsverlag Potsdam.

Fiedler, Ines & Anne Schwartz (eds.). 2010. *The expression of Information Structure. A documentation of its diversity across Africa* (Typological Studies in Language 91). Amsterdam: John Benjamins.

Gómez González, María de los Ángeles. 2000. *The Theme-Topic interface. Evidence from English* (Pragmatics and Beyond 71). Amsterdam: John Benjamins.

Gundel, Jeanette K., Nancy Hedberg and Ron Zacharski. 1993. Cognitive status and the form of referring expressions in discourse. *Language* 69. 274–307.

Gundel, Jeanette K., Nancy Hedberg and Ron Zacharski. 2012. Underspecification of cognitive status in reference production: Some empirical predictions. *Topics in Cognitive Science (TopiCS)* 4(2). 249–268.

Lambrecht, Knud. 1994. *Information Structure and sentence form. Topic, focus and the mental representations of discourse referents.* Cambridge: Cambridge University Press.

López, Luis. 2009. *A derivational syntax for information structure* (Oxford Studies in thoretical linguistics). Oxford: Oxford University Press.

Mereu, Lunella (ed.). *Information structure and its interfaces* (Interface explorations 19). Berlin: Mouton de Gruyter.

Miller, Jim and Regina Weinert. 2009 [1998]. *Spontaneous spoken language* (Oxford Linguistics). Oxford: Oxford University Press.

Van Valin, Robert. 2005. *Exploring the syntax-semantics interface.* Cambridge: Cambridge University Press.

I Theoretical Approaches to IS

M.M.Jocelyne Fernandez-Vest
1 Detachment Linguistics and Information Grammar of Oral Languages

Abstract: This chapter concentrates on three arguments: 1/ An ambitious semantics of human language should take into account two kinds of typologies: i) discourse typology, based on criteria of genre / context / relations between interlocutors; ii) language typology, apt to explain what kind of ressources are mobilized in individual linguistic systems for building meaningful constructions. 2/ In order to increase their relevance regarding language use, word order studies should replace the analysis of "neutral" sentences with that of dialogic utterances taken from various discourse genres. The methodology, developed from the study of some Samic and Finnic languages still prototypical of pure orality, lays stress on Answers (A) as primary elements of Information Structuring. A short rhematic A, taken as the Minimal Communicative Utterance, is in impromptu speech the pivot of 2 binary information strategies involving Initial and Final Detachments, Theme-Rheme and Rheme-Mneme respectively. With examples borrowed from different discourse genres, I will claim that a typology of Question-Answer pairs not only permits to tackle //context / co-text / sentence combining//, but can challenge the traditional word order classifications. A research question remains open: if the method is extended to describing typologically the information structuring beyond short utterances, can detachment constructions be used for evaluating the degree of orality of a text?

Note: This chapter is a synthesis of the PhD seminars I have conducted about Information Structuring and related subjects in diverse universities (Universités René-Descartes, Paris V; Ecole Pratique des Hautes Etudes, EPHE; Paris-Sorbonne, Paris IV; and particularly Sorbonne Nouvelle, Paris III) after my Doctorat d'Etat (1984). It would be impossible to thank all the PhD students who have helped me to progress from field to theory, or all the participants in the CNRS-Federation Typologie et Universaux Linguistiques' international project ISTY (*Information Structuring and Typology*, http://www.typologie.cnrs.fr/spip.php?rubrique48) with whom 8 Workshops were arranged between 2008 and 2012 (see LSA 2011, Boulder, https://verbs.colorado.edu/LSA2011/workshops/WS1.html; http://infostructuring.wikidot.com/, and SLE 2012, Stockholm, http://www.sle2012.eu/listofworkshops).

M.M.Jocelyne Fernandez-Vest, CNRS-LACITO (UMR 7107) and Université Sorbonne Nouvelle – Paris III

1 Introduction

The goal of this chapter is, as announced in the abstract above, two-fold:

(i) to scrutinize from a functional and typological perspective the pre- and post-rhematic detached constructions that reflect the natural segmentation of spoken language, and to theorize about their status within the process of Information Structuring (IS);
(ii) to analyze the Initial Detachments (ID) and specifically the Final Detachments (FD) collected from impromptu conversations in some Indo-European languages (mainly French) compared with two Finno-Ugric languages (Northern Sami and Finnish). While doing so, I intend to argue in favor of a conception of Information Structuring that takes into account the situation and co-text, and also questions the underlying cognitive processes. This implies some reflection about what we mean by "typology".

If the descriptive analysis of oral and spoken data lays claims toward theorization, it must in my view distinguish two kinds of typologies:

1/ *discourse typology*, which defines cross-linguistically different types of discourse (also called "genres", even though the word is ambiguous) and language-internally different registers;
2/ *language typology*, which explains, through comparing the structural systems of individual languages, what kind of resources (phonological, morpho-syntactic, lexical) are mobilized for building oral meaning.

One has good reasons to consider that the first kind of typology is a prerequisite for the second one, in spite of the prominent place occupied nowadays in language science by the second one.

Within the scope of the present chapter, I shall limit myself mainly to two prototypical forms of oral discourse: *impromptu speech* on the one hand and *argumentative speech* on the other, while some subcategories may be referred to sporadically.

2 Information Structuring of oral discourse

Enunciation theories (Benveniste 1966–74, Kerbrat-Orecchioni 2009 among others) have shown that the main characteristic of oral exchange is the anchoring of the speech. Orality is characterized by a situational dependency resulting from the co-presence of interlocutors: defining is thus the unavoidable contextualization of oral and spoken languages (Fernandez-Vest 1987: 217–230, 1994: 118–119; Hagège 1986, 1993: 3–4). Some recurrent language features can be attributed to this oral motivation: an oral exchange is marked by an improvised construction (lack of time for planning) and a strong redundancy necessary for decoding. Conversely, the typological evolution of an orally transmitted language that acquires the status of a written language proves its gradual "oral demotivation" (see Section 4.3.). Paradoxically enough, after establishing the solid anchoring of speech to the enunciative situation, research centered on orality, crossed with discourse situations and with language typology, cannot ignore the Detached Constructions. The term "dislocation", popularized by early generative studies and integrated into the "cartographic" approach initiated by Rizzi (1997), is therefore inadequate

> [Left dislocation?] This metaphor is entirely inappropriate for the analysis of spontaneous spoken language in which the principal idea is that speakers produce a sequence of short constituents which are interlinked by deixis and by discourse relations. (Miller & Weinert 2009 [1997]: 238)

I totally agree with this remark.

2.1 Detachment Constructions[1]

The term "detachment construction" is not so well established in the English-speaking linguistic world, but one should notice that Lambrecht's book from 1994, which remains one of the references most regularly quoted by Information Structuring experts, reserves an entire section to DETACHMENT CONSTRUCTIONS:

> From a certain degree of pragmatic accessibility on, it is possible in many languages to code a not yet active topic referent in the form of a lexical noun phrase which is placed in a syntactically autonomous or "detached" position to the left or, less commonly, to the right of the clause which contains the propositional information about the topic referent. (Lambrecht 1994: 181)

I have constantly since I defended my first thesis (Fernandez-Vest 1977 [1982]) rejected the term "dislocation" as inferred from the exclusive observation of a standardized written register's short utterances. Detachment Constructions

---

[1] Abbreviations: DECS = Detachment Constructions, DIP = Discourse Particle, FD = Final Detachment, ID = Initial Detachment, IS = Information Structure/Structuring, MCU = Minimal Communicative Uttterance; Mn = Mneme/mnematic, Rh = Rheme/rhematic, Th = Theme/thematic; En = English, Fi = Finnish, Fr = French, Sa = Sami; ACC = accusative, ADESS = adessive, ELAT = elative, GEN = genitive, NOM = nominative, PART = partitive.

(DECs) is what I will look at in the following sections, even though I do not exclude a comparison of the results of this analysis with those of other theories using a different terminology.

Detachment Constructions have been studied mainly within two theoretical frameworks: Information Structuring and Detachment Linguistics (see Fernandez-Vest 2015: 15–22 and references therein). Information Structuring (IS) theories were renewed under this label from the 1980s in American linguistics after a long tradition of European Theme-Rheme studies promoted specially by the Prague School functionalists. As for Detachments, IS theories have concentrated on the "left periphery" but the "right periphery" has recently got more attention. Detachment Linguistics was initiated by French syntacticians – who tried to characterize "detachment" with stylistic aims – distinct from "apposition". It has developed rapidly after Bonnard's encyclopedia article (1972), reinforced by diachronic works that invalidated the hypothesis of a transformed structure: "Neither on the theoretical nor on the psycholinguistic level can that label of 'detachment' be used for concluding too hastily that there has been a transformation, a dislocation, of a basic construction" (Combettes 1998: 10 [translation mine]). Enriched with dimensions of prosody and cognition, this syntactic notion, detachment, has spread gradually to other Romance studies. The collective volume published in 2009 after an international conference presents a synthesis of *Les linguistiques du détachement*. The editors emphasize the specific position of their domain, at the interface between syntax and discourse: "The question of detachment constructions is notably related to the organization of information (…) and to the communicative and interactional value of the utterances. It participates thereby in the problem set of discourse coherence". (Apothéloz, Combettes & Neveu (eds.) 2009: 1 [translation mine]). My personal conception is more radical than the editors', and it goes beyond the choices made by the majority of the book's authors: I identify the Detachment Constructions as a core device of Information Structuring, and I want to apply this analysis to the clause and sentence constituents of whole texts (Fernandez-Vest 2009b and 6.2. below).

2.3 Information Structuring from a textual perspective

Adopting, at an early stage, the principle of a triple organization of the utterance – recognized by several language theoreticians (Pierce 1978, Daneš 1974, Hagège 1993 among others) – with a textual and interactional definition of the Theme/Topic ("what is spoken about") and Rheme/Focus ("what is said about it"), I have dedicated several of my corpus studies to the least investigated element, the third one, Mneme in my terminology. This Post-Rheme is characterized by formal properties (generally a flat intonation) and semantic values (e.g. reference to some supposedly shared knowledge – Fernandez-Vest 1994: 197–200). Such a conception meets the definition of Lambrecht's Antitopic (1994: 184–191) but differs from it as two essential points: IS is relevant at the enunciative level, and should also be analyzed beyond the sentence.

Doubly tripartite (3 levels – enunciative, morphosyntactic, distributional semantic –, 3 enunciative constituents), this methodology has served to bring out two basic strategies[2]

- the *Binary strategy 1* (Theme – Rheme), with a 1st element frequently detached (Initial Detachment, ID)
- and the *Binary strategy 2* (Rheme – Mneme), where the 2nd constituent is detached (Final Detachment, FD). It is a typical construction for Impromptu Speech, mostly absent from written style.

A/ *Binary strategy 1* (Th – Rh)
(1) [The guard tries to prevent Captain Haddock from opening the window]
Les fenêtres [ID], *elles ne s'ouvrent pas, señor.*
'The windows [ID], they do not open, señor.'
(Hergé 1976: 17, *Tintin et les Picaros*; 1980)

B/ *Binary strategy 2* (Rh – Mn)
(2) [Captain Haddock sees that the guard brandishes his pistol]
– *Ça part vite, ces machins-là!* [FD]
it goes off quickly, these things
translated 'These things have a habit of going off!'
(Hergé 1976: 17, *Tintin et les Picaros*; 1980)

The published translation of example (2) shows a tendency observed cross-linguistically: Binary strategy 1 is more generally accepted in the world's languages than Binary strategy 2.

If we now combine these binary strategies, we get a figure that is very recurrent in oral and spoken languages:

A/ + B/ = C/ *Circular cohesion* (Fernandez-Vest 1995, 2009b) – see 3.2. below.

---

[2] As a counterpart to the broadly spread Anglo-American terminology (topic – focus), I have kept using Theme – Rheme while elaborating a theoretic frame since my first field experiments. Indebted to the Prague School's textualist methodology, I am also aware of the European source of theme-rheme theories, long before the inventive label of "IS" (see Enkvist 1976, chap. 5; Newmeyer 2001).

Analyzing Initial Detachments and Final Detachments, I allow myself to use as synonyms, whenever a unitary formal description is not at stake, the detachment processes and their linguistic products (detached Theme and Mneme respectively). The analysis of these binary strategies would not be possible without the methodological stabilization of the enunciative pivot around which they are potentially articulated. Viewed from this perspective, a Minimal Communicative Utterance (MCU) is shaped by the only constituent necessary for an utterance to exist, i.e. the Rheme, which, in ordinary conversations, is often, but not obligatorily, a short Answer, morphosyntactically variable, marked in the languages where it has been studied by a terminal intonation, falling in French, which I signal arbitrarily with a falling arrow ↓, ex.[3].

(3) Q. – *Tu comprends ?*
 'Do you understand?'
 A. – *Oui* ↓, or – *Oui / je comprends* ↓
 'Yes ↓', or 'Yes / I understand ↓' ('I do ↓')

This analysis can be applied to the Information Structuring of dialogic pairs, but also to the circular cohesion brought about, even in monologic discourse, by the combination of the two binary strategies (see ex. (12)). A further domain of research is the Information Structuring of complex sentences, with each clause considered an enunciative constituent – see Section 5 below.

3 Detachment Constructions in dialogue

It is broadly recognized today that, for establishing from a typological perspective an information grammar of oral or spoken languages, the study of dialogues is indeed a prerequisite (see Fernandez-Vest 2012b).

Why should an Information Structuring theory be based on Answers?

3.1 The Answer as Minimal Communicative Utterance

The word "dialogue" often refers to the Question-Answer pair, that has mostly been studied in this order, partly for methodological reasons. The Question is

---

[3] The use of ↑ ↓ → arrows for characterizing the Theme, Rheme and Mneme implies an oversimplification. Yet, disregarding critics from phoneticians and experimental phonologists, I insist using them as having an acoustic reality, distinctly perceived by a native speaker.

characterized by easily spotted morphological and syntactical properties, that, in spite of some differences, have much in common in all the languages where they have been studied: the inventory includes interrogative particles, reverse word order, special constructions (e.g. French "est-ce que?"), a specific intonation. Many IS theoreticians have given particular importance to the analogy between Question-Answer pairs and the assumed "focus" (/Rheme) meaning in the establishment of the linguistic category of focus. The Question-Answer test as the focus-triggering context, that is the widespread practice of using the short-hand definition of focus as "what is asked about" (launched by Halliday 1967: 207 ff.) is discussed in a recent critical article, which concludes:

> This procedure is fallacious (...): it presupposes that a pragmatic effect – the regular appearance of a structure in certain contexts – necessarily follows from the existence of a primitive category (...), disregarding the possibility that this effect can have multiple causes and neglecting the differences that may exist between structures that display the same effect. (Matić & Wedgwood 2013: 134)

Although not disregarding the Q–A test, my method proceeds in the reverse order: starting from a Minimal Communicative Utterance, that is often an Answer (see below), I will investigate its extensions and what they imply for Information Structuring in a dialogic exchange. From the point of view of IS theory, and particularly of Detachment Constructions, the Answer is far more interesting than the Question. Whereas the Question generally induces an Answer (the absence of which, felt abnormal, can lead to diverse interpretations), a Minimal Communicative Utterance can occur without being preceded by a linguistic Question, as a reaction or comment to the present situation of enunciation, in which case it is still a response, ex. in French

(4) [At the dinner table, a mother to her child]
 – Fr. *Ton verre* ↓
 'Your glass.'

Whatever the exact meaning of (4) depending on the actual context (the mother has noticed that the glass is on the verge of falling down, or she reminds that a glass has been discussed, that should be fetched from the bedroom, etc.), this utterance is a clear Rheme, which can be seen as a sub-category of Answer, inferred by the context or situation (Fernandez-Vest 2004). The idea of considering Answers as primary units essential for the functioning and understanding of oral exchanges, and consequently of basing on them an Information Structuring theory, emerged from the field corpora I first collected

1/ An interlanguage, Sami Finnish, ex.[4].

(5) Q. – *Oli/ko hän sun opettaja?*
'Was (+ interrog. *-ko*) he your teacher?'
A. – *Oli* ↓
'Was'. i.e. 'Yes'.
(Fernandez-Vest 1982: 233)

Note that the Answer of (5), that is a Minimal Communicative Utter- ance at the enunciative level both in Finnish and in English, involves a different constituent at the morphosyntactic level. Both Questions contain an existential verb, but whereas in Finnish the repetition of the verb is, according to grammars, the most correct minimal A to a total Q, in English this repetition would be an addition, that transforms the MCU into a binary utterance (Rh–Mn) : – Yes ↓ he was →

2/ An *orally transmitted language, Northern Sami* (henceforth Sami), where the most striking observation was, beside the omnipresence of Discourse Particles [DIPs] and the reverse proportion of syntactic vs. iconic cohesion (according to the degree of schooling and written praxis of the informants), the high proportion of Final Detachments in the speech of old Sami. FDs were found both in simple Answers (Rheme – Mneme), and in "Multiple Answers"[5], ex.

(6) [And your parents' house was made of...?]
– *Hirsa .... hirsavisti* =>> *Guđa dumá aso* [Rh] *dat hirssat* [FD-Mn].
'Log .... a log-hut =>> Six thumbs thick [Rh] the logs [FD-Mn].'
(Fernandez-Vest 1987: 552)

This type of comment or explanation as a second utterance might, in another theoretical frame, be considered simply as an independent declarative utterance – would not it be for the frequency of such rapid chained utterances, integrated

---

4 In line with earlier choices (Fernandez-Vest 1987, 2005), my system of transcription includes utterances delimited by a capital letter at the beginning and a full stop at the end. Two types of pauses are indicated (short, less than 3 seconds,.., or longer,....). Overlapping turn segments are framed by 2 equals signs (=...=). "Interlanguage" (Finnish spoken by (partly) bilingual Sami) is used with a functional value, slightly different from that of second language acquisition studies.
5 Part of the typology of Qs and As originally built upon a Sami corpus (Fernandez-Vest 1987: 443–460), Multiple Answers appear as sequences of utterances linked by a quick tempo (double arrow =>>).

into an Answer-unit, that seem to be typical of impromptu dialogue, in connection with Detachment Constructions.

3.2 DECs and Circular cohesion

Let us now turn to spoken French, where a systematic inquiry into the dialogic functions of the two Binary strategies has been conducted. Some examples, slightly modified from my corpus of Southwestern French (from Bordeaux and Bassin d'Arcachon), analyzed previously from the point of view of cognitive processes underlying Information Structuring (Fernandez-Vest 1995), illustrate how a Question can be answered with either of the two Binary strategies:

(7) [At an old people's home, a resident (F2) to her visitor: "I get visits from my grandchildren every day!"]
 Q. – F1 *Le lundi / c'est qui?*
 'On Mondays / who is it?'

(7a) A. – F2 *Le lundi* ↑ *c'est Josette* ↓
 'On Mondays   /   it is Josette.'   [Th – Rh] Binary 1

or

(7b) A. – F2 *C'est Josette* ↓ *le lundi* →
 'It is Josette   /   on Mondays.' [Rh – Mn] Binary 2

Circular cohesion, which combines those two strategies, occurs frequently in a single speech turn (Th – Rh – Mn), but even in two successive utterances, in order to refute a potential implication (8a), or to explicitly express a contrast (8b):

(8) Q. – F1 *C'est Josette / le lundi?*
 'It is Josette / on Mondays?'
 A. – F2 *Oui / lundi* ↑ *c'est Josette* ↓
 'Yes / (on) Mondays / it is Josette.'

+(8a) A. – F2 *C'est pas Riquet* ↓ *le lundi* →
 'It is not Riquet / on Mondays.'

or

+(8b) A. - F2 *Le mardi* ↓ *c'est Riquet* →
'On Tuesdays / it is Riquet.'

Dialogic collaboration ("co-uttering") also produces circular cohesion in pairs of turns:

(9)   – F1 *Et les plus jeunes* ↑ *vous les voyez jamais* ↓
– F2 *Jamais* ↓ *les petits* →

F1 'And the younger ones / you never see them.'
F2 'Never / the small ones.'

Another text excerpt will serve as illustration. It is taken from a special corpus[6] of Southern French (Montpellier): street dialogues about itineraries, exchanges between two investigators (E1, E2) and passers-by (Informants, I1, I2) about the way to get to a church named *Saint-Roch*.

Looking for Detachment Constructions in these exchanges, I verified my initial hypothesis (a low proportion of Minimal Communicative Utterances vs. a higher proportion of Answers repeating the thematic data of the Question – possibly with a different enunciative status), but I was particularly puzzled by the Mnemes. At first sight, Mnemes were indeed numerous, but only a very low proportion of them (1–2%) could be analyzed within a short utterance. The sole occurrences of this type were the ones where the message was co-built, co-produced by two or three speakers. In other words, this Mneme, if it could constitute with the Rheme a Binary strategy 2 in a single turn *stricto sensu*, was obviously inserted into a textual strategy of dialogic meaning construction. Let us take first one of the few examples of Mnemes as utterance internal elements in a sequence of speech turns (utterances, U)

(10) U1. – E2 *Excusez-nous / l'église Saint-Roch s'il vous plaît?*
'Excuse-us / Saint-Roch church please?'

U2. – I1 *L'église?*
'The church?'

U3. – E2 *L'église Saint-Roch.*
'Saint-Roch Church.'

---

6 Collected by the Praxiling research group (UMR 5267, CNRS & Université Montpellier 3), and studied within a collective project from different angles (syntax, pragmatics, conversation analysis).

U4. – I2 *L'ÉGLISE SAINT-ROCH.*
'SAINT-ROCH CHURCH.'

U5. – I1 *Ah oui c'est par là-bas* (gesture) / <u>*l'église Saint-Roch*</u> [FD-Mn].
'Oh yes it's over there (gesture) / <u>Saint-Roch church</u> [FD-Mn].'

In this short exchange, the enunciative status of the main topic changes twice: first uttered as a Theme – simply thematized because the Question is elliptic, but detached if one replaces the politeness formula with a complete clause (*L'église Saint-Roch / on y va comment?* 'Saint-Roch church / how does one get there?'], it turns into a Rheme in E2's Answer, repeated with emphasis by I2. In the speech turn 5, it is a Mneme, that, following a Rheme clarified by an orienting gesture, echoes the Theme of 1. Well identified as an internal Mneme of 5., this Final Detachment thus bounds the dialogic text within a figure of circular cohesion co-constructed by the three participants of the exchange.

Such a corpus of spontaneous exchanges recorded in the street also contains lexical variants that partially blur the profile of the enunciative constituents: (10) is followed by a monologic development, which finishes with a complete subordinate clause, achieved with a flat intonation as a variant of the elliptic preposition phrase found in some other final utterances (*pour Saint-Roch* 'for Saint-Roch' or *pour l'église* 'for the church').

(11) [– E2 So I just turn to the first one there?]
– I2 *Oui.* =>> *Mais i vous faut monter (…) et après vous la voyez. I faut partir à gauche et puis i faut / remonter un peu /* <u>*pour trouver l'église*</u> [FD].

'Yes. =>> But you must go up (…) and then you see it. You must go to the left and then you must / go up a little / <u>in order to find the church</u> [FD].'
(other examples in Fernandez-Vest 2007, and 2015: 182–188)

The main results of this study were thus the following:

1. The *textual* function of Mnemes was to insure a closed cohesion of the entire dialogue exchange, as a final echo to the initial Theme (explicitely expressed or implicitly referred to), a Theme several times changed meanwhile into a Rheme, either nominal or gestual.
2. The *interactive semantic* function of the Mneme was to confirm the identity of the goal of the described itinerary – a device for disambiguing after a longer Answer (explanation or comment) of monological type.

In conclusion, two sub-questions arise:

1/ Is circular cohesion restricted to Detachment Constructions?

Certainly not. This cohesion device, repeating with a rhythmic pattern made up of two predications (often a subordination of paratactic type), the second of which repeats the constituents of the first one in a reverse order, also occurs in oral tradition corpora. Circular cohesion, although it rarely achieves a formal perfection (because of lexical variation and/or syntactic truncating) is more effective than a simple iconic cohesion for highlighting the informational hierarchy. This circular pattern, which closes a longer sequence through permuting enunciative constituents, has however a privileged relation with Detachment Constructions (Fernandez-Vest 1994: 125–126).

2/ Is the figure /Detachment Constructions + Circular cohesion/ restricted to Question-Answer pairs?

Certainly not. As a reaction to monological structuralism, Linguis- tics is today excessively concentrated on dialogues. But monological parts must be recognized as constitutive parts of dialogues (see life stories as digressions within interviews), and the role of Detachment Constructions is not identical in both parts, as many examples of internal contrastivity can show (see for Finnish ex. (13)). An excerpt from the already mentioned corpus of Southwestern French illustrates how the DECs, building a circular cohesion, organize and clarify around its leading topic (a stepladder) an anecdote which would otherwise suffer by the relative confusion of impromptu speech:

(12) [– Hasn't your husband had a problem with a stepladder?]
– *OUI! Alors il est tombé / un jour il a voulu monter <u>sur un escabeau</u>* [Rh].
Et pis il avait pas vu que <u>l'escabeau</u> [ID-Th] *il avait pas la corde! Tu sais / on met une ficelle (– Ah!) pour pas que ça s'ouvre / <u>l'escabeau</u>* [FD-Mn].

'YES! You see he fell / one day he wanted to climb <u>on a stepladder</u> [Rh]. And then he had not seen that <u>the stepladder</u> [ID-Th] it did not have the rope! You know / they put a string (– Oh!) for that it doesn't open / <u>the stepladder</u> [FD-Mn].'

This organization can be explained by the cognitive dimension of speech: the successive components of the story are activated by different kinds of (working, long term…) memory. Resuming a referent first stated as a Rheme (*un escabeau*), the Initial Detachment of the third utterance does not result from the transformation of an originally linked syntactic structure but, on the contrary, from the adjustment of the predication clause to the Theme. Even though neither the identity nor the localization of the main topic are questioned, the functioning of the Final Detachment is rather similar to that of example (10): it closes this excerpt of the narrative and disambiguates the concrete referent of a neutral pronoun after an unclear referring to a pretendedly general practice about stepladders (Fernandez-Vest 1995).

4 DECs and internal contrastivity

Following the terminology I adopted in the early stages of my project, the term "internal contrastivity" will refer to two types of language variations: 1/ language register; 2/ discourse typology. Both have a general cross-linguistic basis, but they will be applied here to a few language-internal observations. The conditions of production of oral discourse are core criteria for drawing up an inventory of the defining criteria of Impromptu Speech, as a prototype of natural spoken language. Impromptu Speech is regulated by the necessity of production in real time: the quantity of information must be limited in each sentence and clause. The syntax is "unintegrated", fragmented into successive stages. Several attempts have been made at establishing a correlation between grammatical categories and text types (Biber 1988, Enkvist 1982, Fernandez-Vest 1994: 117–172). Unfortunately, in the majority of studies, Detachment Constructions are reduced to referential Initial Detachments, i.e. in practice NPs (see for English Biber, Johansson, Leech, Conrad & Finegan 1999). My point here will be to suggest that, if one includes (both) Detachment Constructions as an essential parameter, the correlation between enunciative categories and text types can be used for evaluating the degree of oral vs. written register.

4.1 Language registers: Oral vs. written

A speech situation is, by definition, unique and non-replicable, which explains why comparing the oral and written versions of a discourse/text word for word is not an easy task: the mechanisms of reformulation from one register to the other remain poorly investigated, in spite of many attempts to theorize the relations oral-written in English and a few other European languages (Biber 1988, Miller & Fernandez-Vest 2006).

4.1.1 Oralized written texts

If one takes for example a scientific paper about Automatic Translation, one notices that the lecturer, standing in front of the audience, tries to constantly adapt his talk to his hearers, which results into a difference of length: the oral presentation is about 30% longer than the final publication, 12 lines of transcribed text instead of 4 lines of edited text before reaching the same conclusion. What about Detachment Constructions? The talk does not use a single Final Detachment, but a new Initial Detachment occurs at the beginning of each longer utterance, thus achieving a sequential thematic distribution of all topics (the difficulty, the implicitness, the paradox…) – concentrated into two sentences in the written version. In this scientific text, there are 100% more Detachment Constructions in the oral presentation than in the published text (0 DECs!), and all of them are Initial Detachments (Fernandez-Vest 1994: 143–158, 2015: 108–112)[7].

4.1.2 Edited conversations

Yet another half-experimental situation for studying the relation /oral- written/ is the comparison of two versions of a collection of Finnish artists' private interviews. The introduction of the book published by the Finnish Literature Society (SKS) proclaims its close faithfulness to the face-to-face conversations recorded, but the systematicity of the changes (/corrections) achieved in the edited text testify to an educated native speaker's conception of how an informal style should be offered to book-readers. Although not impromptu style in a strict meaning, subjectivity is vivid in the oral formulation of "Creative processes", and Final Detachments are regularly put in charge of avoiding possible misunderstandings:

(13) [– Doesn't the creativity process evolve with time?]
 [ORAL] – *Kyl siin varmasti vähän eri eri eri mekanismi / mekanismi on hiukan ehkä muuttunut / tän* [GEN.SG] *luovan* [GEN.SG] / *prosessin* [GEN.SG] / *mekanismi* [NOM.SG].

 'Yes there surely a little diff different mechanism / the mechanism has slightly maybe changed / of this creative / process / the mechanism.'

---

[7] Another approach of the comparison /oral-written/ consists in bringing together an argumentative text and its oral commentaries, or discussions about it: DECs are most generally absent from the published text, but reappear in the authentic dialogic exchanges (Fernandez-Vest 2015: 113–123).

[WRITTEN] – *Luulisin myös luovan* [GEN.SG] *prosessin* [GEN.SG] *mekanismin* [ACC.SG] *iän mukana muuttuneen* [PAST.PART ACC.SG]
'I would also believe that the mechanism of the creative process along with age has changed.'

In the edited version, a clear Question is followed by a clear Answer – a verb of opinion followed by a completive participial clause, a Non-Finite Construction (Fi. *lauseenvastike*, generally considered as typical of written style) that integrates syntactically the Final Detachment of the oral version.

In the oral version (my transcription), the proportion of Initial Detachments and Final Detachments is balanced, due to the long monologic parts (more than 70% ID for less than 30% FD). The dialogic parts have a reversed proportion of ID (less than 20%), and FD (more than 80%). But in the edited corpus, Initial Detachments are very rare (around 0,5% of the Themes), and Final Detachments don't exist (Fernandez-Vest 2006: 185–191, 2015: 123–127).

4.2 Type of discourse

4.2.1 Everyday conversation

Impromptu Speech can be defined in terms of context (situational features), intratextual features (specific syntax, types of reference) or discourse production (processual, with memory limitations). The degree of improvisation can be evaluated through a number of parameters (degree of preparation, of macro-structural fixity...); the inventory of certain features (visibility, familiarity, instantaneousness of the feed-back, empathy...) allows us to situate the discourse between the two poles of a scale //dyad vs. talk// (Enkvist 1976, 1982).

Examples will be taken again from my Southwestern French corpus. Detachments are found in over 80% of the utterances – nearly equally in Questions and Answers[8].

– *Initial Detachment*

Logically, Initial Detachment occurs regularly as the first NP of the Questions: it introduces "old" Themes directly connected with the preceding utterances (– *Mais ce poisson* [ID] / *c'est pas lui qui allait le pêcher?* 'But that fish [ID] /

---

[8] Only the first utterance (U1, U2...) of a series of speech turns is numbered. Transcription system: see Note 4.

didn't he go himself to fish it?), as well as, after a short break, Themes that are apparently new but actually related to the context of the conversation. Ex.:

(14) – F1 *Et alors ces huîtres* [ID] / *ya plus de maladies là / maintenant?*

– F1 'And what about these oysters [ID] / is there no sickness there / now?'

One notices in this colloquial exchange the use of spatio-temporal deictics (*ces, là, maintenant*) that neutralize the impression of newness of the Theme (oysters had not been mentioned before) through anchoring it implicitely into a local problem that has recently got a lot of media attention (the sale of oysters has been officially forbidden because of water pollution).

The function of Initial Detachments is not limited to Questions. They play an important role in the monological developments that complete short Answers:

(15) – F2 *Non non. La pêche* [ID] / *c'était surtout Arcachon (...). Et ici* [ID] *c'était les huîtres.*

– F2 'No no. The fishing [ID] / it was mostly Arcachon (...). And here [ID] it was the oysters.'

The spoken syntax of this colloquial explanation strings together two iconic constructions where the NP of the second one is replaced by a proximal deictic adverb (referring to another toponym, Gujan-Mestras, already mentioned).

– *Final Detachment*

The Final Detachment mostly occurs in declarative utterances, general comments or conclusions where one should expect an Answer:

(16) [– F2 So you didn't want to eat mussels?]

– F1 *C'est quand même dangereux / les moules* [FD].

– F1 'It is all the same dangerous / the mussels [FD].'

This declarative utterance avoids a direct Answer: while referring to the Question-Theme, the Final Detachment extends the semantic scope of the lexeme "mussles", a widening that is reflected at the morphosyntactic level by the change of article from indefinite partitive to definite: Q. *de(s) moules* > A. *les moules* (other examples Fernandez-Vest 2015: 130–135).

4.2.2 Political debate

Situation: TV program, FR2 channel, *Droit de réponse* [« Right to reply »] 21.09.2009; Daniel Cohn-Bendit (DCB), a European deputy, debates with Arlette Chabot (AC), a woman journalist.

The journalist principally uses a more formal style than the deputy. As a result, none of her Questions begin with an Initial Detachment. Conversely, Final Detachments are numerous (≈ 30% of the utterances). On the one hand, she tries to bring her own register into alignment with the deputy's colloquial style (DCB – 'I know it poses piles of security problems', AS – (...) *C'est ça qui est un peu casse-pied à votre avis quoi / la sécurité* 'That's what is a little annoying for you all right / security'). On the other hand, she interrupts DCB's long developments by slipping a direct short Question with a tone of complicity – and a flat Final Detachment intonation:

(17) – AC *C'est une bonne idée / selon vous / Nicolas Hulot[9]* [FD]?

– DCB *Ben ça dépend (– ah!). Je sais pas.*

– AC 'It is a good idea / you think / Nicolas Hulot [FD]?'

– DCB 'Well it depends (– oh!). I don't know.'

The deputy's experienced and self-confident rhetoric does not rely upon short NPs as Detachments – neither Initial nor Final. He rather prepares the blow of the final Rheme-block with a long-term strategy that accumulates arguments as appositions of varied syntactic forms, ex.

(18) – DCB *Ce côté ∂ / ISOLÉ / je sais tout / c'est moi qui décide / c'est moi qui arbitre* [ID] */ c'est quand même / disons / A- démocratique.*

– DCB 'This side ∂ / ISOLATED / I know all / it's me who decides / it's me who arbitrates [ID] / it is anyway / let's say / A- democratic.'

After a flexible construction – an initial NP followed by a series of unusual appositions (a sentence-lexis and two cleft sentences) – the Rh-block, signaled by a change of prosody, is itself subdivided into two enunciative segments separated by two Discourse Particles. This type of strategy, manipulated by an experienced speaker, relies totally on the infrastructure of oral devices: Detachment Constructions cannot be dissociated from the prosodic achievement. The meaning is framed and oriented by Discourse Particles that, besides marking

---

9 Nicolas Hulot, a popular reporter-journalist supported by a part of the ecologists, was going to declare his candidacy for the presidential campaign of 2012.

the point of junction between the two main enunciative blocks, can also introduce a further segmentation into each block – as is the case here in the rhematic part.

The frequency of occurrence of such constructions will lead us to go beyond the bounds of simple utterances and raise an important research question regarding the analysis of whole clauses as enunciative constituents, and possibly Detachments.

4.3 Languages in transition

From the point of view of its register change, Northern Sami is a language in transition: traditionally oral, it has for three decades had to gradually move into the communication sphere of written style and massmedia. But this change happens at the same time under the influence of Indo-European languages. This influence is exerted nowadays both directly through standardization (lexical loans), indirectly through syntax formatting and information structuring in view of writing that ignore the oral typological specificity of the Samic languages.

In traditional Sami, information strategies shaped by orality are prominent: paratactic subordination and numerous Discourse Particles – some specialized in the thematization of NPs and VPs, others in charge of marking the articulation of thematic and rhematic constituents. The recent development (1979 – unified Nordic orthography, revised in 1985) of the written mode in Sami is accompanied by the gradual decline of certain grammatical and semantic categories: spatio-temporal deictics and Discourse Particles in the first rank. The impoverishment of these categories, which can be explained by the reduction of the semantic fields they used to connote, has a strong influence on the Information Structuring profile of the language. In the course of such a typological evolution, Detachment Constructions are inevitably endangered: Initial Detachments are replaced by clefts, a new type of analytical construction that even excludes the thematizing DIPs, e.g.

(19) *Dat   leat   dat   riiddut,   mat   hehttejit   dán   áigge*
      they   are   these   quarrels,   that [RELAT.PR.PL]   prevent   this time
      áššiid   ovdáneami.
      of-things [GEN.PL]   progress [ACC]

instead of

(19') *Dat   riiddut   dat   hehttejit   dán   áigge   áššiid   ovdáneami.*
       these quarrels   [Th-DIP]   prevent   this   time   of-things   progress
       'They are these quarrels that nowadays prevent things from progressing.'

As for Final Detachments, their present survival is still attested by the dialogues of many fiction works, but their disappearance is probably a question of relatively short time (Fernandez-Vest 2005, 2009a, 2009b, 2011b).

5 Detachment Constructions and external contrastivity

External contrastivity is taken here as a cross-linguistic comparison, in opposition to "internal contrastivity" (section 4. above) but with an equal requirement of authentic corpora. In order to question, within the limits of this chapter, the impact of the type of text and the text strategy on the quantitative evaluation of Detachment Constructions, let us borrow some examples from a non-Indo-European language, both agglutinative and inflecting: Finnish.

An interesting point, which cannot be developed here, is the evolution of the conception of Detachment Constructions (*lohkeamat*) in Finnish grammars. Already present in Hakulinen & Karlsson's Finnish Syntax (1979), in connection with the grammaticalization of processual sentences, these constructions are given a thoroughful treatment in the voluminous "Comprehensive Grammar of Finnish" (*Iso suomen kielioppi*, ISK 2004).

- Initial Detachment, the first part of which is named a "syntactic omen" (*syntaktinen etiäinen*), is described as a stabilized construction, the main function of which is to lighten the information load, ex.

(20) NP1 + NP2   + DIP   + PRON.PL + V   + x [ELAT.PL]
      Fil ja Dzeni [ID]   *niin* /   *ne*   *tykkäsi*   *niistä runoist.*
      'Fil and Dzeni well / they liked these poems.'

Note however that the frequent use of relative clauses immediately following the Initial Detachment – see Laury and Helasvuo's chapter (this volume) – is partly at variance with such a lightening, ex.

(21)   *Tää aineisto jotta mä kaytän tänään* / *se* on teille etupäässä uutta.
      'This material that I use today / it is for you mainly new.'
      (adapted from ISK 2004: 972)

- Remarkable is the official recognition of a status for the Final Detachment: *lohkeama eteenpäin* ("detachment forward"), a stabilized construction, a grammaticalized addition of syntagmatic type, ex.

(22) *Neljä viikkoa / sitte otamme sen pois vaan sen kipsin*
'Four weeks / then we'll take it away simply this plaster cast.'
(other examples, ISK 2004: 1013–1016).

If one compares dialogues of standard spoken Finnish (with some local variations) – excerpts from the NPM, *Nykysuomalaisen puhekielen murros* [The transformation of spoken Finnish], a project of the Academy of Finland (1976–1981), transcribed with my own system – one notices that Initial Detachment seems to be more frequent (60% on average, up to 70% in some narrative sections) than Final Detachment, but the proportion of Final Detachments increases in the dialogical sections. Moreover FDs contribute to the thematic progression of whole texts in much the same way as the equivalent French Mnemes (examples (10) and (11) above). Whereas the detached Theme must be followed by a Rheme, the Mneme can, in the linearity of the narrative text, refer to a Rheme as well as a Theme, ex.

(23) – *Nämä lasinsirut jotka siis* [DIP] *ikkunasta / tuli sisälle SILLÄ puolella* [ID] / *niin* [DIP] *ne / ne jäi seiniin kiinni* [Rh] / *se oli / se oli ihan täys / lasia / seinät* [Mn-FD].

'These glass splinters that you know [DIP] from the window / came in ON THAT side [ID] / well [DIP] they / they stuck to the walls [Rh] / it was / it was all packed with / glass / the walls [[Mn-FD].'

[Those splinters of glass that, you know, came in from the window on that side, well they got stuck in the wall, it was, it was cram-full of glass, the walls.]
(Fernandez-Vest Archives / Helsinki Corpus, NPM Project)

In terms of universal features, the fact that the relation between Initial Detachment / Final Detachment and the information triad is dissymetric provides us with an additional argument in favor of the functionality of a tripartite analysis of the enunciative strategy (including the enunciative independence of the Mneme). What is the most obvious typological difference between these constructions in French and Finnish? It is of morphological nature, due to the rich morphology of Finnish. In Finnish, the detached NP of the Initial Detachment is often in nominative (more than 90% of the occurrences), while the pronominal resumption adopts the case of its function, including some of the numerous local cases (6 internal, 6 external), especially in existential and possessive constructions. See in (24) how a detached NP is resumed with an external local case, imposed upon by the "have construction" (ADESS + V *olla* 'be'):

(24) – *Siis nää ihmiset* [NOM] *jotka nytte / KASVAA / nämä näi siis mulla .. lapse/ni* [NOM/POSS] */ niil* [ADESS] */ niil on niin paljon parempi ravinto*
'You know these people who are now / GROWING / these these you know I have .. my children / they / they have a much better diet'.

In contrast, the Final Detachment has no syntactic function of its own: it adopts the case of its announcing pronoun. These remarks apply naturally to the internal structure of a single utterance; they do not apply to separate postponed utterances, that can by no means be called "Final Detachments", but are generally the expression of "afterthoughts"[10].

6 Conclusion

6.1 The enunciative status of clauses

The enunciative status of clauses is an important research question. A comparison of the total set of adverbial clauses in diverse corpora shows that several categories of adverbial clauses can function as Theme-clauses as well as Mneme-clauses – or even Rheme-clauses. Such is the case of *conditional clauses*.

Some of the conditional clauses do play their basic role of "hypothetic" utterances and occur indeed in the thematic initial part of the utterance, but it is far from being the general rule – even if the written version of the turns, obliterating the prosody, can be fallacious. This variety of enunciative functions can be clearly seen in periods where a morphosyntactically identical clause is repeated in different positions, and with different intonations, e.g., in our French political corpus:

---

[10] This is for instance the case of example (2) in Laury and Helasvuo's chapter (this volume). The second utterance (line 5), clearly separated from the first one (lines 2 and 3) by a terminal mark of punctuation (a full stop rendering a terminal intonation) – and further more by a feedback marker (line 4)) – is not a FD. There is consequently no reason for its NP (here in nominative) to adopt the case of a pronoun present in the preceding utterances. This second utterance, a typical afterthought meant to clarify (or remind of) a principally shared knowledge, has a rhematic status (usually signalled by a falling intonation).

(27) — AC [When French are asked you will see / they have divided opinions though isn't it they say .... Here it is (shows the results of an opinion poll)].

Qui souhaitez-vous? Alors / ça c'est <u>si vous n'êtes pas candidat</u> [Rh-clause]. *Ça veut dire que / vous soutiendrez Nicolas Hulot / <u>si vous n'allez pas à l'élection présidentielle vous-même</u>* [Mn-clause 1] / <u>*si vous n'êtes pas candidat*</u> [Mn-clause 2]?

— AC 'Whom do you wish? Well / this one is <u>if you are not a candidate</u> [Rh-clause]. Does it mean that / you will support Nicolas Hulot / <u>if you don't go to the presidential election yourself</u> [Mn-clause 1] / <u>if you are not a candidate</u> [Mn-clause 2]?'

In the second Question, the first clause "If you don't go yourself" and its immediate reformulation ("if —— not candidate", marked by a flat intonation), shape a pattern of circular cohesion with the explaining rhematic clause of the Answer-utterance (an excerpt from a poll). Whereas the first occurrence of conditional clause has a pure rhematic function (informing the presentative segment "this one it is"), the second occurrence is intended to remind the addressee of the situation projected on the wall table through repeating the rhematic segment of the preceding utterance — itself much clearer than the somewhat awkward formulation "if you don't go to the election". This disambiguing function, coupled with a flat intonation, is indeed one of the main characteristics of the mnematic constituents — which is a further argument in favor of extending the enunciative study of Information Structuring to broader co-texts.

6.2 Detachments and Information Grammar

Detachment Linguistics has tried to clearly distinguish detachments and appositions, the latter one being framed by two comas in the written style and segmented by prosody in speech. But things are more complex in natural discourse, even when not strictly impromptu. Let us illustrate this with a new excerpt of political debate:

(28) *Situation:* May 2012, French Presidential campaign, final TV debate between the two election rounds (between the two remaining candidates, conducted by a journalist)

[The journalist — François Hollande / what kind of president do you intend to be? FH — A president who / first of all / respects French people (...).

U1. – <u>Moi</u> / président de la République / <u>je</u> ne serai pas le chef de la majorité (...).
'<u>I</u> president of the Republic / <u>I</u> will not be the leader of the majority (...).'

U2. – <u>Moi</u> / président de la République / <u>je</u> ne traiterai pas mon premier ministre de collaborateur (...).
'<u>I</u> / president of the Republic / <u>I</u> will not call my Prime Minister a "collaborator".'
(+ U3, U4, U5 with an identical segmentation)

U6. – <u>Moi</u> président de la République / <u>il</u> y aura un code de déontologie pour les ministres (...).
'<u>Me</u> president of the Republic / <u>there</u> will be a code of deontology for the ministers (...).'

U7. – <u>Moi</u> président de la République / <u>les ministres</u> ne pourront pas cumuler à leurs fonctions avec un mandat à local (...).
'<u>Me</u> president of the Republic / <u>the ministers</u> will not be allowed to cumulate à their functions with a local à mandate (...).'
(+ U8, U9 with an identical segmentation)

In the first five utterances, the detached segment is twofold: a Th-pronoun + an apposition to the co-referring S-pronoun *je* of the main clause. In the following utterances (U6–U9), a shift is carried out. The Initial Detachment, integrating the Th-pronoun without any internal segmentation, has no co-reference with the S (pronoun, U6; substantive, U7) of the main clause. This yet another type of detachment, syntactically independent and semantically richer than "our" Detachment Constructions, is a thematic clause comparable to the "absolute construction" typical of the syntax of older Indo-European languages, that can be analyzed as containing "old, or backgrounded information" (Holland 1986).

Summary

This chapter has shown that Detachments are not pure accidents of oral and spoken languages: far from marginal, they testify to the fact that Impromptu Speech is organized around unintegrated syntactic structures, whose sequence is correlated with the order in which the referents and their story are activated in the speaker's mind. In this sense, Detachments and their constructional variants in different types of discourse are not "agrammatical": they should be investigated as essential elements of oral grammar, ie. a grammar that takes into account criteria of situation anchoring, relevance and planning of the conveyed information. Such an investigation should obligatorily include the broader co-text of utterances and, despite its inherent difficulties, transpose therefore to complex utterances and whole texts the three basic enunciative constituents and the two binary strategies that have been defined above.

References

Apothéloz, Denis, Bernard Combettes & Franck Neveu (éds.). 2009. *Les linguistiques du détachement. Actes du Colloque International de Nancy (7–9 juin 2006)* (Sciences pour la communication 87). Bern & Berlin: Peter Lang.

Benveniste, Emile. 1966–74. *Problèmes de linguistique générale*, 1–2. Paris: Gallimard.

Biber, Douglas. 1988. *Variation across Speech and Writing*. Cambridge: Cambridge University Press.

Biber, Douglas, Stig Johansson, Geoffrey Leech, Susan Conrad & Edward Finegan. 1999. *Longman Grammar of Spoken and Written English*. Harlow: Pearson Education Ltd.

Bonnard, Henri. 1972. Détachement. In *Grand Larousse de la langue française*. Paris: Larousse.

Daneš, Frantisek. 1974. Functional sentence perspective and the organization of the text. In Daneš (ed.), *Papers in Functional Sentence Perspective*, 106–128. Prague: Academia.

Enkvist, Nils-Erik. 1975. *Tekstilingvistiikan peruskäsitteitä* [Fundaments of Textual Linguistics]. Helsinki: Gaudeamus.

Enkvist, Nils-Erik. 1982. Introduction Coherence, composition and text linguistics. In Nils-Erik Enkvist (ed.), *Impromptu speech: a symposium* (MSÅAF 78), 11–26. Åbo: Åbo Akademi.

Fernandez-Vest, M.M.Jocelyne. 1982 [1977]. *Le finnois parlé par les Sames bilingues d'Utsjoki-Ohcejohka (Laponie finlandaise). Structures contrastives, syntaxiques, discursives* [Finnish spoken by bilingual Sami in Utsjoki-Ohcejohka (Finnish Lapland). Contrastive, syntactic, discourse structures] (L'Europe de Tradition Orale 1). Paris: SELAF.

Fernandez-Vest, M.M.Jocelyne. 1987 [1984]. *La Finlande trilingue. 1. Le discours des Sames. Oralité, contrastes, énonciation*. Préface de Claude Hagège. Paris: Didier Erudition.

Fernandez-Vest, M.M.Jocelyne. 1994. *Les Particules Énonciatives dans la construction du discours* (Collection Linguistique nouvelle). Paris: PUF.

Fernandez-Vest, M.M.Jocelyne. 1995. Morphogenèse orale du sens: de l'espace des langues aux objets de discours. In M.M.Jocelyne Fernandez- Vest (dir.), *Oralité et cognition: invariants énonciatifs et diversité des langues; Intellectica* 20 (1). 7–53.

Fernandez-Vest, M.M.Jocelyne. 2004. Mnémème, Antitopic – Le Post-Rhème, de l'énoncé au texte. In M.M.Jocelyne Fernandez-Vest & Shirley Carter- Thomas (éds.), *Structure Informationnelle et Particules Enonciatives – essai de typologie* (Grammaire & Cognition 1–2), 65–104. Paris: Editions L'Harmattan.

Fernandez-Vest, M.M.Jocelyne. 2005. Information structure and typological change: Northern Sami challenged by Indo-European models. In M.M.Jocelyne Fernandez-Vest (dir.), *Les langues ouraliennes aujourd'hui: approche linguistique et cognitive – The Uralic Languages today: a linguistic and cognitive approach* (Bibliothèque de l'Ecole des Hautes Etudes 340), 563–576. Préface de Claude Hagège. Paris: Editions Honoré Champion.

Fernandez-Vest, M.M.Jocelyne. 2006. Vers une typologie linguistique du détachement à fondement ouralien d'Europe. *Bulletin de la Société de Linguistique de Paris* C1 (1). 173–224.
Fernandez-Vest, M.M.Jocelyne. 2007. Structure Informationnelle et genre discursif: décrire un itinéraire piéton en français. In J.M. Barbéris & M.C. Manes-Gallo (dir.), *Parcours dans la ville. Description d'itinéraires piétons* (Collection Espaces Discursifs), 188–210. Paris: Editions L'Harmattan.
Fernandez-Vest, M.M.Jocelyne. 2009a. Vers une typologie informationnelle des constructions à détachement. In Denis Apothéloz, Bernard Combettes & Franck Neveu (éds.), *Les linguistiques du détachement. Actes du Colloque International de Nancy (7-9 juin 2006)* (Sciences pour la communication 87), 251-262. Bern & Berlin: Peter Lang.
Fernandez-Vest, M.M.Jocelyne. 2009b. Typological evolution of Northern Sami: spatial cognition and Information Structuring. In Jussi Ylikoski (ed.), *The Quasquicentennial of the Finno-Ugrian Society* (SUST 258), 33–55. Helsinki: Suomalainen Seura.
Fernandez-Vest, M.M.Jocelyne. 2011. Detachment constructions as fundaments of Information Structuring – evidence from French, Finnic, Samic. Paper presented at the International Workshop Information Structure and Spoken language. Cross-linguistic studies, convenors M.M.Jocelyne Fernandez-Vest & Robert D. Van Valin, Jr., July 9–10, LSA Linguistic Institute, Boulder, Colorado. www.http://infostructuring.wikidot.com/
Fernandez-Vest, M.M.Jocelyne. 2012a. *SAMI. An introduction to the language and culture, with a Sami-English-Sami lexicon*. Helsinki: Finn Lectura. Fernandez-Vest, M.M.Jocelyne. 2012b. Detachments and circular cohesion: what status in language/discourse typologies? Paper presented at the International Workshop Detachment constructions [dislocations] and typology in languages of Europe and beyond, convenors M.M.Jocelyne Fernandez-Vest & Ricardo Etxepare, 45th Annual Meeting of the Societas Linguistica Europaea (SLE 2012), Stockholm, August 28–September 2.
Fernandez-Vest, M.M.Jocelyne. 2015. *Detachments for Cohesion – Toward an Information Grammar of Oral Languages* (Empirical Approaches to Language Typology, EALT 56). Berlin & Boston: De Gruyter Mouton, XVI–290 p.
Hagège, Claude. 1986 [1985]. *L'Homme de paroles* (Collection Folio Essais). Paris: Fayard.
Hagège, Claude. 1993. *The Language Builder. An Essay on the human signature in linguistic morphogenesis* (Amsterdam Studies in the theory and history of linguistic science, ser. IV, Current issues in linguistic theory 94). Amsterdam & Philadelphia: John Benjamins.
Hakulinen, Auli & Fred Karlsson. 1979. *Nykysuomen lauseoppia* [Syntax of modern Finnish] (SKST 350). Helsinki: SKS.
Hakulinen, Auli, Maria Vilkuna, Riitta Korhonen, Vesa Koivisto, Tarja-Riitta Heinonen & Irja Alho. 2004. *Iso suomen kielioppi* [The comprehensive grammar of Finnish]. Helsinki: SKS. [ISK]
Halliday, M.A.K. 1967-68. Notes on transitivity and theme in English. *Journal of Linguistics* 3 (1), 3 (2), 4 (2). 37–81, 199–244, 179–215.
Hergé (Georges Prosper Rémi). 1976. *Tintin et les Picaros* (Les Aventures de Tintin 23. English translation 1980). Tournai: Casterman.
Holland, Garry B. 1986. Nominal sentences and the origin of Absolute Constructions in Indo-European. *Zeitschrift für vergleichende sprachforschung* 99 Band (2. Helft). 161–193.
Horlacher, Anne-Sylvie & Gabriele M. Müller. 2005. L'implication de la dislocation à droite dans l'organisation interactionnelle. In Simona Pekarek Doehler & Marie-José Béguelin (éds.), *Grammaire, discours, interaction. La structuration de l'information; TRANEL* (Travaux Neuchâtelois de Linguistique) 41. 127–145.

ISK. 2004. See Hakulinen, Auli, Maria Vilkuna, Riitta Korhonen, Vesa Koivisto, Tarja-Riitta Heinonen & Irja Alho. 2004.

Kerbrat-Orecchioni, Catherine. 2009 [4, 1980]. *L'énonciation. De la subjectivité dans le langage* (Collection Linguistique). Paris: Armand Colin.

Lambrecht, Knud. 1994. *Information structure and sentence form. Topic, focus and the mental representations of discourse referents.* Cambridge: Cambridge University Press.

Lambrecht, Knud. 2001. Chap. 80. Dislocation. In Martin Haspelmath, Ekkehard König, Wulf Oesterreicher & Wolfgang Raible (eds.), *Language typology and language universals. Sprachtypologie und Sprachliche Universalien. Typologie des langues et universaux linguistiques. An international handbook*, vol. 2, 1050–1078. Berlin & New-York: Walter de Gruyter.

Matić, Dejan & Daniel Wedgwood. 2013. The meaning of focus: The significance of an interpretation-based category in cross-linguistic analysis. Journal of Linguistics 49. 127–163.

Miller, Jim & M.M.Jocelyne Fernandez-Vest. 2006. Spoken and written language. In Giuliano Bernini and Marcia L. Schwartz (eds.), *Pragmatic organization of discourse* (Empirical Approaches to Language Typology, Eurotype 20-8), 9–64. Berlin & New York: Mouton de Gruyter.

Miller, Jim & Regina Weinert. 2009 [1998]. *Spontaneous spoken language* (Oxford Linguistics). Oxford: Oxford University Press.

Newmeyer, Frederick J. 2001. The Prague School and North American Functionalist Approaches to Syntax. *Journal of Linguistics* 37. 101–126.

Peirce, Charles Sanders. 1978. *Écrits sur le signe, rassemblés, traduits et commentés par Gérard Deledalle* (L'ordre philosophique). Paris: Seuil.

Rizzi, Luigi. 1997. The fine structure of the left periphery. In L. Hagerman (ed.), *Elements of grammar*, 281–337. Dordrecht: Kluwer.

Jeanette K. Gundel and Nancy Hedberg
2 Reference and Cognitive Status: Scalar Inference and Typology

1 Introduction

The term 'information structure' has been used in two distinct, and logically independent senses in the literature, which we refer to as 'relational givenness/newness' and 'referential givenness/newness' (see Gundel 1988, 1999, 2012). 'Relational givenness/newness' describes a relation between two complementary parts of a single level of representation–syntactic, semantic, or pragmatic, where the first part of the pair is informationally given in relation to the second and the second part is informationally new in relation to the first. Relational givenness/newness 'reflects how the informational content of an event or state of affairs expressed by a sentence is represented and how its truth value is to be assessed' (Gundel and Fretheim 2004). Examples include notions like psychological subject and predicate (Paul 1880), logical subject and predicate (Chao 1968), presupposition and focus (Chomsky 1971, Jackendoff 1972), topic-comment (Gundel 1974), theme-rheme (Vallduvi 1992), topic-predicate (Erteschik-Shir 1997), topic-focus (Lambrecht 1994, van Valin 2004, Gundel 2012), and Question Under Discussion (QUD) (Roberts 1996) inter alia.

Referential givenness/newness, on the other hand, describes a relation between the intended interpretation/referent of a linguistic expression and its informational status in the speaker/hearer's mind, the discourse (model), some real or possible world, etc. Examples include existential presupposition (Strawson 1964b) and concepts such as salience, activation, familiarity, identifiability, specificity, etc. (Prince 1981, Ariel 1990, Gundel, Hedberg and Zacharski 1993, Chafe 1994 inter alia). In this paper, we will be concerned with referential givenness/newness, specifically within the Givenness Hierarchy theory proposed in Gundel, Hedberg and Zacharski (1993 and subsequent work), which attempts to explain the distribution and interpretation of different nominal expressions, and the fact that such forms succeed in picking out a speaker's intended interpretation even though the conceptual information they encode rarely, if ever, determines a unique referent.

Jeanette K. Gundel, University of Minnesota
Nancy Hedberg, Simon Fraser University

We begin by briefly summarizing the Givenness Hierarchy theory. We then correct some misconceptions and misinterpretations that have appeared in the literature on the predictions of the theory. Finally, we discuss some cross-linguistic and typological facts about the ways in which languages can differ and ways they appear to be alike with respect to encoding cognitive statuses on the Givenness Hierarchy.

2 The role of information status in the interpretation of referring expressions: The Givenness Hierarchy

A central problem for theories of reference is to explain how forms that encode different conceptual/descriptive content can have the same interpretation, as in (1a–c), and forms that encode the same conceptual/descriptive content can have different interpretations, as in (2a–c).

(1) A1   *You've only known **the dog** how long did you say?*
     B1   *Well, about a year, I guess.*
         a.   A2   *Oh well, it is uh, how old is **the dog**?*
                    (Switchboard corpus "Dogs")
         b.   A2' *Oh well, it is uh, how old is **it**?*
         c.   A2" *Oh well, it is uh, how old is **this animal**?*

(2) A1: *uh, do you have a pet, Randy?*
     B1: *uh yeah, currently we have **a poodle***
     A2: ***a poodle**, miniature or, uh, full size*
     B2: *yeah, uh, it's a full size*
     A3: *uhhuh*
     B3: *yeah*
         a.   A4: *I read somewhere that **the poodle** is one of the most intelligent dogs around* (Switchboard Corpus, "Dogs")
         b.   A4' *I read somewhere that **this poodle** is one of the most intelligent dogs around*
         c.   A4" *I read somewhere that **that poodle** is one of the most intelligent dogs around*

In (1a), the phrase 'the dog', which appeared in the original Switchboard dialogue, is easily interpreted as the dog which A and B have been talking about, i.e. B's dog. But A could also have used the pronoun 'it' to refer to the dog as in (1b) or 'this animal' as in (1c), and the interpretation would have been the same, even though the conceptual content encoded in the three examples is different.

In (2a), on the other hand, the phrase 'the poodle' in A's statement could have a specific interpretation where it would be interpreted as referring to B's poodle or a generic interpretation referring to the whole class of poodles. The generic interpretation, which makes the most sense in this context, is the one that comes to mind first. And this is likely the one that speaker A intended. However, using the phrase 'this poodle', as in (2b) or 'that poodle', as in (2c), which encode the same conceptual content, could more easily be understood as referring to B's poodle, even though this interpretation makes less sense in the context of this sentence.

The Givenness Hierarchy theory attempts to explain such facts by proposing that nominal expressions encode two kinds of information: (1) procedural information about how to mentally access a representation of the intended referent/interpretation, its (assumed) cognitive status in the addressee's mind; and (2) conceptual/descriptive information about the referent/interpretation. The former is encoded by the determiner/pronoun[1] head of the DP and the latter is encoded by the rest of the phrase.

The Givenness Hierarchy comprises the cognitive statuses in (3), where each status entails all lower statuses, but not vice-versa.

(3) The Givenness Hierarchy and associated English forms.

in focus	> activated	> familiar	> uniquely identifiable	> referential	> type identifiable
it[2]	this/that/this NP	that NP	the NP	indefinite this NP	a NP

Within a given language, individual determiners/pronouns encode different cognitive statuses. For example, in English, unstressed personal pronouns, such as 'it' in (1b), overtly signal that their referent is in focus for the addressee, which B's dog would be at this point since it is part of the content of the previous two utterances and is the topic of conversation; and, since the statuses are in a unidirectional entailment relationship, where each status entails all lower statuses

---

[1] A pronoun may be analyzed as a determiner with no NP complement (c.f. Postal 1966, Abney 1987); but for the purpose of this paper we will continue to use the more traditional term 'pronoun'.

[2] 'it' here stands for all unstressed personal pronouns.

(statuses to the right on the hierarchy), the referent is also necessarily activated, familiar, uniquely identifiable, and so on, which is why the determiner 'the' as in (1a) and 'this' as in (1c) are perfectly appropriate in referring to speaker B's dog as well. Linguistic forms that encode cognitive status provide procedural information about how to mentally access the referent, as described in (4).

(4)
it	associate representation in focus of attention	(in focus)
this/that/this NP	associate representation in working memory	(activated)
that NP	associate representation in memory	(familiar)
the NP	associate unique representation with DP	(uniquely identifiable)
indefinite this NP	associate unique representation	(referential)
a NP	associate type representation	(type identifiable)

Thus, the pronoun 'it' in (1b) instructs the addressee to associate a representation in his current focus of attention; but 'the dog' (the form actually used in this dialogue) is appropriate here as well since it only instructs the addressee to associate a unique representation with the DP, which he could easily do since the dog is in focus and therefore uniquely identifiable; and 'this animal' in (1c) is possible as well, since a dog is an animal and the determiner 'this' is an instruction to associate a referent which is activated; and anything in focus is also activated, i.e. in working memory.

While cognitive statuses on the Givenness Hierarchy further restrict possible referents from among those that satisfy the conceptual content encoded in the phrase, the Givenness Hierarchy interacts with general pragmatic principles to arrive at the interpretation the speaker actually intended. Thus, in (1b), the linguistic content of the phrase 'the dog' alone does not pick out the intended referent here (as would the pronoun 'it' which explicitly instructs the addressee to associate a referent in his focus of attention); it is simply consistent with the speaker's intended referent since it instructs the addressee to associate a unique representation of a dog, and anything in focus is also uniquely identifiable. The cognitive/pragmatic tendency to pick out the most relevant interpretation, the one that yields an adequate contextual effect with minimal cognitive effort (Sperber and Wilson 1986/1995, Gundel and Mulkern 1998), explains why the in-focus dog is the one that comes to mind first. On the other hand, in (2a), the phrase 'the dog' is much more likely to be interpreted as referring to the kind 'dog' than to the specific dog A and B have been talking about, because interpreting it as B's dog would not be as relevant in this context, as it would not yield an adequate contextual effect.

Interaction of the cognitive statuses signaled by different determiners and pronouns with general pragmatic principles also explains so called 'scalar implicatures' that arise from using different determiners and pronouns. Thus, although using an indefinite article is consistent with any context that allows a definite article, since anything that is uniquely identifiable is also type identifiable, use of the weaker indefinite article, which is unspecified for unique identifiability, often implicates that the referent is not uniquely identifiable (and therefore also not familiar, activated, or in focus). For example, the definite article in the phrase 'the dog' in A's question in (1) above, repeated here as (5a), is interpreted as referring uniquely to B's dog, which they have been talking about and which is therefore uniquely identifiable with minimal cognitive effort in this context. But if the definite article is replaced with an indefinite article, as in (5b), the preferred interpretation is one where 'a dog' is at most type identifiable, i.e. not uniquely identifiable, since the question of how long the addressee has known any member of the class of dogs is also relevant in this context. It yields a contextual effect with minimal cognitive effort.[3]

(5) a. You've only known **the dog** how long did you say?

    b. You've only known **a dog** how long did you say?

In (6), on the other hand, which occurs later in the same dialogue, 'a nose' and 'a tongue' in line 45 are most naturally interpreted as the unique nose and tongue of B's dog, i.e. using 'a N' does not implicate that the referent is not uniquely identifiable; uniqueness simply remains unspecified since it is not necessary to specify it in this context. The unique interpretation is the only one that would be relevant in this case and using the definite article would provide more information about cognitive status than necessary.

(6) 40 Speaker A: ... *it's such a pleasure to come home at night and you can see her smiling from ear to ear. She's so happy to see me*

    41 Speaker B: *yeah, definitely*

    42 Speaker A: *and uh I don't know if you get that kind of greeting or not*

    43 Speaker B: *I can honestly say we do uh we just recently put a security system in our house and so now uh in order to uh to accommodate the motion detectors we have to keep her uh locked up in the master bedroom during the day and the she's got the bedroom and the bathroom to for free run during the day but*

    44 Speaker A: *uhhuh*

    45 Speaker B: *we've always got **a nose** and **a tongue** pressed up against the window when we come walking up to the front door*

---

3 We state the basis for the pragmatic inference here in relevance theoretic terms rather than in terms of Grice's Cooperative Principle, but the difference is not important for purposes of this paper.

Pragmatic principles thus further influence the likelihood of interpretations of referring expressions depending on the relevance of procedural information conveyed by pronouns and determiners in particular contexts.

3 The Givenness Hierarchy as a big Horn scale

3.1 Background

In Gundel, Hedberg and Zacharski (1993), we called upon Grice's (1967/1975) Maxim of Quantity, shown in (7) below, in explaining how general pragmatic principles interact with the Givenness Hierarchy in accounting for particular reference interpretations in context.

(7) Q1: Give as much information as required for current purposes of the exchange.

Q2: Do not give more information than is required.

We pointed out that since the Givenness Hierarchy exhibits a unilateral entailment relation between the statuses, that relationship could thus be expected to give rise to scalar quantity implicatures (Horn 1972, 1984) pertaining to the forms and statuses, as noted in section 2 of the current paper. In our 1993 paper, we proposed that cognitive status implicatures can be explained by appealing to both parts of Grice's Maxim of Quantity. First, Q1 can be called upon to explain focus shift effects of demonstrative pronouns as opposed to unstressed personal pronouns. Examples from the 1993 paper and from Hedberg (2000) showing that use of the demonstrative pronoun, which explicitly signals only activation, can lead to the inference that the referent is not in focus are given in (8):

(8) (a) *Anyway going on back from the kitchen then is a little hallway leading to a window, and across from the kitchen is a big walk-through closet. On the other side of **that** is another little hallway leading to a window. ...* [personal letter]

    (b) Karen: *You know I've tried several times to take, take pictures of the library in Linden Hills. I, sometimes I think it must be haunted or something, because it won't uh ... develop on some film.*

        Neil: *Weird ... I took in the =*

        Karen: *= Isn't **that** supposed to be symbolic of something?* [Frederickson tapes]

In (8a), both the kitchen and the walk-through closet are activated and using 'that' to refer to either one of them would be licit. But since the kitchen is in focus and therefore activated, whereas the closet is at most activated, use of 'that' is relevant here in disambiguating between the two interpretations and therefore gives rise to the Q1 implicature that the referent is the 'not in focus' closet. Likewise in (8b), use of 'that' shifts focus of attention from the library (currently in focus and therefore also activated) to the fact that it doesn't develop on film (activated, but not in focus).

A second cognitive-status-based Q1 implicature proposed in our 1993 paper was the 'not uniquely identifiable' interpretation often associated with indefinite expressions, as discussed in section 2. This again can be viewed as a Q1 implicature, generated through use of a weaker form (one that simply instructs the hearer to associate a particular type interpretation) implicating that a higher status does not obtain. Thus, use of the indefinite article often conveys that the referent is not uniquely identifiable, and therefore also not familiar, activated or in focus, as in examples like (9).

(9) a. *I went with my husband to the park and sat down on a bench.* **A man** *sat down next to me.*

If it were the activated husband who sat down next to the speaker in (9), this referent could have been encoded with a form that explicitly picks out the husband, such as 'he' or 'my husband'. Since the speaker used a relatively weak indefinite 'a' phrase, which explicitly signals only type identifiability, she implicates that the man is not uniquely identifiable and therefore not her husband.

In our 1993 paper, we suggested that such inferences behave similarly to the scalar implicatures discussed in Horn (1972) as applying when a lexical semantic relation, now called a "Horn scale", obtains between a stronger and weaker form, e.g. 'all' and 'some'. When interacting with Grice's Maxim of Quantity, use of a weaker form, as in (10a), often results in the implicature indicated in (10b).

(10) a. *Some of the students passed the exam.*
 b. *Not all of the students passed the exam.*

The focus shift function of demonstrative pronouns and the "new referent" interpretation of indefinite article phrases are well supported by both naturally occurring and constructed examples, and seem to be insightfully characterized as scalar implicatures. They do not always arise, as shown in (6) above; but since implicatures are pragmatic inferences and not conventional meanings associated with the lexical items in question, they are context dependent; so we do not expect them to always arise.

Two features of conversational implicature as distinct from entailment are widely taken to be true of scalar implicatures. They can be cancelled without contradiction and they can be reinforced without redundancy (Levinson 1983), as shown in (11):

(11) a. *Some, if not all, of the students passed.* (cancellation)

b. *Some, in fact all, of the students passed.* (cancellation)

c. *Some, but not all, of the students passed.* (reinforcement)

Gundel et al. 1993 point out that the pragmatic Q1 implicature associated with indefinite articles can be cancelled, as in (12a); and it can be reinforced without redundancy, as in (12b).

(12) a. *I met **a student** before class. **A student** came to see me after class as well – in fact it was the same student I had seen before.* [Hawkins 1991]

b. *I met **a student** before class. **A student**, not the same one, came to see me after class as well.*

The focus-shift inference of demonstrative pronouns can also be cancelled or reinforced, as shown in (13).

(13) a. *The kitchen is next to a big walk-through closet. On the other side of **that**, the kitchen, I mean, is a little hallway leading to a window.* (cancellation)

b. *The kitchen is next to a big walk-through closet. On the other side of **that**, the closet, I mean, is a little hallway leading to a window.* (reinforcement)

We also proposed in our 1993 paper that cognitive status implicatures can arise from the second part of Grice's Maxim of Quantity, Q2 (don't give more information than necessary) which also emerges from the unilateral entailment relationship between the statuses on the hierarchy. With this type of implicature, we explained the tendency found in our corpus data for 'the NP' phrases, which explicitly signal only the status 'uniquely identifiable', to be used extensively for referents that also have a higher cognitive status, e.g. familiar, activated, or even in focus. We suggested that the choice of a relatively weak form, the definite article, arises from lack of a need to signal that a higher status obtains, because the stereotypical uniquely identifiable phrase is uniquely identifiable because it is familiar, or even activated or in focus, appealing to Atlas and Levinson's 1981 proposed explanation for why Q2 rather than Q1 is applicable in explaining the common strengthening of the conditional 'if' to 'if and only if' (see also Levinson (2000)). Hence we get examples like (1a) above and (14), where a relatively weak form is used to refer to a referent that also has a higher cognitive status.

(14) a. *The man wins this time, and the fish that he selects is a big goldfish, which is, at the point when he selects it, hidden in a rocky formation in the tank, and it's impossible for the man conducting the game to get at **the fish** with the net.* [Goldfish stories].

Since uniquely identifiable phrases are also stereotypically familiar (or even activated), it is often not necessary to convey that a higher status obtains, since simply signaling unique identifiability will generally enable the hearer to resolve reference to a familiar or activated entity.[4]

3.2 Response to Kehler and Ward's (2006) criticism of the Givenness Hierarchy account of scalar implicatures

Kehler and Ward (2006) argue against the idea that the Givenness Hierarchy forms a Horn scale and therefore gives rise to scalar implicatures of the type discussed above.[5] They note that Horn scales have been proposed to involve

---

[4] The fact that definite article phrases are frequently interpreted as having referents that are not only uniquely identifiable but also activated and in focus also receives a natural explanation under a Relevance Theory account, as in Gundel and Mulkern (1998), since the activated and in focus interpretations, assuming they yield an adequate contextual/cognitive effect, do so with minimal cognitive effort. In any case, the explanation for the inference is pragmatic and relies on the scalar nature of statuses on the Givenness Hierarchy, in this case the fact that anything which is in focus is also activated, familiar and uniquely identifiable.

[5] The name 'Givenness Hierarchy', and its frequent confusion with other referential hierarchies, such as Ariel's Accessibility Hierarchy (1990). may have contributed to the misinterpretation that would prevent it from giving rise to scalar implicatures. However, cognitive statuses on the Givenness Hierarchy, unlike in other referential hierarchies, are not mutually exclusive since each cognitive status entails all lower statuses; and they do not convey *degree* of accessibility. Rather, they convey procedural information about *manner* of accessibility, specifically on how to access a referent/interpretation. See Gundel, Hedberg and Zacharski (2012).

equally lexicalized forms which vary along a single semantic dimension, a point on which Kehler and Ward challenge the Givenness Hierarchy; and they maintain that several properties in the data on referring expressions, which would be predicted from the premise that the Givenness Hierarchy is a Horn scale, are in fact missing. We agree that the Givenness Hierarchy does not form a scale based on semantic/conceptual meaning directly analogous to scales like <all, most, many, some>, or <necessary, probable, possible>. However, the differences that Kehler and Ward claim to distinguish the Givenness Hierarchy from standard Horn scales have their origins in the distinction between conceptual information relations, which most standard Horn scales encode, and the procedural information relations that the Givenness Hierarchy encodes. The Givenness Hierarchy still forms a unidirectional entailment scale in the sense that the addressee's ability to associate a representation based on a higher status necessarily implies their ability to associate a representation based on all lower statuses, but not vice-versa. Thus anything in focus of attention is necessarily activated (in short term memory); anything activated is necessarily familiar (in memory); anything familiar is necessarily uniquely identifiable (the addressee can associate a unique representation with the referring phrase); anything uniquely identifiable is necessarily referential (the addressee can associate a unique referent by the time the whole sentence is processed); and anything referential is necessarily type identifiable (the addressee can associate a type representation). Since Kehler and Ward base their arguments entirely on the 1993 paper, which, unlike later work (e.g. Gundel 2009) did not explicitly articulate cognitive statuses as encoding procedural information, this misunderstanding is partly understandable. However, we maintain that some of Kehler and Ward's arguments are misplaced in that they do not sufficiently take into account the role of relevance in modulating the inducement of scalar inferences and the cancellation of them.

Kehler and Ward agree with Gundel et al. 1993 that definite article phrases do not always convey familiar information, but rather encode unique identifiability. They also concede that 'the' and 'a' form a Horn scale, <the, a>, citing examples from Larry Horn that show that typical uses of 'a'-phrases can convey that the referent is not unique, an inference that can be cancelled without contradiction or reinforced without redundancy, as shown in (15):

(15) a. *Over the nineteenth century, Britain became **a, if not the**, world power.* [eserver.org/cultronix/sigel/] (cancellation)

   b. *Decision making is **a, but not the**, fundamental construct in design.* [dbd.eng. buffalo.edu/papers/DR.position.htm] (reinforcement)

We would argue that the information encoded in 'the' vs. 'a' that distinguishes the two determiners in the usage cited in (15) is both conceptual and procedural, which is why cancellation and reinforcement using the determiners alone, without following conceptual content, is possible. It is conceptual because it can be formulated as a unique vs. non-unique interpretation, which is a matter for truth conditions to determine. Thus, 'the' in such examples means 'the only' and in fact can be paraphrased as such, which would not be the case for typical, unstressed uses of 'the' that convey purely procedural information (associate a unique representation).

Kehler and Ward also give some examples that do seem to show the possibility of cancelling an implicature that a higher status does not obtain when a form that explicitly encodes only a lower status has been used, as our theory would predict.

(16) **A student** came by. In fact it was that weird guy who sits in the back of the class.

(17) **The book that John is currently reading** [not necessarily familiar] – in fact the one I showed you yesterday when we were at the bookstore...

In (16) 'in fact' is followed by a cancellation of the Q1 implicature that the referent is not uniquely identifiable (and therefore also not familiar) through use of a 'that NP' phrase, which is necessarily familiar according to the Givenness Hierarchy. (17) is felicitous because the complement of 'the' in the clause following 'in fact' contains conceptual information identifying the book as not only uniquely identifiable but also familiar. Kehler and Ward conclude from examples like these that 'a' and 'the' phrases can give rise to non-familiarity implicatures, but they argue that these are the only cognitive-status-type implicatures that can arise.

Thus, they claim that (18) is infelicitous when the 'the' phrase in the 'in fact' clause is uniquely identifiable but not familiar.

(18) #**A student** came to see me after class as well – in fact it was the student I met with three days ago [not familiar].

We disagree with the judgment that this phrase cannot felicitously be interpreted as non-familiar. While it may be difficult to imagine a context in which this phrase would be intended as non-familiar to the addressee, other examples can be constructed where the phrase used in the cancellation clause can more easily be interpreted as uniquely identifiable, but non-familiar, e.g. (19).

(19) **A student** came to see me after class as well – in fact it was the winner of the biggest scholarship on campus.

We also dispute their conclusion about (20), an example from Barbara Abbott, which they give in a footnote. They claim that this does not constitute cancellation of a non-referentiality implicature, because the 'in fact' phrase could include a second 'a' determiner, instead of indefinite 'this'.

(20) *I'm going to buy **a car** today, in fact, this blue sportscar that's at John's car dealership, and it's in great condition.*

Note, however, that nothing in the Givenness Hierarchy framework prevents an 'a' phrase from including conceptual information that would indicate its referentiality. The Givenness Hierarchy simply predicts that 'a' is unspecified for referentiality; it does not exclude an 'a' phrase from being referential, since anything referential is necessarily also type identifiable.[6]

Kehler and Ward point out that a similar example, shown in (21), is infelicitous and here we agree.

(21) *#I'm going to buy **a car** today, in fact this car* [indefinite (and therefore unstressed) 'this'].

Here, we note that the attempted cancellation is infelicitous because the 'in fact' phrase does not convey any additional conceptual information and thus the reformulation is not relevant. The felicitous examples in (16)–(20) all have in common that the 'in fact' phrase contains additional conceptual information about the interpretation of the referring phrase. We maintain that this is an essential property of felicitous use of 'in fact'.

The same explanation can be given for the infelicity of Kehler and Ward's examples in (22) and (23).

(22) *#**That dog**, in fact it, kept me awake last night.*

(23) *#**That dog that bit you last year**, in fact, that/this dog/that dog, won't be able to get out of the yard anymore.*

---

[6] Gundel et al. 1993 claim that 'a' does not typically implicate non-referentiality because the only form that explicitly signals this status is indefinite 'this', which is restricted to certain registers of colloquial English.

Note that if the referential expression following 'in fact' were stressed and would thereby convey conceptual deictic information (e.g. the dog over there, or the dog you are looking at), the cancellation would be felicitous.

Kehler and Ward give no account of cases, such as those illustrated above in (8), where demonstrative pronouns are used to indicate a focus shift. They presumably would draw the conclusion from the lack of cancellability of focus shift inferences using 'in fact' phrases that such focus shift inferences are not Q1 implicatures. We suggest, on the contrary, that the lack of cancellability has to do with it not being possible to cancel with only procedural content following 'in fact'. It is true, as mentioned above, that there are contexts in which such inferences do not arise: e.g. 'that' can be used for an in-focus entity in some contexts, even stressed 'that'; but the fact that an inference does not necessarily arise in all contexts is also a criterion for identifying it as a quantity-based implicature rather than as an entailment arising from the conventional meaning of the lexical item in question.

In sum, we maintain that determiners and pronouns which signal cognitive statuses on the Givenness Hierarchy convey procedural information about how to access a representation of the speaker's intended referent/interpretation, and that this explains why implicatures associated with forms on the hierarchy sometimes appear to have different properties from standard scalar implicatures associated with forms that convey conceptual content. It also explains why the 'in fact' cancellation phrases that involve forms which signal cognitive status are often infelicitous, because the phrase following 'in fact' must convey additional conceptual meaning in order to be felicitous.

4 Typological facts: Cross-linguistic differences and similarities

Cognitive statuses on the Givenness Hierarchy are assumed to be universal. Given that conceptual content alone rarely determines a unique referent, it is expected that all languages have determiners and pronouns that encode cognitive status of the referent, assisting the addressee in picking out the actually intended referent from among the possible ones which satisfy the conceptual content of the phrase.

While all languages investigated within the Givenness Hierarchy framework thus far do indeed have pronouns and determiners that encode cognitive status of the intended referent, not all languages have forms that explicitly encode every status. Few languages have forms that distinguish all three of the statuses on the lower end of the Givenness Hierarchy – type identifiable, referential, and uniquely identifiable. This is also as expected, given the unidirectional entailment relation of the hierarchy, where lower statuses are entailed by higher ones, but not vice-versa, and forms that explicitly encode the lower statuses thus provide less information about how to access the referent. In English, for example, the definite article explicitly signals the status 'uniquely identifiable' and the indefinite article explicitly signals only type identifiability. Indefinite 'this', which explicitly signals referentiality, occurs only in colloquial English. Also, as is well known, many languages lack a definite or indefinite article, and the indefinite article in many languages explicitly signals referentiality, not type identifiability. This was true in earlier forms of English, for example. Non-referential phrases such as predicate nominals, as in 'She is a teacher' could be produced as a bare nominal. And it is also true in Modern Spanish (Bolinger 1980). In languages, like Mandarin, where the numeral 'one' is developing into an indefinite article, it is used only for referential phrases (Gundel et al 1993). Moreover, if a language has only one article, it is more likely to be a definite article than an indefinite article. Hedberg, Görgülü and Mameni (2009b) discussed the referring expression system of Salish languages. Salish languages do not contain definite articles that indicate unique identifiability or indefinite articles that indicate type identifiability, but they do have a system of frequently used articles that indicate referentiality, also called 'specificity'(Matthewson 1998, Gillon 2006). The feminine referential article in the Salish language Sechelt (Sháshísháłh) is illustrated in (28), where the data is drawn from a story, 'The Beaver', published in Beaumont (1985). The important character of the snake woman is introduced in (28a) using the feminine form of the referential article. Here the DP is referential but not uniquely identifiable. Later in the story, as in (28b), when the snake woman is referred to, the referential article is again used, here for a familiar or activated referent.

(28) a. tí   súx^w-t-as   **le**   ʔulqay   **slánay**...
      AUX   see-TR-3ERG   ART snake   woman
      'He saw a snake woman.'...

b. tí   ƛum   s-q^{w}ál-s   **le**   **slánay**...
    AUX then NOM-speak-3SG.POSS ART woman
    'Then the woman said ...'

The Sechelt (Sháshísháłh) referential article behaves like definite articles in English and Spanish and like bare NPs in Chinese, Japanese, and Russian in that it does not induce Q1 implicatures. This can be seen by comparing distribution of uses of those three forms in the three languages across cognitive statuses in discourse, as shown in (29); where the English and Chinese data is taken from Gundel et al. 1993, and the Sechelt data is taken from the Beaver story.

(29)
	FOC	ACT	FAM	UID	REF	TID
English *the* NP:	30	95	47	108		
Sechelt *te/łe* NP:	4	5	6	2	7	
Chinese Ø NP:	12	17	14	49	2	10

In all three languages, the forms that are given in (29) are also distributed across statuses higher than the ones they explicitly encode, as only pronouns and demonstrative determiners encode a higher status in the respective languages.

Hedberg, Görgülü, and Mameni (2009a) discuss the relationship between definiteness and referentiality in Turkish and Persian.[7] Turkish and Persian do not have definite or referential articles but they do have ways of differentially marking referential as opposed to non-referential objects through accusative case marking in the case of Turkish, or the object marker –RA in the case of Persian. Without accusative marking, Turkish indefinite objects get a non-referential (at most type identifiable) reading, as shown by the contrast in (30). Likewise, Persian marks referential direct objects with the suffix –RA, as shown by the contrast in (31)[8]. The referentiality markers co-occur here with the numeral meaning 'one' and hence the DPs are indefinite.[9]

(30) Turkish:
    a. *Bugün* **bir** *avukat-ı gör-üyor-um.*
       today one lawyer-ACC see-PROG-1SG
       'I am seeing a (particular) lawyer today.'

    b. *Bugün* **bir** *avukat gör-üyor-um.*
       Today one lawyer see-PROG-1SG
       'I am seeing a lawyer today (some lawyer or other).'

---

7 Referentiality in our sense is often called 'specificity' in the literature.
8 Some scholars (e.g. Sadrai 2014) analyze –RA as a definiteness marker, specifically a marker of unique identifiability, rather than a referentiality marker because a DP marked with –RA in the absence of the numeral 'one' (*ye*) or the marker –I (see footnote 10) must be interpreted as definite.
9 Turkish also allows a bare noun to appear in object position (Öztürk, 2005). Persian allows this too. However, these nouns do not have an argument status. In (i) it is possible that the speaker is seeing more than one lawyer.

(i) *Bugün* **avukat** *gör-üyor-um*
    today lawyer see-PROG-1SG
    'I am lawyer-seeing today.'

(31) Persian:
   a. *Emruz* **ye** **vakil-(i)-o** *mi-bin-am.*[10]
   today a/one lawyer-I-RA DUR-see-1SG
   'I am seeing a (particular) lawyer today.'

   b. *Emruz* **ye** **vakil** *mi-bin-am.*
   today a/one lawyer DUR-see-1SG
   'I am seeing a lawyer today (some lawyer or other).'

Referentiality has sometimes been discussed in the literature as a category orthogonal to definiteness, e.g. by von Heusinger (2002), which contradicts the entailment relation between uniquely identifiable and referential encoded in the Givenness Hierarchy. Von Heusinger proposes that definite NPs interpreted as attributive (Donnellan 1966) are non-referential ("non-specific"). However, data from Turkish and Persian show that at least in these languages, any DP interpreted as definite (uniquely identifiable in the sense that one can associate a unique referent, whether the exact identity is known or not) is necessarily marked referential. Examples from each language of uniquely identifiable attributive DPs are shown in (32) and (33). If they are to be interpreted as definite, referentiality marking is obligatory.[11]

(32) Turkish:
   katil-*(i) *bul-malı-yız*
   murderer-ACC find-MOD-1PL
   'We must find the murderer (whoever it is)'.

---

[10] In spoken Persian, –RA is realized as –*o* following consonants, and –*ro* following vowels. Ghomeshi (2003) calls the suffix –I an 'indefinite' marker, but Hedberg et al. (2009a) show that –I has other functions. It contrasts with a suffix –E (used in (33) below), which indicates that the DP is familiar; hence –I is used in uniquely identifiable but not familiar DPs as well as in indefinite DPs that are at most referential. *ye* 'a/one' and –I are both optional in (31a), but one of the two morphemes is necessary if the –RA marked DP is to be interpreted as indefinite (at most referential).'

[11] In fact, the murderer in (33) is marked with the –E suffix as familiar, but unfamiliar uniquely identifiable examples also are marked for referentiality, as in (i):

(i) *Jân* **avval-in mâshin-(i)-ro** ke did *az-ash* *xosh-esh* *umad.*
John first-DEF car-I-RA that saw from=CL:3SG good=CL:3SG came.3SG
'John liked *the first car that he saw.*' (speaker cannot necessarily identify the car)

The DP is definite here because it refers to a unique referent and the addressee can assign a unique representation. There can only be one car that is the first one that John saw. It is not necessary, however, that the addressee already has a representation of the car in memory. (The example in (i) is modeled after a Turkish example discussed in Görgülü (2009).)

(33) Persian:
    bayad   **qatel-(a)-*(ro)**   peyda   kon-im
    must   murderer-E-RA   find   do-1PL
    'We must find the murderer (whoever it is)'.

While many languages lack a form that explicitly signals one or more of the three lowest statuses on the Givenness Hierarchy – type identifiable, referential and uniquely identifiable, all languages that have been investigated within the Givenness Hierarchy appear to overtly encode the distinction between the two highest statuses – activated and in focus. This is true for the five languages investigated by Gundel et al 1993 (English, Japanese, Mandarin Chinese, Russian and Spanish) and also for the four languages investigated in Gundel, Bassene, Gordon, Humnick, and Khalfaoui (2010) – Eegimaa, Kumyk, Ojibwe and Tunisian Arabic.

Again, while this fact doesn't follow necessarily from the Givenness Hierarchy, the Givenness Hierarchy provides a natural explanation for it. The higher the functional load of a given status, the more likely a language is to have a form that overtly signals that status. Since statuses are in a unidirectional entailment relation, with higher statuses entailing lower ones, but not vice-versa, languages are more likely to encode the distinction between higher statuses than they are to encode the distinction between lower statuses. And languages are most likely not to have forms that explicitly encode the status type identifiable, which is entailed by all other statuses.

In addition to the fact that not all languages distinguish between every cognitive status on the Givenness Hierarchy, corresponding forms (i.e. pronouns and determiners) across languages do not necessarily encode the same status in every language.[12] This is especially true for demonstratives. Thus, in Russian, which like English has a two-way demonstrative distinction (often called 'proximal' and 'distal'), the distal demonstrative determiner ('to') is used primarily to encode contrastive conceptual information about spatial distance, as distinct from procedural information about cognitive distance. The distal form is thus rarely

---

[12] This is partly true because types of determiners and pronouns do not have clear language independent definitions. For example, although many languages lack a form that would be clearly classified as a definite article, in some languages the distal or proximal demonstrative, though not obligatory, is beginning to function like a definite article in that phrases headed by this determiner only have to be uniquely identifiable, not necessarily familiar. This is true in Mandarin Chinese for example. See Gundel et al 1993 for further discussion. Also, as noted above, some languages have referential determiners that behave like definite articles except that they encode only referentiality and can occur with phrases whose referents are at most referential, and not necessarily uniquely identifiable.

used, and the so-called proximal demonstrative determiner ('eto'), unlike its counterpart 'this' in English, explicitly encodes only familiarity, though like the proximal demonstrative determiner in English and other languages, it can be used for activated referents, since anything activated is also familiar. The proximal form is thus possible, and in fact preferred, in examples like (34) even if the dog has not been recently mentioned and is not present in the immediate visual context, i.e. if it is familiar, but not activated.

(34) Russian:
Eta sobaka u soseda mne vsju noč' ne davala spat'...
this dog at neighbor me all night not allow sleep.INF
'I couldn't sleep last night. That dog next door kept me awake...'
(Gundel et al 1993, p. 286)

Finally, of the languages investigated, none explicitly encode the set difference between two cognitive statuses on the Givenness Hierarchy with a single lexical item, for example one that means 'type identifiable but not uniquely identifiable', or 'activated but not in focus,' just as there is apparently no language that has a single lexical item which means 'some but not all'. This again is as expected given the unidirectional entailment of statuses on the Givenness Hierarchy since such meanings can be derived by pragmatic inference, when relevant.

5 Conclusion

The Givenness Hierarchy is a set of six cognitive statuses in a unidirectional entailment relation that specify procedural information to the addressee about how to mentally access representations associated with the intended interpretations of nominal expressions. Different pronominal and determiner forms explicitly encode different statuses on the hierarchy as part of their conventional meaning. The hierarchy interacts with general pragmatic principles to give rise to quantity implicatures similar to the quantity implicatures triggered by standard Horn scales, which are mainly based on conceptual meaning. The Givenness Hierarchy and the general pragmatic principles that it interacts with are universal, although different languages have referring forms that map onto the Givenness Hierarchy in different ways, with higher, more informative statuses being more likely to be mapped onto specific forms than lower, less informative ones. Thus, the theory can explain differences as well as similarities in referring expression systems across languages.

References

Abney, Steven Paul. 1987. *The English Noun Phrase in its Sentential Aspect*. Cambridge, MA: Masachusetts Institute of Technology dissertation.

Ariel, Mira. 1990. *Accessing Noun-Phrase Antecedents*. London: Routledge.

Atlas, Jay D. and Stephen C. Levinson. 1981. It-clefts, informativeness and logical form. In Cole, Peter (ed.), *Radical Pragmatics*, 1–61. New York: Academic Press.

Beaumont, Ronald C. 1985. *She shashishalhem, the Sechelt language: Language, stories and sayings of the Sechelt Indian people of British Columbia*. Penticton, British Columbia: Theytus Books.

Bolinger, Dwight D. 1980. Syntactic diffusion and the indefinite article. Bloomington, Indiana: Indiana University Linguistics Club.

Chafe, Wallace. 1994. *Discourse, Consciousness and Time*. Chicago: University of Chicago Press.

Chao, Wynne, 1968. *On Ellipsis*. New York: Garland.

Chomsky, Noam. 1971. Deep structure, surface structure, and semantic interpretation. In Steinberg, Danny D. and Leon A. Jakobovits (eds.). *Semantics: An Interdisciplinary Reader in Philosophy, Linguistics and Psychology*, 180–216. Cambridge: Cambridge University Press.

Donnellan, Keith. 1966. Reference and definite descriptions. *Philosophical Review* 75. 281–304.

Erteschik-Shir, Naomi. 1997. *The Dynamics of Focus Structure*. Cambridge: Cambridge University Press.

Ghomeshi, Jila. 2003. Plural marking, indefiniteness and the noun phrase. *Studia Linguistica* 57. 47–74.

Gillon, Carrie. 2006. *The Semantics of Determiners: Domain Restriction in Skwxwu7mesh*. Vancouver BC: University of British Columbia dissertation.

Grice, H. Paul. 1975. Logic and conversation. In Cole, Peter and Jerry Morgan (eds.), *Speech Acts*, 41–58. New York: Academic Press.

Görgülü, Emrah. 2009. On definiteness and specificity in Turkish. In Shibagaki, R. and R. Vermeulen (eds.). *MIT Working Papers in Linguistics 58. Proceedings of the 5th Workshop on Formal Altaic Linguistics*. Cambridge, MA: MIT.

Gundel, Jeanette K. 1974. *The Role of Topic and Comment in Linguistic Theory*. Austin, TX: University of Texas dissertation.

Gundel, Jeanette K. 1988. Universals of topic-comment structure. In Hammond, M., E. Moravscik and J. Wirth (eds.), *Studies in Syntactic Typology*, 209–239. Amsterdam: John Benjamins.

Gundel, Jeanette K. 1999. On different kinds of focus. In Bosch, Peter and Rob von der Sandt (eds.), Focus: Linguistic, Cognitive and Computational Perspectives, 293–305. Cambridge: Cambridge University Press.

Gundel, Jeanette K. 2009. Children's use of referring expressions. What can it tell us about theory of mind? *Cognitive Critique* 1. 1–28.

Gundel, Jeanette K. 2012. Pragmatics and information structure. In Keith Allen and Kasia M. Jaszczolt. *Cambridge Handbook of Pragmatics*, 585–599. Cambridge: Cambridge University Press.

Gundel, Jeanette K., Mamadou Bassene, Bryan Gordon, Linda Humnick and Amel Khalfaoui. 2010. Testing predictions of the Givenness Hierarchy framework: A crosslinguistic investigation. *Journal of Pragmatics* 42. 1770–1785.

Gundel, Jeanette K. and Thorstein Fretheim. 2004. Topic and focus. In Horn, Laurence R. and Gregory Ward (eds.). *The Handbook of Pragmatics*. Oxford: Blackwell. 175–196.

Gundel, Jeanette K., Nancy Hedberg and Ron Zacharski. 1993. Cognitive status and the form of referring expressions in discourse. *Language* 69. 274–307.

Gundel, Jeanette K., Nancy Hedberg and Ron Zacharski. 2012. Underpecification of cognitive status in reference production: Some empirical predictions. Topics in Cognitive Science (TopiCS) 4(2), 249–268.

Gundel, Jeanette K. and Ann E. Mulkern. 1998. Quantity implicatures in reference understanding. *Pragmatics and Cognition* 6. 21–45.

Hawkins, John A. 1991. On (in)definite articles: Implicatures and (un)grammaticality predictors. *Journal of Linguistics* 27. 405–442.

Hedberg, Nancy. 2000. The referential status of clefts. *Language* 76. 891–920.

Hedberg, Nancy, Emrah Görgülü, and Morgan Mameni. 2009a. On definiteness and specificity in Turkish and Persian. *Proceedings of the 2009 Annual Conference of the Canadian Linguistic Association.* http://homes.chass.utoronto.ca/~cla-acl/actes2009/actes2009.html.

Hedberg, Nancy, Emrah Görgülü and Morgan Mameni. 2009b. More on specificity and definiteness in English, Turkish and Persian. Paper presented at MOSAIC (Meeting of Semanticists Active in Canada), University of Ottawa, Ottawa, Ontario, 26 May.

von Heusinger, Klaus. 2002. Specificity and definites in sentence and discourse structure. *Journal of Semantics* 19. 245–276.

Horn, Laurence R. 1972. *On the Semantic Properties of Logical Operators in English*. Los Angeles, CA: University of California at Los Angeles dissertation.

Horn, Laurence R. 1984. A new taxonomy for pragmatic inference: Q-based and R-based implicature. In D. Schiffrin (ed.), *Meaning, Form and Use in Context (GURT '84)*, 11–42. Washington: Georgetown University Press.

Jackendoff, Ray. 1972. *Semantics and Generative Grammar*. Cambridge, MA: MIT Press.

Kehler, Andrew and Gregory Ward. 2006. Referring expressions and conversational implicatures. In Birner, Betty J. and Gregory Ward (eds.), *Drawing the Boundaries of Meaning: Neo-Gricean Studies in Pragmatics and Semantics in Honor of Laurence R. Horn*, 183–200. Amsterdam: John Benjamins.

Lambrecht, Knud. 1994. *Information Structure and Sentence Form*. Cambridge: Cambridge University Press.

Levinson, Stephen C. 2000. *Presumptive Meanings: The Theory of Generalized Conversational Implicature*. Cambridge, MA: MIT Press.

Matthewson, Lisa. 1998. *Determiner Systems and Quantificational Strategies: Evidence from Salish*. The Hague: Holland Academic Graphics.

Öztürk, Balkız. 2005. *Case, Referentiality and Phrase Structure*. Amsterdam: John Benjamins.

Paul, Hermann. 1880. *Prinzipien der Sprachgeschichte*. Tübingen: Niemeyer.

Postal, Paul. 1966. On so-called 'pronouns' in English. In Reibel, David A. and Sanford A. Schane (eds.), 1969, *Modern Studies in English*, 201–224. Englewood Cliffs, NJ: Prentice-Hall.

Prince, Ellen. 1981. Toward a taxonomy of given-new information. In Cole, Peter, *Radical Pragmatics*, 223–255. New York: Academic Press.

Roberts, Craige. 1996. Information structure in discourse: Towards an integrated account of formal pragmatics. In *Papers in Semantics, OSU Working Papers in Linguistics*, volume 49. Columbus, OH: Department of Linguistics, the Ohio State University.

Sadrai, Mahmoud. 2014. Cognitive status and *ra*-marked referents of nominal expressions in Persian discourse. Minneapolis, MN: University of Minnesota dissertation.
Sperber, Dan and Deidre Wilson. 1986. *Relevance: Communication and Cognition*. Cambridge, MA: Harvard University Press. [2nd edition, 1995, Oxford: Blackwell]
Strawson, Peter. 1964. Identifying reference and truth values. *Theoria* 30. 96–118.
van Valin, Robert D. Jr. 2005. *Exploring the Syntax-Semantics Interface*. Cambridge: Cambridge University Press.
Vallduvi, Enric. 1992. *The Information Component*. New York: Garland.

Mitsuaki Shimojo
3 Saliency in discourse and sentence form: Zero anaphora and topicalization in Japanese

Abstract: This study examines relationship between zero anaphora and topicalization with the post-nominal marker *wa* in Japanese, the two commonly used means to represent saliency in discourse, with respect to how speakers' choice of the forms is made and how the morphosyntactic coding should be represented in the linking algorithm in Role and Reference Grammar (Van Valin & LaPolla 1997). Utilizing the framework of Centering Theory (Grosz, Joshi, & Weinstein 1995), picture and animation-elicited Japanese narratives were analyzed and the following observations were made: (i) *wa* is typically used for a new topic in a (topicalized) subject switch and for a persisting (topicalized) subject that signals an episodic shift, and (ii) zero anaphora is not associated with any particular transition type. These observations lead to the conclusion that *wa* is assigned when the corresponding focus structure contains a *subordinate focus* (Erteschik-Shir 2007), and zero anaphora is assigned elsewhere, when no other form is assigned. The study provides discourse evidence for the linking algorithm and sheds light on the plausibility of subordinate focus structure, a potentially abstract notion without empirical applications.

1 Introduction

It has been observed cross-linguistically that saliency of information in discourse affects the speaker's choice of reference forms as well as sentence forms. Although salient information tends to be represented by reduced form and marked word order, the exact mechanism as to how particular choices are made in discourse is more or less language specific and requires a careful observation of discourse in each language.

This paper examines zero anaphora (argument ellipsis) and topicalization (left-dislocated, with the post-nominal marker *wa*) in Japanese, the two commonly used forms that represent saliency in discourse. While zero anaphora is omission of an element that represents salient information, topic-*wa* overtly presents such an element. The two forms that are associated with similar discourse properties raise a cardinal research question with respect to the relation-

---

Mitsuaki Shimojo, University at Buffalo, The State University of New York

ship of the two forms in speakers' usage. Are there discourse regularities which reflect speakers' choice of one form or the other? And how can such regularities be captured in a theory of syntax? The present study probes these questions with (1) quantitative and qualitative analyses of Japanese narrative discourse (the quantitative analysis utilizes Centering Theory, cf. Grosz, Joshi, and Weinstein 1995), and (2) the application of the empirical findings to Role and Reference Grammar (Van Valin and LaPolla 1997) combined with Erteschik-Shir's (1997, 2007) f(ocus)-structure representations.

2 Scope and previous studies

Japanese is well known for its wide range of ways to morpho-syntactically differentiate the coding of arguments on the discourse-pragmatic basis. The so-called topic marker *wa* is one of the commonly used forms, in which the topic element is left-dislocated and marked with *wa*, as shown in (1a, b).[1]

(1) a. *hanako-wa   taroo-to   eega-o   mita*
       Hanako-TOP   Taro-with   movie-ACC   saw
       'Hanako saw a movie with Taro.'

   b. *sono eega-wa   taroo-ga   maeni   mitakotogaatta*
       that movie-TOP   Taro-NOM   before   had.seen
       'The movie, Taro had seen (it) before.'

Zero anaphora is also a very common form, in which arguments are coded in the fully attenuated zero form, as exemplified by (2b), where "Hanako" is anaphorically identifiable.

(2) a. *hanako-ga   taroo-to   eega-o   mita*
       Hanako-NOM   Taro-with   movie-ACC   saw
       'Hanako saw a movie with Taro.'

   b. *sorekara   Ø   kaimono-ni   itta*
       then   shopping-to   went
       'Then, (she) went shopping.'

---

[1] The following abbreviations are used for the interlinear glosses: ACC = accusative, LK = linker, NOM = nominative, TOP = topic. Omitted elements in zero anaphora are indicated by Ø in the examples and the corresponding translation is given in the parentheses within the translation of the whole clause.

While there may be discourse genre-specific usage of these forms,[2] previous studies generally have pointed to the functional properties that zero anaphora represents continuation of a topic (Hinds and Hinds 1979; Tanimura and Yoshida 2003) and *wa* represents discourse prominence such as highlighted referents (Maynard 1980) and contrastivity, especially in spontaneous discourse (Clancy and Downing 1987; Shimojo 2005). Overall, the common property of these two forms lies in their representation of non-focus elements of a sentence, as focus elements are typically represented by an overt element marked with a case marker or a focus particle.[3] Furthermore, they also share the property of representing salient elements in discourse. Shimojo's (2005) analyses of spontaneous Japanese conversation have revealed that zero anaphora is typically used for referents that continue from the anaphoric context to the cataphoric context, i.e. "salient" referents that continue to be activated in the context. In the same conversation data, topic-*wa* was found to be associated with saliency also, but in a somewhat different way. It is not recency of anaphoric reference that predicts the use of *wa* (for example, a referent given for the first time may be marked with *wa*), but *wa* is used regularly when a referent is contrasted with others, while as in the case of zero anaphora, *wa*-marked elements tend to persist in the cataphoric context. Despite the underlying difference in their functional properties, zero anaphora and *wa* both create coherence by linking textual elements and either form may be acceptable in the same sentence in some contexts, which makes it obscure how a speaker's choice is made between the two forms.

How are the observed regularities in discourse captured in a syntactic theory with respect to speakers' choice of forms? In Role and Reference Grammar, Shimojo (2011: 289) has set a step forward to layout the linking algorithm to formalize how zero anaphora and topic-*wa* are differentiated in speakers' coding of the arguments. The relevant part of the algorithm is given in (3).[4]

---

[2] For discussions of *wa* in different types of discourse, see Hinds, Maynard, and Iwasaki (eds.) (1987) inter alia.
[3] However, the topic marker *wa* may mark a focus element as shown in the linking step (3i). Likewise, a case marker, especially the nominative *ga*, may mark a non-focus element as shown in the linking step (3ii). See Shimojo (2011) for discussion of these marked cases of (de)focusing.
[4] In this paper, we do not discuss how the argument forms play a role in the mapping from sentence forms to semantic representations. See Shimojo (2011: 290–1) for the linking algorithm from syntax to semantics.

(3) Linking algorithm: semantics → syntax
Determine the morphosyntactic coding of the arguments.

b. Assign the arguments the appropriate case markers and/or postpositions.

  (i) If an argument has the f-structure [{x$_{foc}$, y}$_{top}$]$_{top}$ or [{x$_{foc}$, ...}$_{top}$]$_{top}$, or if it is a matrix focus but needs to be defocused, assign *wa* to the argument(s).

  (ii) If an argument is a matrix focus, or if it is a matrix topic but needs to be focused, assign appropriate case markers, based on the case assignment rules for accusative constructions.

  (iii) If neither (i) nor (ii) above applies, use no morphosyntactic instantiation for the argument (i.e. zero anaphora).

As indicated in (3i), the linking algorithm incorporates the notion of subordinate focus (Erteschik-Shir 1997, 2007) and represents contrastivity associated with topic-*wa* in its subordinate f-structure. A *wa*-marked element *x* may be contrasted either with an element *y* which is overtly specified in the context ([{x$_{foc}$, y}$_{top}$]$_{top}$), or with an implied element ([{x$_{foc}$, ...}$_{top}$]$_{top}$). In (4), for example, sentence (a) specifies the set [*ani* 'older brother', *imooto* 'younger sister'] and in sentence (b), only the subset *older brother* is singled out as a topic and predicated. Thus, the topic phrase of sentence (b) represents the f-structure [{ani$_{foc}$, imooto}$_{top}$]-WA$_{top}$.

(4) a. watasi-wa   ani-to   imooto-ga   imasu
       I-TOP   older.brother-and younger.sister-NOM   exist
       'I have an older brother and a younger sister.'

    b. ani-wa   tookyoo-ni sundeimasu
       older.brother-TOP   Tokyo-in   is.living
       '(My) older brother lives in Tokyo.'

As stated above, a non-topicalized subset can be only implied, as shown in (5).

(5) ima watasi-no ani-wa   tookyoo-ni sundeimasu
    now I-LK   older.brother-TOP   Tokyo-in   is.living
    'My older brother lives in Tokyo now.'

In this case, the set is not defined but implied, hence, [{watasi-no ani$_{foc}$, ...}$_{top}$]-WA$_{top}$. In this focus type, unlike in the case of (4), the complement of the selected set is not eliminated. For example, the sentence in (5) can be followed by a sentence 'And my younger sister lives in Tokyo too'. On the other hand, the same continuation would be very awkward after (4b), where the set is clearly defined and one subset is singled out and topicalized. It should be noted that the two types of f-structure that represent topic-*wa* discussed above capture the inherent contrastive property of *wa*. Whether a set of referents is contextually specified or unspecified, topic-*wa* singles out a subset and therefore brings out contrastiveness.

In terms of the linking algorithm in (3), zero anaphora represents the default option because it is the form used when any of the other options do not apply. *Wa* is used for a matrix topic that contains a subset focus (i.e. step (3i)) and a case particle (or an appropriate focus particle) is used for a matrix focus (x_{foc} [predicate]) (i.e. step (3ii)). If an element to be coded is neither a subset-containing topic nor a matrix focus (i.e. if element x represents the f-structure, x_{top} [predicate]$_{foc}$), zero anaphora is used for the element. The implication here is unmarkedness associated with zero anaphora. First, the zero element represents a topic of simple f-structure, which lacks a focus, whether it is a matrix focus or a subordinate (i.e. subset) focus. Also, in text counts, zero anaphora is often the most common form used in discourse. Fry (2003: 86) reports in his analysis of the CallHome Japanese corpus that the overall ellipsis rate for all arguments was 70%. In Shimojo's (2005: 64) spontaneous conversation data, zero anaphora was used most frequently for both subjects and objects, amounting to 64% of the total 5087 cases, exceeding the absence of a post-nominal marker (18%), *wa* (9%), the nominative *ga* (7%), the accusative *o* (2%). Lastly, zero anaphora is unmarked in form because of the morphological and phonological absence.

3 Issues

Despite the previous studies summarized above, there are some issues remaining to be investigated. One of the issues is concerned with how the notion of focus used in f-structure representations is linked with previous discourse observations. Shimojo's (2011) linking algorithm assumes the notion of focus as focal information in the way it is defined by Dik (1997: 326), namely, "information which is relatively the most important or salient in the given communicative setting". The notion is more formally put by Erteschik-Shir (1997: 11) as follows:

(6) The FOCUS of a sentence S = the (intension of a) constituent c of S which the speaker intends to direct the attention of his/her hearer(s) to, by uttering S.

Focus has commonly been associated with newness of information since new information contained in an utterance typically makes the utterance informative for its purpose in a given context. However, it is often the case that previously given information represents an informative part of an utterance, which is expected to attract the hearer's new attention. In (4b), for example, *older brother* is given in the preceding context, but it represents focus (though it is not the sole focus of the utterance) since it requires the hearer's attention, as the subject referent is shifted from the whole set to the subset.

Given the definition of focus provided above, empirical support for the claim made in the linking algorithm in (3) must come from a discourse analysis in a framework which examines the speaker and hearer's local attentional state as they process a discourse. Previous discourse observations used in studies of syntax are insufficient to show whether an attention-based focus structure theory is empirically supported. Shimojo's findings (2005), which are assumed in the linking algorithm in (3), are primarily based on textual measures of topic continuity, such as anaphoric referential distance and cataphoric persistence (see Givón 1983). Recency of anaphoric reference and cataphoric frequency of reference provide a rough approximation of how a referent is focused and defocused in a given stretch of discourse, but they fall short of capturing relationships between choice of referring expression and local-level attentional state, as a referent continues to draw attention (i.e. stays salient) or attention is shifted away from the referent.

The discussion thus far leads us to the fact that the formalization of argument coding proposed in the linking algorithm lacks empirical support. The present study attempts to evaluate the formalization by adopting Centering Theory, which allows us to examine relationships between choice of referring expression and types of transition from one utterance to the next in terms of center of attention. The primary empirical questions for this study are: (a) What discourse conditions warrant the proposed contrastivity of topic-*wa*?, and (b) is zero anaphora used in its unique discourse conditions or is it better captured as an unmarked form that is used elsewhere? These questions are not trivial because the linking algorithm would be a mere stipulation without empirically pinpointing discourse properties associated with particular f-structures in the speaker's coding process.

4 Centering Theory

While discourse segments exhibit both local coherence (among the utterances within a discourse segment) and global coherence (with other segments in the discourse) (Grosz and Sidner 1986), Centering Theory (Grosz, Joshi, and

Weinstein 1995) is particularly concerned with local coherence. "Centering" models the discourse participants' focus of attention (i.e. attentional state) at the local level, as they continuously update their local attentional state in processing a discourse. In this theory, each utterance in a discourse segment has two structures of local focus: forward-looking centers [Cfs] and a backward-looking center [Cb]. Cfs are elements contained in the current utterance U_i and ranked in terms of relative salience as in (7).

(7) Cf ranking for Japanese (Walker, Iida and Cote 1994)
(GRAMMATICAL OR ZERO) TOPIC > EMPATHY > SUBJECT > OBJECT2 > OBJECT > OTHERS

The highest ranked member of the Cfs(U_i) is called the preferred center [Cp] and it is the expected focus of the following utterance U_{i+1}. Cb is a special member of Cfs, which is defined as the highest ranked Cf in the preceding utterance U_{i-1} and also realized in the current utterance U_i. With the Cb and Cp, the theory captures both looking back to the previous discourse and projecting preferences for the subsequent discourse and assumes that these properties are updated at every utterance as the discourse segment is processed.

The theory also assumes that different ways of updating the Cb (i.e. transition) affect coherence in the discourse segment and some transition types are preferred over others. Transition types are defined by two criteria: whether the Cb of the preceding utterance is kept in the current utterance (8a), and whether the Cb in the current utterance is also the highest ranked entity (8b).

(8) a. $Cb(U_i) = Cb(U_{i-1})$, or there is no $Cb(U_{i-1})$

b. $Cb(U_i) = Cp(U_i)$

If both (8a) and (8b) hold, it is a continue [CON] transition, which represents a situation in which the speaker has been talking about an entity and shows an intention to continue talking about the entity in the subsequent utterance. If (8a) applies but (8b) does not, it is a retain [RET] transition, in which the speaker shows an intention to shift to a new topic in the subsequent utterance, because the current Cb is no longer the Cp. If (8a) does not apply, then it is a shifting [SHIFT] state, in which the speaker has shifted attention to a new entity.[5] These transition types are exemplified by the examples in (9), which are

---

[5] In the Centering literature, SHIFT is further divided into smooth-shift and rough-shift, depending on whether (8b) applies or not. This distinction is not used in the current study, however.

from Tanimura and Yoshida (2003: 59). The Cb, Cfs and transition type for each utterance are indicated in Table 1.

Centering Theory assumes that discourse segments which continue with the same center are more coherent (and require less processing) than those that shift; thus, the theory stipulates that transition states are ordered: CONTINUE is preferred to RETAIN, which is preferred to SHIFT (Walker, Iida, and Cote 1994: 7). A CONTINUE transition requires the hearer to keep track of only one main discourse entity, unlike the other transition types, which involve a shift of attention between main entities.

(9) 1. *and the man with the hat runs back,*
    2. *and gives the hat to the boy,*
    3. *and so the boy gives him three pears, to thank him for bringing the hat,*
    4. *so the boys who got the pears takes the three pears back,*
    5. *and the three boys share the three pears,*

Table 1

Utt.	Cb	Cf*	Transition type
1	none	the man with the hat(s)	NULL**
2	the man with the hat	zero(= the man with the hat)(s), the boy(o), the hat(o)	CON
3	the man with the hat	the boy(s), him(= the man with the hat)(o), three pears(o), the hat(ot)	RET
4	the three pears	the boys(s), the three pears(o), the pears(ot)	SHIFT
5	the boys	the three boys(s), the three pears(o)	SHIFT

*s = subject, o = object, ot = others, **NULL represents a case in which there is no Cb for the utterance.

Given the outline of Centering Theory, it should be noted that the notion of center (or center of attention) used in the theory needs to be kept separate from the notion of focus used in f-structure representations discussed in Section 3. Walker, Iida and Cote (1994: 6) state that "[t]he Cb is the discourse entity that the utterance most centrally concerns, what has been elsewhere called the 'theme'"; thus, the Cb represents saliency as represented by the topic of f-structures, though it may represent a subordinate focus embedded in a matrix topic.

5 Data

The data for the current study consists of picture and animation-elicited Japanese narratives written by 73 native speakers. The picture-elicited narratives were given by 11 speakers on the basis of a cartoon strip consisting of 12 pictures (see Appendix), which was used by Brown and Yule (1983) in their study of English narratives. Each speaker was asked to write a coherent story in any way they chose on the basis of the pictures, using at least one sentence per picture. The cartoon strip contains three main characters depicted in a series of events such that a man bored with his wife meets a young woman ending up living together but is left alone in the end.

The animation-elicited narratives were written by 62 speakers on the basis of a five-minutes episode of a claymation Pingu, entitled *Pingu Runs Away*.[6] The speakers were asked to write a story at their own pace while they watched the video. The episode contains three characters, Pingu and his parents, concerning Pungu's running away from home after he ruined the dinner table and getting lost in the icy field until he was finally taken home safely by his father.

The pictures and animation served as a useful guideline to control the overall storyline in the speakers' writing, yet allowing the leeway to use their own discourse and sentence structures. The written narratives were divided into clausal units for the centering analysis, and for each clausal unit, the Cb, Cfs, and transition type were identified and the data was tagged in terms of Cb form (i.e. zero anaphora and *wa*). Adverbial subordinate clauses were considered as independent clausal units; however, noun modifying clauses, subject and object complement clauses were considered as part of the matrix clausal unit. The data contains 1862 clausal units in total.

6 Results and discussion

The discussion of the results deals with the property of Cb and Cp: their forms, the associated transition types, and structural properties of the clausal units.

6.1 Overall frequency by Cb form and transition type

Table 2 shows the frequency counts in terms of the transition types and Cb forms (or Cp forms for NULL). Overall, zero anaphora and *wa* are the two most frequently used forms and of almost equal frequency. It is not surprising that, in

---

6 The Pingu data was provided by Mitsuko Yamura-Takei, Etsuko Yoshida, and Miho Fujiwara, who also collaborated on data coding used in this study.

NULL, zero anaphora is noticeably less frequent than *wa*, since there is no Cb in the current clause, or there is even no preceding clause in the case of the first clause of a narrative, which negatively affects the identifiability of the referent if omitted. For this reason, we will exclude the NULL transition type in the subsequent discussions. In the CONTINUE transitions, zero anaphora is more frequent than *wa*, which is expected due to the continuation of the center. On the other hand, in the RETAIN transitions, *wa* is far more frequent. A clause in the RETAIN transition represents a complex information structure because the clause contains a prospective new center in addition to the Cb. In the SHIFT transitions, zero anaphora and *wa* are of almost equal frequency; both are used for over 40% of the total.

Table 2

Transition type	Zero anaphora	Wa	Other[7]	Total
NULL	20 (.13)	98 (.63)	38 (.24)	156 (1.00)
CON	478 (.62)	273 (.36)	14 (.02)	765 (1.00)
RET	70 (.17)	262 (.62)	90 (.21)	422 (1.00)
SHIFT	258 (.50)	224 (.43)	37 (.07)	519 (1.00)
Total	826 (.44)	857 (.46)	179 (.10)	1862 (1.00)

The observations concerning the overall frequencies are summarized in (10).

(10) Frequency in terms of the three transition types
 CONTINUE zero anaphora > *wa*
 RETAIN   *wa* > zero anaphora
 SHIFT   zero anaphora, *wa*

It is noteworthy that zero anaphora is as common as *wa* in SHIFT, which is inconsistent with a previous claim that the use of zero anaphora is most acceptable in CONTINUE, where relative inferential demand is low to process the utterance (Yamura-Takei 2005, Yamura-Takei and Fujiwara 2007). The present findings suggest that it is not the case that zero anaphora is characterizable solely by the particular transition type. In the subsequent sections, we will examine the relationship between transition types and some structural properties of clauses.

---

[7] "Other" consists of arguments marked with case markers (such as *ga* 'nominative' and *o* 'accusative') and adjuncts.

6.2 Persisting (topicalized) subject center

When a (topicalized) subject persists from one clausal unit to the following, the two units may be contained in the same sentence or separate across a sentence boundary. In (11), for example, the center *Pingu* persists for three clauses, from (b) to (d), within a single sentence in which clauses are connected with the conjunction *tari* "and". *Pingu* continues to be a center in (e) as well; however, (e) is a separate sentence. This section examines the relationship between the structural properties and a persisting center for the CONTINUE and SHIFT transitions.[8]

(11) a. *pinguu-wa [NULL] ryoosin-to issyoni yuusyoku-o tabeteiru*
Pingu-TOP   parents-with together dinner-ACC is.eating
'Pingu is having dinner with his parents.'

b. *sikasi pinguu-wa [CON] yasai-o   nokositari*
but   Pingu-TOP   vegetable-ACC leave.and
'But, Pingu is leaving vegetable (on his plate) and'

c. *Ø [CON] isu-o   yurasitari*
           chair-ACC rock.and
'(Pingu) is rocking his chair and'

d. *Ø [CON]   gyoogi-ga   warui*
              manner-NOM   bad
'(Pingu) is misbehaving [lit. (Pingu's) manner is bad].'

e. *sonotoki pinguu-wa [CON] teeburu-o hikkurikaesitesimau*
then   Pingu-TOP   table-ACC end.up.knocking.over
'Then, Pingu ends up knocking over the table.'

Table 4 presents the frequency counts of zero anaphora and *wa* that represent a persisting center in CONTINUE in terms of the two structural types. In this transition type, persisting centers are common in both structural types; however, most of the same-sentence centers are realized as zero anaphora (93%), and *wa* is typically used for a center that persists from a preceding sentence (148 out of 174, i.e. 85%).

---

8 In RETAIN, the backward-looking center is not the preferred center (i.e. (topicalized) subject); therefore, only CONTINUE and SHIFT transitions are considered here.

Table 4: Inter/intra-sentential persisting (topicalized) subject center in CONTINUE

	Persisting from a preceding clause of the same sentence	Persisting from a preceding sentence
Zero anaphora	362 (.93)	105 (.42)
Wa	26 (.07)	148 (.58)
Total	388 (1.00)	253 (1.00)

X^2 (1) = 205.145, $p < .001$

A similar pattern is found for the SHIFT transitions (cf. Table 5). Intra-sententially persisting centers (297 cases) are three times more frequent than inter-sententially persisting centers (93 cases), which means that the same (topicalized) subject sequence in SHIFT is more likely to occur within the same sentence. As in CONTINUE, the former is almost always realized in zero anaphora (96%), and most of *wa* is used for sentence-initial persisting centers (50 out of 62, i.e. 81%).

Table 5: Inter/intra-sentential persisting (topicalized) subject center in SHIFT

	Persisting from a preceding clause of the same sentence	Persisting from a preceding sentence
Zero anaphora	285 (.96)	43 (.46)
Wa	12 (.04)	50 (.54)
Total	297 (1.00)	93 (1.00)

X^2 (1) = 127.272, $p < .001$

To summarize, in both CONTINUE and SHIFT, intra-sententially persisting centers are mostly coded in zero anaphora, while *wa* used for persisting centers is found mostly for a new sentence. There is a simple structural explanation for this asymmetry. By default, the topic of a sentence is dislocated in the left-detached position, which gives it scope over the entire sentence; thus, the same topic element is not repeated for each clause (if repeated, the sentence would sound redundant and unnatural).

Whether CONTINUE or SHIFT, both zero anaphora and *wa* are common for centers persisting across sentences; however, a qualitative examination of the data suggests discourse-organizational grounds for the use of *wa*. The data contains many cases in which an overt NP-*wa* is used for a sentence that shifts to a new *episode* (van Dijk 1981), a different global event or action, which typically represents a new time, place (or scene), and/or participants. In (12), for example, the transition from (d) to (e) represents an episodic boundary, as the narrative shifts from the couple's discord at home to the husband's new life with the young woman. In (e), *husband* is topicalized with *wa*, despite the continuation of the referent from the preceding context.[9]

(12) a. *tuma-wa [SHIFT]   heya-ni   tozikomotte*
         wife-TOP   room-in   shut.herself.in.and
         'The wife keeps to her room and'

   b. *Ø [CON]   naiteiru*
               is.crying
      '(she) is crying.'

   c. *otto-wa [NULL]   nimotu-o   matomete*
      husband-TOP   baggage-ACC   pack.up.and
      'The husband packed up his baggage and'

   d. *Ø [CON]   deteikukotoninatta*
               decided.to.leave
      '(he) decided to leave.'

   e. *otto-wa [CON]   disuko-de   siriatta   zyosei-to   kekkonsita*
      husband-TOP   disco-in   got.to.know   woman-with   married
      'The husband married the woman whom (he) got to know in the disco.'

6.3 (Topicalized) subject center switch

When (topicalized) subjects switch from one clause to the next, the switch may occur within a sentence or across a sentence boundary. In (13), there is a switch from *Pingu's parents* in (a) to *Pingu* in (b) and these conjoined clauses form a single sentence. On the other hand, the switch from *Pingu's mother* in (c) to *Pingu* in (d) spans two sentences. The token counts for the Cp's in the three transition type are shown in Tables 6, 7, 8.

(13) a. *pinguu-no   ryoosin-wa [RET]   tanosiku   syokuzi-o   siteimasitaga*
        Pingu-LK   parents-TOP   happily   meal-ACC   were.doing.but
        'Pingu's parents were having dinner happily, but'

   b. *pinguu-wa [CON]   dandanto   kigen-ga   warukunattesimaimasita*
      Pingu-TOP   gradually   mood-NOM   ended.up.becoming.bad
      'Pingu became upset gradually.'

---

[9] A similar observation is made by Clancy and Downing (1987) in their oral narrative data, in which NP-*wa* that represents a continuing referent is used at a turning point of a story. The example in (12e) can be taken as such.

[8 clauses omitted]

    c. *suruto pinguu-no hahaoya-wa [NULL] kare-o donaritukemasita*
        then   Pingu-LK mother-TOP   he-ACC shouted.at
       'Then, Pingu's mother shouted at him.'

    d. *pinguu-wa [CON] ie-o tobidasitesimaimasita*
        Pingu-TOP   house-ACC ended.up.rushing.out
       'Pingu rushed out of the house.'

In CONTINUE (Table 6), inter-sentential switch is more frequent than sentence-internal switch (77 out of 110, 70%), and *wa* is far more frequent than zero anaphora in both types of switch (with no statistical significance).

Table 6: New (topicalized) subject center in CONTINUE

	New (topicalized) subject in intra-sentential switch	New (topicalized) subject in inter-sentential switch
Zero anaphora	5 (.15)	5 (.06)
Wa	28 (.85)	72 (.94)
Total	33 (1.00)	77 (1.00)

In RETAIN (Table 7) as well, inter-sentential switch is more frequent than sentence-internal switch (194 out of 259, 75%), and in both cases, *wa* is more frequent than zero anaphora. The use of *wa* is even more robust for inter-sentential switch.

Table 7: New (topicalized) subject center in RETAIN

	New (topicalized) subject in intra-sentential switch	New (topicalized) subject in inter-sentential switch
Zero anaphora	16 (.25)	19 (.10)
Wa	49 (.75)	175 (.90)
Total	65 (1.00)	194 (1.00)

$X^2 (1) = 7.927, p < .01$

As in the other transition types, in the SHIFT transitions (Table 8), inter-sentential switch is more frequent than sentence-internal switch (171 out of 248, 69%) and *wa* is more common than zero anaphora with inter-sentential switch. Again, the use of *wa* is more robust with inter-sentential switch (about 80% of the total).

Table 8: New (topicalized) subject center in SHIFT

	New (topicalized) subject in intra-sentential switch	New (topicalized) subject in inter-sentential switch
Zero anaphora	33 (.43)	36 (.21)
Wa	44 (.57)	135 (.79)
Total	77 (1.00)	171 (1.00)

X^2 (1) = 11.507, $p < .001$

In summary, the frequency counts for (topicalized) subject switch have revealed the following: (i) (topicalized) subject switch is more likely to occur across sentences than within a sentence, and (ii) *wa* is used more frequently than zero anaphora for a new (topicalized) subject. The dominance of *wa* is more robustly observed for a new (topicalized) subject that appears in a new sentence, which coincides with the observation that an episodic shift occurs with a new sentence, though an episodic shift does not always involve a (topicalized) subject shift.

6.4 Potentially contrastive context

As discussed in Section 2, the linking algorithm in (3) indicates that *wa* is assigned to an argument if it has the f-structure $[\{x_{foc}, y\}_{top}]_{top}$ or $[\{x_{foc}, ...\}_{top}]_{top}$, and this means that, for *wa* to be assigned, topic referents must be present, or implied to be present, in the preceding context. To test this assumption, frequency counts were conducted for zero anaphora and *wa* in the Cp's that are preceded by a potentially contrastive context. For this purpose, "potentially contrastive context" was defined as an immediately preceding clause which contains a referent that can be taken as a subset of a shared set. For example, *parents* in (14a) can be taken as a subset of Pingu family; thus, *Pingu* in (14b) is considered as one that is in a potentially contrastive context. Table 9 shows the number of zero anaphora and *wa* appearing in such contexts in terms of the three transition types.

(14) a. *pinguu-wa [NULL]   ryoosin-to   issyoni   yuusyoku-o   tabeteiru*
   Pingu-TOP   parents-with   together   dinner-ACC   be.eating
   'Pingu is having dinner with his parents.'

   b. *sikasi   pinguu-wa [CON]   yasai-o   nokositari*
   but   Pingu-TOP   vegetable-ACC   leave.and
   'But, Pingu is leaving vegetable (on his plate) and'

Although the percentage of the two forms significantly differed by the transition types, the observed frequency does not necessarily reflect the assumed "subset" requirement for *wa*. In the CONTINUE and SHIFT transitions, both *wa* and zero anaphora are commonly used in the potentially contrastive contexts. In RETAIN, however, *wa* is clearly the preferred form. Overall, it is safe to conclude that the "potentially contrastive context" in the way it was defined does not constitute grounds for the use of *wa*. Yet the dominance of *wa* in RETAIN indicates that *wa* is preferred for a new Cp (which is different from the Cb of the clause). This may also explain the use of *wa* in some of the SHIFT cases because in ROUGH-SHIFT, the Cp is not the Cb, as in the case of RETAIN.

Table 9

	CON	RET	SHIFT
Zero anaphora	101 (.47)	1 (.07)	81 (.62)
Wa	113 (.53)	14 (.93)	49 (.38)
Total	214 (1.00)	15 (1.00)	130 (1.00)

Zero anaphora, *wa*, CON, SHIFT: X^2 (1) = 6.818, $p < .01$
Zero anaphora, *wa*, CON, RET: Fisher's exact test, $p = .0021$
Zero anaphora, *wa*, RET, SHIFT: Fisher's exact test, $p < .0001$

7 Application of discourse observations and linking algorithm

On the basis of the results from the Centering analysis presented thus far, the following generalizations are proposed. First, the CONTINUE transition is not associated with zero anaphora such that it serves as a condition for the choice of the form. Zero anaphora was found to be dominant only for sentence-internal persistence of centers (Table 4), and there is a structural explanation for this, as discussed earlier. On the other hand, *wa* is associated with two related properties: (i) a new center in a (topicalized) subject switch, and (ii) a persisting center which represents the onset of a new episode. As stated in (10), zero anaphora outnumbers *wa* in the CONTINUE transitions; however, it is not the case that the continuation of a center per se is linked with the use of zero anaphora. The prominence of zero anaphora in CONTINUE is due to the low frequency of (topicalized) subject switch in this transition type and the high frequency in sentence-internal continuation of a center. Overall, the discourse observations point to the specialized property of *wa* as a marker of new (topicalized) subject, either as a new topic in a (topicalized) subject switch or a "new" topic which re-presents a persisting referent and signals an episodic boundary. Our observations also point to the general property of zero anaphora as default marking which is used when *wa* is not available structurally or the conditions for the *wa* use are not met. This is in line with the linking algorithm (3iii).

With respect to contrastive properties of *wa*, the present analysis has revealed that it is not mere presence of potential subsets in the preceding context that warrants the use of *wa*, but it is a switch from a previous center (Cb or Cp) to a new center. This observation leads us to assuming that for a potential subset in the preceding context to be a subset of the subordinate f-structure represented by a topic-*wa* (i.e. the *y* element in (3i)), the subset needs to be salient such that it is a Cb or a Cp. In other words, if a potential subset is not salient enough, the corresponding set would not be made salient enough to be realized as a set at the time the new topic (i.e. another subset) is given. In terms of f-structure, the saliency of the set, including the non-focus subset *y*, is indicated by the subordinate TOPIC set $\{x_{foc}, y\}_{top}$ which is embedded in the matrix topic. The TOPIC indicates that the subsets are required to be salient enough to be topical.

The last puzzle piece to fit in the linking algorithm is the use of *wa* at an episodic boundary. We claim that this is captured by the same subordinate f-structure for *wa*. We assume that an episodic shift is a type of topic shift and, as in the case of a (topicalized) subject shift, it involves a shift from one subset topic to another. While a (topicalized) subject shift from one clause to the next represents a shift in a very local-level discourse, an episodic shift may span a broader range as the discourse is shifted from a more global level topic, i.e. a prominent entity of one event to a prominent entity of another event, as exemplified by a shift from *wife* of the *family discord* episode to *husband* in the *new life* episode in (12).

By way of summary, the linking algorithm given earlier is revised in (15). Step (ii) includes the saliency requirements for the subsets. Also, steps (i) and (ii) in the original version are reversed in the revision so that they are arranged in terms of a topic-focus scale, with $[\ ]_{foc}$ (a matrix focus for a case marker) being most focal and $[\ ]_{top}$ (a matrix topic for zero anaphora) being most topical. The f-structure for *wa* sits squarely in the middle due to the topic-focus ambivalence, as indicated by the matrix topic that contains a subordinate focus.

(15) Revision of (3) linking algorithm: semantics → syntax
Determine the morphosyntactic coding of the arguments.
   b. Assign the arguments the appropriate case markers and/or postpositions.
      (i) If an argument is a matrix focus, or if it is a matrix topic that needs to be focused, assign appropriate case markers, based on the case assignment rules for accusative constructions. If it is a matrix focus that needs to be defocused, follow step (ii).
      (ii) If an argument has the f-structure [{x_{foc}, y}$_{top}$]$_{top}$ or [{x_{foc}, ...}$_{top}$]$_{top}$ (the specified or implied non-focus subset(s) within { }$_{top}$ must be salient), or if it is a matrix focus that needs to be defocused, assign *wa* to the argument(s).
      (iii) If neither (i) nor (ii) above applies, use no morphosyntactic instantiation for the argument (i.e. zero anaphora).

8 Conclusions

This study was an attempt to show how observations in discourse may be applied to a theory of syntax with respect to morphosyntactic coding of arguments in Japanese. We hope to have demonstrated that the findings from our study have provided empirical support for the linking algorithm and particularly shed light on plausibility of subordinate f-structure, a potentially abstract notion without empirical applications.

Given the observation of topic-*wa* in signaling an episodic shift, one may wonder how this relates to the long-known discourse effects in the use of the nominative marker *ga* for a topic, which is captured by step (15i) of the linking algorithm (i.e. "... or if it is a matrix topic that needs to be focused, assign appropriate case markers,..."). It has been observed, particularly in narrative discourse, that an entity that has already been salient may be re-introduced as if new (as part of a new proposition represented by the whole sentence) to signal a shift such as a temporal change in discourse and a perspective shift in narration. In Maynard's (1987) terms, it represents the narrator's staging strategy, in which the avoidance of *wa*-marking (hence, the use of *ga* for a subject) achieves non-thematization of the referent, as it draws the hearer's new attention by being presented as if new. The critical difference between this use of *ga* and the use of *wa* in episodic boundaries lies in cohesion with an earlier discourse element. The *ga*-marking cancels cohesion so that the whole proposition containing a previously given element can be presented as new. On the other hand, *wa* maintains cohesion with an earlier element while signaling a shift in discourse structure. This contrast is captured by the subordinate f-structure in the linking algorithm because a non-focus subset required for *wa* represents the link with an earlier element.

Lastly, the present analysis was based solely on certain written narratives. Because the exact usage of zero anaphora and *wa* may be genre specific, a future study would be appropriate to investigate different genres of discourse, such as spoken narratives and conversations, and to capture variations in the linking algorithm. Furthermore, the present findings may be fed into a future cross-linguistic study of topic marking. A recent cross-linguistic study in Japanese and Korean (Lee and Shimojo, forthcoming), for example, suggests that different discourse-functional properties are employed for topicalization in the two typologically similar languages, and such cross-linguistic findings warrant future studies to further develop the empirical basis of a syntactic theory.

References

Brown, Gillian & George Yule. 1983. *Discourse analysis*. Cambridge: Cambridge University Press.

Clancy, Patricia M. & Pamela Downing. 1987. The use of *Wa* as a cohesion marker in Japanese oral narratives. In John Hinds, Senko K. Maynard & Shoichi Iwasaki (eds.), *Perspectives on topicalization: The case of Japanese WA*, 3-56. Amsterdam & New York: John Benjamins.

Dik, Simon C. 1997. *The theory of Functional Grammar: Part 1: The structure of the clause*. Berlin: Mouton de Gruyter.

Erteschik-Shir, Nomi. 1997. *The dynamics of focus structure*. Cambridge: Cambridge University Press.

Erteschik-Shir, Nomi. 2007. *Information structure: The syntax-discourse interface*. Oxford: Oxford University Press.

Fry, John. 2003. *Ellipsis and wa-marking in Japanese conversation*. New York & London: Routledge.

Givón, Talmy. 1983. Topic continuity in discourse: An introduction. In Talmy Givón (ed.), *Topic continuity in discourse: A quantitative cross-language study*, 4–41. Amsterdam & New York: John Benjamins.

Grosz, Barbara J. & Candace L. Sidner. 1986. Attentions, intentions and the structure of discourse. *Computational Linguistics* 12: 175–204.

Grosz, Barbara J., Aravind K. Joshi & Scott Weinstein. 1995. Centering: A framework for modeling the local coherence of discourse. *Computational Linguistics* 21(2). 203–225.

Hinds, John & Wako Hinds. 1979. Participant identification in Japanese narrative discourse. In George Bedell, Eichi Kobayashi & Masatake Muraki (eds.), *Explorations in linguistics: Papers in honor of Kazuko Inoue*, 201–212. Tokyo: Kaitakusha.

Hinds, John, Senko K. Maynard & Shoichi Iwasaki (eds.). 1987. *Perspectives on topicalization: The case of Japanese WA*. Amsterdam & New York: John Benjamins.

Maynard, Senko K. 1980. *Discourse functions of the Japanese theme marker – wa*. Evanston, IL: Northwestern University dissertation.

Maynard, Senko K. 1987. Thematization as a staging device in the Japanese narrative. In John Hinds, Senko K. Maynard & Shoichi Iwasaki (eds.), *Perspectives on topicalization: The case of Japanese WA*, 57–82. Amsterdam & New York: John Benjamins.

Lee, EunHee & Mitsuaki Shimojo. forthcoming. Mismatch of topic between Japanese and Korean. *Journal of East Asian Linguistics*.

Shimojo, Mitsuaki. 2005. *Argument encoding in Japanese conversation*. Hampshire & New York: Palgrave Macmillan.

Shimojo, Mitsuaki. 2011. The left periphery and focus structure in Japanese. In Wataru Nakamura (ed.), *New perspectives in Role and Reference Grammar*, 266–293. Newcastle: Cambridge Scholars Publishing.

Tanimura, Midori & Etsuko Yoshida. 2003. *Pear story saikoo: nichieigo parareru koopasu ni okeru shijihyoogen no sentaku to sono yooin nitsuite* [Reconsidering the Pear Story: The choice of referring expressions and its factors in Japanese-English parallel corpora]. *English Corpus Studies* 10. 55–72.

van Dijk, Teun. 1981. Episodes as units of discourse analysis. In Deborah Tannen (ed.), *Analyzing discourse: Text and talk*, 177–195. Georgetown: Georgetown University Press.

Van Valin, Robert D. Jr. & Randy J LaPolla. 1997. *Syntax: Structure, meaning & function*. Cambridge: Cambridge University Press.

Walker, Marilyn, Masayo Iida & Sharon Cote. 1994. Japanese discourse and the process of centering. *Computational Linguistics* 20(2). 193–232.

Yamura-Takei, Mitsuko. 2005. *Theoretical, technological and pedagogical approaches to zero arguments in Japanese discourse: Making the invisible visible*. Hiroshima: Hiroshima City University dissertation.

Yamura-Takei, Mitsuko & Miho Fujiwara. 2007. Japanese native speakers' intuition of ZERO use: An account by Centering Theory. In Masahiko Minami (ed.), *Applying theory and research to learning Japanese as a foreign language*, 213–239. Newcastle: Cambridge Scholars Publishing.

Appendix

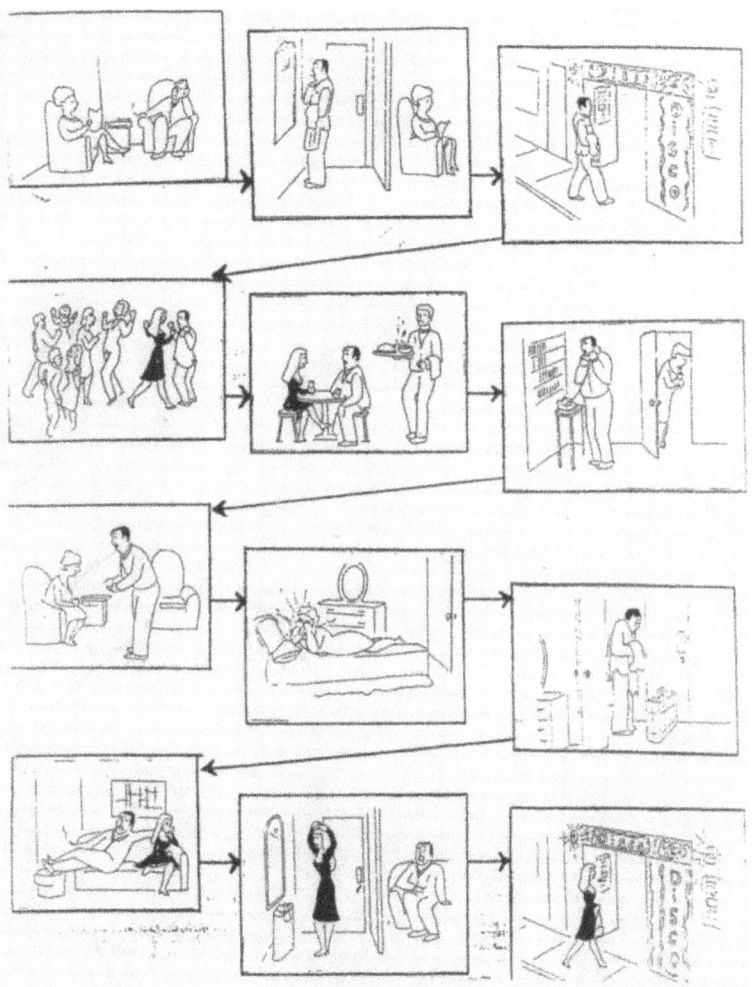

Appendix

Robert D. Van Valin, Jr.
4 An Overview of Information Structure in three Amazonian Languages

Abstract: Information structure has become a central topic in linguistic theory and description over the past two decades, with much of the initial work focused on familiar Indo-European languages and much studied non-Indo-European languages like Hungarian, Japanese and Mandarin Chinese. This chapter summarizes the main results of a project in which information structure was investigated in three unrelated Amazonian languages: Banawá (Reinbold 2004, 2007), Wari' (Turner 2006), and Karitiâna (C. Everett 2008). Data were collected on morphosyntactic and prosodic aspects of information structure and, importantly, their interaction. It will be shown that each language exhibits some unique attributes, the most striking being that Karitiâna does not use prosody to signal information structural distinctions. Most of the data discussed in these papers is available in the form of sound files on the project website, as well as additional data.

1 Introduction

Information structure has become a central topic in linguistic theory and description over the past two decades, with much of the initial work focused on familiar Indo-European languages and much studied non-Indo-European languages like Hungarian, Japanese and Mandarin Chinese. This paper summarizes the main results of a project in which information structure was investigated in three unrelated Amazonian languages: Banawá (Reinbold 2004, 2007), Wari' (Turner 2006), and Karitiâna (C. Everett 2008). Data were collected on morphosyntactic and prosodic aspects of information structure and, importantly, their interaction. Most of the data discussed in these papers is available in the form of sound files on the project website, as well as additional data.

Note: This work was supported in part by grant BCS-0344361 from the US National Science Foundation (jointly with Daniel Everett) and in part by a fellowship from the Max Planck Society (2008–2014).

Robert D. Van Valin, Jr., Heinrich Heine University Düsseldorf & University at Buffalo, The State University of New York

In this paper I will present an overview of the information structural phenomena in these three languages and will compare them with each other. In this first section, I will lay out some of the relevant descriptive and theoretical concepts that are employed in the analyses. In the second, I will give brief typological sketches of the languages, and in the third section the comparative discussion will be given, organized in terms of information structure phenomena.[1] The conclusion will include a comparison table summarizing the similarities and differences across the three languages.

The basic conception of clause structure assumed in these discussions is taken from Role and Reference Grammar [RRG] (Van Valin & LaPolla 1997, Van Valin 2005). Clause structure is represented in a semantically-based model known as the 'layered structure of the clause'. The essential components of this model of the clause are (i) the NUCLEUS, which contains the predicate, (ii) the CORE, which contains the nucleus plus the arguments of the predicate in the nucleus, and (iii) a PERIPHERY for each layer, which contains adjunct modifiers. These aspects of the layered structure are universal. The structure of a simple English clause is given in Figure 1. The structure in Figure 1 is the constituent projection of the clause; grammatical categories like tense and modality are represented in a separate projection, which is not included here.

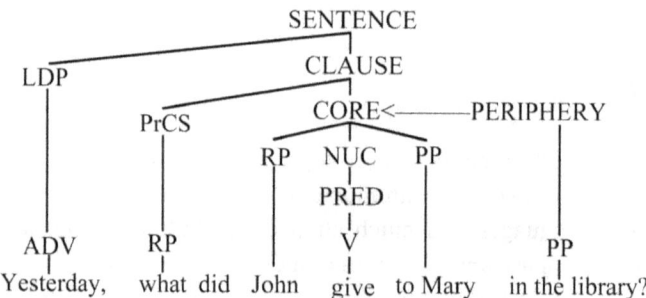

Figure 1: The layered structure of the clause[2]

---

1 Additional text materials and sound files for all three of the languages can be found on the Information structure in Amazonian languages website: http://wings.buffalo.edu/linguistics//people/faculty/vanvalin/infostructure/Site/Intro.html.
2 Abbreviations: ABS 'absolutive', AUX 'auxiliary', CNTR 'contrastive', COLL 'collective', COP 'copula', DEC 'declarative', EPIS.EVID 'epistemic evidential', EQU 'equative', F 'feminine', FUT 'future tense', IU 'information unit', LDP 'left-detached position', M 'masculine', N 'neuter', NFUT 'non-future tense', NSAP 'non-speech act participant', NUC 'nucleus', O 'object', OFC 'object-focus construction', POSS 'possessive', PrCS 'precore slot', PRED 'predicate', PROX 'proximate', PSA 'privileged syntactic argument', Q 'question', RF 'realis future', RP 'reference phrase', RP/P 'realis past & present tense', S 'subject', SAP 'speech act participant', TRANS 'transitive', VFC 'verb-focus construction', VIC 'verbal inflectional clitic'.

In addition to the universal layers of the clause, there are two additional structures that are important for this discussion, the precore slot [PrCS] and the left-detached position [LDP]. They are not universal, in the sense that some languages have them and others do not. The PrCS is prototypically the location of displaced WH-expressions, although non-WH-expressions may also occur in it, e.g. *That book I wouldn't buy*. The LDP is the location of dislocated topic expressions, set off from the following clause by an intonation break; if the element in the LDP is an argument of the verb, then there is typically a resumptive pronoun in the core, e.g. *As for John, I haven't see him in two weeks*. Some languages have a postcore slot, e.g. Japanese, and some have a right-detached position for right-dislocated expressions.

The theory of information structure assumed in these analysis is that presented in Lambrecht (1994), as adapted in RRG. Lambrecht proposes that there are recurring patterns of the organization of information across languages, which he calls 'focus types'. The three main types are presented in (1), with data from English and Italian; focal stress is indicated by all caps.

(1) Focus structure in English and Italian (Lambrecht 1994, Bentley 2008)

    a. Q: *What happened to your car?*   Predicate Focus
        A: i. *My car/It broke DOWN.*   English
            ii. *(La mia macchina) si è ROTTA.*   Italian

    b. Q: *What happened?*   Sentence Focus
        A: i. *My CAR broke down.*   English
            ii. *Mi si è rotta la MACCHINA.*   Italian

    c. Q: *Did your motorcycle break down?* Narrow Focus
        A: i. *No, my CAR broke down./*   English
               it's my car that broke down.
            ii. *No, si è rotta la mia MACCHINA./* Italian
               è la mia MACCHINA che si è rotta.
               (Lit: 'broke down my car'/
               'it's my car that broke down')

Predicate focus corresponds to the traditional topic-comment distinction, with a topical subject RP and a focal predicate phrase which receives the focal stress. It is universally the least marked or default focus structure. In English, the subject would most likely be an unstressed pronoun, while in Italian it would most likely not occur at all; if it were overt, it would be preverbal in Italian. Sentence focus is a topicless construction in which the entire sentence is focal. In English, the subject receives the focal stress, while in Italian the subject appears postverbally and with focal stress. Narrow focus involves focus on a single constituent, in these examples, the subject. In English this is signaled by focal stress on the element or by a cleft, and Italian likewise has two options: postposing the subject, when it is the focused element, or a cleft.

There is an important distinction between unmarked and marked narrow focus. All languages have an unmarked focus position in the clause; in English it is the last constituent of the core, whereas in verb-final languages it is the position immediately before the verb. Consider the following English sentence with different focal stress options.

(2) a. *Dana sent the package to LESLIE yesterday.*
 b. *Dana sent the package to Leslie YESTERDAY.*
 c. *Dana sent THE PACKAGE to Leslie yesterday.*
 d. *Dana SENT the package to Leslie yesterday.*
 e. *DANA sent the package to Leslie yesterday.*

Focal stress on *Leslie* in (a) is a case of unmarked narrow focus, while focal stress on any other constituent of the clause, as in (b)–(e), yields marked narrow focus. The most marked narrow focus is on the subject, as in (e).

There is a further component to the RRG account of information structure, which is not part of Lambrecht's original account, namely, the contrast between the actual focus domain and the potential focus domain. Languages differ as to constraints on where the actual focus domain can be in a clause. In some like English, it can fall on any word or phrase, as (2) shows. In others, e.g. Italian, it is excluded from the preverbal core position and can only include the nucleus and what follows (see Van Valin & LaPolla 1997, §5.4, Van Valin 1999, Bentley 2008 for detailed discussion). The potential focus domain is a feature of the grammar of the language, while the actual focus domain is contextually determined. In a sentence like the one in Figure 1, the LDP element is outside of the potential focus domain, while the WH-expression in the PrCS is within the potential focus domain and is the actual focus domain, in this case, a type of narrow focus.

2 Basic typological features

Banawá (Arawan family) is a verb-final language, but it is not strictly verb-final; adjuncts and indirect objects may follow the verb. The privileged syntactic argument [PSA] ('subject') normally occurs initially, but not necessarily. Nouns fall into two gender classes, masculine and feminine, and this is important for agreement both within the RP and with the verb or auxiliary. One of the most striking features of Banawá syntax is the contrast between what Dixon (2000) (with respect to the closely related language Jarawara) calls 'A-constructions' and 'O-constructions'. In the A-construction, the actor is the PSA and normally occurs in initial position in the core; the optional mood marker agrees with it in gender. In the O-construction, on the other hand, the undergoer is the PSA; it is signalled by the third-person prefix on the verb or auxiliary. This is illustrated in (3).

(3) a. A-construction
Biri   karabowa   mowa-na-ka.
name.M   blowgun.F   make-AUX-DEC.M
'Biri is making a blowgun.'

b. O-construction
Karabowa o-ka   abi   mowa hi-na-ni   ama-ke.
blowgun.F 1sg-POSS father.M   make 3sg-AUX-? EQU-DEC.F
'My father made the blowgun.'

Dixon (2000) argues that the choice of construction in Jarawara is influenced by discourse, in that the PSA is the most topical argument; consequently, according to Dixon, the A-construction is used when the actor is the primary topical participant, while the O-construction is used when the undergoer is more topical. Reinbold investigates Dixon's claim for the corresponding construction in Banawá.

Wari' (Chapakuran family; D. Everett & Kern 1999) is verb-initial and PSA-final, i.e. V (PP) (RP) RP. There is no case marking on RPs. The nucleus is immediately followed by a clitic complex (the 'verbal inflectional clitic' [VIC]) which expresses the person, number and gender features of the direct core arguments, as well as tense-aspect. Wari' is a head-marking language, as the nucleus plus VIC alone can constitute a complete utterance.

(4) a. Mi'   non-on   con   hwam hwijima' mon   tarama'.
give   3pls.RP/P-3plO.M   PREP.3sgM   fish children COLL man
'The men gave the children fish.'

b. Mi'   non-on.
give   3pls.RP/P-3plO.M
'They gave them something.'

Wari' exhibits a secondary object pattern, as the recipient is the undergoer in (4a) and the theme an oblique core argument.

Karitiâna (Tupi) is verb-medial, with the unmarked order in transitive clauses being actor (PSA)-nucleus-undergoer; the single argument of an intransitive verb can occur before or after it. This is illustrated in (5).

(5) a. *Irip naka-ɨ-j kojpa.*
    tapir NSAP-eat.TRANS-FUT pineapple
    'The tapir will eat the pineapple.'

  b. *Taso na-aŋgar-i.*
    man NSAP-stand.up-FUT
    'The man will stand up.'

  c. *Na-aŋgar-i taso.*
    NSAP-stand.up-FUT man
    'The man will stand up.'

Karitiâna is a head-marking language with no case marking on RPs.

3 Aspects of information structure in Banawá, Wari' and Karitiâna

3.1 Banawá

The focus structure contrasts introduced in (1) are signalled in Banawá by prosody and morphosyntactic devices. In predicate focus, the subject can be a clitic pronoun, as in the sequence of clauses in (Reinbold 2004:56–7, lines 28–30), an unstressed RP, as in (6a), or is omitted altogether, as in (6b, c).

(6) a. *Yumai-ba tonwiyei matamona.* (Reinbold 2007:13)
    jaguar-FUT change.M PST.REP.M
    'The jaguar changed a long time ago.'

  b. *Yama yete-nei to-kei.*
    thing hunt-AUX.M away-go.M
    'He went away hunting.'

  c. *Kamai kobo-na-mai mowei matamona.*
    come.M arrive-AUX-MOT.M do.M PST.REP.M
    'He came back. He returned.'

In (6a) the subject 'jaguar' has lower pitch relative to the following predicate complex, and it functions as the topic expression for this sentence and the two following, in which it is omitted and indicated only by the masculine agreement on the predicate complexes. In all of these sentences is the predicate accented. In sentence focus, every word in the sentence is accented, as shown by the pitch-track of (7) in Reinbold (2007), unlike in English and many other languages, in which only the subject is accented.

(7) *Enemede nafi-rei yamakabani-ya to-kei.* (Reinbold 2007:12)
child big-NEG.M jungle-LOC away-go.M
'A little boy went to the jungle.'

In both broad focus types the predicate expression is accented, with the subject accented in sentence focus and unaccented (if expressed) in predicate focus.

It was mentioned above that Dixon (2000) claims that the choice of the privileged argument ('pivot' in Dixon's terms) is influenced by information structure in that when the actor is more topical, then the A-construction is used, and when the undergoer is more topical, the O-construction is used. While Reinbold (2007) finds general support for this view, there are clear exceptions as well. The 'pivot' is focal in the sentence-focus construction in (7). Furthermore she gives examples of yes-no questions with the focus on the 'pivot', e.g. [26a, b], pp. 19–20. Hence the core-initial RP 'pivot' in both A- and O-constructions may, but need not be, topical. Overt topics, both RPs and PPs, may occur in the left-detached position.

(8) a. *FUNASA me FUNAI me fa, ere me keye fora okune.* (Reinbold 2004:38, 56)
3pl 3pl ? 1plo 3pls lie often ?
'FUNASA and FUNAI people, they often lie to us.'

b. *Pirei-ya meketima, me yama-me daani moa...* (Reinbold 2004:56)
River.Pirei-LOC upstream 3pl things-PL sell do
'On the river Pirei, they used to sell things...'

In (8a) there is a left-detached topic expression set off by an intonation break and followed by a clause in which there is a clitic pronoun (*me* '3pl') serving as a resumptive pronoun, whereas in (8b) there is an initial locative PP set off by an intonation break. Thus, there seems to be clear evidence that Banawá has a LDP for dislocated topic expressions.

There also seems to be clear evidence for a PrCS position as well. There is a strong preference for WH-expressions to occur clause-initially (Reinbold 2007:16–17), although there are a few examples of in situ WH-expressions as well. The following question-answer pair illustrates that not only does the WH-expression occur in the PrCS, but the focus of the answer may, too.

(9) a. *Hikei badue tao-hi-kanei-no yamakabani-ya?* (Reinbold 2007:18)
who deer.M shoot-3sg-AUX.M-IP jungle-LOC
'Who shot the deer in the jungle?'

b. *Batao badue tao-hi-kanei-no yamakabani-ya.*
Batao.M deer.M shoot-3sg-AUX.M-IP jungle-LOC
'Batao shot the deer in the jungle.'

The pronominal prefix *hi-* '3sg' signals that these are both O-constructions, and therefore *badue* 'deer' is the undergoer 'pivot' in core-initial position. In (9a) *hikei* 'who' occurs in the PrCS, before the core-initial 'pivot', and likewise in (9b) the answer *Batao*, the completive focus, is in the same clause-initial position. Hence focal expressions, both WH-expressions and non-WH RPs, can occur in the PrCS. (See also Reinbold 2004:57, lines 30–32.) It is not necessary for the completive focus to occur in the PrCS; [21b] in Reinbold (2007: 18) exemplifies post-verbal completive focus in an adjunct question.

Completive focus is a type of narrow focus; another important type is contrastive focus. There is a contrastive focus particle *taa* which can mark contrasting phrases in any grammatical function. Reinbold (2007) has an extensive discussion of it; only one example will be given here.

(10) *Yifari taa nofi maditowei kaira taa non-nofa-ra manei.*
banana.F CNTR like very.M guava CNTR RED-like-NEG AUX.M
'Bananas he likes a lot, but guava he doesn't like a lot.' (Reinbold 2007:23)

It is not clear in this example whether the RPs marked by *taa* are in the PrCS or not, since there is no overt core-initial 'pivot' RP, but there are clear examples of core-internal RPs marked by *taa*, e.g. [32] and [36] on p. 23. There are other morphosyntactic devices, as well as prosody, which are used to signal contrast.

To sum up, Banawá distinguishes all three major focus constructions via prosody, although not in the same way as English and many other languages do. In predicate focus, the subject, if overt, is not accented, while the predicate is. In sentence focus, every word in the clause is accented, not just the subject. Reinbold notes that "it is sometimes difficult to distinguish predicate focus from the other focus structures in the language, as the predicate is also accented in other focus structures" (2007:13). In narrow focus, the focus constituent is accented, as is the predicate. In addition to prosody, there are morphosyntactic means for signalling information structure contrasts: a LDP for dislocated topic expressions, a PrCS for WH-expressions, completive foci, and possibly contrastive foci, and a contrastive marker *taa* for indicating contrastive focus.

3.2 Wari'

Turner (2006) presents an investigation of information structure and intonation in Wari', building on the earlier description of the language in D. Everett & Kern (1999). As mentioned in §2, Wari' is a head-marking language, with the direct core arguments coded on the clitic cluster (VIC) immediately following the nucleus. Hence a highly activated referent need not be coded by an independent RP, nominal or pronominal, and therefore in predicate focus the nucleus + VIC would normally constitute the whole clause. This can be seen clearly in the 'How to make a basket' text. The second line is (11) below, which includes a left-detached topic expression 'the(se) women' (Turner 2006:73); for additional examples of left-detached topic expressions, see D. Everett & Kern (1999: 212–14).

(11) Oro   narima   cwa   'ara   nana-in   wao.
     COLL   woman   this.M/F   make   3plRP/P-3N   basket
     'The women, they make baskets'

In subsequent clauses in the text, neither the women nor baskets are mentioned explicitly again; they are coded as the third-person plural subject and third neuter object on the VIC. Examples of subsequent clauses are given in (12). (*Wao* is both the word for 'basket' and the name of the plant which is the source of the leaves for weaving baskets.)

(12) a. Mama   nana-in   mi   noro   ci'   nana-in   wao.
        go.pl   3plRP/P-3N   jungle   look   pull/take   3plRP/P-3N   wao.palm
        'They went to the jungle, to pull the leaves of the wao palm out'

     b. Wiritik   pin   nana-in   pixi   nein.
        pull.out   completely   3plRP/P-3N   spines   3sgN
        'They pulled its spines completely out'

     c. Ten   cira   nana-in.
        dry.out   put.in.sun   3plRP/P-3N
        'They dry them out in the sun.'

In (12a) there are predicate focus constructions, the two clauses having the topical subject 'the women' coded on the VIC only with the focal object of the second clause explicitly mentioned, since a different sense of the word *wao* is intended here. In (12b) there is likewise a predicate focus construction, with the object RP 'its spines' and the verbal complex in focus. Finally, in (12c) the core arguments are expressed only in the VIC, and hence this is an instance of narrow focus on the nucleus, which consists of two verbs.

According to D. Everett & Kern (1999), the primary sentence accent falls on the last syllable of the predicate expression in the nucleus, and other words are stressed on their final syllable and count as secondary sentence accents; Turner confirms this. This rigidity of stress pattern suggests that prosody could not be the primary indicator of focus, and Turner makes exactly this point: "prosody is not a sufficient indicator alone to indicate focus" (2006:85). Given that Wari' is head-marking, as shown in (11) and (12), activated referents are normally expressed by clitic pronouns in the VIC, and consequently the expression of a referent as an overt RP is in itself an indicator that it is focal. Focal RPs can occur in the normal post-nuclear positions, as in (11) and (12) with object RPs. An example with a subject RP is given in (13), from Turner 2006:85–6).

(13) a. *Ma   wari'   co   cao   na-on   hwam?*
       that.PROX.HEARER person M/F.RP/P eat 3sgRP/P-3sgM   fish
       'Who ate (the) fish?'

   b. *Cao   na-on   Elizeu.*
       eat   3sgRP/P-3sgM
       'Elizeu ate it.'

In the question in (13a), 'who' is expressed by a deictic element + the word for 'person'; it occurs in the PrCS and is followed by a kind of 'pre-VIC' which agrees with the RP in the PrCS in gender and expresses tense/aspect. In the answer in (13b) the subject *Elizeu* is the completive focus, and it occurs in a core-internal, post-nuclear position.

Contrastive focus may be expressed prosodically, by a focus particle, or by putting the focal RP together with an emphatic pronoun in the PrCS, according to D. Everett & Kern 1999:205–6, 303). Contrastive focal stress, indicated by all caps, is illustrated in (14).

(14) a. TO'   'ina   xe.
         hit   1sgRP/P   firewood
         'I *chopped* firewood.'

   b.   To'   'ina   XE.
        hit   1sgRP/P   firewood
        'I chopped *firewood*.'

   c.   *To'   'INA   xe.
        hit   1sgRP/P   firewood
        '*I* chopped firewood.'

In (14a) the contrastive stress is on the verb, while in (14b) it is on the object RP. For subject emphasis, however, it is not possible to stress the VIC. Rather, the particle *pan* must be used, and no special prosody is involved.

(15) a. To'   pan   'ina   xe.
         hit   CNTR   1sgRP/P   firewood
         '*I* chopped firewood.'

   b.   Pi'   pan   nana   hwijima'.
        dance CNTR   3plRP/P   children
        'The *children* danced.'

The PrCS option involving an emphatic pronoun is illustrated in (16), from D. Everett & Kern 1999:206–7, 303).

(16) a. Wirico Xijam   co   'oin'   na   mapac.
         EMPH.3sgM   M/F.RP/P   plant   3sgRP/P   corn
         'It was Xijam who planted corn.'

   b.   Wata'   tara   co   tomi'   na.
        EMPH.1sg   3sgRF   M/F.RP/P   speak   3sgRP/P
        'It shall be I who speaks.'

This construction seems to be parallel to the one in (13a), and the proper name *Xijam* receives a contrastive interpretation in (16a).

To sum up, Wari' seems to use morphosyntactic devices as the primary means of indicating information structural contrasts. Highly activated, i.e. topical, referents are normally expressed by means of clitic pronouns on the VIC, and the expression of a referent by a full RP is normally indicative of focus. Prosody seems to play at best a secondary role in signaling focus and seems to be most important for contrastive focus. There is a LDP for dislocated topic expressions, and there is a PrCS in which WH-expressions in questions occur and in which non-WH RPs may occur to signal contrastive focus.

3.3 Karitiâna

C. Everett (2008) presents an analysis of constituent focus in Karitiâna, building on his earlier description of the language (C. Everett 2006). Karitiâna is a verb-medial language and seems to make primary use of morphosyntactic devices to signal information structural contrasts, rather than prosody; in this regard it seems to be more like Wari' than Banawá. In a predicate focus construction, there is a pronominal subject, realized either as a prefix on the verb, as in (15a) or as an unstressed independent pronoun, as in (15b), and the object follows the verb. The examples in (17) are from C. Everett (2008:15–16).

(17) a. *I-ta-piso-t epesap-asok.*
  1sgABS-SAP-take-NFUT leaf-OBL.CONTACT
  'I took the leaf.'

 b. *ĩn naka-pɨdn-aj mãŋga.*
  1sg NSAP-kick-FUT mango
  'I will kick the mango.'

The intonation in both sentences is flat, with a fall on the last syllable of the last word. In discussions of focus structure in English, it is often suggested that an SVO sentence with falling intonation on the object is ambiguous between predicate focus and (unmarked) narrow focus on the object RP. This does not seem to be the case in Karitiâna, however, as there is a special object-focus construction which involves occurrence of the object in the PrCS and an 'object focus' prefix (*ti-*) on the verb. This is illustrated in (18), from C. Everett (2008:29).

(18) *Kojpa an-ti-okẽŋ-Ø.*
 pineapple 2sg-OFC-cut-NFUT
 'You cut a pineapple', 'A pineapple you cut' or 'It was a pineapple you cut.'

Everett argues that this is an instance of unmarked narrow focus on the object, unlike the structurally analogous English translations. This construction is also used in WH-questions when the question word is an object; this is illustrated in

(19b), from C. Everett (2008:28). It is not found in (19a), a subject WH-question, from C. Everett (2006:374).

(19) a. *Mõrãmõn   a-ta-pisok-Ø   (an-o)   (hĩ)?*
       what/who   2sgABS-SAP-pierce/stab-NFUT   2sg-Q.NOM   Q
       'Who stabbed you?'

   b. *Mõrãmõn   sopãm ti-mʔa-tiɲã-t   (hĩ)?*
       what/who   OFC-make-PROG-NFUT   Q
       'What is Sopaõm [person's name] making?'

Example (19b) is significant, for two reasons. First, it shows that WH-expressions occur in the same initial position and take the same object focus marking (when they are objects) that non-WH RPs do. Second, the occurrence of the overt subject *Sopām* between the WH-expression and the verb shows that the WH-expression is in the PrCS, not in a core-internal position, since the prenuclear core-internal position is occupied by the subject RP. The answers to WH-questions also occur in the PrCS, which supports Everett's conclusion that in Karitiâna a focal element in the PrCS represents unmarked narrow focus.

(20) a. *Mõrãmõn   a-ti-hĩrã?*   (C. Everett 2006:325)
       what   2sgABS-OFC-smell
       'What did you smell?'

   b. *Epo:si:d   ĩn   ti-ti-hĩra-t.*
       flower   1sg   OFC-smell-NFUT
       'I smelled a flower.' ('A flower I smelled.')

Everett notes that the intonation pattern on this construction is basically the same as that on the predicate focus examples in (17), i.e. flat with a fall on the final syllable. He comments:

> Karitiâna clauses with unmarked or default narrow constituent focus, like clauses with broad predicate focus, are consistent prosodically. They may vary syntactically, in that some constituents such as question words and objects may be placed in the precore slot, and may also vary morphologically via the presence or absence of a focus marker. Their pitch, however, is remarkably consistent. The clauses we habe observed, taken from Karitiâna discourse and from elicitation sessions, display generally flat intonation during the majority of the clause (though there is sometimes an increase in pitch on question words, followed by a noticeable fall in pitch of the final syllable of the clause. (2008:30).

Narrow focus on the verb is not signaled prosodically but rather by a special verb-focus construction, in which the verb is marked with a special prefix *piri-* and occurs obligatorily in clause-initial position. It is illustrated in (21), from C. Everett (2008:36).

(21) Pirí-tãm-ĩn   pat.
     VFC-fly-NFUT   macaw
     'The macaw flew.'

Given that no elements within the clause can occur before the verb in this construction, Everett suggests that the verb occurs in the PrCS, just like the RPs in the object-focus construction. This is not unattested in other languages; in German, for example, it is possible for the verbal nucleus to occur in the PrCS, as in (22).

(22) Waschen   muss Johannes   jetzt   das   Auto.
     wash   must   now   the   car
     'Johannes must wash the car now.'

Intonationally, the construction in (21) follows the pattern seen in the other examples, i.e. flat with a fall on the final syllable. In particular, the verb in the PrCS receives no special accentuation.

Contrastive narrow focus is expressed via a cleft construction. An example with contrastive focus on the subject is given in (23a), and on an adjunct, in (23b), from C. Everett (2008:41–2).

(23) a. Õwã   na-aka-t   pirí-taktaŋ-ĩn   i.
        child   NSAP-COP-NFUT   VFC-swim-NFUT   3
        'It is the child that is swimming.'

     b. Kiri   di:p   i-taka-tat-ason.
        soon   night   1sgABS-SAP-go-EPIS.EVID
        'It's tonight I think I'm going.'

The first example involves a copula, the second one does not. Everett shows that in both the initial phrase ('child + copula' in (a) and 'tonight' in (b)) has a distinct intonation pattern (rise-fall-rise) independent of the following verbal expression, which has the typical 'flat + final fall' seen above in other constructions. He suggests that this is in fact a paratactic construction, in which both components are independently asserted. Evidence in favor of this interpretation comes from the fact that the verb in (23a) is itself focused, using the verb-focus construction.

Finally, detached topic expressions can be expressed in the LDP in Karitiâna, just as in the other two languages. The following example is from C. Everett (personal communication).

(24) Onɨ   taso   aka, i   naka-ɨ-t   pikõm.
     DEM.DIST   man   DEF   3   NSAP-eat-NFUT   wooly.monkey
     'That man over there, he ate the wooly monkey.'

The initial topic expression, 'that man over there', is set off by an intonation break, and there is a resumptive pronoun in the following clause referring to it.

To sum up, Karitiâna does not employ prosody as its primary means of signaling information structural contrasts; rather, it has special object-focus and verb-focus constructions to indicate narrow focus on the object or the verb; both involve the focussed constituent occurring in the PrCS. It also has a paratactic 'cleft' construction to signal contrastive focus. As in the other two languages, there is the possibility of left-dislocating topic expressions in the LDP.[3]

4 Summary

The main properties of information structure in the three languages are summed up in Table 1.

Table 1: Comparison of information structure properties of Banawá, Wari' and Karitiâna

	Banawá	Wari'	Karitiâna
Basic word order	Verb-final	Verb-initial	Verb-medial
Topic in LDP	Yes	Yes	Yes
PreCore Slot	Yes	Yes	Yes
–WH-elements	Yes	Yes	Yes
–Non-WH-elements	Yes	Yes	Yes
–Focus only	Yes	Yes	Yes
–Answer to WH-Q in PrCS	Possible	No	Yes
Prosody as main cue for focus	Yes	Contrastive only	No
Special verb-focus construction	No	No	Yes

---

3 Storto (2011) presents an analysis of information structure in Karitiâna within a generative framework. While her analysis differs from C. Everett's on a number of points, she is in agreement with the existence of what in RRG terms is the PrCS and agrees that both RPs and nuclei can occur in it; furthermore, she also concludes that prosody is not used to signal focus.

The main differences among the three languages concern the last three properties. Banawá allows and Karitiâna seems to require the answer to WH-questions to occur in the PrCS. Prosody seems to play a much more important role in signaling focus in Banawá than in Wari' or Karitiâna, and Karitiâna has a special verb-focus construction that has no analog in the other two languages. From a theoretical perspective the data from these three languages support the cross-linguistic validity of the Lambrecht-based RRG approach to information structure.

References

Bentley, Delia. 2008. The interplay of focus structure and syntax: Evidence from two sister languages. In Robert Van Valin, ed., *Investigations of the syntax-semantics-pragmatics interface*, 263–84. Amsterdam: John Benjamins.
Dixon, R.M.W. 2000. A-constructions and O-constructions in Jawawara. *IJAL* 66. 22–56.
Everett, Caleb. 2006. *Patterns in Karitiâna: Perception, articulation and grammar*. Houston, TX: Rice University dissertation. [on ISAL web site]
Everett, Caleb. 2008. Constituent focus in Karitiâna. Unpublished ms. [On ISAL web site]
Everett, Daniel & Barbara Kern. 1999. *Wari'*. London: Routledge.
Lambrecht, Knud. 1994. *Information structure and sentence form*. Cambridge: Cambridge University Press.
Reinbold, Julia. 2004. *Intonation and information structure in Banawá*. Manchester: University of Manchester M.A. dissertation. [On ISAL web site]
Reinbold, Julia. 2007. Summary of the results on the research on intonation and information structure in Banawá. Unpublished ms. [On ISAL web site]
Storto, Luciana. 2011. Information structure in Karitiâna. Proceedings of the Conference on Indigenous Languages of Latin America-V, UT Austin. [available at http://www.ailla.utexas.org/site/cilla5_toc.html]
Turner, Ingrid. 2006. *Intonation and information structure in Wari'*. Manchester: University of Manchester M.A. dissertation. [on ISAL web site].
Van Valin, Robert. 1999. A typology of the interaction of focus structure and syntax. In E. Raxilina & J. Testelec, eds., *Typology and linguistic theory: from description to explanation*, 511–524. Languages of Russian Culture: Moscow. [available on RRG web site]
Van Valin, Robert. 2005. *Exploring the syntax-semantics interface*. Cambridge University Press.
Van Valin, Robert & Randy LaPolla. 1997. *Syntax: Structure, meaning and function*. Cambridge: Cambridge University Press.

II IS and Spoken language

Delia Bentley, Francesco Maria Ciconte, Silvio Cruschina, and Michael Ramsammy

5 Micro-variation in information structure: *There* sentences in Italo-Romance

1 Introduction

In this article we report original findings from an investigation of *there*-sentences in Italo-Romance dialects. By *there*-sentence we mean a construction which is formed as in (1).

(1) (adpositional phrase) + (proform) + copula + NP + (adpositional phrase)

Italo-Romance is a branch of the family of Romance languages whose members are primarily spoken in Italy. Exception being made for Italian, these languages are usually referred to as **dialects** because they have very little, if any, official recognition in socio-political terms. Importantly, the Italo-Romance dialects are not varieties of Italian, but rather daughters of Latin, which have developed independently alongside Italian. Our evidence was collected within a large-scale research project, which involved fieldwork in 138 survey points in Italy. The data reported in this article were gathered in 20 survey points, situated in the North, the Centre, and the South of Italy, including Sicily.[1]

Note: This research was financed by the Arts and Humanities Research Council (research grant AH/H032509/1, http://existentials.humanities.manchester.ac.uk/, November 2010 to June 2014). This funding is gratefully acknowledged. Special thanks go to our informants and helpers in the field. Bentley, Ciconte and Cruschina were in charge of the analysis of the discourse-syntax interface. Ramsammy was in charge of the intonational analysis expounded in Sect. 4.1, which was carried out with Praat.

[1] The relevant localities are the following: Acquaro (Calabria), Anacapri (Campania), Ascoli Piceno (Marche), Badalucco (Liguria), Felino (Emilia), Ferrara (Emilia), Gallo (Marche), Gambettola (Romagna), Grosio (Lombardy), Grosseto (Tuscany), Guardiagrele (Abruzzo), Gubbio (Umbria), Milano (Lombardy), Modica (Sicily), Polignano a Mare (Apulia), Premosello Chiovenda (Piedmont), Soleto (Apulia), Santa Croce di Magliano (Molise), Squinzano (Apulia), and Tursi (Basilicata).

Delia Bentley, The University of Manchester
Francesco Maria Ciconte, University of Puerto Rico
Silvio Cruschina, University of Vienna
Michael Ramsammy, The University of Edinburgh

In Section 2 we introduce a typology of *there*-sentences (cf. Cruschina 2012a) which will be relevant to our analysis. In Section 3 we discuss the shared trends in the encoding of information structure which emerge from the analysis of the dialects of our sample, in particular, the syntactic position of two types of topic, as well as, in all but few dialects, the position of foci and the marking of the construction with a CI-proform.[2] We then consider the microvariation in information structure which was uncovered by our investigation (Section 4). This was found in the licensing of narrow focus in preverbal syntax, in prosody, and, more conspicuously, in the expression of information structure in number inflection on the copula. Some conclusions are drawn together in Section 5. Our analysis is couched in the theoretical framework of Role and Reference Grammar (Van Valin and LaPolla 1997, Van Valin 2005).

2 Four types of *there*-sentence

Our point of departure is Cruschina's (2012a) fourfold typology of *ci*-sentences in Italian: existentials proper (cf. (2a)), inverse locatives (cf. (2b)), deictic locatives (cf. (2c)), and presentationals (cf. (2d)).[3]

(2) a. *Ci sono molti fiori bianchi sul prato* (type I)
    PF be.3PL many flowers white on-the lawn
    'There are many white flowers on the lawn.'

  b. *C'è tua sorella, in cucina* (type II)
    PF-be.3SG your sister in kitchen
    'There's your sister in the kitchen.'

  c. *Guarda! C'è Maria* (type III)
    look.IMP.2SG PF-be.3SG Maria
    'Look! Maria is here / Lit.: Look! There's Maria.'

  d. *C'è il figlio di mia sorella che canta alla televisione stasera*
    PF-is the son of my sister who sing.3SG at-the television tonight
    'There's my sister's son singing on television tonight.' (type IV)

---

[2] We use lower case *ci*, in *ci*-sentence, to refer specifically to Italian, while with CI-sentence we refer to this type of structure in Italo-Romance.
[3] The abbreviations used in the glosses are as follows: EXPL = expletive; F = feminine; IMP = imperative; INF = infinitive; M = masculine; NEG = negation; PF = existential or locative proform; PL = plural; PRT = partitive; PP = past participle; SCL = subject clitic; SG = singular.

All four types share the two main morpho-syntactic properties of the existential construction, namely, the presence of the proform *ci*, cliticised to the copula 'be' (hence the name *ci*-sentence), and the post-copular position of the noun phrase. However, as is shown in Table 1, each type also has distinctive features, correlating with (a) a specific kind of information structure, here defined in terms of the actual domain of focus (Van Valin 2005: 75),[4] (b) the function of the proform *ci*, and (c) the semantic and syntactic function of the postcopular noun phrase, which is subject to a loose specificity restriction.

Table 1: Italian *ci*-sentences

TYPE	STRUCTURE	FOCUS	PROFORM *ci*	NP
I	existential	sentence/predicate	pro-argument	predicate (typically non specific)
II	inverse locative	argument	pro-predicate	argument (typically specific)
III	deictic locative	argument	pro-predicate	argument (typically specific)
IV	presentational	sentence	grammaticalised	argument (typically specific)

Let us now examine the properties of each type individually. In line with previous syntactic and semantic studies (Williams 1984, 1994, La Fauci and Loporcaro 1997, Zamparelli 2000, Hazout 2004, Francez 2007), the postcopular noun phrase of the existential construction is assumed to be a predicate. Drawing upon a tradition which is established in the semantics literature, we use the term **pivot** to refer to the noun phrase which, in English and Italo-Romance existential constructions, occurs by default in the immediately post-copular position. In this sentence type, *ci* is not an anaphoric locative clitic, but has to be interpreted as a pro-argument, namely, a pronominal form that spells out an abstract argument which provides the spatio-temporal co-ordinates of the predication (Parry 2010, Pinto 1997, Tortora 1997, Francez 2007). Importantly, the proform is not referential, that is, it does not encode a location in these structures (see Ciconte 2008, in prep., for a diachronic account of the proform and the loss of its locative meaning across constructions).

From the point of view of information structure, existential sentences are sentence-focus structures (Lambrecht 1994: 233–235), although they may exhibit

---

[4] The **Actual Focus Domain** is the part of a given sentence which is in focus, whilst the **Potential Focus Domain** is the syntactic domain in the sentence in which focus elements can occur in a given language.

a clause-initial **aboutness topic**, in which case they are internally organised as topic-comment structures.⁵

(3) IN   QUESTA   FRUTTA   CI   SONO   TANTI   SEMI   (Italian)
     in   this   fruit   PF   be.3PL many   seeds
     'In this fruit there are many seeds.'

The reader should note that aboutness topics (e.g., *in questa frutta* 'in this fruit' in (3)) are not established discourse referents, but rather new discourse referents which indicate what the proposition is about. Existentials proper need not have a coda, i.e., a prepositional phrase or an adjectival phrase, in which case the only focal information unit is the pivot, i.e., the predicate. With respect to the loose specificity restriction on the pivot (see Table 1), we note that, in a limited set of cases, definite pivots are admitted in the existential construction (type I) and that, at the same time, non-specific noun phrases are not entirely excluded from the other types of *ci*-sentences, although specific noun phrases typically occur in those constructions. A well-known exception to the Definiteness Effect is the so-called list reading, where one or more definite pivots are used to convey new information in the form of a single list (Milsark 1974, Rando and Napoli 1978, Lumsden 1988, McNally 1992, Abbott 1992, 1993, 1997, Ward & Birner 1995). List existentials may also indicate or remind the hearer/reader that an individual or a set are available or suitable to fulfil some purpose.

As for type II, it has often been pointed out that Italian putative existential sentences with a definite pivot have a strong locative flavour and should thus not be considered to be genuine existential sentences (Zucchi 1995, Moro 1997, Zamparelli 2000). Following these observations, Cruschina (2012a) shows that, in conjunction with a definite post-copular argument, *ci* can preserve the properties of a locative pronoun and act as a resumptive clitic that is co-referent with a detached locative phrase (see also Leonetti 2008 and Remberger 2009). In this type of *ci*-sentence, the post-copular argument is in focus, whereas the locative phrase conveys information that has already been introduced in discourse. We therefore call the locative phrase a **referential topic**.

---

5 The proposition is construed and understood as being about the **topic** and increases the addressee's knowledge of it (Lambrecht 1994: 131). The topic is part of the pragmatic presupposition, i.e., the set of propositions which are linguistically evoked in a sentence and can be taken for granted in discourse. We further differentiate between **aboutness** and **referential topics** (see below). By contrast with topics, **foci** do not belong to the presupposition, but rather to the assertion, i.e., the proposition which the hearer is expected to know as a result of a sentence being uttered (Lambrecht 1994: 52). We indicate focus with small caps.

(4) a. Chi   c'è   in   cucina?   (Italian)
       who   PF-be.3SG   in   kitchen
       'Who is there in the kitchen?'

   b. C'è   TUA   SORELLA,   in   cucina
       PF-be.3SG   your   sister   in   kitchen
       'Your sister is in the kitchen.'

Type II is thus an argument-focus structure (Lambrecht 1994: 228–233). Sentence (4b) is characterised by two independent strategies related to information structure: post-verbal focalization of the subject, and anaphoric agreement with a right-detached locative phrase through the locative pronoun *ci*. From a purely semantic viewpoint, this sentence is equivalent to the corresponding canonical locative predication (i.e. *Tua sorella è in cucina* 'Your sister is in the kitchen'). The topic can be omitted altogether, which proves to be the option that is preferred by most speakers. In fact, shared knowledge or knowledge that is situationally available should be subsumed within the notion of referential topic. Resumptive clitics resume topics, but are incompatible with foci (Rizzi 1997: 289). The locative function of *ci* in type II is thus confirmed by its incompatibility with a focal locative phrase, such as a locative *wh*-phrase (5a), or a prepositional phrase co-occurring within the clause and bearing focus in the answer of a question-answer pair (5b). The symbol # flags examples that are infelicitous in a given context.

(5) a. DOVE   (*c')   è   tua   sorella?   (Italian)
       where   PF   be.3SG   your   sister
       'Where (*there) is your sister?'

   b. #C'è   (mia   sorella)   IN   CUCINA
       PF-be.3SG   my   sister   in   kitchen
       'My sister is in the kitchen.'

In type II, *ci* functions as a pro-predicate, replacing the locative predicate within the clause (in fact, within the Nucleus, see Note 6). The complementary distribution of *ci* and a full locative phrase or a locative adverb is therefore expected.

Type III *ci*-sentences exhibit similar properties to type II, the only difference consisting in the deictic function of the proform. If no location is active or salient in discourse, the locative clitic does not refer anaphorically to a locative phrase, but rather it takes a strong deictic value, that is, a default interpretation of 'here and now'. Type III *ci*-sentences, thus, do not require any discourse background and are generally uttered in out-of-the-blue contexts. In this type too the focus is on the argument, which tends to be specific, as specific referents are more easily located in space and time.

Whereas the proform is locative in types II and III, no locative function can be detected or indeed envisaged in type IV: presentational *ci*-sentences. Semantically, type IV *ci*-sentences are equivalent to canonical predications. Even though they may at first sight appear to be similar to inverse locatives, especially when they involve a locative phrase, information structure keeps them distinct from type II: while inverse locatives are argument-focus structures, presentational sentences are sentence-focus structures. Type IV is peculiar to spoken and colloquial Italian and has a particular discourse function (Berruto 1986). It marks a new proposition as relevant to the discourse context, i.e., the situation in which the conversation takes place, further providing the justification for an immediately preceding or following statement, or an explanation for the previous assertion or the next one. The second part of the presentational sentence serves as the predicate of the post-copular argument. It can be a clause (cf. (6a–b)), an adjective (cf. (6c)), or a locative phrase (cf. (6d)).

(6) a. C'È   GIANNI   CHE   STA   MALE   (Italian)
       PF-be.3SG   Gianni   who   stay.3SG sick
       'Gianni is sick.'

   b. C'È   MIO   FIGLIO   CHE   HA   LA   TONSILLITE
      PF-be.3SG   my   son   who   have.3SG   the   tonsillitis
      'My son has tonsillitis.'

   c. OGGI   C'È   IL   DIRETTORE   ARRABBIATO
      today   PF-be.3SG   the   director   angry
      'Today the director is angry.'

   d. CI   SONO   I   PIATTI   DI   PORCELLANA   NEL   LAVANDINO
      PF   be.3PL   the   plates   of   porcelain   in-the   sink
      'The porcelain plates are in the sink.'

In Section 3.2, we will argue that the discourse function of type IV requires sentence focus, which is flagged by the pseudo-existential construction, specifically, the proform and the copula.

3 Shared trends in the encoding of information structure

3.1 Syntactic position

We are now able to discuss the findings of our investigation into Italo-Romance. We will begin with the encoding of topic and focus (see Note 5). The twenty dialects under examination here exhibit a clear tendency towards the encoding of the topic-vs.-focus contrast by means of syntactic position. Adopting Van Valin's (2005: 3–8) **Layered Structure of the Clause** (LSC),[6] clause-internal topics only occur in a pre-nuclear position, whereas foci strongly tend to occur in a post-nuclear position. When we take the extra-clausal positions into account, we find that both referential and aboutness topics can occur in the Left-Detached Position, but only referential topics are found in the Right-Detached Position.

(7) a. Indo   èn-i   i   sugaman?   (Felino, Emilia)
      where be.3PL-SCL.PL the towels

      i   sugaman   i   èn   int   al   caset
      the   towels   SCL.PL be.3PL inside the   drawer

      #a   gh'è   i   sugaman int   al   caset
      EXPL PF-be.3SG the towels   inside the   drawer
      'Where are the towels? The towels are in the drawer'

   b. Co   gh'è   sot   al   let?
      what PF-be.3SG under the   bed

      A   gh'è   AL   PANTOFLI sot   al   let
      EXPL PF-be.3SG the slippers under the   bed

      #Al   pantofli i   èn   sot   al   let
      the   slippers SCL.PL be.3PL under the   bed
      'What is there under the bed? There are the slippers under the bed.'

---

6 The LSC is based on the semantically-motivated contrasts between (a) predicating and non-predicating elements, and (b) those noun and adpositional phrases which are arguments of the predicate of the clause and those which are not. The locus of the predicate is the Nucleus, whereas the arguments of the predicate occur within the Core. Any noun and adpositional phrases which are not arguments in the semantic representation of the predicate occur in a Periphery of the Core.

(i) [$_{Core}$ Chris [$_{Nucleus}$ saw] Bill] [$_{Per}$ in the library]

Whereas all human languages are assumed to have the syntactic layers shown in (i), there are a number of more external positions, which are not taken to be universal. These can be associated with specific constructions or discourse functions. The Pre-Core Slot is the locus of *wh-* words in English, as well as many other languages. The Pre-Core Slot can have a counterpart after the core, the Post-Core Slot, which has been argued to be the locus of post-nuclear contrastive foci in Italian (Bentley 2008: 280–281). The syntactic layer called Clause is formed by the Core, its Periphery (or peripheries), and the Pre- and Post-Core Slots. The positions which are external to the Clause typically host constituents which are topical in discourse, as is the case with the Left Detached Position in (ii), and afterthoughts, as is the case with the Right Detached Position. The detached positions can be reiterated within a single sentence.

(ii) *A scuola Piero ci va ancora* (Italian)
    to school Piero PF go.3SG still
    [$_{LDP}$ A scuola] [$_{Clause}$ [$_{Core}$ Piero ci [$_{Nucleus}$ va] *ancora*]]
    (Lit.: To school, Piero still goes there)

c. *Co   è   suces?*
   what be.3SG   happen.PP.SG.M

   I   ÈN   PASÈ   DU   FURASTER
   SCL.PL   be.3PL   pass.PP.PL.M   two   strangers

   #*Du   foraster   i   èn   pena   pasè*
   two   strangers   SCL.PL   be.3PL   just   pass.PP.PL.M
   'What happened? Two strangers just passed by.'

In the replies to the (a) question, the argument is a referential topic. In the felicitous member of the given pairs, the noun phrase which encodes this argument precedes the copula immediately (in (7a), a subject clitic is proclitic on the copula). There is no pause between the noun phrase and the rest of the sentence, and we therefore assume that the argument takes the core-internal immediately pre-nuclear position. We thus propose the syntactic structure in (8) for these structures.

(8)   [Core I sugaman [Nucleus i èn int al caset]]⁷

In the alternative realisations of the same replies, the topic figures in post-nuclear position. These realisations were deemed to be infelicitous in this context. The structures with an immediately post-copular argument were selected as felicitous replies to the (b) questions, where the argument is focal. There is no pause between the copula and the post-copular noun phrase, and thus we take the latter to be core-internal.⁸ It appears that there can be a break between the postcopular noun phrase and the coda, in agreement with Leonetti's (2008: 142) hypothesis on Italian *ci*-sentences. Assuming that the predicate of this structure is the locative phrase (see Section 2), it would seem that the predicate is detached from the clause because it is a referential topic. For the felicitous replies to the (b) questions we thus propose the syntactic structure in (9), where the locative predicate occurs in the clause-external Right Detached Position, while being co-referent with the core-internal locative proform that is pro-clitic to the copula and spells out the predicate inside the Nucleus.

(9)   [Clause [Core [Nucleus A gh'$_i$ è] AL PANTOFLI]] [RDP sot al let$_i$]

---

[7] We abstract away from the syntactic position of the subject clitic, the copula, as well as any tense, aspect or mood operators in the constructions under investigation.
[8] While the data show that there is no period of silence between the copula and the pivot, there may nevertheless be pitch changes reflecting the realisation of different intonational targets.

Comparable word order characterises the felicitous replies to the (c) questions. Again, there is no pause between the nucleus and the post-nuclear argument. We thus assume that the post-nuclear argument occurs within the Core, as is the case with (9). In this case, however, the predicate figures in its default, nuclear, position, as is shown in (10).

(10) [Core [Nucleus I ÈN PASÈ] DU FURASTER]

The above data suggest that, in the dialects under investigation, the core-internal immediately post-nuclear position is the default position of focal arguments. The copular structure in (7b) classifies as a type II *ci*-sentence. We will not discuss the syntax of type IV here, as we will deal with it in Section 3.2. As for types I and III, interestingly, they also exhibit the encoding of the focal noun phrase in immediately post-copular position. Type I is exemplified in (11).

(11) A   GH'È   AL SIT PER FER   D'ALTRI CÀ   (Felino, Emilia)
      EXPL PF-be.3SG the site for do.INF of-other houses
      'There's space for other houses in this town.'

This example was produced as a follow-up to the protasis of a conditional construction of the speech-act type (Sweetser 1990: 113–125): 'if you want to move here...'. It is thus a sentence focus construction whose relevance in discourse is explained by the preceding utterance. The focal pivot 'space to build other houses' follows the copula immediately without an intervening break. We thus take it to be core-internal. Recall now that, following Francez (2007), we assume that in existential constructions proper there is no predicate other than the pivot. In accordance with this analysis, we propose that the syntax of type I differs from that of type II, in that the nucleus is core-final. The proform is not referential in this case, but rather encodes an abstract argument which determines the contextual domain of the predication.

(12) [Core [Nucleus A GH'È AL SIT PER FER D'ALTRI CÀ]]

As for the syntactic encoding of focus in (12), we note that this is core-final, as is the case with type II, although here the core-final focal pivot provides the predicate in semantics and the nucleus in syntax. Since type I constructions are typically sentence-focus constructions, if there is a coda, this is within the Actual Focus Domain. The coda does not play any role in the predication, but rather it is a contextual modifier, in the sense that it modifies the contextual domain that is an implicit argument of the existential predicate (Francez 2007,

2009). Accordingly, we propose that the coda figures in a periphery of the Core, the default position of locative adpositions.

(13) [_Core_ [_Nucleus_ Cə STA   SPAZIJə PE L'ATI   CASə]] [_Per_ DEND' E STU PAESə]
      PF stay.3SG space   for the-other houses   inside of this town
                                                   (Santa Croce di Magliano, Molise)

Type III is exemplified by the sentence in (14), which was solicited with the question 'If you realise that Mary is here, how do you warn me about this?'

(14)   *Guerda:*   *a*   *gh'è*   *LA*   *MARIA*   (Felino, Emilia)
        look.IMP.2SG EXPL PF-be.3SG the Maria
        'Look: Maria is here.'

In this structure, the immediately post-copular noun phrase is not a predicate, but rather the argument of a speaker-oriented locative predicate, which is spelled out by the deictic proform (**be-Loc'** (*gh'* / *ce*, (la) Maria)). The argument of this predicate is in focus and is not separated intonationally from the copula. Once again, therefore, the focus turns out to be core-final.

(15)   [_Core_ [_Nucleus_ a gh'è] LA MARIA]

So far we have observed that the core-final position is a focal position in the dialects under investigation, and that, typically, this position is taken by a post-nuclear focal argument (cf. (9), (10)), although deviations from this pattern are attested (cf. (12), (13)). We discuss further deviations in the position of foci in Section 4.1.

    The other pattern discussed above concerns topics. If these are aboutness topics, and hence are not detached, they are typically found in a clause-internal pre-nuclear position, whilst they do not occur in a post-nuclear position. In (8) we illustrated a core-internal pre-nuclear topical subject. In (16) we illustrate an existential construction with a peripheral aboutness topic.

(16)   [_Clause_ [_Per_ TUN STA FRÔTTA] [_Core_ [_Nucleus_ C'È   TANT SEM]]]
                   in   this fruit   PF-be.3PL many seeds
        'In this fruit there are many seeds.'   (Gallo, Marche)

We will now mention the case of topicalised pivots, such as those occurring in the second member of the following sentence pair.

(17) *A   N   GH'È   ED DUBI   – Invece di dubi   G   N'È*
    EXPL NEG PF-be.3SG of doubts   instead of doubts PF PRT-be.3SG
    'There are no doubts – Actually, of doubts there are some.' (Felino, Emilia)

The first member of this example is a sentence-focus structure of type I. The focal pivot occurs in the core-final position discussed above.

In the second member of the sentence pair, the truth value of a negated existential construction is itself negated. Given that the pivot is here a referential topic, a number of dialects resort to cliticisation with the outcome of Latin INDE 'of it, of them' to encode the pivot as part of the presupposition and of the assertion at the same time. This is the case with (18), where *n(e)* resumes the topicalised complement (*di dubi* 'of doubts') of an understood asserted quantifier 'some' (Bentley 2004). We indicate this quantifier with Ø in (18), since it is lexically unrealised (although it is realised prosodically, with stress on the copula). Since the pivot can be separated from the rest of the clause by another clause ('doubts, as I said to you, there are some'), we assume that it occurs in the clause-external Left-Detached Position. This is thus another example of a pre-verbal topic, although here this topic is clause-external.

(18)   [LDP Di dubi] [Core [Nucleus G N'È Ø]]   (Felino, Emilia)

By contrast, another group of dialects does not provide any evidence of there being a focal pivot within the nucleus (the silent quantifier in (18)). Interestingly, in these dialects the copula agrees with the pre-copular pivot, whether or not it would normally agree with post-copular pivots (see Section 4.3). This is testified by the contrast in (19).

(19) a. *Sta   tenta   che   TUN STA FRÔTTA   C'È   TANT SEM*
       stay.IMP.2SG careful that in this fruit   PF-be.3SG many seeds
       'Be careful that there are many seeds in this fruit.'   (Gallo, Marche)

   b. *SU QUEST EN   C'È   I   DUBI   / EN   C'EN   I   DUBI*
       on this NEG PF-be.3SG the doubts   NEG PF-be.3PL the doubts
       'There are no doubts about this.'

   c. *E   invece scé, i   dubi   C'EN   /* C'È*
       and instead yes the doubts PF-be.3PL   PF-be.3SG
       'On the contrary, the doubts are there.'

Examples (19a–b) indicate that post-copular – i.e., focal – pivots do not necessarily control agreement in the dialect of Gallo. The topic *i dubi* 'the doubts', however, does control agreement obligatorily in (19c). We thus assume that this is not a predicative pivot, but rather the topical subject of a focal existential predicate **exist'** (Van Valin 2005: 55), which is here spelled out by the proform and the copula, but could otherwise be spelled by the lexeme for <exist>.

(20) a. **exist'** (i dubi) (Gallo, Marche)

b. [Core I dubi [Nucleus C'EN]]

The structures with a topicalised pivot thus provide evidence that topics cannot occur in a post-nuclear position within the clause, whereas foci typically do.

3.2 The proform

In addition to being encoded by syntactic position, information structure can be spelled out by the clitic pronominal form which we have referred to as the proform.[9] The Italian proform *ci*, and its Italo-Romance alloforms (*ce*, *cə*, *nci*, *ncə*, etc.), are etymologically locative, from Latin ECCE HIC (Rohlfs 1969, but see also Maiden's 1995 proposal that the same proforms derive from HINCE). Diachronic evidence suggests that the proform is progressively generalised from type III to type II and type I *CI*-sentences (Ciconte 2008, 2011, in prep.). In this process, the proform undergoes the loss of its locative function in some constructions, though not others. While in type II and type III *CI*-sentences the proform retains its locative meaning, in type I the proform has come to spell out the abstract argument which provides the contextual domain of the predication.

The proform has a clear role in discourse in type IV (which is not attested in the early Italo-Romance vernacular texts). In this type of *CI*-sentence, the proform bears no semantic function whatsoever. As was explained in Section 2, this type of *CI*-sentence signals that a statement is relevant to discourse, providing the justification for an immediately preceding or following utterance (Berruto 1986, Cruschina 2012a). What interests us in this context is how exactly this discourse function is expressed in type IV. We claim that it is expressed through the explicit encoding of sentence focus by the proform, as well as the copula. Observe (21B), which is a type IV *CI*-sentence, as it does not predicate the pivot,

---

[9] The present discussion is not based on evidence from Anacapri (Campania), Polignano a Mare (Puglia), and Soleto (Puglia), since in these dialects the proform does not figure in the same constructions as in the other dialects and does not appear to play a role in information structure.

but rather introduces an event into discourse. This event is relevant in the context of the utterance in (21A).

(21) A: *Vue   u   nìasci   cu   nui u   sabbatu   a   sira?*
       want.2SG that go-out.2SG with us the Saturday at evening
       (Acquaro, Calabria)

   B: *No   pìanzu.   Nc'è   sùarma   chi canta   a   chiazza e*
      NEG think.1SG PF-be.3SG sister-my who sing.3SG at square   and

      nu   bogghju   m'   a   pìardu
      NEG want.1SG that her miss.1SG

   'A: Do you want to go out with us on Saturday evening?

    B: I don't think so. My sister is singing in the square and I don't want to miss her.'

The *CI*-sentence in (21B) has a grammatical counterpart with the argument in pre-nuclear position (cf. (22a)). However, this counterpart is not as felicitous as (21B), in the given discourse context, since it does not encode sentence focus explicitly. In fact, it exhibits the syntactic structure which usually encodes focus on the predicate. Similarly, the counterpart with the argument in post-nuclear position (cf. (22b)) indicates contrastive focus on the argument, thus proving to be even more infelicitous.[10]

(22) a. *No   pìanzu.   Sùarma   canta   a   chiazza*   (Acquaro, Calabria)
        NEG think.1SG sister-my sing.3SG at square
        'I don't think so. My sister sings in the square.'

     b. *No   pìanzu. #Canta   SÙARMA   a   chiazza*
        NEG think.1sg sing.3SG sister-my at square
        'I don't think so', lit.: # sings MY SISTER in the square.'

As is the case with constructions with activity or active accomplishment predicates (cf. (22a–b)), in copular constructions, sentence focus is not readily encoded by word order alone. Rather, it can be encoded explicitly by embedding the construction in a *CI*-sentence (cf. (21B)), a syntactic strategy which signals that the argument is in non-contrastive focus, on a par with the rest of the proposition.

---

10 By contrastive focus we mean a type of focus which involves a choice among the members of a finite set.

This strategy is reminiscent of the serial verb construction with the existential verb *yôu* of Mandarin Chinese (Lambrecht 2000: 654) and of locative-possessive and locative-copula constructions with pseudo-clausal complements in Swahili (Marten 2013: 68–70). In turn, sentence focus signals the relevance of the whole proposition (hence the whole statement) in the given discourse context.

We can now return to the issue of the syntax of *ci*-sentences. We propose that, in type IV, the nucleus is filled by the proform and the copula, which are necessary for the formation of this structure, but are not predicating elements themselves (see Van Valin 2005: 14 for a comparable case). The noun phrase occurs in post-nuclear position, the default focal position, being modified by an adjectival or clausal predicate that occurs in its periphery (see the notion of peripheral or ad-subordination in Van Valin 2005: 194). We represent the layered structure of type-IV *ci*-sentences in (23a) and that of their argument in (23b).

(23) a. [$_{Core}$ [$_{Nuc}$ c'è Ø$_i$]   MIA SORELLA [(CHE È)   MALATA$_i$]]   (Italian)
         PF-be.3SG   my sister   who be.3SG sick

b. [$_{NP}$[$_{CoreN}$ MIA SORELLA]] [$_{Per}$ (CHE È)   MALATA]
              my sister   who be.3SG sick

According to (23b), the noun phrase and the following predicate constitute a noun phrase and its periphery. In the next section, we provide evidence from Sicilian which supports this analysis.

4 Micro-variation in information structure

The results of our investigation indicate that the position of topics is remarkably consistent across dialects. Typically, this is the core-internal immediately pre-nuclear position (cf. (8)), although topicalised constituents also occur in peripheral (cf. (16)) or left- (cf. (18)) and, less commonly, right-detached positions. This finding is robust across the twenty dialects of the sample considered here. The micro-variation attested in our survey concerns the encoding of focus. It was seen above that all the dialects under investigation exhibit a strong tendency towards the post-nuclear or core-final placement of foci. Within this broadly uniform pattern we found two kinds of micro-variation: the one concerning intonation, the other concerning word order.

4.1 Intonation

With respect to intonation, we extracted pitch measurements from five sentences from each dialect (i.e., each interview): four of these contained post-copular definite and indefinite existential pivots, while the remaining one contained a post-nuclear subject; f_0 measurements were taken across the region spanning the onset of the primary stressed syllable of the pivot/subject up to the boundary between the end of the pivot and the beginning of the coda (e.g., *Ci sono* [$_{\text{PIVOT}}$*le pan{tófole}*][$_{\text{CODA}}$*sotto il letto*]). Raw pitch values (in Hz) extracted from each token were $\log_{10}$-transformed and submitted to a linear regression. Analysis of regression-slope values (i.e., β-coefficients) provides an indication of whether f_0 has a rising or falling contour over the measurement region, and of the relative magnitude of the rise or fall. We hypothesised that differences in the *direction* of the intonational contour (i.e., rise vs. fall) or the *magnitude* of the rise/fall may potentially function as important phonetic cues of focus in different types of sentence. To test this hypothesis statistically, regression-slope values from each token were subjected to a two-way ANOVA with Dialect and Sentence Type as predictors.

Inferential testing revealed significant main effects of Dialect ($F_{(19,63)}$ = 1.916, $p < 0.05$) and Sentence Type ($F_{(4,63)}$ = 3.942, $p < 0.01$) on f_0 contours. Post-hoc pairwise *t*-tests (Bonferroni adjusted) showed that, in some dialects (Anacapri, Ferrara, Gambettola, Guardiagrele, Gubbio, Polignano a Mare, Santa Croce di Magliano, Soleto, Tursi), the f_0 contour in the post-nuclear subject tokens patterns differently from the pivot constructions (see Figure 1). With the exception of Anacapri and Gubbio, there is a pre-coda intonational fall (i.e., negative f_0 slope) in each of the pivot sentences, whereas we observe a clear intonational rise (i.e., positive f_0 slope) in the postverbal subject tokens. For Anacapri and Gubbio, the intonational target in the postverbal subject construction is also notably different from the pivot construction: whereas we observe a clear pre-coda fall over the pivot tokens, there is almost no change in f_0 in the postverbal subject tokens in these two dialects. In other words, whilst f_0 has a strongly negative contour in the pivot sentences, the postverbal subject tokens are characterised by a lack of pitch movement (i.e. flat intonation, cf. Figure 1).

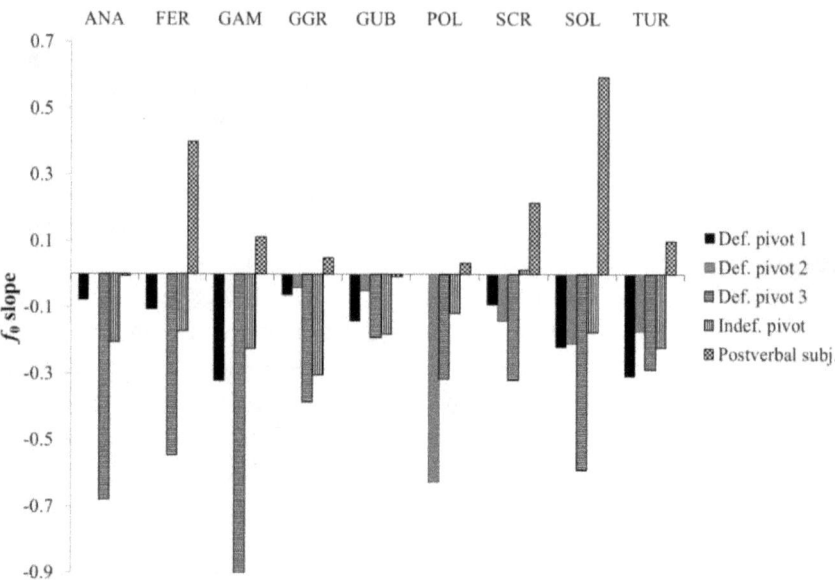

Figure 1: Dialects in which f_0 slope in post-nuclear subjects differs from pivot constructions

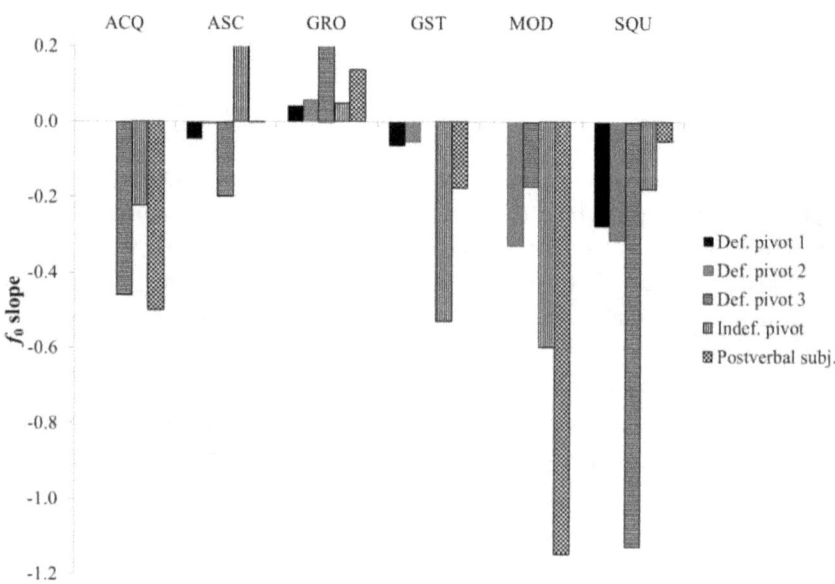

Figure 2: Dialects in which f_0 slope in post-nuclear subjects does not differ from pivot constructions

In comparison to these dialects, a number of other dialects (Acquaro, Ascoli Piceno, Grosio, Grosseto, Modica, Squillaci) show a different pattern: observe in Figure 2 that postverbal subject tokens do not pattern separately from the pivot tokens with regard to f_0 slope in these dialects. For example, we see here that all test sentences for which data were available in the Acquaro, Grosseto, Modica and Squinzano varieties have a strong falling f_0 slope preceding the coda boundary (i.e., including the postverbal subject tokens). Conversely, all sentences display an intonational rise in the Grosio dialect, and the Ascoli Piceno variety displays a strong rise in the indefinite pivot token which contrasts to falling or level f_0 trajectories that occur in the definite pivot and postverbal subject tokens.

4.2 Syntax

With respect to word order, we found that pre-nuclear foci are admitted by the Sicilian dialect of Modica (cf. (24) to (26)) under certain conditions. In this dialect, *ci*-sentences with post-copular focus have counterparts with a pre-copular argument. In terms of the syntactic position of the pre-copular focal constituent, in the absence of any prosodic or syntactic evidence of a break between the focal constituent and the copula, we propose that this is the core-internal pre-nuclear position (see also Bentley 2008).

(24) [Core I   TAPPINI [Nucleus ci$_i$ su]]   [RDP sutta ô lièttu$_i$]
     the slippers   PF be.3PL   under to-the bed
  'There are the slippers, under the bed.'   (Modica, Sicily)

Interestingly, the core-initial position is not available to all foci. In particular, this position is associated with special kinds of emphasis (Leone 1995: 59, Sornicola 1983), which Cruschina (2012b: 57–60) characterises in terms of relevance (Sperber & Wilson 1995: 48).[11] This is typically associated with narrow argument focus. With respect to the four types of *ci*-sentence, core-initial focus is readily available with types II and III, both of which involve narrow focus. Type III is illustrated in (25).

---

[11] In Relevance Theory (Sperber & Wilson 1995), the term relevance refers to the relationship between utterances, on the one hand, and pragmatic interpretations and implicit inferences on the other. Narrow focus is relevant in that it gives rise to various 'contextual effects', which are created by the interplay between the new information conveyed by the focus and the old information already available according to the specific context and the hearer's assumptions.

(25) Talìa: MARIA   c'è!   (Modica, Sicily)
      look.imp.2SG Maria   PF-be.3SG
      'Look: Maria is here.'

Contrastingly, types I and IV involve wide focus, and the core-initial position is subject to other syntactic and interpretive restrictions. To begin with, in type IV, the focal information unit (the argument and its predicate) must both occur in pre-copular position.

(26) a. Talè!   MARIA CA   CANTA   N'CHIESA   c'è   stasira
        look.IMP.2SG Maria who sing.3SG in-church PF-be.3SG tonight
        'Look! There's Maria singing in the church tonight.'   (Modica)

    b. Talè!   *MARIA c'è   CA   CANTA   N'CHIESA stasira
       look.IMP.2SG Maria PF-be.3SG who   sing.3SG in-church tonight
       'Look! There's Maria singing in the church tonight.'

Secondly, in type IV CI-sentences, as well as sentence focus constructions in general, the availability of the core-initial position is limited to a special interpretation, which Cruschina (2012b) describes in terms of mirativity. In linguistic typology, mirativity is defined as 'a grammatical category whose primary meaning is speaker's unprepared mind, unexpected new information, and concomitant surprise' (Aikhenvald 2004: 209). With a mirative interpretation, the core-initial position is generally occupied by a single constituent ((25) may in fact have a mirative value in the relevant context), but, interestingly, it may also host a larger constituent, like the argument and its predicate of type IV CI-sentences (26a). If an appropriate context is set up, an existential sentence may express mirativity and thus exploit the core-initial position, but in that case the sentence would be ambiguous between a genuine existential reading (type I) and a presentational one (type IV).

(27) Minchia! DU CRISTIANI DAVANTI Â   PORTA   ci sunnu. Scappamu!
     damn   two people   in front to-the   door   PF be.3PL run.IMP.1PL
     'Damn! There are two people in front of the door. Let's run!'   (Sicilian)

Sentence (27) would be pragmatically felicitous in a context in which two burglars have broken into a house and one of them notices two men at the door and shouts to the other to run. This context, and in particular its introductory character with respect to the main assertion (i.e. *let's run!*), would certainly favour a presentational reading of the CI-sentence.

The contrast between types II and III, on the one hand, and types I and IV, on the other, indicates that core-initial focus is normally constrained to argument-focus, with possible exceptions in the case of sentence focus constructions with mirative value, especially for type IV, where the core-initial information unit must be a syntactic constituent, i.e. the argument and its periphery.

Although the other dialects do not offer robust evidence of core-initial focus, we should report a result which stands out in the context of the evidence provided by these dialects. Specifically, in four dialects (Squinzano, Polignano a Mare, Acquaro, Gubbio), the structure in (28b) was chosen as the most natural, if not the only grammatical, reply to (28a). This structure exhibits a focal argument in immediately pre-nuclear position (cf. (28c)).

(28) a. *Ce stè sott' u ghittə?* (Polignano a Mare, Apulia)
what stay.3SG under the bed
'What is there under the bed?'

b. *I CHIAVATTƏ stòunə sott' u ghittə*
the slippers stay.3PL under the bed
'THE SLIPPERS are under the bed.'

c. [Core I CHIAVATTƏ [Nucleus stòunə]] [RDP sott'u ghittə]

The findings in (28) contrast with the systematic selection of the core-final position as the syntactic locus of focus in sentence focus constructions.

(29) a. *Mannagghjə! M' ANNƏ CADÉUTƏ I PJATTƏ!*
damn to.me have.3PL fallen.PP the plates
'Damn! The plates fell on me!' (Polignano a Mare)

b. *STÒUNƏ DÒ CRƏSTJÉNƏ A LA PORTƏ*
stay.3PL two people at the door
'There are two people at the door.'

Although this result should be investigated further, ideally with evidence from spontaneous spoken discourse, we note that the contrast between (28), on the one hand, and (29), on the other, parallels the Sicilian contrast between argument (narrow) and sentence focus, insofar as the former more readily lends itself to core-initial focus.

To return to the dialect of Modica, and to Sicilian in general, in addition to exhibiting non-contrastive argument focus in core-initial position, Sicilian allows contrastive argument focus in a pre-nuclear position, which Bentley (2008) claimed not to be core-internal. Unlike the former structure, the latter is also found in a number of other dialects as well as in Italian (Benincà 1988, Frascarelli 2000, Rizzi 1997, among others).

By contrast with the dialects discussed above in this section, the variety of Premosello Chiovenda bans pre-nuclear focus altogether (30), thus providing a clear example of pragmatic rigidity, in the sense of Van Valin (1999), in Italo-Romance.

(30) a. *Cus   a   gh'è   sut   al   letc?*
       what   EXPL   PF-be.3SG   under   the   bed
       'What is there under the bed?'   (Premosello Chiovenda, Piedmont)

   b. *Al   gh è   I   PANTUFUL,   sut   al   letc*
      EXPL-SCL   PF-be.3SG   the   slippers   under   the   bed
      'There are the slippers, under the bed.'

(31) A: *La   Luisa   l'   à   rot   al   vaas*
        the   Luisa   SCL.3SG.F   have.3SG   broke.PP   the   vase

   B: *No,   (*LA DELIA)   l'   à   rot   LA   DELIA*
      no   the   Delia   it   have.3SG   broke.PP   the   Delia
      '– A: Luisa broke the vase. – B: No, it was Delia who broke it.'

We refer to Cruschina (2012b) and Paoli (2003) for comparable evidence from other Piedmontese dialects.

4.3 Inflection

In addition to being spelled out by syntactic position, the contrast between presupposition and assertion can also be spelled out by finite number agreement on the copula. The finite form of the verb is the one which carries the same person and number features as the subject in predicate-focus constructions. These features can be spelled out in affixal or clitic form or both. We constrain the discussion to number agreement, in that structures with a third person singular copula and a third person plural post-copular noun phrase can be argued to exhibit person agreement (Manzini and Savoia 2005/III: 34). The encoding of information structure in finite verb agreement is exemplified in (32).

(32) a. *Indu é-i   i   sugamen?*   (Grosio, Lombardy)
       where be.3PL-SCL.3PL.M the towels

   I   sugamen i   é   INDE 'L CASÉT
   the towels SCL.3PL.M be.3PL inside the drawer
   'Where are the towels? The towels are in the drawer.'

b. *Cus a   gh'é-l   sota 'l letc?*
   what EXPL PF-be.3SG-SCL.3SG.M under the bed

   Al   gh'é   I SCIUÀTI, sota 'l letc
   EXPL-SCL PF-be.3SG the slippers under the bed
   'What is there under the bed? There are the slippers, under the bed.'

c. *Cus é-l   sucès?   –L'É   PASÈ   DU FURÈST*
   what be.3SG-SCL.3SG.M happen.PP SCL.3SG.M-be.3SG pass.PP two strangers
   'What happened? Two strangers passed by.'

d. *AI   DO A-L'   É   RIVÀ   EL PÀ   E   LA MAMA*
   at-the two EXPL-SCL be.3SG arrive.PP the father and the mother
   'At two o' clock the parents arrived.'

In the dialect of Grosio the third person of ESSE 'be' does not vary for number. In the third person, therefore, agreement is marked by the alternation of the subject proclitic *l* (singular) and *i* (plural). In (32a) we find the agreeing clitic *i*, which contrasts with non-agreeing *l* in (32b) (*a* is another clitic, for which we refer to Benincà 1983). The evidence from sentence-focus constructions (cf. 32c–d) further indicates that the status of the potential controller as topic or focus is a condition on agreement (Corbett 2006) in Grosio: topical potential controllers trigger agreement, whereas focal ones do not.

In the southern dialects, and in the majority of the dialects of the Centre of Italy, finite verb agreement is not sensitive to information structure. In the dialects of the North, instead, we also find another pattern of agreement that is driven by information structure. This is not indicative of the status of the potential controller as part of the presupposition or the assertion (cf. 32b–d), but rather to the status of the referent of the potential controller in the minds of the discourse participants (Lambrecht 1994: 93ff.).

(33) a. *Maria l'   é   miga de per lé*   (Grosio, Lombardy)
       Maria SCL.3SG.F be.3SG NEG by for she
       'Maria is not on her own / alone.'

b. *Te   gh'es   TI*
   SCL.2SG PF-be.2SG you
   'There's you / Lit.: There are you.'

c. *An   ghe se   NUIALTRI*
   SCL.1PL PF be.1PL we
   'There's us / Lit.: There are we.'

d. *I   gh'é   LOR*
   SCL.3PL PF-be.3PL they
   'There's them / Lit.: there are they.'

Whereas the existential copula does not exhibit agreement with the pivot in (32b–d), it does exhibit such agreement with the pivot in (33b–d). In particular, in (33b) and (33c) the pivot controls both clitic and affixal agreement on the copula. Although the third person of ESSE 'be' is invariant, agreement is spelled out by the clitic *i* in (33d), which contrasts with *l* in (32b–d). The pivots of (33b–d) differ from the post-nuclear arguments of (32b–d) in that they are personal pronouns (tonic *ti* 'you', *nuialtri* 'we', and *lor* 'they'). Personal pronouns encode **active identifiable** discourse referents. A discourse referent is identifiable if the speaker can assume that the hearer has a cognitive representation for it, and will be able to pick it out among all the referents that can be designated with the same linguistic expression (Lambrecht 1994: 77, Chafe 1976). The activation of a discourse referent depends on its being in the current focus of consciousness (Chafe 1987). It turns out, therefore, that, in the dialects of Grosio, agreement is not only sensitive to whether the potential controller is topical or focal, but it is further constrained by the status of the potential controller in the minds of the discourse participants. Personal pronouns control finite verb agreement regardless of topicality, in that they encode active identifiable discourse referents (cf. Saccon 1993, where they are defined in terms of presupposition).

A slightly different pattern was found in the dialect of Gallo. Here finite verb agreement is obligatory with topical controllers (cf. 34a), and optional with focal controllers (cf. 34b). Focal first and second person pronouns (but not third person pronouns) do not follow the pattern in (34b), but rather they control finite agreement obligatorily (35b–c).

(34) a. *Du   en i   sciugamen? – I   sciugamen *è/ en tel   caset*
        where   are the towels   the towels   is are in-the   drawer
        'Where are the towels? The towels are in the drawer.'   (Gallo, Marche)

b. *Cu   c'è   sota   'l   let? – C'è / en   le   ciavat,   sota   'l   let*
what PF-is under the bed   PF-is are the slippers   under the bed
'What is there under the bed? There's / there are the slippers under the bed.'

(35) a. *Maria en'è   da per lìa*   (Gallo, Marche)
Maria NEG-be.3SG by for she
'Maria is not on her own / alone.'

b. *C   si   TO*
PF be.2SG you
'There's you / Lit.: There are you.'

c. *C   sen   NO*
PF be.1PL we
'There's us / Lit.: There are we.'

d. *C'è   LOR / C'en   LOR*
PF-be.3SG they   PF-be.3PL they
'There's them / Lit.: There is/are they.'

Thus, in the *ci*-sentences of the dialect of Gallo, only the speech act personal pronouns control agreement obligatorily. By speech act personal pronouns, we mean personal pronouns which encode referents that are active and identifiable within the context of the speech act. As was mentioned above, the agreement alternations illustrated in this section are unknown to the dialects of the South of Italy, as well as the majority of the dialects of the Centre. We thus conclude that here agreement does not contribute a strategy for the encoding of information structure.[12]

5 Conclusion

Differentiating between four types of *there*-sentence, we analysed the encoding of information structure in twenty Italo-Romance dialects from the North, the Centre and the South of Italy. Within a broadly uniform tendency towards the encoding of the opposition between presupposition and assertion in word order, we identified three principal patterns of micro-variation in (i) preverbal syntax, (ii) the prosody of copular and non-copular sentences with postverbal pivots/subjects, and (iii) number agreement or lack thereof in the verbal inflection.

---

[12] For a detailed account of agreement in Italo-Romance existential constructions, we refer to Bentley, Ciconte & Cruschina (2013).

References

Abbott, Barbara. 1992. Defniteness, existentials, and the 'list' interpretation. In *Proceedings of SALT II*, C. Barker, D. Dowty (eds.), Columbus, OH: Ohio State University.

Abbott, Barbara. 1993. A pragmatic account of the definiteness effect in existential sentences. *Journal of Pragmatics* 19 (1), Amsterdam: Elsevier.

Abbott, Barbara. 1997. Defitniteness and existentials. *Language* 73, Washington, DC: Linguistic Society of America.

Aikhenvald, Alexandra. 2004. *Evidentiality*. Oxford: Oxford University Press.

Benincà, Paola. 1983. Il clitico *a* nel dialetto padovano. In *Scritti linguistici in onore di Giovan Battista Pellegrini*, Pisa: Pacini.

Benincà, Paola. 1988. L'ordine degli elementi della frase e le costruzioni marcate. In *Grande grammatica italiana di consultazione*, L. Renzi, G. Salvi (eds.), Vol. 1, Bologna: Il Mulino.

Bentley, Delia. 2004. *Ne*-cliticisation and split intransitivity. *Journal of Linguistics* 40, Cambridge: Cambridge University Press.

Bentley, Delia. 2008. The interplay of focus structure and syntax: evidence from two sister languages. In *Investigations of the Syntax-Semantics-Pragmatics Interface*, R. D. Van Valin Jr (ed.), Amsterdam and Philadelphia: Benjamins.

Bentley, Delia; Francesco Maria Ciconte; Silvio Cruschina. 2013. Micro-variation in subject agreement: The case of existential pivots with split focus in Romance. *Italian Journal of Linguistics* 25 (1): 15–43.

Berruto, Gaetano. 1986. Un tratto sintattico dell'italiano parlato: il c'è presentativo. In *Parallela 2. Aspetti della sintassi dell'italiano contemporaneo*, K. Lichem, E. Mara, S. Knaller (eds.), Tubingen: Narr.

Chafe, Wallace. 1976. Givenness, contrastiveness, definiteness, subjects, topics, and point of view. In *Subject and Topic*, C. Li, (ed.), New York: Academic Press.

Chafe, Wallace. 1987. Cognitive constraints on information flow. In *Coherence and grounding in discourse* (Typological studies in language 11), R. Tomlin (ed.), Amsterdam and Philadelphia: Benjamins.

Ciconte, Francesco Maria. 2008. Existential Constructions in Early Italo-Romance Vernaculars. In *Proceedings of the Oxford Postgraduate Conference LingO 2007*, M. Kokkonidis (ed.), Oxford: University of Oxford.

Ciconte, Francesco Maria. 2011. The emergence and the reanalysis of the existential proform: evidence from Early Italo-Romance. *Transactions of the Philological Society* 109 (3), Oxford: Blackwell Publishing.

Ciconte, Francesco Maria. In prep. Historical Context. In D. Bentley, F.M. Ciconte, and S. Cruschina. *Existentials and Locatives in Romance Dialects of Italy*. Oxford: Oxford University Press.

Corbett, Greville G. 2006. *Agreement*. Cambridge: Cambridge University Press.

Cruschina, Silvio. 2012a. Focus in existential sentences. In *Internet Celebration for Luigi Rizzi's 60th Birthday*, V. Bianchi, C. Chesi (eds.), Siena: Centro Interdipartimentale di Studi Cognitivi sul Linguaggio (http://www.ciscl.unisi.it/gg60/).

Cruschina, Silvio. 2012b. *Discourse-related Features and Functional Projections*. Oxford/New York: Oxford University Press.

Francez, Itamar. 2007. *Existental propositions*. Stanford: Stanford University. PhD Dissertation.

Francez, Itamar. 2009. Existentials, predication, and modification. *Linguistics and Philosophy* 32, Dordrecht: Springer.
Frascarelli, Mara. 2000. The Syntax-Phonology Interface in Focus and Topic Constructions in Italian. *Studies in Natural Language and Linguistic Theory* 50, Dordrecht: Kluwer Academic Publishers.
Hazout, Ilan. 2004. The syntax of existential constructions. *Linguistic Inquiry* 35, Cambridge, MA: MIT Press Journals.
La Fauci, Nunzio; Michele Loporcaro. 1997. Outline of a theory of existentials on evidence from Romance. *Studi italiani di linguistica teorica e applicata* 26: 5–55. Pisa: Pacini.
Lambrecht, Knud. 1994. *Information Structure and Sentence Form*. Cambridge: Cambridge University Press.
Leone, Alfonso. 1995. *Profilo di sintassi siciliana*. Palermo: Centro di Studi Filologici e Linguistici Siciliani.
Leonetti, Manuel. 2008. Definiteness effects and the role of the coda in existential constructions. In *Essays on Nominal Determination*, H. Høeg Müller, A. Klinge (eds.), Amsterdam: John Benjamins.
Lumsden, Michael. 1988. *Existential Sentences: Their Structure and Meaning*. London: Croom Helm.
Maiden, Martin. 1995. *A Linguistic History of Italian*. London: Longman.
Manzini, Maria Rita; Leonardo Savoia. 2005. *I dialetti italiani e romanci. Morfosintassi generativa*. Alessandria: Edizioni Dell'Orso.
Marten, Lutz. 2013. Structure and interpretation in Swahili existential constructions. *Italian Journal of Linguistics* 25 (1): 45–73. Pisa: Pacini.
McNally, Louise. 1992. *An Interpretation for the English Existential Construction*. Santa Cruz: University of California Ph.D. Dissertation.
Milsark, Gary. 1974. *Existential Sentences in English*. Cambridge, MA.: MIT. PhD Dissertation.
Moro, Andrea. 1997. *The Raising of Predicates*. Cambridge: Cambridge University Press.
Parry, Mair. 2010. Non-canonical subjects in the early Italian vernaculars. *Archivio Glottologico Italiano* 95 (2), Firenze: Le Monnier.
Paoli, Sandra. 2003. *COMP and the left-periphery: Comparative Evidence from Romance*. Manchester: The University of Manchester. PhD Dissertation.
Pinto, Manuela. 1997. *Licensing and interpretation of inverted subjects in Italian*. Utrecht: Universiteit Utrecht. PhD Dissertation.
Rando, Emily; Donna Jo Napoli. 1978. Definites in *there*-sentences. *Language* 54, Washington, DC: Linguistic Society of America.
Remberger, Eva-Maria. 2009. Null subjects, expletives and locatives in Sardinian. In *Null subjects, expletives and locatives in Romance, Konstanzer Arbeitspapiere des Fachbereichs Sprachwissenschaft 123*, G. Kaiser, E. Remberger (eds.), Konstanz: Universität Konstanz.
Rizzi, Luigi. 1997. The fine structure of the left periphery. In *Elements of Grammar*, L. Haegeman (ed.), Dordrecht: Kluwer.
Rohlfs, Gerard. 1969. *Grammatica storica della lingua italiana e dei suoi dialetti. Sintassi e formazione delle parole*. Torino: Einaudi.
Saccon, Graziella. 1993. *Post-verbal subjects: A study based on Italian and its dialects*. Harvard: Harvard University. PhD Dissertation.
Sornicola, Rosanna. 1983. Relazioni d'ordine e segmentazione della frase in italiano. Per una teoria della sintassi affettiva. In *Scritti linguistici in onore di Giovan Battista Pellegrini*, Pisa: Pacini.

Sperber, Dan; Deirdre Wilson. 1995. *Relevance: Communication and Cognition*, Oxford: Blackwell.

Sweetser, Eve. 1990. *From Etymology to Pragmatics. Metaphorical and Cultural aspects of Semantic Structure*. Cambridge: Cambridge University Press.

Tortora, Christina. 1997. *The Syntax and Semantics of the Weak Locative*. Newark, DE: University of Delaware. PhD Dissertation.

Van Valin Jr, Robert D. 1999. A typology of the interaction of focus structure and syntax. In *Typology and linguistic theory from description to explanation: For the 60th birthday of Aleksandr E. Kibrik*, E. V. Rachilina, J. G. Testelec (eds.), Moscow: Languages of Russian Culture.

Van Valin Jr, Robert D. 2005. *Exploring the Syntax-Semantics Interface*. Cambridge: Cambridge University Press.

Van Valin Jr, Robert D.; Randy J. LaPolla. 1997. *Syntax: Structure, Meaning, and Function*. Cambridge: Cambridge University Press.

Ward, Gregory; Betty Birner. 1995. Definiteness and the English existential. *Language* 71, Washington, DC: Linguistic Society of America.

Williams, Edwin. 1984. *There*-insertion. *Linguistic Inquiry* 15, Cambridge, MA: MIT Press Journals.

Williams, Edwin. 1994. *Thematic Structure in Syntax*. Cambridge, MA: MIT Press.

Zamparelli, Roberto. 2000. *Layers in the Determiner Phrase*. New York: Garland.

Zucchi, Alessandro. 1995. The ingredients of definiteness and the definiteness effect. *Natural Language Semantics* 3(1), Dordrecht: Springer.

Ricardo Etxepare
6 How does adjacency arise? Grammatical conditions on focus-verb adjacency in Basque

Abstract: The adjacency between focused expressions and the finite verbal complex in Basque has been traditionally taken to reflect a configurational relation. The received analysis in the generative approach has the focus in a Specifier-Head relation with the finite verbal complex. To the extent that agreement, a feature matching relation, underlies Spec-Head configurations, that configuration is held to reflect the existence of a formal syntactic feature F (for Focus) which is licensed by a matching feature F residing in the focal operator. Although there are good reasons to sustain the idea that a syntactic focus feature may exist as a grammatical formative, I would like to defend the idea that adjacency relations, at least in the domain of Basque focal syntax, do not constitute supporting evidence for this (see Laka and Uriagereka 1987; Uriagereka 1999, for an earlier discussion of this idea). The adjacency relation between the focus and the finite verbal complex does not reflect a configurational relation mediated by the purported feature F, but the output of a set of different factors working together, some morpho-phonological, concerning the linearization of the finite auxiliary, some others syntactic, reflecting the feature constitution of the left periphery and its relation to elements inside the Inflectional Phrase. The arguments that I will develop to sustain this claim are twofold: on the one hand, I will show that the adjacency required between the focus and the finite verbal complex in the preverbal domain follows either from the clitic status of the auxiliary or from independent cartographic restrictions in the placement of focus and polarity; on the other, I will show that the adjacency requirement itself is just a preverbal phenomenon, not an obligatory condition on foci. As observed by Irurtzun (2007), the adjacency of focus and verb only holds in finite clauses, and as shown by Etxepare and Ortiz de Urbina (2003), it is not required in the postverbal domain.

Ricardo Etxepare, CNRS-IKER (UMR5478)

1 Some basic structural properties of focus in Basque

Basque is a so-called free word order language, in which informationally unmarked sequences are of the SOV type (see De Rijk 1968; Elordieta 2001). (1) represents a relatively complex sentence, with a ditransitive auxiliary and three independent arguments preceding a verbal modifier. It is meant to reflect the unmarked ordering of those elements in the sentence:[1]

(1) *Mirenek   gaur   Anderri   garbigailu   berria*
    Miren.ERG   today   Ander.DAT   wash.mashine   new.ABS
    kotxez   eraman   dio
    car.by   carried   AUX.3sA.3sD.3sE
    'Miren brought Ander the new washing machine by car today.'

Basque grammarians have noted long ago (Azkue 1891; Altube 1929) that the apparent "free word order" of the language (characterized by the fact that it allows a rich set of permutations in the relative order of syntactic constituents), obeys a restriction that associates information structural concepts to syntactic configurations. This restriction can be characterized as in Altube (1929:6, translation mine):

(2) "The main rule concerning the use in the sentence of the inquired nominal element is that it must be placed immediately before the verb"

The "inquired term" or the "question-target" is how the focus has been designated in the Basque grammatical tradition. The free permutations of the relevant elements in (2) thus obey a constant rule: the element that precedes the verbal complex is the focus of the sentence (focus in capitals).[2] Thus, the unmarked

---

[1] The abbreviations used correspond to the Leipzig list of standard abbreviations. For those items which are not represented in that list, I will use PART for the partitive determiner, HAB for habitual aspect, AFF for affirmative particle, and POL for a functional projection including both negation and affirmation.
[2] Focus-verb adjacency is a relatively widespread phenomenon, noted in Turkish (Kennelly, 1999), Hungarian (Horvath, 1986; Kiss, 1998; Puskás, 2000), Hindi-Urdu (Kidwai, 2000), Kashmiri (Manetta, 2011), Malagasy (Keenan, 1976), Georgian (Skopeteas and Fanselow, 2010) or Nagh-Daghestanian languages (see Forker and Belyaev, this volume), among many others. In reference to the placement of wh-pronouns, typically parallel to that of focused elements in those languages, Dryer (2013) observes in the WALS that "placement of interrogative phrases in immediately preverbal position is found in a number of verb final languages in Europe and Asia, although it doesn't seem to be common outside this area" (Dryer, in Dryer and Haspelmath, online WALS).

word order in (3a) exists alongside the possible marked orders illustrated in (3b–d):³ **(S IO O V AUX)**

(3) a. Jonek   Mireni   eskutitz   bat   idatzi   dio
       Jon.ERG   Miren.DAT   letter   DET.ABS   written   AUX.3sE.3sD.3sA
       'Jon wrote a letter to Miren.'   **(S IO O V AUX)**

   b. JONEK idatzi dio Mireni eskutitz bat   (S$_{focus}$ V+AUX...)
      'It is JON who wrote a letter to Miren.'

   c. MIRENI idatzi dio Jonek eskutitz bat   (IO$_{focus}$ V+AUX...)
      'It is to MIREN that Jon wrote a letter.'

   d. ESKUTITZ BAT idatzi dio Jonek Mireni   (O$_{focus}$ V+AUX...)
      'It is A LETTER that Jon wrote to Miren.'

The descriptive rule in (2) accounts for the absence of structures like (4):

(4) *MIRENI   Jonek   idatzi   dio   eskutitz   bat
    Miren.DAT   Jon.ERG   written   AUX.3sE.3sD.3sA   letter   DET.ABS
    'It is to MIREN that Jon wrote a letter.'   (IO$_{focus}$ XP V+AUX...)

All elements to the left of the preverbal focus constituent are interpreted as topics (possibly giving rise to multiple topicalization structures, see Elordieta 2001), with raising intonation at the accented syllable of the constituent immediately preceding the focus:

(5) a. Mireni   eskutitz   bat,   JONEK   idatzi   dio
       Miren.DAT   letter   DET   Jon.ERG   written   AUX
       'To Miren a letter, it is JON who wrote it.'

   b. Eskutitz   bat   Mireni,   JONEK   idatzi   dio
      letter   DET   Miren.DAT   Jon.ERG   written   AUX
      'A letter to Miren, it is JON who wrote it.'

---

3 (3a), illustrating the unmarked word order, gives rise to "focus projection" (see Reinhart, 2006 and references therein). In other words, it may be interpreted as having focus on the object, the predicate or the whole sentence, as an answer to "what happened". (3d) only represents narrow focus on the object. The narrow foci are not necessarily contrastive. In fact, heavily contrastive foci may marginally allow disruption of the adjacency between focus and verb, as noted by Etxepare (1997:112).

The postverbal elements are typically arranged in the unmarked order, but alternative orders are possible (see Albizu 1993 for an analysis of the word order variation in postverbal domains in terms of scrambling):

(6) a. *MIRENI   idatzi   dio   Jonek   eskutitz bat*
       Miren.DAT written   AUX.3sE.3sD.3sA Jon.ERG   letter   DET.ABS
       'It is to MIREN that Jon wrote a letter.'

   b. *MIRENI   idatzi   dio   eskutitz bat   Jonek*
       Miren.DAT written   AUX.3sE.3sD.3sA letter   DET   Jon.ERG
       'It is to MIREN that Jon wrote a letter.'

No focal effect has been claimed to arise from word order permutations in the post-auxiliary domain. With its rigid assignment of focus and topic slots, Basque word order thus ideally corresponds to what Kiss (1995) has called a "discourse configurational language". In a linear representation, basque word order can roughly be described as in (7):

(7) TOPIC FOCUS V INFL [backgrounded material]

Structurally, (7) translates into a configuration in which both topic and focus are external to the IP, or the phrase headed by the inflected verb. Topic and focus precede negation, which in turn licenses ellipsis of the finite clause (Laka 1990):

(8) *Jonek   LIBURUA   erosi   du   baina   Peruk*
    Jon.ERG   book.DET   bought   AUX.3sE.3sA   but   Peru.ERG

    ez   [IP du   liburua   erosi]
    NEG   AUX.3sE.3sA   book.DET   bought
    "Jon bought a BOOK, but Peru didn't"

Focus can also directly license IP-ellipsis, as shown in (9):

(9) *Jonek   LIBURUA   erosi   du*
    Jon.ERG   book.DET   bought   AUX.3sE.3sA

    baina   Peruk   ALDIZKARIA   [IP erosi   du]
    but   Peru.ERG   newspaper.DET   bought AUX
    'Jon bought a BOOK, but Peru a NEWSPAPER.'

And it precedes both negation and the auxiliary:[4]

(10) LIBURUA   ez   du   Jonek   erosi
     book.DET NEG   AUX.3sE.3sA Jon.ERG bought
     'It is the book that Jon did not buy.'

We therefore refine (9) in the following terms, with Polarity Phrase the structural projection of positive (marked as AFF below) and negative features (see Laka 1990; Etxepare 2003; Haddican 2004 for arguments in favour of such an independent projection):

(11) TOPIC FOCUS [PolP NEG/AFF [IP AUX backgrounded material]]]

2 Foci and Wh-movement

Ortiz de Urbina's classic work (see in particular 1987, 1989, 1995, 1999), highly influential in the development of an analysis of Basque foci from a generative perspective, argues that focus is represented in the syntax in the same way as other scope taking phenomena are: focused elements target a designated position in the sentence, that he takes to be identical to the one targeted by wh-words. Under this view, focused constituents are syntactic operators, with a behavior parallel to that of wh-words. Let us review some of the arguments for the parallel treatment of focus and wh-phrases.

2.1 Parallels between focus position and wh-position

Foci and wh-phrases occupy the same position vis-à-vis the lexical verb: they require the adjacency of the wh-word and the verb, as shown in (12b,c).[5]

---

[4] Focus can also occupy a syntactic position below negation and the auxiliary. For the existence of two focus positions in Basque see De Rijk (1996), Etxepare (1997) and Etxepare and Uribe-Etxebarria (2008). See also Section 4.2 of this chapter.
[5] Elordieta (2001) notes the following asymmetry in the behaviour of wh-words and focussed constituents, which according to her, weakens the alleged parallelism between wh-words and foci in Basque: whereas IP-internal focus is possible (see recently Etxepare and Uribe-Etxebarria,

(12) a. Jonek   eskutitza   idatzi   du   SOV
       Jon.ERG   letter.DAT written AUX.3sE.3sA
       'Jon wrote the letter.'

   b. Nork   idatzi   du   eskutitza?   S$_{wh}$VO
      who.ERG   written   AUX.3sE.3sA   letter.DET
      'Who wrote the letter.'

   c. *Nork   eskutitza   idatzi   du?   *S$_{wh}$OV
      who.ERG   letter.DET   written   AUX.3sE.3sA

2.2 Long-distance movement of focus

Both foci and wh-words can be displaced across more than one clause, taking scope over the whole sequence of clauses:[6]

(13) a. Nor   esan   dute   [uste   dutela
       who.ABS   said   AUX   think   AUX.COMP
       [(nor)   etorri   dela]]?
       (who.ABS) come   AUX.COMP
       'Who did they say that they think has come?'

2008), IP-internal wh-words do not seem to be possible. In other words, there is no analogous construction to the one in (ia) in the domain of partial questions (ib):

(i) a. Ez   da   Xabier etorri (Miren baizik)
       Neg AUX Xabier come Miren but
       'It is not Xavier who came, but Miren.'

   b. *Ez   da   nor   etorri?
       NEG AUX who.ABS   come
       'Who did not come?'

I take this asymmetry to illustrate the fact that partial questions must satisfy other syntactic constraints beyond those applying to focus-phrases. One possibility is that wh-words must be in the local domain of an interrogative feature in the left periphery of the clause and that this is only possible if they rise to a higher position than the one exemplified by IP-internal focus.

6 For wh-words, this movement is related to the scope of the question, which may be enforced by grammatical elements such as (selected) complementizers (see Ortiz de Urbina, 1990). Focus movement also determines the scope of the assertion with regard to other operators in the clause, but is not limited in the same way. Focus movement is not easy to accommodate in purely stress-based approaches to focus marking in Basque, such as Arregi's (2003a). See also van Valin (this volume) for related general discussion.

b. JON   esan   dute   [uste   dutela
    Jon.ABS   said   AUX   think   AUX.COMP
    [(JON)   etorri   dela]]
    (Jon.ABS)   come   AUX.COMP
    'It is JON who they said that they think has come.'

Their movement triggers subject-verb inversion in each of the intermediate clauses, which suggests the displacement of both foci and wh-phrases operates in a successive cyclic fashion:

(14) a. Nor   esan   du   Mikelek   uste   duela
         who.ABS   say   AUX   Mikel.ERG   think   AUX.COMP
         Jonek   [(nor)   etorriko   dela]?
         Jon.ERG   (who.ABS)   come.FUT   AUX.COMP
         'Who did Mikel say that Jon thinks will come?'

     b. *Nor   esan   du   Mikelek   [Jonek   uste   duela
         who.ABS   say   AUX   Mikel.ERG   Jon.ERG   think   AUX.COMP
         [(nor)   etorriko   dela]]?
         (who.ABS)   come.FUT   AUX.COMP
         'Who did Mikel say that Jon thinks will come?'

(15) a. JON   esan   du   Mikelek   [uste   duela   Aitorrek
         Jon.ABS   say   AUX   Mikel.ERG   think   AUX.COMP   Aitor.ERG
         [(Jon)   etorriko   dela]]
         (Jon.ABS)   come.FUT   AUX.COMP
         'It is JON that Mikel said that Aitor thinks will com.'

     b. *JON esan du Mikelek [Aitorrek uste duela [etorriko dela]]

Focus and wh-phrases interact in movement relations, in the sense that each of them induces locality restrictions on the other in extraction out of finite clauses:[7]

---

[7] For unclear reasons, verbal focus does not seem to interfere with extraction:

(i) Zer   ez   dakizu   IRAKURRI   ere   egingo   duten ?
    what   NEG   you.know   read   do.FUT   AUX.COMP
    « What is the thing such that you don't know whether they will even READ? »

Whatever the underlying motivation of this asymmetry, it cannot be due to any special status of verbal focus vis à-vis long distance extraction. The latter is also possible with focused verbs, as shown in (ii):

(ii) IRAKURRI   ere   ez   dakit   egingo   duten
     READ   even   NEG   know   do.FUT   AUX.COMP
     'I don't know whether they will even READ it.'

(16) *Zer   uste   du   Mikelek
    what.ABS think   AUX   Mikel.ERG
    [ETXEAN   (zer)   aurkitu   duela   Jonek]
    home.DET.LOC (what.ABS)   find   AUX.COMP   Jon.ERG
    '*What does Mikel think that it is at HOME that John has found?'

(17) *Zer   galdetu du   Mikelek
    what.ABS asked   AUX   Mikel.ERG
    [non   (zer)   aurkitu duen   Jonek]?
    where   (what.ABS) find   AUX.COMP   Jon.ERG
    'What did Mikel ask where Jon had found?'

Both foci and wh-words optionally trigger massive Pied-piping (a term coined by Ross 1967; see Ortiz de Urbina 1993; Etxepare 1997; Etxepare and Ortiz de Urbina 2003; Arregi 2003 for Basque). Under the pied-piping mode, wh-phrases and foci trigger the displacement of the clause in which they are embedded. (18a) illustrates the displacement of the wh operator; (18b) illustrates pied-piping.

(18) a. Nor$_i$ esan   duzu   [$_{CP}$ uste   dute-la
         who.ABS   say   AUX   think   AUX-COMP
         [(nor)   etorri   d-ela]]?
         who.ABS   come   AUX-COMP
         'Who did you say they think has come?'

    b. [$_{CP}$ nor   etorri   d-ela]$_i$ esan   duzu
                who.ABS come   AUX-COMP   say   AUX
         [$_{CP}$ uste   dutela   t$_i$]?
                 think   AUX.COMP
         'Who did you say they think has come?'

The same phenomenon arises with embedded foci:

(19) a. JON$_i$ esan   dute   [$_{CP}$ uste   dute-la
         JON.ABS   say   AUX   think   AUX-COMP
         [t$_i$ etorri   d-ela]]
                 come   AUX-COMP
         'It is JON who they said they think has come.'

b. [_CP_ JON   etorri d-ela]$_i$ esan dute
JON.ABS come AUX-COMP say AUX

[_CP_ uste   dute-la   t$_i$]
think AUX-COMP

'It is JON who they said they think has come.'

2.3 Focus as operator

The parallel behaviour of wh-phrases and foci invites the conclusion that focus is a syntactic operator, akin to wh-questions, possessing quantificational value, and yielding operator-variable chains at the interpretive component. Semantically, both wh-questions and foci give rise to open propositions (Ortiz de Urbina 1989). Under a certain view of the semantics of questions, the meaning of a question is an unsaturated proposition (20a,b). A congruent answer to the question saturates this proposition (the structured meaning approach to the semantics of questions, see Krifka 2001 and references therein):

(20) a.   Who came?

     b.   λx[x came]

The semantic contribution of focus can be taken to be parallel to the question denotation, in that the focus gives rise to an open sentence (an unsaturated proposition giving rise to an existential presupposition, see Herburger 2000), and an assertion which establishes the identity of the open variable (see Zubizarreta 1998). This identificational relation tells you, from a given set of potential fillers of x, which one should constitute the assertion. Both the focused sentence and the question share the background or presuppositional part:

(21) a.   λx [x came]   (Presupposition, Jackendoff 1972)

     b.   x is Jon   (Assertion)

One potential argument against a unitary semantic analysis of foci and wh-questions in Basque is raised by Elordieta (2001: 145-149). She notes that unlike wh-words, which cannot cross an embedded coreferential pronoun in their way to CP (the so-called "weak crossover condition"), foci in Basque do not seem to be sensitive to such configurations (Elordieta 2001: 146):

(22) a. *Nor$_i$ jo   du   bere$_i$ amak   t$_i$?
       who.ABS   beat AUX   his   mother.ERG
       '*Who$_i$ did his$_i$ mother beat?'

   b. JON$_i$ jo   du   bere$_i$ amak   t$_i$
       Jon.ABS   beat AUX   his   mother.ERG
       'It is Jon who his mother beat.'

The configuration in (22a) is identical to the English (23). In English, wh-movement cannot cross a coindexed pronoun, either (Wasow 1972):

(23)   *Who$_i$ did his$_i$ mother love t$_i$?

Chomsky (1976) extends the weak crossover condition to (24a,b), arguing that the relevant operators in (24) (focus and quantifier) are raised to a clausal scope position at an abstract derivational component called LF, which yields a configuration identical to the one apparent in (23):

(24) a. ??His$_i$ mother saw JOHN$_i$ -> LF: JOHN$_i$ his$_i$ mother saw t$_i$

      b. *His$_i$ mother loves every child$_i$ -> LF: Every child$_i$ his$_i$ mother loves t$_i$

The offending structures share a quantificational antecedent which, in the given configuration, is not allowed to bind the embedded pronoun (a "crossover configuration").[8] Following Lasnik and Stowell's work (1991), Elordieta proposes that focus in Basque is not quantificational, and therefore is not subject to the crossover condition, unlike wh-phrases which are irreducibly quantificational. The absence of crossover conditions in Basque focus constructions justifies, in her view, a distinct syntactic treatment of focus and wh-movement in that language. There are reasons to think, however, that this asymmetry is not a significant one. (22b), with a displaced focus, becomes bad if the focus is an indefinite, as the wh-word:

(25) *UME   TTIKI   BAT$_i$ jo   du   bere$_i$ amak   t$_i$
      child   little   one.ABS   beat AUX   his   mother.ERG
      '*His$_i$ mother has beaten a LITTLE CHILD$_i$.'

---

[8] For different analyses of the crossover condition, see Hornstein, 1995; Erteschik-Shir, 1997; Büring, 2005; Portolan, 2005, and references therein.

On the other hand, (22a), which some speakers find relatively acceptable, becomes fully acceptable if the wh-word is a D-linked one (26a) (see Pesetsky 1989, for the concept of *discourse-linking*). The crossover condition arises again if we force a non-D-linked reading (26b), suggesting the relevant generalization must take into account the referential status of the focus or the wh-phrase:

(26) a. Zein   ume$_i$ jo   du   bere$_i$ amak   t$_i$?
        which child   beat AUX   his   mother.ERG
        'Which child$_i$ did his$_i$ mother beat?'

   b. *Nor   arraio$_i$ jo   du   bere$_i$ amak   t$_i$?
        who the.hell   beat AUX   his   mother.ERG
        '*Who the hell$_i$ did his$_i$ mother beat?'

I think therefore that from a descriptive point of view, crossover configurations strengthen the parallelism between wh-questions and focus, rather than weakening it.[9]

2.4 The received analysis of verb-focus adjacency

Why should the focus and the verbal complex be adjacent to each other? Ortiz de Urbina (1987, 1989) suggested that the adjacency of the inflected verb to focus was a case of "residual verb second", of the sort one can see in English partial questions. The relation between the focus and the verbal head can be formalized in terms of a structural agreement criterion, an idea coming from Rizzi's analysis of the adjacency between auxiliary and wh-words in English wh-questions (Rizzi 1990; 1996). Rizzi considers that the adjacency relation between the wh-word and the finite verb in both (27a,b) follows from a condition on agreement. T has

---

[9] In recent work, Portolan (2005) argues that crossover configurations must be accounted for in the larger context of backward pronominalization, a discourse sensitive phenomenon in which relative topicality is a crucial factor. Portolan develops Postal's descriptive generalization on backward pronominalization (1970) extending it to crossover configurations. Let me state the relevant descriptive generalization in the following terms, adapting Postal's original generalization:

(i) If a definite pronoun is to the left of an NP, the NP may serve as the antecedent for the pronoun only if it is D-linked.

In (22–26), the pronoun is to the left of the base position of the antecedent in all cases, and the crossing operator must be of the D-linked type. Under this approach to crossover, the condition is one which must be at least partly formulated in discourse structural terms. See also Erteschik-Shir (1997) for an Information Structure based account of crossover conditions.

a wh-feature which must be in a local relation with a wh-element in order to be licensed. The relevant local relation for the licensing of that feature is a Spec/Head relation, in which the wh-word matches the wh-feature in T. This matching relation can be established in-situ for the subject (which is already in a Spec-Head configuration with the wh-feature in T), but requires the displacement of both the T head and the wh-word in the rest of the partial questions, illustrated by an object question in (27b). The corresponding structural descriptions are given in (28a,b):[10]

(27) a. *Who saw you?*

b. *Who did you see?*

(28) a. [$_{IP}$ *who* I$_{wh}$ [VP *saw you*]]]

b. [$_{CP}$ *Who* C+did [IP *you* (*did*) [VP *see* (*who*)]]]

The condition on the licensing of the wh-feature is formulated by Rizzi (1990) as follows:

(29) Wh-Criterion

A. A wh-operator must be in spec-head configuration with an X0 [+wh]

B. An X0 [+wh] must be in a spec-head configuration with a wh-operator

Brody (1990) proposed to extend (29) to the domain of focus, by formulating a focus criterion analogous to the wh-criterion:

(30) Focus criterion (Brody 1990)

A. A focus-operator must be in a spec-head configuration with an X0 [+f]

B. An X [+f] must be in a spec-head configuration with a focus operator

The focus criterion requires the focus operator to enter into a matching relation with a head possessing a focus feature. In Basque, this head would be the verbal complex, endowed with a focus feature associated with the verb (see Elordieta 2001, for a more recent analysis in those terms):

---

10 Other analyses of the residual verb second effect are available. See for instance Pesetsky and Torrego (2001). I stay deliberately within the set of assumptions of Ortiz de Urbina (1989) and Elordieta (2001).

(31)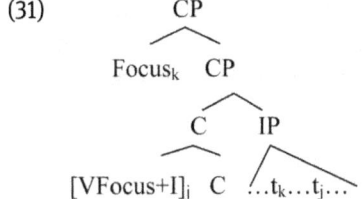

Ortiz de Urbina (1989) proposed to interpret the adjacency of the focus and the verbal complex as the linear product of a Spec/Head configuration, with English residual V-2 in mind. Cast in terms of Rizzi's and Brody's analysis, this configuration reflects agreement, mediated by the presence of a focus feature F both in the Tense/C domain and in the focussed phrase itself. Note however that Ortiz de Urbina's classic analysis requires the adjacency of an object which is more complex than the one we observe in residual V-2 in English. As noted by Uriagereka (1999), the adjacency relation operating on foci involves the sequence lexical verb plus auxiliary. And there is nothing in (30) that requires that.

3 Problems with the received analysis of verb-focus adjacency and a new proposal

3.1 The verbal complex and negation

As concluded above, what moves to F is, arguably, something more than the inflected form. It is a complex head composed by the inflected auxiliary and the lexical verb, which carries aspectual morphology. Ortiz de Urbina's analysis, and all other analyses cast in terms of residual V-2, are forced to claim that the complex head is created by adjunction of V to I, plus movement of the complex head into a left-headed Focus head or Complementizer (see for instance Elordieta 2001). But consider the following paradigm, from Laka (1990):

(32) a. *Jonek   eskutitza   idatzi   du*
          Jon.ERG   letter.DET   written   AUX.3sE.3sA
          'Jon wrote the letter.'

      b. *Jonek   ez   du   eskutitza   idatzi*
          Jon.ERG   NEG   AUX.3sE.3sA   letter.DET   written
          'Jon did not write the letter.'

As (32b) shows, the negative morpheme in root clauses appears to the left of the clause, inmediately preceding the tense bearing element. In order to analyze those facts, Laka proposes the following simplified underlying structure:

(33)
```
        NegP
       /    \
      ez     IP
            /  \
           VP   Infl
```

(33) is the input to the derived structure (34), which has the Auxiliary raise to adjoin to negation:

(34)   [NEG+INFLi ...V...ti]   (auxiliary raising)

The movement of the inflection would be motivated, according to Laka, by the need for Tense to have scope over other clausal operators (her Tense C-Command Condition). The high position of negation vis-à-vis the IP is shown by ellipsis: IP ellipsis is possible in Basque leaving negation unaffected, as shown in (35).

(35)   Jonek   liburua   erosi   du   baina   Peruk   ez
       Jon.ERG   book.Det   buy   AUX   but   Peru.ERG   NEG
       [IP du   liburua   erosi]
            AUX   book.DET   buy
       'Jon bought a BOOK, but Peru didn't.'

But the underlying structure that Laka proposes for sentential negation in Basque presents the following problem for the V-2 analysis: something like (36) is ungrammatical.

(36)   *Ez   etorri   da
        NEG   come   AUX
       'He/she didn't come.'

If the sequence of lexical verb plus auxiliary is the product of head movement, why does the presence of negation (higher than the auxiliary in the clausal structure) preclude the obligatory V-to-I movement? And if the latter is not obligatory, why is (37) not possible?[11]

(37) *Nor/JON da etorri?
 who/Jon AUX come
 'Who came?'
 'JON came.'

Remember also that negation may intervene between the focus and the auxiliary (38). Unless the auxiliary and negation constitute a single head, the focus-criterion based analysis of adjacency cannot be sustained. The purported movement of the auxiliary to negation would in principle allow structures such as (39), which turn out to be impossible:

(38) JONEK ez du batere jan
 Jon.ERG NEG AUX.3sE.3sA anything eat
 'It is JON who didn't eat anything.'

(39) *Jonek LIBURUA erosi du baina Peruk
 Jon.ERG book.DET buy AUX but Peru.ERG
 [$_{PolP}$ ez+du [$_{IP}$ du~~ ~~liburua~~ erosi~~]]
 NEG+AUX AUX book.DET buy
 'Jon bought a BOOK, but Peru didn't.'

3.2 Haddican's alternative analysis

In a series of recent works, Haddican (2001, 2004, 2005, 2008) has argued that the Basque basic word order in both affirmative and negative sentences can have a simpler analysis under the hypothesis that the inflected auxiliary is to the left of the VP. In his approach to the Basque basic word alternations, negation is generated below INFL but higher than VP. From that position, it raises to a higher polarity phrase and ends up preceding the auxiliary (40a). This results in the canonical order for sentential negation (40b).

---

[11] (37) is possible in the Basque varieties spoken in France. I leave those varieties aside, but see Duguine and Irurtzun (2008) and Etxepare (forthcoming). Elordieta (2001: 188, footnote 14) is aware of this problem.

(40) a. [PoIP Pol⁰ [IP Aux [PoIP Neg Pol⁰ [VP...V⁰]]]]
→ Raising of negation to higher Polarity Phrase

b. [PoIP Neg Pol⁰ [IP Aux [PoIP (Neg) Pol⁰ [VP...V⁰]]]]

c. Ez   da   etorri
   NEG AUX come
   'He/she did not come.'

According to Haddican (2004), when the polarity phrase in the vicinity of the VP is not headed by overt negation, but occupied by a silent positive polarity head, it is the whole polarity phrase which raises to the higher polarity phrase, carrying the VP behind (a case of predicate fronting):

(41) a. [PoIP Pol⁰ [IP Aux [PoIP ø Pol⁰ [VP...V⁰]]]]
→ Raising of the inner Polarity Phrase

b. [PoIP [PoIP ø Pol⁰ [VP...V⁰]] Pol⁰ [IP Aux...]]

c. Etorri da
   come   AUX
   'He/she has come.'

Haddican's analysis makes a clear prediction concerning IP-ellipsis: if IP-ellipsis is involved in those cases where the auxiliary is not phonologically realized, we should be able to find instances in which the lexical verb is exempted from elision. This should only happen when no overt polarity marker is present. The prediction is borne out, as shown in (42a), with the partial structural representation in (42b):

(42) a. Ni   joan naiz   eta   zu   etorri
        I.ABS go   AUX.1s and you.ABS come
        'I left and you came.'

b. eta [TopP zu Top⁰ [PoIP1 [PoIP2 etorri] [IP...Aux]

Nothing like that can be constructed with negation in the second term of the coordination:

(43) *Ni   joan naiz   eta   zu   ez   etorri
      I.ABS go   AUX.1s and you.ABS NEG come
      'I left and you didn't come.'

Under Haddican's cartographic analysis of the basic word orders in Basque, the linear adjacency between the focus and the verbal complex is devoid of any significance as an argument for a configurational relation of the Spec-Head sort. This adjacency relation is derived from independent cartographic properties of the left periphery, related to the relative position of polarity features and the way they attract different elements in the structure. The very idea of a verbal complex dissolves, as the lexical verb and the auxiliary are in different phrases.

4 Phonological conditions on the finite form

4.1 The clitic status of the inflected form

The head-movement approach to the adjacency between the verb, the auxiliary and the focus makes wrong predictions regarding the order of the elements and their respective behavior in ellipsis contexts. Haddican's analysis, on the other hand, has the finite auxiliary to the left of the verbal phrase, not an obvious move for a seemingly head-final language like Basque,[12] despite the elegant analysis it allows of Basque basic word order alternations in positive and negative declarative sentences. Haddican's proposal can be enhanced, I think, by data coming from the clitic status of the finite forms in Basque. Let me address this issue by examining the distribution of Basque synthetic verbs. A small set of Basque lexical verbs, called "synthetic verbs", can directly inflect for Tense and agreement, as shown in (44):

(44) a. *Ba-da-ki-t*
AFF-Present-root-1sE
'I know.'

b. *Ba-ne-ki-en*
AFF-Past-root-Past
'I knew.'

The synthetic verbs stand in contrast to the normal periphrastic form of Basque inflected verbal complexes, illustrated for the same verb *jakin* "know" in (45a,b):

---

[12] Ortiz de Urbina's work on wh-movement (1989) already implied the leftward position of Comp in Basque, and Laka (1990) offered arguments to think that negation is a leftward head. Elordieta (2001) reaches the conclusion that whereas functional heads are to the left in Basque, lexical ones are to the right.

(45) a. Jonek   egia   jakin   du
        Jon.ERG   truth.DET   know   AUX.3sE.3sA
        'Jon has come to know the truth.'

   b. Jonek   egia   daki
        Jon.ERG   truth.DET   knows
        'Jon knows the truth.'

As shown in the contrast between (45a,b) the main difference between the periphrastic and the synthetic paradigms is in the presence of morphologically expressed aspect: the periphrastic form requires the lexical verb to adopt one of a restricted set of aspectual markers. In (45a), the aspectual ending corresponds to the participle, which marks perfective aspect. I will adopt Laka's standard analysis (1990) of the synthetic verbs as involving direct head raising of a bound root to inflection. Direct head raising of the bound lexical form is possible precisely because there is no intervening aspectual head, unlike in periphrastic forms:

(46)   [$_{TP/AgrP}$ root+T/Agr [$_{VP}$ (root)...]]

Despite the fact that they are fully inflected verbs and contain a lexical root, synthetic verbs cannot occupy the first position in the sentence. We can show that by enforcing the presence of null arguments in the positions preceding the synthetic verb. The result is an unacceptable sentence:[13]

(47)   *__ __ daki
        'He/she knows it.'

What (47) shows is that inflected verbs in Basque cannot occur in the first position of the clause, even if this is the natural place which would correspond to those forms. But not being able to occur in first position is a typical feature of clitic auxiliaries. A sentence containing a synthetic verb and no other element before it would require an overt preverbal expletive *ba-* (diachronically related to *bai* "yes") to its left:

(48)   Ba-daki
        AFF-s(h)e.knows.it
        'He/she knows (it).'

---

13 Null arguments are perfectly possible with synthetic verbs (cf. 48).

Other elements, such as negation (49a) and foci (49b), can rescue the auxiliary in first position:

(49) a. *Ez   daki*
        NEG   he.knows.it
        'He doesn't know (it).'

   b. *JONEK   daki*
       Jon.ERG he.knows.it
       'It is JON who knows it.'

But not any element preceding the auxiliary can save it (Ortiz de Urbina 1995). Topics for instance, despite occurring before the synthetic verb, cannot save it from first position:

(50) **Jonek,   daki*
       Jon.ERG   he.knows.it
       '(As for) Jon, he knows (it).'

It is well known that topics introduce an independent intonational phrase (see e.g. Nespor and Vogel 1986). This suggests that the synthetic verb requires stricter conditions for phonological integration than ordinary lexical material. In the spirit of the prosodic hierarchy, I will claim that the synthetic verb must be integrated in a phonological phrase. It is a tenet of theories of syntax-prosody correspondence, that only information about the edges of designated syntactic constituents is appealed to in constituency correspondence constraints (see Selkirk 2011 for a general discussion). In the optimality theoretic instantiation of Selkirk (1996), this edge theory is referred to as the Alignment theory of the syntax-phonology interface. In Selkirk's theory two distinct phrase-level constraints Align Right (XP, p) and Align Left (XP, p) are posited as part of the universal syntax-phonology interface constraint repertoire: the first calls for the right edge of a syntactic phrase XP to align with the edge of a phonological phrase, and the second calls for alignment between left edges.[14] The latter corresponds to Basque, as the prosodic constraints involve elements displaced to the left periphery of the sentence. The phonological phrase can be headed by

---

14 In Selkirk (2009, 2011) a more minimalist correspondence rule is proposed, called Match, in which both edges of a prosodic constituent must correspond to the edges of a syntactic constituent. This change is not directly relevant to the piece of data considered in this paper: what comes after the auxiliary is irrelevant for the purposes of its linearization.

negation or affirmation (polarity), or by focus. Both are accented elements that can constitute a phonological phrase by themselves, as in fragments (51a,b):

(51) a. *Nork   daki?   JONEK*
      who.ERG knows Jon.ERG
      'Who knows it? JON does.'

    b. *Ba-daki?   Ez*
      AFF-know   No
      'Does he/she know it? No.'

The phonological approach to the linear restrictions of finite verbal forms in Basque allows us to recast the adjacency requirements of those forms in different terms. Assuming that the Aligning Parameter relevant in the formation of the Prosodic constituent involved in the linearization of inflected verbal forms in Basque (the Phonological Phrase) concerns the left edge of the sentence, it would seem that the basic position of the inflected forms in Basque is to the left end of the clause too.[15] This gives us an elegant way out of the following puzzle:

(52) **Jonek   liburuak   maite ditu, baina Mirenek   ez   ditu*
     Jon.ERG book.DET.PL love AUX but   Miren.ERG NEG AUX
     'Jon loves books but Miren doesn't.'

If the raising of the auxiliary is motivated by the Tense C-command Condition or any such comparable condition, or by formal features of negation which force movement of the auxiliary, then it is not clear why (52) is impossible (see the discussion in Section 3.1). First you raise the auxiliary, adjoining it to Neg, then you do ellipsis. Under the PF motivation for the distribution of the auxiliary, in which the auxiliary is to the left of the verbal phrase, the ungrammaticality of (52) follows from ordinary IP ellipsis, which necessarily includes the auxiliary.

3.3 Synthetic verbs versus auxiliaries

There is at least one aspect of the distribution of finite forms in Basque that does not immediately fall into place in the cartographic approach designed

---

[15] See recently Etxepare and Uribe-Etxebarria (2009) and previously, Haddican (2001, 2008), Artiagoitia (1992), Albizu (1994) and Elordieta (1997, for the hypothesis of leftward Infl in Basque.

by Haddican, and this fact has motivated the hypothesis that the sequence of auxiliary and lexical verb in Basque constitutes a syntactic unit, one of the basic tenets of the "residual V-2" account. The comparison between synthetic verbs and auxiliaries in Basque raises the following issue regarding the linear distribution of finite verbal forms. Auxiliaries can be directly saved from first position by the lexical verb or by negation, but not by focus (53a–c). On the other hand, synthetic verbs can be saved from first position not only by negation, but also by focus (54):

(53) a. Etorri   da   b. Ez   da   etorri
        come   AUX.3s   NEG   AUX.3s   come
        'He/she didn't come.'   'He/she didn't come.'

     c. *JON   da   etorri
        Jon.ABS   AUX.3s come
        'JON came.'

(54) JON   dator
     Jon.ABS   comes
     'JON came.'

It thus seems that synthetic verbs and auxiliaries do not present the same PF requirements. This may be linked to the fact that synthetic verbs and auxiliaries are not deficient to the same extent. Synthetic verbs lack aspectual morphology, but have otherwise a lexical root. Auxiliaries lack both. Synthetic verbs seem to be relatively free as to the kind of element that can determine the Left Edge of their prosodic phrase. Basically, anything that precedes the finite form and does not constitute an independent intonational phrase will do. Auxiliaries seem to be choosier: they can only be preceded by negation or the lexical verb. Focus will not do. Auxiliaries therefore seem to obey restrictions which draw on both phonological and morphological considerations. The latter property is reminiscent of the kind of restrictions arising in the domain of phonological words, which typically affect clitics: as shown by Nespor and Vogel (1986), several phenomena related to cliticization seem to be sensitive to both lexical categories and syntactic structure (see also Hall 1999). The linear requirements operating on synthetic verbs and auxiliaries in Basque can thus be related to different levels of the prosodic hierarchy as they apply to clitic constituents. The relevant prosodic level at which synthetic verbs become integrated in the overall prosodic structure is the phonological phrase. The level at which auxiliaries come to be integrated in the overall prosodic structure is the phonological word.

This idea that the lexical verb and the auxiliary form a phonological word is compatible with the fact that the sequence lexical verb-auxiliary constitutes the relevant domain for a number of phonological processes in some dialects of Basque. Thus, Hualde et al. (1994) show that despite being separate morphological words, the sequence of lexical verb and auxiliary constitutes a single prosodic word as far as accent placement is concerned in Lekeitio Basque. Elordieta (1997) also shows that the sequence constitutes the relevant domain for vowel assimilation in that same variety, a phenomenon which does not apply across words. Elordieta (2001) exploits the special morphophonological status of this sequence to argue in favour of her analysis of verb-focus adjacency. This morphological word would correspond to the complex head involved in the residual V-2 analysis. We saw that this crucial aspect of the residual V-2 analysis cannot be right. Interestingly, Elordieta's (1997) analysis of the phenomenon is embedded in the general idea that operations responsible for the creation of phonological domains are not reducible to prosodic algorithms solely, but "can stem from morphological domains created on the basis of morphosyntactic licensing" (Elordieta 1997: 104)". In the case of the sequence lexical verb-auxiliary, Elordieta argues that the relevant prosodic domain arises from the syntactic relation between V and T. The finite auxiliary has a non-interpretable [V] feature which must be licensed by the lexical verb, as well as an [affix] feature, that it shares with synthetic verbs. The [affix] feature is satisfied by any accented element belonging in the same phonological phrase as the auxiliary. The T-feature embedded in the finite auxiliary, on the other hand, requires a more specific set of licensors. Those licensors are negation and the lexical verb. In Elordieta's account, the relevant syntactic configuration that allows for this licensing requires the displacement of either the lexical verb or negation into the projection of the finite auxiliary containing T. Note that it is crucial for the residual V-2 analysis that this movement is adjunction to the auxiliary head. Only this movement allows the creation of a complex head that can be attracted to a higher Comp or Focus head (cf. 31). But if the kind of licensing relation invoked in this case is syntactic licensing, there is nothing intrinsically wrong with the possibility of moving the verbal predicate or negation via the specifier of the Inflectional head into the higher Polarity Phrase, the ultimate target of predicate fronting or polarity raising in Haddican's analysis:

(55)   [$_{PolP}$ VP Pol^0 [$_{IP}$ (VP) Aux [$_{PolP}$ (Neg) Pol^0 [$_{VP}$...V^0]]]]

Under this analysis, the creation of a complex head along the derivation is not necessary. The relevant relation underlying the morphophonological domain determined by the lexical verb and the auxiliary is agreement between the fronted predicate or negation and T. In the case of synthetic verbs, the T-feature of the Infl is checked directly by the raised verbal root. Since the verbal root is an affix in those cases, it cannot license the [affix] feature of the auxiliary, and something else is required to rescue the finite form from first position. Either focus or negation can do that.[16]

4 In the absence of inflection

4.1 Nominalized clauses

We have already seen that the adjacency of the verbal complex and the focus is a phenomenon arising from a combination of various factors, some cartographic (the position of the focal operator and the Polarity head in the clause structure), and some other phonological, caused by the deficient status of auxiliaries and synthetic verbs in determining the left edge of a prosodic domain. If the presence of inflection is crucial for the adjacency condition to be operative, we expect it to disappear when inflection is absent. One context in which this prediction can be tested is tensed nominalized clauses such as (56).

(56) [Kepak   ardoa   eda-te-a]   arraroa   da
     Kepa.ERG wine.DET   drink-NMLZ-DET   strange.DET   is
     'It is strange for Kepa to drink wine.'

Nominalizations are full clauses: they admit temporal modification, canonical Case marking, and pro-drop (see Artiagoitia 2003, and references therein). Nominalized clauses are in this sense different from control structures, which involve participles or aspectual complements in Basque. Focus can also occur internal to the nominalized clause. In those cases, adjacency is not necessary inside the nominalized clause. Consider the following exchange (from Irurtzun 2007:163):

(57) A: [Kepak   ardoa   edatea]   arraroa   da
        Kepa.ERG   wine.DET   drink.NMLZ.DET   strange.DET   is
        'It is strange for Kepa to drink wine.'

   B: Ez,   [JULENEK   ardoa   edatea]   da   arraroa
      No,   Julen.ERG   wine.DET   drink.NMLZ.DET   is   strange.DET
      'No, it strange for JULEN to drink wine.'

---

[16] This alternative account makes sense within the set of assumptions of Elordieta (1997), but other alternatives exist that do not assume any special morphosyntactic relation between the verb and the auxiliary in Basque, nor the creation of a complex head, and still account for the special phonological relation between auxiliary and verb (cf. Samuels (2009)).

(57A) represents a nominalized clause in Basque, which shows the typical case pattern of ordinary transitive predicates, with an ergative subject and an absolutive object. (57B) represents a reply to (57A), with contrastive focus on the subject. The focus does not need to be adjacent to the verb in the nominalized clause. On the other hand, the whole nominalized clause must be adjacent to the higher finite verb, suggesting that the whole clause has been displaced to the sentence peripheral focus position.

A further argument in support of the irrelevant status of adjacency effects in the domain of focus is that if something else occupies the polarity phrase and allows the finite form to avoid first position, the focus doesn't have to be adjacent to the verb anymore. One such case is illustrated by postauxiliary focus in negated clauses (Etxepare and Ortiz de Urbina 2003):

(58) a. *Ez du JONEK liburua erosi, baizik-eta Mirenek*
NEG AUX JON.ERG book.ABS buy, except-and Miren.ERG
'It is not JON who bought the book, but Miren.'

b. *Ez dut JON etxean ikusi, baizik-eta Miren*
NEG AUX Jon.ABS home.LOC seen, except-and Miren.ABS
'It is not JON who I saw at home, but Miren.'

In (58), negation rescues the auxiliary from first position, and the focus does not have to be adjacent to the lexical verb. This shows that the adjacency of the focus to the verbal complex is not a significant element in trying to construct an argument for the positive existence of a focus feature, as the traditional analysis would have it.

5 Conclusions

The Basque focus-verb adjacency phenomenon has been traditionally taken to correspond to a particular kind of syntactic configuration, one which has the focussed element in the Specifier of a left-peripheral functional head which attracts the verb. This configurational relation is furthermore held to allow agreement between the focus feature in the focussed term and a focus feature embedded in the complex head created as a result of verbal attraction, typically V or T. I have shown that the basic elements of such an approach in Basque, even if we stay within the syntactic assumptions that made it possible, are untenable. Focus-verb adjacency in Basque does not result from attraction of a verbal head to a left peripheral head related to focus licensing, and there is no agreement relation whatsoever relating the verb or the auxiliary and the focus. To the extent that agreement implies an agreeing feature, focus-verb adjacency relations in Basque cannot be used anymore as an argument in favour of the existence of a syntactic focus feature. Since focus-verb adjacency is a widespread phenomenon and the kind of analysis examined here has proved to be resilient and widely adopted (see Cruschina 2011: 104-110, for a brief review), the Basque case can suggest a way of thinking about the adjacency phenomenon in a different way. This does not mean that Basque does not provide reasons to think that a grammatical formative *focus* may exist; it just means that a traditional source of evidence, focus-verb adjacency under the examined analysis, cannot count as valid evidence for that. Whether focus features have or not a place in narrow syntax, must be elucidated in other ways. The paper also allowed us to review a number of general properties and recent analyses of focal constructions in Basque, as well as their relation to wh-constructions.

Bibliography

Albizu, Pablo. 1993. Focus and word order in Basque. Ms. USC.
Altube, Severo. 1929. *Erderismos*. Bermeo: Gaubeka.
Arregi, Karlos. 2003a. *Focus on Basque Movements*. Cambridge, MIT dissertation.
Arregi, Karlos. 2003b. Clausal Pied-Piping in Basque. *Natural Language Semantics* 11(2). 115–143.
Artiagoitia, Xabier. 1992. *Verbal projections in Basque and minimal structure*. Washington, University of Washington dissertation.
Artiagoitia, Xabier. 2003. Complementation. In José Ignacio Hualde & Jon Ortiz de Urbina (eds.) *A Grammar of Basque*. Berlin: Mouton de Gruyter. 634–709.
Azkue, Resurrección María. 1891. *Euskal Izkindea* [Basque Grammar]. Bilbao.
Brody, Michael. 1990. Some remarks on the Focus Field in Hungarian. *UCL Working Papers in Linguistics* 2. 201–225.
Cruschina, Silvio. 2011. *Discourse-Related Features and Functional Projections*. Oxford: Oxford University Press.
Duguine, Maia & Aritz Irurtzun. 2008. Ohar batzuk nafar-lapurterazko galdera eta galdegai indartuez. In Xabier Artiagoitia & Joseba A. Lakarra (eds.) *Gramatika jaietan. Patxi Gonegaren omenez*, 195–207. Bilbao:University of the Basque Country.
Elordieta, Arantzazu. 2001. *Verb movement and constituent permutation in Basque*. Leiden, Holland: HIL Publications.
Elordieta, Gorka. 1997. *Morphosyntactic feature chains and phonological domains*. California: University of Southern California dissertation.
Erteschik-Shir, Noemi. 1997. *The dynamics of focus structure*. Cambridge: Cambridge University Press.
Etxepare, Ricardo. 1997. Two types of focus in Basque. In Brian Agbayani and Sze-Wing Tang (eds.) *WCCFL 16 Proceedings*, 113–128. CA:CSLI.

Etxepare, Ricardo. 2003. Negation. In Jose Ignacio Hualde & Jon Ortiz de Urbina (eds.) *A Grammar of Basque*, 516-562. Berlin: Mouton de Gruyter.

Etxepare, Ricardo & Jon Ortiz de Urbina. 2003. Focalization. In Jose Ignacio Hualde & Jon Ortiz de Urbina (eds.) *A Grammar of Basque*, 459–516. Berlin: Mouton de Gruyter.

Etxepare, Ricardo and Myriam Uribe-Etxebarria. 2009. Hitz hurrenkera eta birregituraketa euskaraz. In Ricardo Etxepare, Ricardo Gómez & Joseba Lakarra (eds.) *A Festschrift for Bernard Oyharçabal*. *ASJU* 43 (1/2). 335–356.

Giannakidou, Anastasia. 1997. *The Landscape of Polarity*. Utrecht, Holland: LOT dissertation series.

Haddican, William. 2001. Basque Functional Heads. In *Linguistics in the Big Apple. Working papers in Linguistics of NYU*. http://web.gc.cuny.edu/dept/lingu/liba/paper.html

Haddican, William. 2004. Sentence polarity and word order in Basque. *The Linguistic Review* 21(2). 81–124.

Haddican, William. 2005. *Aspects of language variation and change in contemporary Basque*. New York: New York University dissertation.

Haddican, William. 2008. Euskal perpausaren espez-buru-osagarri hurrenkeraren aldeko argudio batzuk. In Iñigo Arteatx, Xabier Artiagoitia & Arantzazu Elordieta (eds.) *Antisimetriaren hipotesia vs buru parametroa: euskararen oinarrizko hitz hurrenkera ezbaian*, 69–96. Vitoria-Gasteiz: University of the Basque Country.

Hall, T. Alan. 1999. The phonological word: a review. In T. Alan Hall & Ursula Kleinhenz (eds.) *Studies in the Phonological Word*, 1–22. Amsterdam:John Benjamins.

Herburger, Elena. 2000. *What counts*. Cambridge, MA: MIT Press.

Horvath, Julia. 1986. *Focus in the Theory of Grammar and the Syntax of Hungarian*. Dordrecht: Foris.

Hualde, José Ignacio, Gorka Elordieta and Arantzazu Elordieta. 1994. *The Basque Dialect of Lekeitio*. Bilbao: University of the Basque Country.

Irurtzun, Aritz. 2007. *The Grammar of focus at the interfaces*. Vitoria-Gasteiz: University of the Basque Country dissertation.

Keenan, Edward. 1976. Remarkable Subjects in Malagasy. In Charles Li (ed.) *Subject and Topic*, 247–301. Academic Press.

Kennelly, Sarah D. 1999. The Syntax of the P-Focus position in Turkish. In Georges Rebuschi & Laurice Tuller (eds.) *The Grammar of Focus*, 179–212. Amsterdam: John Benjamins.

Kidwai, Ayesha. 2000. *XP-Adjunction in Universal Grammar. Scrambling and Binding in Hindi Urdu*. Oxford: Oxford University Press.

Kiss, Katalin. 1995. Introduction. In Katalin Kiss (ed.) *Discourse Configurational languages*, 3–27. Oxford: Oxford University Press.

Krifka, Manfred. 2001. For a structured meaning account of questions and answers. In Caroline Féry and Wolfgang Sternefeld (eds) *Audiatur Vox Sapientiae. A Festschrift for Arnim von Stechow*, 287–319. Berlin: Akademie Verlag.

Krifka, Manfred & Renate Musan. 2012. Information structure: Overview and linguistic issues. In Manfred Krifka & Renate Musan (eds.) *The Expression of Information Structure*, 1–44. Berlin: Mouton de Gruyter.

Laka, Itziar. 1990. *Negation in Syntax: On the nature of functional categories and projections*. Cambridge, MA: MIT dissertation.

Laka, Itziar & Juan Uriagereka. 1989. Barriers for Basque and vice-versa. In Joyce McDonough & Bernadette Plunkett (eds.) *NELS* 17 (2). 394–408.

Manetta, Emily. 2011. *Peripheries in Kashmiri and Hindi-Urdu. The Syntax of Discourse Driven Movement*. Amsterdam: John Benjamins.
Nespor, Marina & Irene Vogel. 1986. *Prosodic Phonology*. Dordrecht: Foris.
Ortiz de Urbina, Jon. 1989. *Parameters in the Grammar of Basque*. Dordrecht: Kluwer.
Ortiz de Urbina, Jon. 1995. Residual verb-second and verb-first in Basque. In Katalin Kiss (ed.) *Discourse Configurational Languages*, 99–121. Oxford:Oxford University Press.
Ortiz de Urbina, Jon. 1999. Focus in Basque. In Georges Rebuschi & Laurice Tuller (eds) *The Grammar of Focus*, 311–333. Amsterdam:John Benjamins.
Ortiz de Urbina, Jon. 2003. Word Order. In Jose Ignacio Hualde & Jon Ortiz de Urbina (eds.) *A Grammar of Basque*, 448–454. Berlin: Mouton de Gruyter.
Portolan, Daniele. 2005. *Informational effects. The interrelationship of narrow syntax and Information Structure*. Siena: University of Siena dissertation.
Reglero, Lara. 2003. Non-wh-fronting in Basque. In Cedric Boeckx and Kleanthes Grohmann (eds.) *Multiple Wh-fronting*, 185–227. Amsterdam: John Benjamins.
Reinhart, Tanya. 2006. *Interface strategies*. Cambridge, MA: MIT Press.
Rijk, Rudolf P.D. 1969. Is Basque S.O.V.?. *Fontes Linguae Vasconum* 1. 319–351.
Rijk, Rudolf P.D. 1996. Focus and quasifocus on Basque negative statements. *Revista Internacional de Estudios Vascos* 41(2). 63–76.
Rizzi, Luigi. 1990. *Relativized Minimality*. Cambridge, MA: MIT Press.
Ross, John R. 1967. *Constraints on variables in syntax*. Cambridge, MA: MIT dissertation.
Samuels, Bridget. 2009. *The structure of phonological theory*. Harvard: Harvard University dissertation.
Selkirk, Elisabeth. 1996. The prosodic structure of function words. In James L. Morgan & Katherine Demuth (eds.) *Signal to Syntax: prosodic bootstrapping from speech to grammar in early acquisition*, 186–210. Mahwah, NJ: Lawrence Erlbaum Associates.
Selkirk, Elisabeth. 2009. On clause and intonational phrase in Japanese: the syntactic grounding of prosodic constituent structure. *Gengo Kenkyu* 136. 35–73.
Selkirk, Elisabeth. 2011. The Syntax-phonology Interface. In John Goldsmith, Jason Riggle & Alan Yu (eds.) *The Handbook of Phonological Theory*. Oxford: Blackwell Publishing.
Skopeteas, Stavros & Gisbert Fanselow. 2010. Focus in Georgian and the expression of contrast. *Lingua* 120(6). 1370–1391.
Uriagereka, Juan. 1999. Minimal Restrictions on Basque Movements. *NLLT* 17. 403–444.
Zubizarreta, Maria Luisa. 1998. *Prosody, Focus and Word Order*. Cambridge, MA: MIT Press.

Ritva Laury and Marja-Liisa Helasvuo
7 Detached NPs with relative clauses in Finnish conversations

Abstract: The article discusses detached NPs with relative clauses in Finnish conversation. The NPs discussed here include both so-called left and right dislocations and other types of detachments (Neveu 2010). We show that functioning as heads of relative clauses is an important use of detached NPs and that relativizing on detached NPs is a robust relativization pattern in Finnish.

It has been suggested that right and left dislocations function to organize new information in discourse. While Finnish detachments clearly serve functions that are relevant for information structure, they do not serve as escape valves for new information or function in topicalization of referents. Instead, they are responsive to local contingencies and serve in formulation and negotiation of reference in a variety of ways.

The article shows that the direction of continuation of reference is highly relevant for the form and function of the DNP+RCs and the way they are treated in the interaction. Those DNP+RCs which project forward in terms of continuation of reference have heads which are definite and specific, and relative clauses which are restrictive. On the other hand, the backward linking ones may also have heads which are generic or nonspecific, and relative clauses which are non-restrictive. The forward projecting ones are embedded in longer turns and are not responded to by other participants, while the backward linking ones, and the ones with no clear relationship to any clause preceding or following, are embedded in sequences with frequent turn transition and are responded to by coparticipants.

1 Introduction

This article presents research which is part of a larger project concerning the structure and use of relative clauses in Finnish conversation (e.g. Helasvuo & Laury 2009). In this article, we focus on relative clauses with an NP head that is not an argument in any clause. We call these constructions detached NPs

---

Ritva Laury, University of Helsinki
Marja-Liisa Helasvuo, University of Turku

with relative clauses, or DNP+RC constructions. These include both so-called right and left dislocations (RDs and LDs) and other types of detachments (Neveu 2010) which include a relative clause. We focus on their morphosyntactic and lexical characteristics and their treatment in interaction.

Our paper shows that detachment constructions are a significant context for the use of relative clauses in everyday Finnish conversation. In fact, the largest group of relative clauses in our collection of some 350 Finnish relative clauses had detached NPs as heads, which indicates that functioning as heads of relative clauses is an important use of detached NPs. Further, as many researchers have pointed out, the function of detachments is closely connected to the context in which they are used (e.g. Fernandez-Vest, this volume), and to the interactional value of the utterance housing the detachment construction (Apothéloz, Combattes and Neveu 2009). We offer an analysis of detachments in the framework of interactional linguistics (Couper-Kuhlen and Selting 2001), and show that besides the management of information structure, the form and function of detachments is linked to their interactional context. Specifically, we will show that DNP+RC constructions have varying lexico-syntactic manifestations depending on their syntactic and sequential environments. With close analysis of DNP+RC constructions in their local contexts, we will show that they are responsive to local contingencies (cf. Pekarek Doehler 2011). It has been suggested that LDs function to organize topics and information structure in English (Geluykens 1992: 53–66) and Italian (Duranti and Ochs 1979). Lambrecht (1994: 128–129) has proposed that LDs are topic expressions, i.e. their referents have a topic relation to the proposition. While Finnish detachments clearly serve functions that are relevant to information structure, they do not offer a regular escape valve for e.g. introducing new information, and they do not develop into discourse topics in ordinary conversation. In addition, they do not appear to be nearly as grammaticized[1] or indeed frequent in Finnish as they are, for example in French, or even English (e.g. Pekarek Doehler 2011: 51). Neither do they serve a topicalizing function similar to the one described by Geluykens (1992) for English and Ashby (1988) and Horlacher and Müller (2005) for French. We will show that instead, Finnish detachments function in formulation and negotiation of reference in a variety of ways. Thus, while our analysis of the DNP+RC constructions in Finnish conversation supports earlier research on detachments in a range of languages, it also offers new observations which were not possible to make based only on restricted contexts of occurrence.

---

[1] Lambrecht (1984: 231) shows that in his data from spoken French, constructions with RDs and LDs (Topic and Antitopic Constructions in Lambrecht's terminology) are more frequent than regular SVO sentences. Whether dislocations are grammaticized in French is a matter of debate. We thank the editors of the volume for pointing this out to us.

We will analyze the functions of DNP+RC constructions in their wider syntactic and interactional contexts. We have divided the DNP+RC constructions into three groups depending on the direction of referential continuity. These three groups differ significantly in the ways in which participants treat the DNP+RCs. First, forward projecting DNP+RCs (e.g. LDs) are typically embedded within a longer turn, and do not get recognitional (or any other) responses from other participants. Secondly, backward linking detached DNP+RCs (e.g. RDs) are embedded in sequences with frequent turn transitions, and are responded to by coparticipants. Finally, DNP+RCs with no clear link to either preceding or following clause also get responses.

2 Data

Our data consist of more than 11 hours of audiotaped and videotaped conversations from the Conversation Analysis archives of the Department of Finnish, Finno-Ugric and Scandinavian Studies at the University of Helsinki and the archives of the Department of Finnish at the University of Turku. From these data we have extracted all relative clauses for closer inspection. There are 342 relative clauses in the data.

Table 1 below shows the relative clauses in the data classified according to the syntactic function of the head of the relative clause. The table shows that relative clauses whose heads are detached NPs, that is, NPs which have no syntactic function in any clause, form the largest group in the data. They represent

Table 1: Syntactic function of the head of the relative clause.

Syntactic function of the head	Relativizer							
	joka		*mikä*		*kun*	*kuka*	Total	
	N	%	N	%	N	N	N	%
A	3	3	0	0	0	0	3	1
S	16	14	15	8	2	0	33	10
O	23	20	32	16	1	0	56	16
Existential NP	23	20	49	25	5	4	81	24
Predicate nominal	9	8	23	12	5	1	38	11
Obliques and adverbials	8	7	15	8	5	0	28	8
Clause	3	3	5	3	0	0	8	2
Headless	0	0	3	2	1	0	4	1
Detached NPs	22	20	54	28	6	0	82	24
Other	6	5	2	1	0	1	9	3
Total	113	100	198	100	25	6	342	100

24% of all the relative clauses in the data. It should also be noted that the percentage of free NPs, a subclass of detached NPs which excludes appositions (Tao 1996; Helasvuo 2001), among the heads of relative clauses in our corpus is relatively high (60/342, or 18%), and much higher than their frequency in conversational discourse (cf. Helasvuo 2001: 90). This shows that functioning as heads of relative clauses is an important use of detached NPs and that relativizing on detached NPs is a robust relativization pattern in Finnish.

From now on, we will focus on relative clauses which have detached NPs as their heads. As can be seen from Table 1, there are 82 such cases in the data.

3 Analysis

In what follows, we will analyze the detached NPs with relative clauses in our data with regard to, first, referential continuity; that is, the direction of linkage to a coreferential mention either forward or backward. We will also discuss the type of head NP, whether it is pronominal or lexical, has a specific referent, and whether it is definite. The function of the relative clause as restrictive, classifying, or predicating, as well as the sequential context in which the DNP+RC occurs are also discussed.

3.1 Linking forward

In this section of the article, we will discuss those DNP+RCs which project forward in terms of referential continuity, that is, those that are followed by a subsequent coreferential mention or mentions. These DNP+RCs typically create specific new referents which are made identifiable by a restrictive relative clause. Their heads tend strongly to be definite and are often pronominal. In spite of these characteristics, the identifiability of the referent does not seem to be an issue to the participants: as we will show, the recipients of the turn containing the DNP+RC do not ratify or acknowledge or in other ways respond to the mention of the referent in terms of its identifiability in our data. An important exception to this are those DNP+RCs which do not have any connection to a preceding or following clause.

In terms of sequential context, and differing from the other DNP+RCs in our data, forward linking DNP+RCs project more talk to follow by the same participant. They occur in extended turns and are seldom responded to by other participants. The referent of the head NP of the relative clause in this group of DNP+RCs does not become topical.

There were altogether 17 detached NPs with relative clauses of this type in our data. We classified them into two subtypes. The first group was made up of DNP+RCs which included a coreferential mention in a following clause, in other words, those which might be called left dislocations. In addition, there were four forward-looking DNP+RCs which occurred before a predication, but where the predication was not as clearly tied to the preceding detached NP; there may have been a lengthy pause between the detached NP and the following predication, or the anaphoric link to the following mention was ambiguous.

As is typical of the DNP+RCs which project forward, the heads of DNP+RCs in the first group were typically definite and specific, and often pronominal, with a subsequent, coreferential pronominal mention. The relative clause was restrictive. The head of the relative clause could be in the same case or in a different case than the coreferential mention which followed. The following clause containing the coreferential mention was initiated with the connector *ni* 'so', which has been characterized as an indicator of continuation (Vilkuna 1997). The head NP constituted the first mention of its referent in the conversation.

These DNP+RCs occurred in extended turns in the conversations in our data; typical environments were narratives and other reportings. In contrast to what has been reported for left dislocations in languages in which they are highly grammaticized (e.g. Pekarek Doehler 2011 on French, Gelyukens 1992 on English, Lambrecht 1994 on French), these mentions are not followed by recognitional responses and co-constructions are rare (cf. Pekarek Doehler 2011). In keeping with earlier studies on left dislocations, these DNP+RCs may involve contrast with other referents, and they may also be involved in list construction.

Our first example illustrates this type of DNP+RC. It comes from a conversation among two middle-aged couples who have gathered at the home of one of the couples to celebrate the approach of the Christmas holidays. Jaana is discussing the recent division of the estate of a relative. The DNP+RC is in line 5.

Example (1) SG 355 Glögi[2,3]

1	Jaana:	*tää*	*ol-i*		*ihan*	*täynnä*	*tavara-a,*
		DEM1	be-PST+3SG		quite	full	stuff-PAR
		'This was completely full of stuff)'					

2	Mikko:	*siis*	*ol-i-k-s*		*[ne-*		
		PTC	be-PST-3SG-Q		DEM3+PL		
		'so were they-'					

---

2 Glossing symbols in addition to the ones mentioned in the Leipzig glossing rules: ADE – adessive; CONNEG – connegative; ELA – elative; ILL – illative; PAR – partitive; PTC – particle; PX – possessive suffix; WH – question word.

3 Jaana: [tääl   ol-i   ne   tavara-t
         DEM1+LOC be-PST+3SG DEM3+PL thing-PL
         'There were those things here'

4   mi-tä   mei-lle   on   tua-tu,
                REL-PAR   1PL-ALL   be+3SG   bring-PASS+PTCP
                'that had been brought to us'
                (.)

5 Jaana: kaikki   ne   mi-tä   on   Veiko-lla   <=
          all   DEM3+PL   REL-PAR   be+3SG   MaleName-ADE
          'all those that Veikko has'

6   nii   nii-stä   ei   puhu-ttu   mittää,
                 so   DEM3+PL-ELA NEG   talk-PASS+PTCP   WH+PAR
                 'so no one said anything about those.'
                 (.)

7 Jaana: >ja kaike-n   se   ve-i↑   mi-tä   se   irti   sa-i,
          and all-ACC DEM3 take-PST+3SG REL-PAR DEM3 loose get-PST-3SG
          'And he took everything he could pry loose.'
          (.)

In this example, as is typical of the DNP+RCs in this group, the head of the relative clause is definite and specific, and the relative clause is restrictive. There is a coreferential mention in the following clause, here in a different case (elative) than the head of the relative clause (nominative), but there are no further mentions of the referent in the conversation; it does not become topical. On the other hand, the referent contrasts lexically and morphosyntactically with the NP containing a relative clause in the previous clause, *ne tavarat mitä meille on tuatu* 'the things that have been brought to us'.

This DNP+RC is embedded in a lengthy complaint. There is no response from coparticipants to the new, definite mention, even though the speaker pauses briefly after the clause containing the coreferential mention.

---

3 Transcription symbols: *(.)* – micropause (0,2 seconds or less); *(1.2)* – length of pause in seconds; *WORD* or <u>word</u> loud talk or syllable; >*TALK* <– faster than surrounding talk; <*TALK*> – slower than surrounding talk; : – lengthened syllable; @...@ – marked voice quality; £ – smiley voice; *ta-* – interrupted word; = – latching; .hh – inhalation; *[...]* – overlap; ? – rising intonation at utterance end; . – falling intonation at utterance end; , – slightly falling or level intonation at utterance end; ↑ – rising pitch within utterance; (–) – unhearable talk.

The DNP+RCs before a predication resemble the first group in most of the characteristics mentioned above. However, the following clause is not as likely to be linked to the DNP+RC with a *ni* 'so' connector, and there is not as clear an anaphoric link between the mention in that clause and the head of the RC as there is with the first group. However, they closely resemble the DNP+RCs in the first group in that they are embedded in lengthy, often complex turns, and are not responded to by other participants.

In this section we have seen that the DNP+RCs which project forward in terms of continuation of reference involve new, definite referents which, while being predicated upon in the next clause, do not become topics in the conversation. This is interesting in light of the fact that when examined at the sentence level, topicalization has been shown to be a central function of LDs (see, e.g. Fernandez-Vest, this volume). The relative clauses in this group are restrictive. These DNP+RCs are embedded in longer turns and are typically not responded to by the participants.

3.2 Linking backward

The majority of DNP+RCs in our data link backward in terms of referential continuity. They constitute subsequent mentions of an already mentioned referent or classify, characterize or comment on it in various ways. They differ in several respects from the forward-projecting DNP+RCs (see section 3.1 above), but they do not constitute as coherent a group.

Backward linking DNP+RCs include three subtypes: First, there are cases where there is a coreferential pronominal in the preceding clause. These cases meet the criteria traditionally described as being characteristic of right dislocations ("RDs"). This is a very small group as there are only 3 such cases in the data (for similar observations, see Fernandez-Vest, this volume). Secondly, there are 15 DNP+RCs where there is a coreferential lexical NP in the preceding clause. These are similar to RDs except that the coreferential mention is lexical, not pronominal as in the case of "RDs". Thirdly, there are 22 cases where the DNP+RC functions as an apposition in the larger sentence.

Example (2) illustrates cases where there is a coreferential pronominal in the preceding clause (so-called "RDs"). The example comes from a sequence where the participants who are members of a band discuss upcoming performances and rehearsals.

Example (2) SG141-3 1a4 Keikka

1 Mikko: [Joo]   se-kin   tota   se (0.2) se   et
         PTC   DEM1-CL   PTC   DEM1   DEM1   COMP
         'Yeah also the thing is'

2   mu-l   ei   ok-kaan   sunnuntaina   si-tä
         I-ALL   NEG   be+CONNEG-CL   on.Sunday   it-PAR
         'I don't have it on Sunday'

3   mä   sa-i-n   se-n   peru-ttua,
         I   get-PST-1SG   it-ACC   cancel-PASS+PTCP
         'I was able to cancel it'

4 Kati: Joo,
         PTC
         'Yeah'

5 Mikko: Se   yks esiintyminen   mikä piti   olla   tuolla,   <=
         DEM3   one performance.NOM   REL must-PST   be-INF   DEM2+LOC
         'The performance that was supposed to be at that,'

6 Kati: Kiva.=
         nice
         'Good deal.'

7 Mikko: =Et   sikälis   mutta   e:i   se   nyt   o-is
         COMP   in.that.way   but   NEG   DEM1   now   be-COND+CONNEG
         paljon   mitään
         much   else+PAR
         'So that as far as that goes but it wouldn't have hardly any'

8   vaikutta-nuk-kan   to-hon   mutta,
         affect-PCP-CL   DEM2-ILL   but
         'effect on that but,'

9 Kati: Joo   mut   ihan (.)   hauska-a.
         PTC   but   quite   fun-PAR
         'Yeah but good thing.'

In ex. (2), the DNP+RC construction is in line 5. There are two coreferential mentions in the prior sequence, and they are both pronominal, namely *sitä* (line 2) and *sen* (line 3). The head of the DNP+RC is (*se yks esiintyminen* 'the performance', line 5) is lexical, definite and specific, and the RC functions to restrict the reference of the head. Syntactically, the DNP+RC construction is not completely integrated into the syntax of the preceding clausal unit: the cases of the coreferential pronouns in Mikko's two-clause turn (lines 2 and 3) are partitive and accusative, but the head NP of the relative clause (line 5) is nominative.[4]

Sequentially, the pronominal mentions preceding the DNP+RC (lines 2 and 3) are followed by a response token. The response particle *joo* (line 4) could be taken as an indicator that the responding coparticipant has enough information for the prior speaker to go on, and that she has understood the background assumptions (Sorjonen 2001), but that continuation by the prior speaker is relevant. Thus, Mikko's turn containing the DNP+RC in line (5) can be seen as prompted by this response in line 4. Consequently, in response to the DNP+RC construction, Mikko receives a positive evaluation from Kati in line 6 (cf. Horlacher and Müller, 2005). We may note that the response does not deal with the identifiablity of the referent.

Example (3) comes from a recording where young men have gathered to have dinner together. This example represents those cases in our data where the preceding coreferential mention is lexical and the referent is generic.

Example (3) SG 396 Viini-ilta_Kerava-tossut

1	Riku:	*on-k-s*		*se*	*siis (.)*	*teekookoo-n*
		be+3SG-Q-CL		DEM1	so	Name-GEN
		'Is it from HUT (Helsinki University of Technology)'				

| 2 | | (0.2) |

3	Lauri:	£*joo*£
		PTC
		'Yeah'

| 4 | All: | ((laughter)) |

5	Taavi:	£*teekookoo-n l(h)aulukirj(h)a-sE*
		Name-GEN song.book-INE
		(from the HUT song book)

| 6 | Riku: | *m(h)m(h)* |

7	Taavi:	[*sit se*
		then it
		'then it'

---

[4] This example is in contrast to the observation made by Fernandez-Vest (this volume) regarding the form of final detachments in Finnish.

8   Lauri: [me   laite-taan   sellase-t   niin   sano-tu-t   karjalanpiiraka-t
              1PL   put-PASS   DEM.ADJ-PL   so   call-PTCP-PL   carelian.pie-PL
              jalko-i-hin
              foot-PL-ILL
              'we'll put on like what they call carelian pies on our feet'

9   sellase-t
              DEM.ADJ-PL
              'like'

10 Aapo: m(h)m(h)m(h)

11 Lauri: s(h)ella[se-t
              DEM.ADJ-PL
              'like'

12 Aapo: [m(h)m(h)m(h)

13 Lauri: £Kerava-tossu-t   mitkä   vede-tään   [niinku ((groans)) <=
              PlaceName-slipper-PL   REL+PL   pull-PASS   like
              'Kerava-slippers that you like pull'

14 Aapo: [m(h)m(h)m(h)

15 Lauri: [sit   men-nään   istu-ma-an
              then   go-PASS-   sit-INF-ILL
              'Then we'll get seated'

16 Aapo: [m(h)m(h)m(h)m(h)m(h)

17 Lauri: piiri-in ja   (.)   @laulu   alka-a   hiljaisuude-sta@
              circle-ILL and   song   begin-3SG   silence-ELA
              'in a circle and the song begins from silence'

Just prior to the sequence presented in ex. (3), the participants have talked about what songs were popular with their primary school classmates. One participant then suggests that the last song mentioned comes from the song book of his university (line 1). He then goes on to present a parody of students in his college getting together to sing like young children (lines 8–17). The scene of primary school children in music classes is obviously familiar to all and evokes hilarity.

The DNP+RC is in lines 9 and 13. The head of the RC is lexical (*Keravatossut*, l. 13) and includes a demonstrative adjective *sellaset* used as a determiner (l. 9). The prior mention of the same referent is in line 8, and the case of the head of the RC matches that of the prior mention. The referent is generic, as is typical of cases where the prior mention is lexical. The RC functions to classify the referent. The DNP+RC gets an overlapping response in line 14, accompanied by laughter.

The sequence given in (3) involves reference negotiation. The first mention of the referent (line 8) is tentative, prefaced with *niin sanotut* 'so called'. It is received with laughter encouraging continuation. The DNP+RC (lines 9 and 13) gets an overlapping response (lines 12 and 14), which is again laughter. The whole sequence involves playful portrayal of an imaginary situation.

To summarize, the backward linking DNP+RCs do not form a coherent group in terms of form and function. The RDs have specific referents, the heads are definite and the RCs are restrictive, while for appositions and those with a coreferential mention in a prior clause, the referents are generic, and the RCs are classifying and predicating. In terms of their sequential contexts, backward linking DNP+RCs resemble each other. They are embedded in sequences with frequent turn transitions. The initial, lexical mentions are often followed by responses which receive the turn as understood but make continuation relevant. The backward linking DNP+RCs also receive responses from coparticipants.

3.3 No clear relationship to any clause preceding or following

Our data also contained a fairly large group of detached NPs with relative clauses which had no clear relationship to any clause either preceding or following it. This group included two subtypes, DNP+RCs which were used in contexts of referent negotiation, and ones which commented on a prior action or situation. There were 14 examples of the first type and 8 examples of the second type in our data.

For the first group, there is typically a prior, lexical, specific NP coreferential with the head of the RC. The head of the RC is specific and pronominal; the RC is restrictive. In contrast, in the second type, there is no prior mention. The DNP+RC creates a referent, characterizes or classifies or evaluates it, or comments on an earlier action or situation. The head NP often consists of or contains an adjective, an extreme case formulation (e.g. *ainoo* 'the only'). Like the DNP+RCs which are backward-looking, these DNP+RCs are also embedded in sequences with frequent turn transition, and a response from a co-participant normally follows. The responses to the first type deal with identifiability, while the responses to the second type involve amusement and often agreement.

Example (4) below illustrates the first group, which links backward to an earlier mention and involves referent negotiation. It comes from a phone conversation between two young women. Vikke is telling about a dream she had.

Example (4) SG112 1a3_Suolapala_Uni

```
1 Vikke:   mä nä-i-n          un-ta         koulu-sta-ki?,
           1SG dream-PST-1SG  dream-PAR     school-ELA-CL
           'I dreamed about school too?'

2 Missu:   mitä      sää    nä[it.
           WH-PAR    2SG    see-PST-2SG
           'What did you dream (about).'

3 Vikke:   [(ku)  alko, .hhh (.)  no siel       ol-i, (.)
           when  begin+PST+3SG   PTC DEM+LOC   be-PST+3SG
           'When (it) begain, well there was'

4          khm (0.3) .mt mu-n    ↑serkku-ni      <Salla>,
                         1SG-GEN cousin-1SGPX   FemaleName
           'my cousin Salla,'

5 Missu:   nii.
           PTC
           'Yeah.'

6 Vikke:   Rantalan       Anni,
           LastName-GEN   FemaleName
           'Anni Rantala.'

7 Missu:   £joo-o£?,
           PTC
           'Yeah?'

8          (.)

9 Vikke:   ja    sit   se    yks  poika:    Lahde-sta. (.)
           and  then  DEM3  one  guy.NOM   PlaceName-ELA
           'and then another guy from Lahti.'

10         mikä on, (0.6)  ol-i<,      v- vaihto-oppilaa-na.h
           REL be+3SG      be-PST+3SG  exchange-student-ESS
           'who is, was, away as an exchange student'

11         (0.3)

12 Vikke:  just vuade-n?,  =se,  Mäkelä-n       Kimmo-n         kaveri.
           just year-ACC   DEM3  LastName-GEN   MaleName-GEN    friend.NOM
           'for one year. That friend of Kimmo Mäkelä's.'
```

```
13              (0.3)

14  Missu:  KUka,h
            who
            'Who?'

15  Vikke:  se        mikä  on       se-n,  (0.3)  se-n,     se-n      poliisi-m    <=
            DEM3.NOM  REL   be+3SG   DEM3-GEN      DEM3-GEN  DEM3-GEN  police-GEN

16          [poika.   <=
            son.NOM
            'the one who is the son of that, that, that policeman.'

17  Missu:  [.hhh  se         Vehviläine,h
                   DEM3.NOM   LastName.NOM
            'that Vehviläinen.'

18  Vikke:  >nii<.
            PTC
            'Right.'
```

The DNP+RC in this example is in lines 15–16. There is not only one, but two prior specific, lexical mentions of the referent, the first in lines 9–10 and 12, and another one also in line 12. The first mention, which forms part of a list, also includes a relative clause. The referent of the DNP+RC in lines 15–16 is specific. The head of the RC is pronominal, the RC is restrictive. In contrast with the examples in the preceding sections, this DNP+RC has no relationship to any clause preceding or following it. It is embedded in a sequence with frequent turn transitions, and, similarly to the backward linking DNP+RCs in the previous section, the mention is responded to by the coparticipant. Here, the response is recognitional; it consists of an NP, a name, indicating that Missu is able to identify the referent.

The next example illustrates the second type, that is, those DNP+RCs which comment on a prior action or situation. It comes from a conversation among three young women. In example (5), Miia is describing an alarm clock by animating the sound it makes. The DNP+RC is in lines 6 and 9, and functions to characterize the sound which Miia has just produced as 'the absolutely last sound one would want to hear in the morning'.

Example (5) SG151B

1 Miia: *Se   sa[no-o] sillee .hh @?ä ?ä ?ää ?ä[ä]*
         DEM3 say-3SG like.that
         'It says like .hh ä ä ää ää' (= Cock-a-doodle-doo))

2 Susa: *[.hh]*

3 ():   *[tshh]*

4 Miia: *käsittämättömän sit s- (.) kovaa,   sit   ku   sitä   painaa*
         unbelievably   then loud-PAR then when DEM3-PAR press-3SG
         'unbelievably loud, then when you press it'

         (tää) Mikki   sanoo (.) @good morning@. he >he he he<h
         DEM3 Mickey say-3SG
         'this Mickey Mouse says "Good morning"'

5   (0.7)

6 Susa: *mts hh £aa[mul   varmaa vihon vii]me£-*
                  morning-ADE surely very last
         'In the morning, surely the very last'

7 Anne: *[(– – –)]*

8 Miia: *Mm,*
         PTC
         'Mhm'

9 Susa: *.hh ääni   mi-tä   halua-a   £kuul-la£. .hh <=*
         voice.NOM REL-PAR want-3SG hear-INF
         'sound that one wants to hear'

10   (.)

11 Susa: *[.nsss]*

12 (Miia): *[Mm,]*
            PTC
            'Mhm,'

Note that in example (5), there is no preceding NP that would be coreferential with the NP in lines 6 and 9, and the referent is not mentioned subsequently in the conversation either. The head NP, as is typical of these DNP+RCs, contains an extreme case formulation (*vihon viime* 'the absolutely last'). The head NP is specific, and the RC is restrictive. The DNP+RC is responsive to the prior turn and is evaluative in nature. The coparticipants respond even while the DNP+RC is being produced, but their responses do not deal with identifiability of the referent.

This section concerned those DNP+RCs which have no clear relationship to any clause preceding or following. Their referents are identifiable and specific. For the first group, the head NP is typically pronominal, while for the second one, it is typically lexical. The relative clause is restrictive. We saw that for the first group of these, the ones which remention a referent, are the only ones in the data in which identifiability is at issue. For both types, the sequences in which they occur involve frequent turn transitions, and the DNP+RC is responded to by the coparticipants. In this way, they resemble the backward-looking DNP+RCs. In fact, these DNP+RCs could also be considered backward-looking since the first type involves a coreferential mention, while the second type comments on an earlier action or situation.

4 Conclusions

We have seen that there are various types of detached NPs with RCs in Finnish conversation. The majority are not clearly classifiable as LDs or especially as RDs.

To summarize our findings concerning form and function: The forward projecting DNP+RCs form a coherent group in terms of form and function. The heads of the RCs are pronominal and the referents are specific. The RCs are restrictive. In contrast, the backward linking DNP+RCs are more heterogeneous. For RDs, the referents are specific and RCs are restrictive, while for appositions and cases where the coreferential NP is in a prior clause, referents are much more likely to be generic or nonspecific and to involve lexical prior mentions. They are also more likely to have RCs which are non-restrictive. Our last group, namely those DNP+RCs which have no relationship to any clause, serve to classify, characterize or predicate. Their heads are specific, and the RCs are restrictive. They remention an earlier referent in the context of referent negotiation or comment on an earlier action or situation.

To summarize our sequential findings, the forward linking DNP+RCs are in extended turns and are followed by more talk by the same participant. They may come early in the turn. In the literature it has been suggested that LDs may function as 'turn-entry devices' (Mondada 1995; Pekarek Doehler 2001, 2003), and our forward linking DNP+RCs may function similarly, but not always. They serve to introduce a referent which will be predicated upon in the upcoming turn. Often they occur in complex turns, as described by Pekarek Doehler 2011 for LDs in French. They may involve construction of lists or expressions of contrast. These are both functions identified for LDs (for English, see Gelyukens 1992; for French, see Pekarek Doehler and Müller 2006).

The backward linking ones are found in sequences with frequent turn transitions, and are typically followed by responses from coparticipants. The earlier mentions of the same referents are followed by responses which make continuation relevant. The backward linking DNP+RCs typically occur in evaluations or assessments, which are sequential contexts found to be typical of RDs in French (see Horlacher and Müller 2005).

The DNP+RC constructions which have no relationship with any clausal unit are also backward linking in the sense that they occur in referent negotiations (for example, they remention an already mentioned referent when recognition has not taken place) or comment on an earlier situation or event (cf. Fernandez-Vest, this volume). The ones which specifically deal with reference negotiation are the only ones where the responses deal with the identifiability of the referent.

To conclude, our data indicate that the direction of continuity of reference is relevant for detached NPs with relative clauses in several ways: The treatment of those DNP+RCs in our data which project forward in terms of continuity of reference are a manifestation of clausal orientation from the part of the participants: a heavy NP with a restrictive relative clause referring to a specific referent projects a predication to follow. Those DNP+RCs which project backward in terms of referential continuity are prompted by participant responses which make continuation relevant. They also receive responses from the coparticipants.

References

Apothéloz, Denis, Bernard Combettes & Franck Neveu (eds.). 2009. *Les linguistiques du détachement, Actes du Colloque International de Nancy (7–9 juin 2006)*. Bern-Berlin: Peter Lang.

Ashby, William J. 1988. The syntax, pragmatics, and sociolinguistics of left- and right-dislocations in French. *Lingua* 75. 203–229.

Couper-Kuhlen, Elizabeth & Margret Selting. 2001. Introducing interactional linguistics. In Margret Selting & Elizabeth Couper-Kuhlen (eds.), *Studies in interactional linguistics*, 1–22. Amsterdam: John Benjamins.

Duranti, Alessandro & Elinor Ochs. 1979. Left-dislocation in Italian Conversation. In Talmy Givón (ed.), *Syntax and Semantics, vol. 12: Discourse and Syntax*. 377–416. New York: Academic Press.

Geluykens, Ronald. 1992. *From discourse process to grammatical construction*. Amsterdam: John Benjamins.
Givón, Talmy. 1983. *Topic continuity in discourse: A quantitative cross-language study*. Amsterdam: John Benjamins.
Helasvuo, Marja-Liisa. 2001. *Syntax in the Making*. Amsterdam: John Benjamins.
Helasvuo, Marja-Liisa & Ritva Laury. 2009. Relative clause structures in context. Paper given at the International Pragmatics Conference, Melbourne, Australia, July 12–17.
Helasvuo, Marja-Liisa & Aki-Juhani Kyröläinen. 2011. Ilmisubjekti vai nolla? Syntaktisen variaation kontekstuaaliset piirteet tarkastelussa. [Pronominal or zero subject? Exploring contextual features of syntactic variation.] Paper given in the conference "Kielioppia lypsämässä", Tartu Ülikool, April 1–2, 2011.
Hopper, Paul J. 1988. *Emergent grammar and the a priori grammar postulate*. In D. Tannen (ed.), *Linguistics in context*. Norwood, NJ: Ablex.
Horlacher, Anne-Sylvie & Müller, Gabrielle. 2005. L'implication de la dislocation à droite dans l'organisation interactionnelle. *TRANEL* (Travaux Neuchâtelois de Linguistique) 41, 127–145.
Koivisto, Aino, Ritva Laury, & Eeva-Leena Seppänen. 2011. Syntactic and actional characteristics of Finnish *että*-clauses. In Ritva Laury & Ryoko Suzuki (eds.) *Subordination in Conversation. A cross-linguistic perspective*, 69–102. Studies in Language and Social Interaction. Amsterdam: John Benjamins.
Lambrecht, Knud. 1981. *Topic, antitopic, and verb agreement in non-standard French*. Amsterdam: Benjamins.
Lambrecht, Knud. 1984. On the status of SVO sentences in spoken French. In Russell Tomlin (ed.), *Coherence and grounding in discourse*, 217–261. Amsterdam: John Benjamins.
Lambrecht, Knud. 1994. *Information structure and sentence form*. Cambridge: CUP.
Neveu, Franck. 2010. La linguistique du détachement en français. Paper given in the Symposium Grammaire de l'information et typologie. Université Paris III, Paris. March 25–27
Pekarek Doehler, Simona. 2011. Emergent grammar for all practical purposes: The on-line formatting of left- and right dislocations in French conversation. In Peter Auer & Stefan Pfänder (eds.), *Constructions: Emerging and Emergent*, 45–87. Berlin: Mouton.
Pekarek Doehler, Simona & Müller, Gabrielle M. 2006. Zur Rolle von Linksherausstellungen bei der interaktiven Konstruktion von Auflistungen: Linksversetzungen und Pseudo-Clefts im gesprochenen Französischen. In Deppermann, A., Fiehler R. & Spranz-Fogasy, T. (eds). *Grammatik und Interaktion. Untersuchungen zum Zusammenhang von grammatischen Strukturen und Gesprächsprozessen*, 245–277. Radolfzell: Verlag für Gesprächsforschung.
Sorjonen, Marja-Leena. 1999. Dialogipartikkelien tehtävistä. [On the functions of dialogue particles] *Virittäjä* 103: 170–194.
Sorjonen, Marja-Leena. 2001. *Responding in conversation*. Amsterdam: John Benjamins.
Tao, Hongyin. 1993. *Units in Mandarin Conversation*. Amsterdam: John Benjamins.

Dejan Matić
8 Tag questions and focus markers: Evidence from the Tompo dialect of Even[1]

1 Introduction

It is well known that cleft structures are the major diachronic source of focus markers, where focus is understood as that element of the sentence which carries the main assertion (Harris & Campbell 1995: 151–165, Heine & Kuteva 2002: 95–6, among others). Importantly, the development of focus markers out of a cleft sentence includes the relaxation of clause boundaries, so that an originally biclausal structure is reinterpreted as monoclausal. In this paper, I shall argue that the Northern Tungusic language Even provides an example of a diachronic development in which the source of the focus marker is another common biclausal structure, tag questions. Tag questions in Even minimally include the negative auxiliary verb which copies the agreement, tense and mood of the preceding finite verb.

(1) *E,   tar kụkatmụ   tar nọk-ča   bi-he-nni   **e-he-nni**.*
     INTJ DIST glove.POSS.1SG DIST hang-PF.PTC be-NFUT-2SG NEG-NFUT-2SG
    'Oh, there, you hanged my glove there, didn't you?'   (Top09_GMG_1_013)

This same structure can be used in contexts which seem to indicate that its function is to mark the main assertive point of the utterance, focus.

---

[1] Thanks are due to the Max Planck Society and the Volkswagen Stiftung (DobeS project *Dialectal and cultural diversity among the Evens in Siberia*), whose generous financial support has enabled me to conduct fieldwork with the Even communities for many years. I am also grateful to the audiences of the First Data Session on Information Structure, MPI Nijmegen (2010) and SWL 4, Lyon (2010) for their invaluable input, to Robert Van Valin, Jr. and an anonymous reviewer for their helpful comments, and, first and foremost, to my linguistic consultants for their readiness to share their knowledge with me: Natalia M. Golikova, Elizaveta N. Baramygina, Nikolaj I. Neustroev†, Evdokia V. Semenova, Stepanida F. Protopopova, Tat'jana A. Zabolockaja, Khristina M. Zakharova and Tat'jana V. Zakharova.

Dejan Matić, University of Graz

(2) Adʒit=ta   **e-h-ni**   noŋan   goːn-ni.
    truth=PTL   NEG-NFUT-3SG   he   say-3SG(NFUT)
    'He told the TRUTH. / What he said was the truth.'   (Top09_GNM_4.1_116)

It will be shown that the stages of this development are similar to those postulated for clefts by Harris and Campbell, and that the evolution of tag questions towards a full-fledged focus marker is still on-going.

The connection between tag questions and information structure has to my knowledge not been investigated before. One of the purposes of the paper is therefore to shed light on the information-structural properties of tag questions which allow them to serve as one of the possible sources for discourse-pragmatic markers. Yet another intention of the paper is to contribute to the current discussion on the categorial nature of focus (Matić & Wedgwood 2013) by describing a type of focus marker which carries many of the pragmatic features of its source structure and thus semantically deviates from the better known, European-style foci.

The paper is organised as follows. After a short introduction to the Even language and the data on which the paper is based (Section 2), formal (Section 3) and semantic (Section 4) properties of the tag construction are described. Section 5 is devoted to the diachronic aspects of the development from tag question to focus marker. In Section 6, I take up issue with the nature of the relationship between tag questions and information structure. The corollaries of the Even data for a general theory of focus are addressed in Section 7.

2 Language, data and terminology

Even is a North Tungusic language, closely related to Evenki and Neghidal, spoken by small reindeer herding communities scattered over the huge area of north-eastern Siberia, between the Lena River in the west and the Pacific Ocean in the east, and between the Arctic Ocean and the Aldan River on the north-south axis. Due to the fragmentation of the Even communities, the language is divided into a number of dialects. The dialects display significant phonological, lexical, and grammatical differences, to the extent that some of them are not fully mutually intelligible. In order to provide for the consistency of the data, the material on which this paper is based is restricted to data from one dialect, spoken in the Tompo region of the Sakha Republic (Yakutia), located some 200 kilometres to the north-east of the confluence of the Aldan River into the Lena River, in the Verkhoyansk Range. Examples from other dialects will be adduced only sporadically, for comparison.

Even is a typical northern Eurasian language, with such standard features as vowel harmony, agglutinative suffixing morphology, predominant dependent marking, head-final structure, and a rich array of non-finite verbal forms (see standard descriptions in Novikova 1960, 1980 and Mal'čukov 1999, 2008).

The argumentation is based on data from natural discourse collected during fieldwork with the Even community of the Tompo region and some other parts of north-eastern Siberia and Kamchatka; additional material is provided by elicited and experimental data, as well as grammaticality judgments. All the examples in the text have tags with the format *place.year_speaker(s)_session_clause*. These tags refer to the source of the example, which can in most cases be checked in the DobeS Archive (www.mpi.nl/DOBES).

A word on terminology: following Axelsson (2011), I will use the term *question tag* or simply *tag* to refer to interrogative clausal elements following the main clause, while the main clause itself will be called *anchor*. Thus, in the sentence *He opened the window, didn't he?*, the clause *he opened the window* is the anchor, and the interrogative part, *didn't he*, is the tag.

3 Formal properties of tags

3.1 Negation and questions in Even

Even tags are originally negative interrogative constructions. This section introduces the major structural properties of negative clauses and polar questions.

Negation in Even is expressed with the negative auxiliary *e-*, which carries agreement, tense and mood features, and is complemented by a non-finite form, the so-called negative converb, of the lexical verb.

(3) *Noŋartan   keːńeli-w   ịa-w=da   **e-če-l**   ǫː-r.*
     they   bad-ACC   what-ACC=PTL   NEG-PST(3)-PL   do-NEG.CVB
     'They didn't do anything bad.'   (Top07_NIN_story1_022)

The negative verbal complex is a major exception to the head-final syntax of Even: the negative auxiliary, which is to all intents and purposes the head of the phrase, precedes its complement, the negative converb of the lexical verb. This complement can be left out only under strict adjacency of the negative structure to its positive counterpart.

(4) – *Tar   tarapaka-w   (...) nǫk-kǫːt-ta?*   – ***E-s-ten.***
         DIST ribbon.R-ACC   hang-GNR-NFUT(3PL)   NEG-NFUT-3PL
     '– Did they hang ribbons? – No.'   (Top09_GNM_4.1_620)

Polar questions are marked with a rising-falling intonation (LHL%) on the final accentable syllable; more often than not, an interrogative particle (=*gu* or =*i*) is attached to the focus of the question (Ma'lčukov 2008: 138–9).

(5)   LH L%
    Erek   *bej*   (...)   *i̯a-w=da*   *ule:-ri-n?*
    PROX   man   what-ACC=PTL   sacrifice-PST-3SG
    'Did this man (...) perform some kind of sacrifice?' (Top07_BEN_conv1_168)

(6)   *Hi:=**gu***   *birigeʒir*   *bi-he-nni,*   *eṅehni=**gu***   *birigeʒir?*
    you=Q   foreman.R   be-NFUT-2SG   mother.POSS.2SG=Q   foreman.R
    'Are YOU the foreman of this brigade, or is it your MOTHER?'
    (Top09_GNM_4.1_466)

(7)   *Ta-la*   *i:w-riʒur*   *ečin*   *i̯r-wa:č-kara-ča-l=**gu***   (...)?
    DIST-LOC   bring.in-ANT.CVB.PL   thus   drag-GNR-HAB-PF.PTC(3)-PL=Q
    'After they had brought (them) in, did they have to drag (them) like this?'
    (Top09_PSF&AGA_conv2_217)

Example (6) shows that narrow question focus attracts the interrogative particle; if the question has a broad focus, the particle is attached to the main verb, as in (7).

3.2 The basic structure of tags

It has been claimed that the type of question tag in which the form of the tag co-varies with the form of the predicate of the anchor (*dependent tags*) is unique to English (Culicover 1992), while all other languages have fixed, invariant tags of the French or German type. Recent typological surveys, such as those by Sailor (2010) and Axelsson (2011) show that this is not entirely true: dependent tags are relatively rare cross-linguistically, but they do occur in a wide array of languages across the globe. Tags in Even are also of the dependent type, since the form of the tag depends on the form of the anchor (see (1) and (2)).

    As was indicated in the Introduction, the tag is based on the negative auxiliary *e-*, independently of the polarity of the anchor. Negative tag with a positive anchor is illustrated in (8a); the combination with a negative anchor is given in (8b). Even tags thus belong to the rare subtype of dependent tags – *constant polarity tags* – in which there is no polarity reversal between the anchor and the tag (as is the case in English: *He cried, didn't he.* vs. *He didn't cry, did he?*).

(8) Has she picked berries in the forest?
   a. *Tewli-ri-n*   ***e-če!***
      gather-PST-3SG   NEG-PST(3SG)
      'She has, hasn't she (she obviously has).'

   b. ***E-če***   *tewli-r*   ***e-če!***
      NEG-PST(3SG)   gather-NEG.CVB   NEG-PST(3SG)
      'She hasn't, has she (she obviously hasn't)' (Top11_ZTA_elic1)

Sailor (2010) differentiates two types of dependent tags: *auxiliary-stranding tags*, in which the tag contains only the auxiliary, as in English, and *V-stranding tags*, in which the whole lexical verb from the anchor is repeated in the tag. Tags in the Tompo dialect of Even clearly belong to the auxiliary-stranding type, since the lexical verb is never repeated in the tag. This can be seen in all examples given in this paper.[2]

The negative auxiliary in the tag copies the agreement features (person and number), tense and mood of the predicate in the anchor. Apart from some well-defined exceptions (see Section 5), the congruence between the anchor and the tag is obligatory. I will call this obligatory sharing of features between the predicate of the anchor and the tag *Agreement Condition*.

(9) a. *Adʒit=ta,*   ta-la   ih-***ha**-p*   *c **he** p.*
     truth=PTL   DIST-LOC   arrive-NFUT-1PL   NEG-NFUT-1PL
     'And indeed, we have arrived there, haven't we.' (Top09_GNM_4.1_127)

   b. **Adʒit=ta,*   ta-la   *ih-**ha**-p*   *e-**dʒi**-p.*
                         arrive-**NFUT**-1PL   NEG-**FUT**-1PL

   c. **Adʒit=ta,*   ta-la   *ih-ha-**p***   *e-he-**m**.*
                         arrive-NFUT-**1PL**   NEG-NFUT-**1SG**

Yet another prominent feature pertains to the restrictions on the forms of the negative auxiliary. Non-finite forms of the auxiliary (10a), as well as imperatives (10b), are banned from tags. The exclusion of non-finite forms and imperatives from tags has to do with the interrogative origin of the latter: only those verbal forms which can be used as main predicates in questions can be employed

---

2 Burykin (2004: 89) mentions instances of V-stranding tags, such as *haːram-kka esem haːr* [know-NFUT-1SG NEG-NFUT-1SG know-NEG.CVB], literally 'I know, don't I know'. As his materials mostly come from the dialects of the Pacific and Okhotsk Sea coasts, which are spoken some 2000 kilometres to the east from the Tompo region, I take this to be an instance of dialectal variation. In the dialect of Tompo, this structure is impossible.

in tags (compare the ungrammaticality of the English equivalent of (10b): *Bring me the coat, don't!*). This condition will be labelled *Question Compatibility Condition*.

(10) a. **Dʒep-tidʒi*   **e-tidʒi**   *hor-če.*
      eat-ANT.CVB   NEG-ANT.CVB   go.away-PF.PTC(3SG)
      intended meaning: 'He ate, didn't he, and (then) he left.'

  b. **Teti-w*   *umu-li*   **e-dʒi!**
      coat-ACC   bring-IMP.2SG   NEG-IMP.2SG
      intended meaning: 'Bring me the coat, won't you?' (Top09_SEV_elic1)

Finally, negative auxiliary is very often preceded by the contrastive enclitic particle *=k(k)A* (*-kk-* after vowels, *-k-* after consonants). If the tag is clause-final, the particle is attached to the final word of the anchor, the main verb (11); if it is clause-internal, the host of the particle is the word that precedes the tag (12).

(11) *Ajị-wa-n,*   *amarla*   *ič-ed-dʒi-ndi=**kke**   *e-te-ndi.*
      good-ACC-POSS.3SG   later   see-PROG-FUT-2SG=CONTR   NEG-FUT-2SG
      'That good thing, you will see it yourself later.'   (Top09_GNM_4.1_120)

(12) *Hi:=**kke**   *e-he-ndi*   *erek*   *kụŋa:-w*   *čọrda-ndị.*
      you=CONTR   NEG-NFUT-2SG   PROX   child-ACC   beat-2SG(NFUT)
      'You beat up this child, didn't you?'   (Top11_GNM_elic1)

To summarise: Even tags belong to the class of dependent tags, they have constant (negative) polarity and, at least in the Tompo dialect, consist of the negative auxiliary without a lexical complement. They are subject to two conditions, Agreement Condition and Question Compatibility Condition. More often than not, tags are immediately preceded by the enclitic particle *=k(k)A*.

3.3 Partial grammaticalisation of tags

The properties listed in the previous section qualify Even tags as rather straightforward question tags of the dependent type, i.e. as clauses which are linked to their anchor paratactically and whose dependency on the anchor is regulated by discourse linking rules. However, tags also display a number of characteristics which imply that they have lost some of the properties of independent clauses: they are, at least partially, grammaticalised.

First, tags exhibit symptoms of phonological erosion. The domain of vowel harmony in Even, as in other Tungusic languages, is the phonological word – roughly, stem and affixes plus clitics. When used in the negative construction, negative auxiliary is never subject to vowel-harmonic influences from the preceding words (13); in tags, it can optionally be harmonised with the preceding word (14). This seems to indicate that tags have acquired some properties of clitics.[3]

(13) Ọrọm   e-h-ni /*a-h-nị maː-r.
     reindeer.ACC NEG-NFUT-3SG   kill-NEG.CVB
     'He didn't slaughter the reindeer.'

(14) Ọrọm   maː-n   e-h-ni / a-h-nị.
     reindeer.ACC kill-3SG   NEG-NFUT-3SG
     'He slaughtered a reindeer, didn't he?' (Top09_ZTA_elic5)

Second, in contrast to polarity questions proper, tags don't carry the interrogative tune LHL%, which was illustrated in (5). In tagged sentences, the anchor ends with the declarative tune, L%, while the tag is usually fully deaccented and carries the flat low contour which continues the final L of the last word of the anchor. Thus, in (9), repeated here as (15), the boundary tones look as follows:

(15)   L   L%
     Adʒịt=ta,   ta-la   ịh-ha-p   e-he-p.
     truth=PTL   DIST-LOC arrive-NFUT-1PL NEG-NFUT-1PL
     'And indeed, we have arrived there, haven't we.'

A further indication of the lack of interrogative force of tags is their incompatibility with interrogative particles (cf. Section 3.1, ex. (6) and (7)). While the negative auxiliary can host the particle in proper information-seeking questions (16), it cannot do so if used as a tag (17).

---

[3] In some other dialects, the erosion process appears to have gone further than this. A speaker of the Lamunkhin dialect, spoken some 300 km to the north-west from Tompo, confirmed to me that the negative tag can optionally lose its inital vowel in this variety of Even. This usually occurs in the 3rd person sg. Non-future, so that next to the usual form *ehni* this dialect also has the eroded clitic form *=hni*.

(16) Er-eŋ-en   e-te-n=**gu**   huji   o̱:-da?
     PROX-ALN-POSS.3SG NEG-FUT-3SG=Q   wound   become-NEG.CVB
     'Won't this here cause an injury?' (Top09_GNM_4.1_228)

(17) *Tu̱kar   butun-ni   dehči-n   e-h-ni=**gu**.
     rubbish   all.Y-3SG   lie-3SG(NFUT)   NEG-NFUT-3SG=Q
     intended meaning: 'Rubbish is lying all over the place, isn't it?'
     (Top09_SEV_elic2)

Two syntactic features indicate that Even tags have idiosyncratic features which set them apart from simple negative questions. In Even non-future nominal clauses, the copula is zero if the subject is 3rd person singular (18a). If such a clause is negated, the copula must surface as the complement of the negative auxiliary (18b). This is in accordance with the observation that the complement of the auxiliary can be left out only under strict adjacency of the negative structure to its positive counterpart (ex. (4), Section 3.1): if there is no immediately adjacent positive counterpart of the negative structure, the copular complement of the auxiliary must be overt. However, if the negative auxiliary appears in a tag following a zero-copula clause, the complement is routinely left out (19), even though no overt positive antecedent is present (recall that the copula is zero). This implies that the ellipsis of the complement in tags is not subject to discourse constraints, as is the case with regular negative clauses, but is fully conventionalised.

(18) a. Ammu̱   hagdi̱   Ø.
        father.POSS.1SG   old
        'My father is old.'

     b. Ammu̱   hagdi̱   e-h-ni   **bi-h.**
        father.POSS.1SG   old   NEG-NFUT-3SG   be-NEG.CVB
        'My father is not old.' (Top09_SEV_elic2)

(19) Tar   hamŋi̱han   aji̱=kka   e-h-ni   Ø.
     DIST   fumigation good=CONTR   NEG-NFUT-3SG
     'Fumigation is good, isn't it.' (Top09_GNM_4.1_591)

The second syntactic sign of grammaticalisation is the position of tags. As we have seen above, tags can be clause-final or clause-internal (ex. (2) and (12), repeated here as (20)).

(20) Hiː=**kke**   e-he-ndi   erek   kuŋaː-w   čọrda-ndị.
      you=CONTR   NEG-NFUT-2SG   PROX   child-ACC   beat-2SG(NFUT)
      'You beat up this child, didn't you?'   (Top11_GNM_elic1)

The clause-final position is the position to be expected if the tag construction is analysed as a structure consisting of two paratactic independent clauses bound by discourse linking rules, with the tag clause following the anchor. Clause-internal tags pose a problem for this kind of biclausal analysis, since they would represent an independent clause attached to a constituent of another clause, with which it is bound via discourse linking. I see two ways out of this quandary: clause-internal tags can be analysed as parenthetical clauses, or they can be treated as non-clausal entities, a kind of grammatical marker.

I opt for the latter solution, for following reasons. First, parentheticals are regularly separated from their host sentences by prosodic breaks (Dehé 2009). This is never the case in my corpus of Tompo Even data: clause-internal tags (as well as clause-final ones) are fully integrated in the prosodic frame of the anchor. Second, if clause-internal tags were full-fledged clauses, they would have to obey the Even rules of ellipsis, which allow for zero complements of negative auxiliaries only with immediately preceding positive antecedents (see above). Parentheticals are generally considered to follow the same rules of ellipsis as other non-embedded clauses (see Dehé and Kavalova 2007 for an overview). The tag in (20) is followed by its positive counterpart, not preceded by it, and still, the complement is not expressed. Finally, all the non-clausal properties of tags listed above also apply to clause-internal tags. This renders the analysis in terms of parenthetical clause less plausible. Clause-internal tags thus do not appear to be parenthetical clauses, but rather a kind of grammatical marker, whose meaning will be discussed in the following section.

Even tags display a number of features which indicate that they are currently on the path of losing their status as independent clauses in paratactic relationship with the anchor. They are phonologically eroded (optional vowel harmony, loss of prosodic independence) and are not subject to productive syntactic constraints (obligatory ellipsis of the complement, intra-clausal insertion). They lack the defining properties of polar questions (interrogative tune, question particle). Their conventionalised structure – they are not proper questions and not proper negative structures – implies a certain degree of semantic non-compositionality. In the following section, I shall show that the meaning of tags in Even is not directly calculable from the meanings of negative questions combined with preceding assertions, as has been convincingly argued to be the case in English (Hudson 1975). Instead, tags are related to information-structural and epistemic notions.

4 Meanings of tags

4.1 Focus and tags

The first approximation on the meaning of tags is that they are somehow related to focus. They are often used in contexts which are commonly considered to be focus-sensitive. I will return to the historical connection of tags and focus in Section 6; this section deals with context types which are indicative of the focus-marking nature of tags.

One function tags can fulfil in discourse is to mark the element of the proposition whose identity the hearer should change in her discourse model. The typical context type for this is corrections. Example (21) illustrates the situation where the corrected element is the polarity of the clause. In this case, the tag is clause-final, attached to the finite verb of the anchor. In (22), it is the identity of a participant that is subject to correction. The tag is attached to the argument which denotes this participant, i.e. it is clause-internal.

(21) – *E-he-ndi go:n.* – *Go:n-e-m=ke e-he-m!*
  NEG-NFUT-2SG say.NEG.CVB say-NFUT-1SG=CONTR NEG-NFUT-1SG
  '– You didn't tell me that.' '– I DID tell you!' (Top09_GNM&GVN_note1)

(22) – *Oliki-w ma:-h.* – *Ńọŋčak-ụ=kke e-he-p ma:-ra-p.*
  squirrel-ACC kill-2PL wolf-ACC=CONTR NEG-NFUT-1PL kill-NFUT-1PL
  '– You killed a squirrel.' – 'We killed a WOLF!' (Top09_ZTA_elic2)

These sentences show that tags are used congruently: the tag has to be attached to the element of the clause which is the object of correction. Since the main assertive point of the utterance is the establishment of the correct polarity or reference, it is obvious that tags attach to the element encoding this main point – i.e., they attach to the focus.

Another context in which tags are used congruently and seem to mark focus is question-answer pairs. As in the case of corrective utterances, tags in answers must be attached to the element that is questioned in the preceding utterance. In answers to polarity questions, where the object of inquiry is the truthfulness of the whole proposition, the tag is clause-final and attached to the finite verb (23). If the identity of a participant is questioned, the answer contains a clause-internal tag adjacent to the phrase which denotes the given participant (24).

(23) – *Tara-ŋ-ị ič-endi?* – *It-te-m e-he-m.*
  DIST-ALN-POSS.REFL see-2SG(NFUT) see-NFUT-1SG NEG-NFUT-1SG
  '– Have you seen that?' '– I (obviously) HAVE.' (Top11_ZTV&ZKS_conv1)

(24) – Ḷa-w   taŋa-d-andị?
       what-ACC read-PROG-2SG(NFUT)

    – Kińiga-w **e-he-m**   taŋa-d-da-m.
      book-ACC NEG-NFUT-1SG read-PROG-NFUT-1SG
      '–What are you reading?' '– I'm reading a BOOK.'   (Top09_ZTA_elic)

Tags can also be used with broad predicate focus, in answers to questions of the type 'what is X doing'. In this case, they are placed after the anchor, i.e. they are clause-final, attached to the finite verb of the anchor (25). Note that broad focus structure is identical to polarity focus (24). This seems to indicate that tags as focus markers are able to trigger focus projection: attached to one element of a phrase, they can license focal interpretation for the whole phrase (probably to be defined as VP in (25)).

(25) – Ḷa-ndị?   – Kińiga-w taŋa-d-da-m   **e-he-m**.
       what.do-2SG(NFUT)   book-ACC read-PROG-NFUT-1SG NEG-NFUT-1SG
       '–What are you doing?' '– I'm (obviously) reading a book.'
       (Top09_ZTA_elic)

Congruent use in question-answer pairs is considered to be the key diagnostics for focus (e.g. Büring 2007: 448). Tags in Even obey the rules of congruence quite strictly: for instance, it is infelicitous to attach a tag to the predicate in an answer to a content question inquiring about the identity of one of the participants, as (24') shows.

(24') – Ḷa-w   taŋa-d-andị?
        what-ACC read-PROG-2SG(NFUT)

     – #Kińiga-w taŋa-d-da-m   **e-he-m**.
       book-ACC read-PROG-NFUT-1SG NEG-NFUT-1SG

At first blush, Even tags do seem to encode focus, as they pass two important tests for focushood (congruent use in corrective and Q-A contexts) and behave in a rather typical way with respect to focus projection. There are, however, problems with this account. First, tags are not obligatory in either of the diagnostic context types, unlike typical focus markers; second, some instances of clause-final tags seem to be only indirectly connected to information structure and carry modal meanings. I shall broach these two issues in the following two sections.

4.2 Tags as markers of uncontroversial focus

The non-obligatoriness of tags in typical focus contexts suggests that they do not mark 'focus' per se, but rather a special subtype thereof. On the basis of the evidence at hand, I shall argue that, apart from their function of marking the main assertive point of the utterance, tags encode an additional meaning. This meaning is interactional, i.e. it does not contribute to the truth value of the proposition, but gives instructions to the hearer how to process the utterance instead. Somewhat simplified, tags mark the focal part of the proposition as uncontroversial, as an established fact (see Grosz 2014 for the notion of established fact). Consider the following minimal pair:

(26) a. *Bi: hagdị bi-he-m.*
 I old be-NFUT-1SG
 'I'm old.'

 b. *Q:n ere-w umu-de-ku?*
 how PROX-ACC carry-PURP.CVB-1SG

 Bi: hagdị bi-he-m **e-he-m.**
 I old be-NFUT-1SG NEG-NFUT-1SG
 'How am I supposed to carry this? I'm old (can't you see that)!'
 (Top09_SEV_note2)

While (26a) expresses the proposition 'I am old' without any further modification, (26b), with a tag, conveys the additional information that the interlocutor should be aware of the proposition expressed, an effect the translation tries to capture. Note that the clause-final position of the tag signals that it is the predicate that this additional interactional information pertains to: it is the old age of the speaker that is to be understood as an established fact.

This is one of the major functions of tags in Tompo Even: they signal (a) that the element which is in their scope is the major point of the assertion, but also (b) that the information that it conveys is in one way or another non-controversial and obvious. More technically, tags indicate that the main point of the utterance, focus, either already is or should be a part of the common ground and that the interlocutor is expected to retrieve it in order to grasp the meaning of the message. This analysis applies to most examples adduced in this paper by now (cf. esp. (1), (11), (12) and (15)). Note that there is a tension between the two meanings tags encode: on the one hand, focus is supposed to convey an update to the common ground, new information, as it were; on the other hand, this information is marked as an established, non-controversial and given fact. This tension is resolved through different pragmatically derived interpretations, depending on the context. In (26b), the combination of focus and obviousness results in a reproach. This is not necessarily so. Consider once again example (15), repeated here for convenience as (27):

(27) Adʒit=ta,   ta-la   ịh-ha-p   **e-he-p.**
     truth=PTL   DIST-LOC   arrive-NFUT-1PL   NEG-NFUT-1PL
     'And indeed, we have arrived there, haven't we.'

This sentence occurs in the narrator's story about her grandfather, who was a shaman and able to predict the future. He had prophesied that people will stop working with their hands and that everything will be done by pressing buttons. At this point in the story, the narrator looks at my laptop, turns to me and pronounces (27), which in effect says that we have reached the stage of pressing buttons. The sentence has a clear polarity focus (... *we* HAVE *reached that stage...*), which is expressed with the clause-final tag. At the same time, the information is marked as an obvious fact that is already shared by the interlocutors: we both know that people nowadays spend their time pressing buttons, and the laptop on the table is a vivid proof of that. What comes out as interpretation is not a reproach, as in (26b), but rather an instruction to the hearer to retrieve his own world knowledge and see for himself that the prophesied situation has indeed occurred.

The same interpretive procedure applies to clause-internal tags, i.e. those that do not take the predicate or the polarity into their scope, but indicate that the main point of the utterance is the identification of the reference of an argument or adjunct in the anchor clause.

(28) Deweŋŋit-u   **e-h-ni**   tarakam   dʒep-pe:t-te-n.
     mushroom-ACC   NEG-NFUT-3SG   then   eat-GNR-NFUT-3SG
     'It was mushrooms they used to eat at that time.'
     (Top09_PSF&AGA_conv_288)

The segment of the conversation from which (28) is taken is about the ways people used to graze reindeer in ancient days. One interlocutor, AGA, cannot remember what the main food in late summer was, and the other, PSF, reminds her with this sentence. The focus is obviously on the direct object, *deweŋŋitu*, which is marked with the tag. Since this is a piece of information both speakers should be aware of after having spent their lives living with reindeer, its status as an established fact is also conveyed by the tag. The effect is that of wondering how AGA could forget such a basic thing.

These examples illustrate one important interactional feature of tags.[4] Even tags do not seem to imply that both interlocutors have direct access to the uncontroversial proposition at the utterance time, i.e. they are underspecified as to the current state of consciousness of the interlocutors. The fact that the proposition is an established fact means that the interlocutors either share it or that it is so obvious that they *should* share it. Thus, the use of tags is compatible both with situations in which both interlocutors have a direct access to the uncontroversial proposition and with those in which one of them appears to be unaware of it. The former case is nicely illustrated with (27): both the informant and the interviewer are immediately aware of the fact that the humanity has reached the stage of pressing buttons. The latter type of situation, in which one of the interlocutors seems to be currently unaware of the obvious proposition, is exemplified with (26b) and (28). It is an obvious fact that the speaker is old, but the interlocutor acts is if he didn't know this (26b); it is well known that reindeer eat mushrooms in summer, but the interlocutor has forgotten it (28). This underspecification as to the current state of mind of the interlocutor sets Even tags apart from some other languages, in which uncontroversiality markers make a clear difference between these two types of situations (the best known example is certainly the German particles *ja* and *doch*, cf. Grosz 2014).

The function of tags is thus to mark an element of the proposition as the main assertive point which is non-controversial, because it is assumed to be a given fact established as such independently of the utterance and irrespective of the current state of mind of the interlocutors. They can single out a non-verbal element of the sentence (clause-internal type), its polarity, or they can have a broad scope over the predicate (clause-final type). The semantics of tags can be formalised as follows:

(29) a. *tag*(x), where x is an element filling a slot in the propositional function P, asserts that x is the correct filler of the slot in the presupposed propositional function in the given context (focus).

b. *tag*(x) presupposes that P(x) is uncontroversial, i.e. that ¬P(x) can be discarded in the given context, irrespective of the current state of consciousness of the interlocutor (non-controversiality).

4.3 Epistemic uses of tags

Some rare instances of tags (8 in a corpus of roughly 50,000 words) deviate semantically from the definition given in (29). Instead of uncontroversiality,

---

4 Thanks are due to an anonymous reviewer for drawing my attention to this point.

they seem to encode a kind of epistemic modality. Here are two characteristic examples.

(30) *Erek   ewihken   **e-h-ni**,   gerbe-we-n*
     PROX   toy   NEG-NFUT-3SG   name-ACC-POSS.3SG
     e-he-m   ha:-r (...)
     NEG-NFUT-1SG   know-NEG.CVB
     'This is probably a toy, I don't know what it's called'
     (Top07_GIG_Stative_24)

(31) *Tar   ṅṵːčị-dị-č   goː-mi,   tar,   ọːn   goː-weːt-te*
     dist Russian-ADJ-INS   say-COND.CVB   DIST   how   say-GNR-NFUT(3PL)
     *ṅṵːčị-l,   'čort',   ịak,   goː-weːt-te   **e-s-ten**.*
     Russian-PL   devil.R   what   say-GNR-NFUT(3PL)   NEG-NFUT-3PL
     'To say it in Russian, uhm, how do the Russians say it, 'čort (devil)',
     or something, probably that's what they say'.   (Top07_BEN_story_155)

Examples of this type are invariably interpreted as expressing uncertainty on the part of the speaker about the content of the proposition: the speaker judges his state of knowledge on the basis of which he expresses the assertion insufficient to make a definite claim. The meaning of this type of tag – let's call it *epistemic tag* – is quite different from that of the dominant, *uncontroversial tag* type, described in the previous section: it expresses epistemic uncertainty, as opposed to the dominant tag type, which encodes assumed shared knowledge.

Epistemic tags differ from uncontroversial tags in their distribution: while the latter can be both clause-final and clause-internal, the former are possible only in the clause-final position. Speakers consistently reject epistemic interpretations for clause-internal tags. Furthermore, at least in my corpus, epistemic tags are less prosodically reduced, never display vowel harmony and are never preceded by the particle *=k(k)E*. Even though the evidence is not conclusive (in part due to impossibility of eliciting information on prosodic reduction and vowel harmony), I take this to indicate that epistemic tags are a different species to uncontroversiality tags. Given the lack of conventionalisation symptoms they display, I assume that they are a non-grammaticalised counterpart of the grammaticalised uncontroversiality tags. In other words, Tompo Even has two diachronic stages of the same construction, and these differ both in form and meaning. Interestingly, my field data from the Bystraja dialect of Even, spoken in central Kamchatka, some 2000 kilometres to the east from the Tompo region, show that this dialect only has the epistemic tag. The uncontroversial type, with it combined focus-marking and interactional function, does not occur in natural discourse and is rejected by the speakers. The important issue from the viewpoint of this paper is that epistemic tags, both in Tompo and Bystraja dialects, are not related to information structure: they invariably scope over the whole proposition and cannot mark focus. In Section 6, I will attempt to explain how two disparate types of meanings and structures have developed in Even. For the time being, suffice it to say that both types represent separate developments of two basic types of meanings conveyed by tags across languages, the information-seeking type (epistemic tags) and the positively biased type (uncontroversiality tags).

The important tenets of this section are that there are two types of tags in Tompo Even. The dominant one, uncontroversiality tags, marks foci which are assumed to be already present in the common ground between the interlocutors. The minor type, epistemic tags, is not focus-sensitive and encodes the epistemic stance of the speaker.

5 Diachronic status and emergent developments

As mentioned in the Section 1, it is commonly assumed that the major source of focus morphology is cleft structures. The diachronic path leading from a cleft to a focus morpheme is the gradual relaxation of clause boundaries between the main clause and the relative clause in a cleft, leading ultimately to clause fusion. Harris & Campbell (1995: 166) postulate the following stages of the clause fusion:

> *Stage I*: The structure has all the superficial characteristics of a biclausal structure and none of the characteristics of a monoclausal one.
>
> *Stage II:* The structure gradually acquires some characteristics of a biclausal structure and retains some characteristics of a monoclausal one.
>
> *Stage III*: The structure has all of the characteristics of a monoclausal structure and no characteristics of a biclausal one.

Due to scarcity of data from Tompo Even, epistemic tags are difficult to locate in this scheme. The general impression is that they are closer to Stage I than to Stage II, but this is far from certain. The actual object of this study, uncontroversiality tags with focus interpretation, seem to be at Stage II. The standard type of uncontroversial tag, which has been described by now, still has a number of clausal properties, most importantly the variable person, number, tense and mood features, which co-vary with the features of the anchor clause. It also displays some symptoms of gradual loss of clausal features, as has been shown in Section 3.3. These newly acquired features – phonological weakening, automatic drop of the complement of the negative auxiliary and positional freedom – mostly belong to the so-called *behavioural properties*, i.e. those properties which have no direct reflex in the morphological build-up of the structure (see e.g. Keenan 1976; Croft 2003; Haspelmath 2010 on this notion). The received wisdom at least since Cole et al. (1980) is that these kinds of properties precede the so-called *coding properties*, i.e. those which are reflected in inflexional morphology. We have not seen any changes in the coding properties of tags. Tags in Tompo Even thus seem to be in a transitional stage between a proper question tag and a focus-marking inflexional morpheme.

The change towards the latter is still in progress, however, and tags are currently in the middle of the process of acquiring new coding properties. I shall argue that this process is triggered by the tension between their focus-marking function and the limitations inherited from their clausal past.

Recall that tags are restricted by two syntactic conditions, the Agreement Condition and the Question Compatibility Condition (Section 2.2). The Agreement Condition requires that the agreement, tense and mood features of the tag match those of the anchor; the Question Compatibility Condition excludes all verb forms that are illicit as predicates of independent questions from tags, viz. non-finite forms and imperatives. Both of these conditions reflect the fact that tags were once full-fledged clauses. If a tag clause is to refer to the same proposition as the anchor, it must have the same person and TAM features as the anchor; if it is an interrogative clause, then only those verb forms which are fine as predicates of questions can appear in it.

On the other hand, tags have acquired new expressive possibilities through their positional freedom. They can mark broad and narrow focus domains by being attached to the appropriate expression in the clause – broad focus and polarity focus by adjacency to the verb, narrow term focus by adjacency to any other element of the clause.

There is an obvious conflict between the historically anchored restrictions (Agreement and Question Compatibility Conditions) and the synchronic focus-marking function. There is no way to focus elements of directive clauses and of subordinate predications expressed with non-finite verb forms, since the tag has to agree with the predicate of the anchor, but it cannot be an imperative or a non-finite form (cf. ex. (10a–b), repeated here as (32a–b) in a slightly modified form).

(32) a. **Dʒep-tidʒi* **e-tidʒi**   *hor-če.*
       eat-ANT.CVB neg-ANT.CVB go.away-PF.PTC(3SG)
       intended meaning: 'It was only after he ATE that he left.'

   b. **Teti-w*   **e-dʒi**   *umu-li!*
      coat-ACC   NEG-IMP.2SG   bring-IMP.2SG
      intended meaning: 'Bring me the COAT!'

In its current stage, Tompo Even has two solutions to this problem. First, the Agreement Condition can be relaxed: instead of the ungrammatical non-finite/imperative form of the negative auxiliary, one uses its finite form which has a similar temporal reference to the non-finite form/imperative that functions as the main predicate. For example, in (33), focus is on *dʒulehki* 'in future', which is an element of a subordinate clause headed by a non-finite future-participle form *binnewutnen*, 'in order for them to be'. On strict application of the Agreement Condition, it would be impossible to focus this element with a tag, since the tag would have to be a non-finite, participial form. With a relaxed Agreement Condition, it is enough if the tag has a similar tense reference as the main verb. In this case, it is the Future tense, which is the closest finite equivalent of the future participle.

(33) *Nǫŋǫrtan dʒulehki* **e-te-n**   *ajị-č*   **bi-nne-wu-tnen**
     they   in.future NEG-FUT-3SG good-INST be-FUT.PTC-ACC-POSS.3PL
     goːmi gịːdak (…)   *dʒụgǫh-rịdʒi*   *nǫŋ-ńụn-tan* (…)
     so.that Siberian.crane spend.summer-ANT.CVB they-COM-POSS.3PL
     'The cranes (…) spend the summer with them so that they could be prosperous in the FUTURE.' (Top09_GNM_4.1_032)

The same applies to focusing via tags in directive clauses: the approximately congruent form of the tag is usually one of the Future tense, as shown in (34). Incidentally, this solution is similar to the one found in English with imperative clauses, such as: *Open the window, won't you?*.

(34) *Teti-w*   **e-te-ndi**   *umu-li.*
     coat-ACC NEG-FUT-2SG   bring-IMP.2SG
     'Bring me the COAT!/It is the coat you should bring me.' (Top11_ZTA_elic)

The second way out of the dilemma is to turn the tag into an invariable form. One occasionally finds tokens of tags in which the tag has completely lost its dependent nature, viz. those in which the Agreement Condition has been abandoned altogether. The tag is insensitive to TAM and person features of the main verb and always appears in the unmarked form, 3rd person singular Non-future, *ehni*, sometimes assimilated to *enni* (a phenomenon which bears remarkable similarity to the southern British English reduction of the question tag to the invariable form *innit*, as described in Krug 1998). This option is relatively rarely made use of in Tompo Even (3 instances), but my elicitation data show that it can occur in all positions in which standard uncontroversiality tags occur.[5]

(35) Rọvnọ   badʒịkar   **e-n-ni**   (…) em-gere-če-l.
     straight.R   in.morning   NEG-NFUT-3SG   come-HAB-PF.PTC(3)-PL
     'Of course, they used to come right in the MORNING.'
     (Top07_NIN_story1_02)

The standard uncontroversiality tag is thus still in Stage II on Harris & Campbell's scale, showing both clausal and non-clausal features, the latter being mostly of the behavioural kind. In certain types of contexts, coding properties of the tag have begun to change towards a *bona fide* grammatical morpheme, bringing this construction closer to Stage III on the grammaticalisation scale. Given that Tompo Even also has the non-grammaticalised epistemic tag, this dialect turns out to currently host three historical stages of one construction.

6 Tag questions and information structure

An issue which needs separate explanation is the question of semantic shift from question to focus marker and epistemic modifier. This topic is best introduced by looking into the relationship between evidential and uncontroversiality tags. Synchronically, they obviously do not have much in common. Diachronically, they represent separate developments of two frequent uses of question tags across languages. There has been a lot of discussion on the functions of tags in the literature, with different authors coming up with no less than a dozen discrete functions (see Tottie & Hoffmann 2006 for an overview). I assume, following Hudson (1975), that this diversity can be reduced to two basic

---

[5] The Lamunkhin dialect of Even (cf. footnote 3), seems to use the invariable variant (*ehni* or =*hni*) much more often, according to my informant Raisa P. Kuz'mina. The Bystraja dialect of Kamchatka, which does not have uncontroversiality tags, does not seem to have the invariant tag either (no attestations in my corpus), which is in accordance with the hypothesis that only the uncontroversiality tag, but no the epistemic tag, is a grammaticalised structure.

types: the information-seeking and the positively biased type (Hudson's term is *positively conducive*). All tagged sentences require pragmatic enrichment before they are interpreted, since they convey two contradictory speech acts in one, first an assertion, then a question, the former entailing knowledge and belief, the latter lack thereof. The meaning of the tagged sentence is computed by applying pragmatics to reach a satisfactory interpretation of this apparent inconsistency. The question can cancel the truth-committing effect of the assertion: the tag is understood as a signal that the assertion just made is based on insufficient knowledge, so that the speaker is asking for confirmation or rejection of what has been said. In this case, the tag is of the information-seeking type. The other interpretive possibility functions the other way around, with the assertion cancelling the information-seeking effect of the question. The speaker treats the assertion as valid. The question, requiring from the hearer to consider whether the assertion is valid, must therefore be treated as a rhetorical question. In this way, it comes to implicate that the hearer knows that the assertion is valid, too – the tag is positively biased.

It has become clear by now that the two basic types of the relationship between assertion and tag question have most probably served as separate sources for the two types of tags in Tompo Even: the information-seeking type has developed into the epistemic tag, while uncontroversiality tags have evolved from the positively biased kind. The former has remained a question tag, while the latter has become grammaticalised as an idiosyncratic focus marker.

While the path from a positively biased tag to the general marker of uncontroversiality is rather straightforward, the emergence of the focus-marking function may appear enigmatic at first sight. Recall, however, that the basic function of positively biased tags is to reassert the principle assertion. Thus, if one says *I told you so, didn't I?*, the question tag is there to reinforce the truthfulness (and the common ground status) of the asserted proposition. Assertions regularly contain one element which represents the main point, what the speaker wants to go on record as having said and what is supposed to be added to the stock of information shared by the interlocutors: focus. If the purpose of tags is to reinforce the assertion expressed by the anchor, then they are, at least at the level of interpretation, focus-sensitive. In order to reinforce an assertion, they must reinforce its carrier, the focus of the utterance. Thus, in *I lent YOU a book, didn't I?*, the tag reasserts that that identity of the receiver of the book is 'you', while in *I LENT you a book, didn't I?*, it reinforces the contention of the speaker that the action performed with the book is lending (as opposed to, say, giving for good). The step from this type of focus sensitivity to overt focus marking is not a difficult one. I assume that in Even, the transition from a full tag to focus marker was facilitated, or even made possible in the first place, by the tags' acquisition of positional flexibility. Once it was possible for them to immediately follow that element of the clause whose main-point status they are supposed to reassert, they were able to unequivocally mark that element as the main assertive point, and that's what focus marking is all about. When this functional shift was completed, the formal changes described in the previous sections have further contributed to the obfuscation of the previous clausal nature of the tag, so that it is, as we have seen, on the way to become a kind of focus morpheme. The final stage of that development could be the vowel harmonic invariant tag *ehni/ahnį*, or some weakened form thereof.

7 Summary and a note on the meaning of focus

I aim to have shown that question tags can be a source of morphological focus markers and that the diachronic path in this development is similar to that of the standard source of focus morphemes, cleft sentences. An originally biclausal structure can turn into a single clause through mechanisms of clause fusion. In the initial phases of the fusion, the behavioural properties of the construction are changed, to be succeeded by changes in the coding properties. The historical developments in Tompo Even have resulted in three types of tags: (a) epistemic tags, which are hardly grammaticalised, (b) standard uncontroversiality tags, which have acquired a new function – focus marking – and new behavioural properties, and (c) innovative uncontroversiality tags, which have changed their coding properties in addition to the changes of the standard tags. The simultaneous existence of different diachronic stages comes as no surprise in view of the gradual nature of linguistic change.

The intimate connection of question tags and assertion represents the deeper motivation behind this chain of diachronic transformations. The tag chooses the element of the anchor which carries the main assertive point and reasserts this point. This amounts to focus sensitivity, which can easily be transformed into focus marking. Given the naturalness of this path, it would be surprising if Even were the only language which has grammaticalised its question tags in this way. I am aware of two potential parallels. First, the closest relative of Even, Evenki, seems to have a similar construction, at least in some of its dialects (A. Lavrillier, p.c.). Second, in at least some of the southern dialects of British English, structures of the type *George innit told you that* seem to occasionally occur (Anderson 2001: 133). Of course, further research is needed to confirm these parallels.

I would like to conclude this chapter with a short note on the nature of focus marked by tags. If the analysis presented in Section 4 is correct, then Tompo Even has a highly idiosyncratic semantic category, in which the locus of information update ('focus') is at the same time a given, uncontroversial information. In recent literature (Matić & Wedgwood 2013), it has been argued that 'focus' is rather a type of interpretation than a grammatical category in the narrow sense of the word, an interpretation which can be arrived at through a potentially unlimited number of grammatical means. Thus, panoply of peculiar focus-like entities has been identified, including such categories as evidential focus markers, realis-mood focus morphemes, foci that are encoded as comparatives, etc. The Tompo Even tags can be considered an addition to this list of idiosyncratic focus-like categories. In the ultimate analysis, the meaning of this construction is a product of the grammaticalisation of interrogative clauses attached to different elements of the matrix clause. By conventionalising one pragmatic interpretation of these embedded questions, the positively biased interpretation, and by their ability to take different scopes, they have been re-interpreted as a highlighting device. The outcome of this is their focus-like interpretation. Even tags-as-focus are thus yet another indication of the interpretive nature of information structural categories.

Abbreviations

ACC – accusative; ADJ – adjecitivizer; ALN – alienable; ANT – anterior; COM – comitative; COND – conditional; CONTR – contrastive; CVB – converb; DIST – distal; FUT – future; GNR – general (aspect); HAB – habitual; IMP – imperative; INST – instrumental; INTJ – interjection; LOC – locative; NEG – negative; NFUT – non-future; PF – perfective; PL – plural; POSS – possessive; PROG – progressive; PROX – proximative; PST – past; PTC – participle; PTL – particle; PURP – purposive; Q – question; R – Russian (loan); REFL – reflexive; SG – singular; Y – Yakut (loan)

References

Anderson, Gisle. 2001. *Pragmatic markers and sociolinguistic variation*. Amsterdam: Benjamins.
Axelsson, Karin. 2011. A cross-linguistic study of grammatically dependent question tags. *Studies in Language* 35. 793–851.
Büring, Daniel. 2007. Intonation, semantics and information structure. In Gillian Ramchand & Charles Reiss (eds.), *The Oxford handbook of linguistic interfaces*, 445–473. Oxford: Oxford University Press.

Burykin, Aleksej A. 2004. *Jazyk maločislennogo naroda v ego pis'mennoj forme (na materiale evenskogo jazyka)* [A language of a small people in its written form (on the basis of the material from the Even language)]. St-Peterburg: Peterburgskoe Vostokovedenie.
Cole, Peter, Wayne Harbert, Gabriella Hermon & Shikaripur N. Sridhar. 1980. The acquisition of subjecthood. *Language* 56. 719–743.
Croft, William. 2003. *Typology and universals*, 2nd edn. Cambridge: Cambridge University Press.
Culicover, Peter. 1992. English tag questions in Universal Grammar. *Lingua* 88. 193–226.
Dehé, Nicole. 2009. Clausal parentheticals, intonational phrasing, and prosodic theory. *Journal of Linguistics* 45. 569–615.
Dehé, Nicole & Yordanka Kavalova. 2007. Parentheticals: An introduction. In Nicole Dehé & Yordanka Kavalova (eds.), *Parentheticals*, 1–22. Amsterdam: Benjamins.
Grosz, Patrick. 2014. German *doch*: An element that triggers a contrast presupposition. In *Proceedings of Chicago Linguistic Society 46*. 163–177. Chicago: University of Chicago.
Harris, Alice & Lyle Campbell. 1995. *Historical syntax in cross-linguistic perspective*. Cambridge: Cambridge University Press.
Haspelmath, Martin. 2010. The behaviour-before-coding principle in syntactic change. In Franck Floricic (ed.), *Essais de typologie et de linguistique générale: Mélanges offerts à Denis Creissels*, 493–506. Lyon: ENS Éditions.
Heine, Berndt & Tania Kuteva. 2002. *The world lexicon of grammaticalization*. Cambridge: Cambridge University Press.
Hudson, Richard A. 1975. The meaning of questions. *Language* 51. 1–31.
Keenan, Edward. 1976. Towards a universal definition of 'subject'. In Charles N. Li (ed.), *Subject and topic*, 303–333. New York: Academic Press.
Krug, Manfred. 1998. British English is developing a new discourse marker, innit? *Arbeiten aus Anglistik und Amerikanistik* 23. 145–197.
Matić, Dejan & Daniel Wedgwood. 2013. The meanings of focus. The significance of an interpretation-based category in cross-linguistic analysis. *Journal of Linguistics* 49. 127–163.
Novikova, Klavdija A. 1960–1980. *Očerki dialektov evenskogo jazyka: Ol'skij govor* [Grammatical sketches of the dialects of the Even language: The Ola dialect], Vols. 1–2. Leningrad: Nauka.
Mal'čukov, Andrej L. 1999. *Struktura prostogo predloženija v evenskom jazyke* [The structure of the simple sentence in the Even language]. St-Petersburg: Nauka.
Mal'čukov, Andrej L. 2008. *Sintaksis evenskogo jazyka* [The syntax of the Even language]. St-Petersburg: Nauka.
Sailor, Craig. 2010. VP ellipsis and tag questions: A typological approach. Paper presented at CLS 46. http://cwsailor.bol.ucla.edu/ (accessed 20. October 2013)
Tottie, Gunnel & Sebastian Hoffmann. 2006. Tag questions in British and American English. *Journal of English Linguistics* 34. 283–311.

Victor Junnan Pan
9 Syntactic and Prosodic Marking of Contrastiveness in Spoken Chinese[1]

Abstract: This paper discusses the division of labor between the syntactic and the prosodic marking of Information Structures in spoken Mandarin Chinese. Following the idea that "contrastiveness" should be kept as an independent component in the system of Information Structure (Lambrecht 1994, Erteschik-Shir 2007), the goal of this paper is to show that different informational components are marked by different linguistic ways in Mandarin: topics and foci are only marked by syntax; contrastive elements can be marked either by syntax or by prosody. However, in spoken Chinese, it is much more frequent to mark a contrastive element by word-stress. In this study, I will argue that prosody behaves as a last resort to mark contrastiveness in Chinese. When syntax fails to mark a contrastive element (topic or focus), the prosodic marking is activated by the computational system as a "repair device" in the sense of Reinhart (2006).

1 Information structure in Mandarin Chinese

1.1 Topic and focus structures in Mandarin

Mandarin Chinese is known as a topic prominent language (Chao 1968, Li & Thompson 1981). Much work has been done on the syntax and semantics of the different types of topic and focus structures in Chinese (Tsao 1979, Huang 1982, Xu & Langendoen 1985, Paul 2002, von Prince 2012, Shyu 2013). The sentence initial position is not necessarily occupied by the grammatical subject or by the logical subject of the whole sentence; instead, such a position can host

---

[1] I would like to thank Professor M.M. Jocelyne Fernandez-Vest for providing me with the occasion to present a preliminary version of this article in her doctoral seminar in 2013 and for her insightful suggestion and questions. The article has also benefited from the discussion with the audience after the talk. I likewise want to express my gratitude for the support from Professor Robert Van Valin as one of the editors of this volume. The valuable suggestions from the anonymous reviewers helped me to shape the final version of this paper. Any remaining errors and shortcomings are mine.

Victor Junnan Pan, Université Paris Diderot-Paris 7 & CNRS-LLF (UMR 7110)

a nominal phrase (1a,b), an adverbial phrase (1b), a verbal phrase (1c), or a prepositional phrase (1d), all of which are considered as topics of the relevant sentences. It is worthwhile to notice that there is not necessarily a comma or an intonational pause between these sentence initial elements and the real subjects.

(1) a. [[Top Zhe-jia yinhang] [Comment [Subj. xinyu]   bucuo]][2].
        this-Cl bank   reputation not-bad
   '(As for) this bank, (its) reputation is good.'

  b. [[Top Na   ji   nian] [Comment [Subj. shengyi] bu hao zuo]].
       those several years   business not easy do
   '(During) those years, it was not easy to do business.'

  c. [[Top Changge] [Comment [Subj. ta]   juedui   mei wenti]].
       sing   3SG absolutely Neg. problem
   '(As for) sing(ing), she has no problem.'

  d. [[Top Woshi   li] [Comment [Subj. kongqi] bu   liutong]].
       bedroom in   air   Neg. circulate
   'In the bedroom, there is no fresh air.'

Each of the topics illustrated in (1) is syntactically considered as a 'base-generated' topic. These topics are generated in a rather fixed syntactic position in the sentence, that is to say, the position immediately before the subject. There is no relevant syntactic derivation that is involved in the topic structure.

On the other hand, a topic can be derived by movement/extraction as well. For instance, in (2a), the NP *the syntax class* is base-generated in the direct object position of the verb *teach* in the original sentence and it moves to the sentence initial topic position. After this movement, the topicalized element *the syntax class*$_j$ leaves a trace that shares the same index, noted as t_j. One reasonable question is how we know that the topic in this case must be extracted from the inside the sentence instead of base-generating in the sentence initial topic position? As a matter of fact, this type of movement is not without any constraint. One classical test is based on the locality constraint on this type of movement which is called 'island constraint' (Ross 1967). Concretely, a topicalized element cannot be extracted out of certain subordinate clauses that are

---

[2] The abbreviation used in this paper are glossed as follows: Cl: classifier; DE: the structural particle placed between an NP and its determiner; Exp: experiential aspect; FocP: focus phrase; Neg: negative element; Perf: perfective aspect marker; subj.: subject; TM: Topic Marker; TopP: topic phrase; TP: tense projection.

called 'islands'. (2b) illustrates a typical strong island constructed by a relative clause headed by a complex NP. If we try to extract the subject of this relative clause, *Shakespeare*, to the topic position, the sentence becomes ungrammatical. (2b) is thus viewed as a proof to show that topicalization is essentially derived by movement. Another independent argument that supports the topic status of the fronted elements is that they can be optionally marked by the so-called Topic Markers (TM) in Mandarin, which is shown in (2c). In natural conversation, those topic markers are frequently used and there is always a short pause between those markers and the comment part.

(2) a. [Top Jufaxue de ke]$_j$, [Comment [Subj. wo] mei nian dou jiao t$_j$].
      syntax DE course   1SG every year all teach
   (Lit.) 'As for the syntax class$_j$, I teach (it$_j$) every year.'

   b. *[Top Shashibiya]$_j$, [Comment [Subj. wo] zui xihuan [[t$_j$ xie] de shu].
         Shakespeare   I most like   write DE book
   (intended) ('As for Shakespeare$_j$, I like the books that [(he$_j$) wrote] most.')

   c. [Top [Zhe-ben cidian]$_j$ (ne / a / ba)], [Comment [Subj. wo] jingchang yong t$_j$].
         this-Cl dictionary TM   1SG usually use
   'As for this dictionary$_j$, I use (it$_j$) quite often.'

There are internal topics in Chinese as well. In (3), *Dutch*, which originates in the direct object position, undergoes topicalization to the post-subject preverbal position, which is considered as an internal topic position (Tsao 1979, Paul 2002, Pan 2011a).

(3) [[Subj. wo] [[Top helanyu]$_j$ conglai mei xue-guo   t$_j$]].
         1SG   Dutch   never   not learn-Exp.
   'As for Dutch, I never learnt.'

So far we have introduced two typical ways to form a topic structure in Mandarin: base-generation and movement, both of which are considered as syntactic ways.

Foci in Mandarin are always marked in the sense that special structures are employed to focalize an element in a sentence. Many of the previous studies (Teng 1979, Paris 1979, Paul 2008, Cheng 2008) present and analyze these different focus structures in great detail; for the sake of space, I only give one example for each type of those structures. The *shi* ...*de* construction is taken to be the cleft sentence in Mandarin. In (4a), *shi* 'be' is placed in front of the temporal adverbial phrase *last year*; *de*, as a complementizer, is placed at the sentence final position. In this case, the focus element *last year* stays in-situ without moving anywhere. The focus is realized by means of syntax and no special prosodic form is needed. (4b) illustrates the bare *shi* 'be' focalization structure, in which the presence of the complementizer *de* is not necessary, and *shi* focalizes the subject *I*. The bare *shi* 'be' can also mark the whole sentence as a focus (cf. 4c) and it is paraphrased as 'it is really the case that/ it is true that...' in this case.

(4) a. Wo *shi* [Focus qunian] qu faguo de.
        1SG be   last-year go France DE
        'It was last year that I went to France.'

  b. *Shi* [Focus wo] bu   xiang qu kan zhe-bu dianying.
        be   1SG Neg.   want   go see this-Cl movie
        'It is I that don't want to see this movie.'

  c. *Shi* [Focus xia yu le], bu   pian ni.   (Lü 2000)
        be   fall rain PART Neg. trick 2SG
        'It is really the case that it is raining now, and I am not kidding.'

Another focalization structure involves the movement of the focalized element to the sentence initial position. The fronted element is marked by the focus marker *shi* 'be'. This fronting process leaves a trace in the original site. However, this type of focalization is derived by extraction and therefore, it must obey several syntactic and semantic constraints. One of them, discussed in Pan (2011b, 2014), is that the extraction of a direct object out of an episodic eventuality context is illicit, which means that the direct object of an action verb can hardly undergo this fronting focalization movement, as shown in (5b,c). The main action verbs *zhaodao-le* 'have found sth.' and *qu-guo-le* 'have been in somewhere' create episodic eventuality predicates (Zhang 2002). The extraction of the object out of those contexts makes the relevant sentences ungrammatical.

(5) a. *Shi* [Focus ni-de yizhuo]$_j$, [gongsi de laoban bu   xihuan t$_j$].
        be   your   clothing   company of boss   Neg like
        'It is your way of dressing that the boss of the company doesn't like.'

  b. **Shi* [Focus ni-de gou]$_j$, [wo zai gongyuanli zhaodao-le t$_j$].
        be   your   dog   1SG at   park-in   find-Perf
        ('It was your dog that I found in the park.')

  c. **Shi* [Focus Faguo]$_j$, [wo qunian   qu-guo-le   t$_j$].
        be   France   1SG last-year go-Exp-Perf
        ('It was France that I visited last year.')

Contrary to the *shi* 'be' marked fronting focalization structure, topicalization is not subject to this constraint. (6 a,b) are the topic structure versions of (5b,c). The extraction of the relevant direct objects to the sentence initial topic position does not render the sentences ungrammatical and the extracted elements can also be marked optionally by the topic markers.

(6) a. [Top [Ni-de gou]ⱼ (*ne*)], [wo zai gongyuanli zhaodao-le tⱼ].
        your dog TM 1SG at park-in   find-Perf
    'As for your dog, I found (*it*) in the park.'

   b. [Top [Faguo]ⱼ (*a*)], [wo qunian qu-guo-le   tⱼ].
        France TM 1SG last-yea go-Exp-Perf
    'As for France, I went (*there*) last year.'

The episodic eventuality constraint is thus a crucial diagnostic test that is able to make a clear distinction between a focus and a topic structure when the fronting process is involved.

A *shi* 'be' marked sentence initial focus can be base-generated as well. In (7), *jiao-hao* 'cry "bravo" ' is a true intransitive verb that cannot take any object at all. Therefore, *Mary's performance* cannot be extracted from the comment part of the sentence but must be base-generated in the sentence initial focus position.

(7) *Shi* [Focus Mali de biaoyan], [dajia   zuotian dou jiao-hao].
    be   Mary DE performance everyone yesterday all cry-good
    (Lit.) 'It was (to) Mary's performance that everyone said "bravo!" yesterday.'

An important point in the information structure in Chinese is that a topic or a focus is not marked by prosody. As I will show in Section 2, prosody is used to mark contrastiveness. Therefore, an element that is marked by prosody can be either a topic or a focus. The topic status is determined by either syntactic position (i.e. sentence initial Topic position) or syntactic marking (i.e. topic markers), and the focus status is determined by the relevant syntactic structures that mark it, such as *shi* 'be'...*de*, bare *shi* 'be' and etc.

Table 1: Syntactic marking of topics and foci in Mandarin

	Topics (non contrastive)		Foci (non contrastive)	
	By movement	Base-generation	By movement	Base-generation
Syntactic marking	yes (2, 6)	yes (1)	yes (5)	yes (4, 7)
Prosodic marking	no	no	no	no

1.2 *Wh*-topics and *wh*-foci in Spoken Chinese

Chinese is known as a *wh*-in-situ language, in the sense that in order to form a *wh*-question, the relevant *wh*-phrase stays in-situ (i.e. stays in its original position where its declarative counterpart would stay) instead of moving to the sentence initial scope position.³ However, previous studies show that there are cases where the relevant *wh*-phrases can be fronted to the sentence initial position. Pan (2012a, 2014) shows four basic types of *wh*-ex-situ.⁴ Especially, these four types of *wh*-ex-situ cases are rather productive in spoken Chinese. In this section, I will show how those four types of *wh*-topics and *wh*-foci interact with contrastiveness in Mandarin.

Type I: extracted *wh*-topic (the gap is created by movement)

(8) [TopP Na-yi-bu   dianying, [TP Zhangsan zui bu xihuan kan __]] ?
         which-one-Cl film   Zhangsan most Neg like   see
    'Which movie (is the one that) Zhangsan doesn't like at all?'

The sentence initial element *na-yi-bu dianying* 'which one of those movies' is extracted from the TP and the structure is derived by movement. Many scholars, such as Tang (1988), Wu (1999) and Pan (2011a,b), argue that Type I is not ordinary *wh*-movement. Wu's crucial test is based on the scope-ambiguity. In English, topicalization of the existential quantifier phrase *someone* in (9) can resolve the 'scope ambiguity'; however, *wh*-movement cannot, as shown in (10).

(9) a. Everyone saw someone.
        i) 'Everyone saw a different person.'   (∃ > ∀)
        ii) 'Everyone saw exactly the same person.' (∀ > ∃)

     b. Someone$_i$, everyone saw t$_i$.   *Topicalization*
        i) *'Everyone saw a different person.'   (*∃ > ∀)
        ii) 'Everyone saw exactly the same person.' (∀ > ∃)

---

3 In *wh*-movement languages like English, *wh*-phrases raise to the sentence initial position, CP, which is considered, in the generative framework, as a scope position (the highest position in the sentence). The *wh*-phrase is thus treated as quantifier that raises to the scope position to get its interrogative force in order to be interpreted properly at Logical Form.

4 Adopting the cartographic approach in the generative framework (Rizzi 1997), topics and foci are situated in distinct projections, TopP and FocP, in the left periphery. I will keep the syntactic representation of the original authors in this paper. 'TP' stands for 'Tense Phrase' that corresponds to an independent declarative sentence/ main clause here.

(10) [Which student]$_i$ did everyone see t$_i$? Wh-*movement*
　　 i) 'Everyone saw a different student, who are these students ?' (∃ > ∀)
　　 ii) 'Everyone saw exactly the same student, who is this student ?' (∀ > ∃)

Mandarin *wh*-fronting can also disambiguate the 'scope ambiguity' (cf. 11), just like the English topicalization pattern. Therefore, *wh*-fronting in Chinese is more appropriate to be analyzed as a case of topicalization.

(11) a. Normal in-situ *wh*-question
　　　　Mei-ge　　nansheng　dou　xihuan　na-ben　　shu ?
　　　　every-Cl　boy　　　　all　　like　　which-Cl　book
　　　　'Which book does every boy like?'　　　　　　(∃ > ∀ / ∀ > ∃)
　　b. Topicalized *wh*-question
　　　　[Na-ben　shu]$_i$ [mei-ge　nansheng　dou　xihuan　t$_i$] ?
　　　　which-Cl　book　every-Cl　boy　　　all　　like
　　　　'Which book (is the one that) every boy likes?'　(∃ > ∀ / *∀ > ∃)

Traditionally, topics are associated with *aboutness* and bear *old information*; they should be *given*, and *known* to interlocutors (Chafe 1976). Pronouns, definites, specific indefinites and generics qualify as topics. At first sight, it seems that it is not appropriate to say that a *wh*-element, as a bearer of unknown information, can also qualify as topic. However, it is argued that D-linked *wh*-phrases can be assigned topic status in that the question ranges over a discourse-specified set. Furthermore, a simple *wh*-word can be interpreted as being D-linked if the context provides a set over which it must range (Erteschik-Shir 2007). In Mandarin, only the *wh*-words that apply to restrictive nominal sets can undergo topicalization. Either the nominal range specifier of a complex *wh*-phrase provides a restrictive set (12a,b), or the context implies such a set in the case of simple *wh*-word (cf. 12c). This point has been argued by Wu (1999) and Pan (2011a,b).

(12) a. [Shenme　cai],　Zhangsan　zuotian　chi-le　?
　　　　what　　　dish　Zhangsan　yesterday　eat-Perf
　　　　'What dish (is the one) that Zhangsan ate yesterday?'　(Pan 2011b)
　　b. [Na-ge　cai],　Zhangsan　zuotian　chi-le　?
　　　　which-Cl　dish　Zhangsan　yesterday　eat-Perf
　　　　'Which dish (is the one) that Zhangsan ate yesterday?'　(Pan 2011b)
　　c. ??Shenme　Zhangsan　mai-le ? (A list of things must be presupposed)
　　　　what　　　Zhangsan　buy-Perf
　　　　'What has Zhangsan bought?'　　　　　　　　　(Wu 1999:82)

Second, fronted D-linked *which* + NP questions can be treated as topicalization cases (Cinque 1990, Boeckx and Grohmann 2004, Erteschik-Shir 1997, 2007). For instance, D-linked *wh*-phrases are not subject to the Superiority effect, as shown in (13–14).

(13) a. Who read what?

b. *What$_i$ did who read t$_i$?

(14) a. Which man read which book?

b. Which book$_i$ did which man read t$_i$?

Erteschik-Shir (1997) gives a very detailed analysis of this contrast, which I will not repeat here. The important point is that Chinese shows exactly the same pattern, as is shown in (15). (15a) contains the *wh*-words in simple form, and the superiority effects are observed. (15b) contains the complex *wh*-phrases and the superiority effects disappear.

(15) a. *Shenme$_j$, shei yijing du-guo-le t$_j$?
  what who already read-Exp.-Perf
  (*'What did who already finish reading?')

b. [Na-ji-ben shu]$_j$, na-xie tongxue yijing du-guo-le t$_j$?
  which-several-Cl book which-Pl student already read-Exp.-Perf
  'Which book did which student finish reading?'

Another independent piece of evidence is that as any other ordinary nominal topic in Mandarin, a fronted *wh*-phrase can be marked by the so-called 'topic markers (TM)' as well.

(16) [Na-ge cai] ne /a /ya, ni-erzi zui xihuan chi ?
  which-Cl dish TM /TM /TM your-son most like eat
  'Which dish (is the one) that your son likes eating most?'

Let us turn to other three types of *wh*-ex-situ.

Type II: extracted *wh*-focus (the gap is created by movement)

(17) [$_{FocP}$ Shi na-yi-bu dianying, [$_{TP}$ Zhangsan zui bu xihuan kan __]]?
  be which-one-Cl movie Zhangsan most Neg like see
  'Which movie is it that Zhangsan doesn't like at all?'

In (17), *na-yi-bu dianying* 'which one of the movies' is also extracted from the TP and the structure is derived by movement, leaving a gap. In this case, the fronted constituent *which movie* is marked by the focus marker *shi* 'be', whose presence is obligatory.

Type III: base-generated *wh*-topic (gapless construction)

(18) [_TopP_ Na-ge   guojia, [_TP_ ni   xihuan de dachengshi buduo]]?
         which-Cl country   2SG like   DE big-city   not-many
'Which country is the one (such) that its big cities that you like are not many?'

(18) illustrates a gapless topic structure since there is no gap in the TP. *Na-ge guojia* 'which country' is base-generated in the TP external topic position. Movement is involved (8) but not in (18).

Type IV: base-generated *wh*-focus (gapless construction)

(19) [_FocP_ Shi shei de biaoyan,   [_TP_ dajia   zuotian dou jiao-hao]]?
          be   who DE performance   everyone yesterday all cry-good
'It was (to) whose performance that everyone said "bravo!" yesterday?'

In (19), *jiao-hao* 'cry "bravo"' is a true intransitive verb that cannot take any object at all. Therefore, *shei-de biaoyan* 'whose performance' cannot be extracted from the TP but must be base-generated in the sentence initial focus position.

These four types of *wh*-ex-situ cases are very much like the Topic structure and Focus structure that I presented in Section 1. My claim is that as for the ex-situ type of topics and foci, there is no difference between an ordinary non-*wh* topic/focus (cf. sentences in (b) from (20)–(23)) and *wh*-topic/focus (cf. sentences in (a) from (20-(23)). Their syntactic positions are relatively fixed and they share similar properties.

(20) a. [_TopP_ Na-yi-bu   dianying, [_TP_ Zhangsan zui   bu xihuan kan ___]] ?
              which-one-Cl film   Zhangsan most Neg like   see
       'Which movie (is the one that) Zhangsan doesn't like at all?'

   b. [_TopP_ Hali Bote, [_TP_ Zhangsan zui   bu xihuan kan ___]].
             Harry Potter   Zhangsan most Neg like   see
      'As for Harry Potter, Zhangsan doesn't like at all.'

(21) a. [FocP Shi shei-de taidu, [TP gongsi de laoban zui bu xinshang __]]?
      be whose manner company DE boss most Neg appreciate
   'Whose manner is it that the boss of the company doesn't appreciate at all ?'

   b. [FocP Shi Mali-de taidu, [TP gongsi de laoban zui bu xinshang __]].
      be Mary's manner company DE boss most Neg appreciate
   'It is Mary's manner that the boss of the company doesn't appreciate at all.'

(22) a. [TopP Na-ge guojia, [TP ni xihuan de dachengshi buduo]]?
      which-Cl country 2SG like DE big-city not-many
   'Which country is the one that its big cities that you like are not many?'

   b. [TopP Zhongguo, [TP wo xihuan de dachengshi buduo]].
      China 1SG like DE big-city not-many
   'As for China, its big cities that I like are not many.'

(23) a. [FocP Shi shei de biaoyan, [TP dajia zuotian dou jiao-hao]]?
      be who DE performance everyone yesterday all cry-good
   'It was (to) whose performance that everyone said "bravo!" yesterday?'

   b. [FocP Shi Mali de biaoyan], [TP dajia zuotian dou jiao-hao]].
      be Mary DE performance everyone yesterday all cry-good
   'It was (to) Mary's performance that everyone said "bravo!" yesterday.'

2 Contrastiveness

2.1 Syntactic marking of contrastiveness

This section argues against the point of view that a contrastive element must be analyzed as a focus. Many of the scholars present solid data and analyses to show the existence of the contrastive topics. "Contrastiveness" should be kept as an independent component in the system of Information Structure (Lambrecht 1994, Erteschik-Shir 2007). The existence of contrastive topics in Chinese also supports the idea that a contrastive element should not be exclusively analyzed as being in focus. As in many other languages, a syntactic way to mark a contrastive element in Chinese is to build parallel contrastive clauses. In this case, the contrastive element is not obligatorily marked by prosody. (24a) illustrates a contrastive topic derived by movement/extraction; (24b) illustrates a base-generated contrastive topic. In both examples, the second clause is considered as a syntactic way to give a contrastive reading to the topic of the first clause.

(24) a. <u>Amusitedan</u>, wo yijing qu-guo-le; Naimeiheng, wo hai
       Amsterdam 1SG already go-Exp.-Perf Nijmegen 1SG still
   mei qu-guo.
   not go-Exp.
   'As for Amsterdam, I have already been there before; as for Nijmegen, I haven't been there yet.'

   b. <u>Zhe-ke</u> <u>shu</u> yezi hen duo, na-ke shu yezi hen shao.
      this-Cl tree leave very many that-Cl tree leave very few
      'As for this tree, it has many leaves; as for that one, it has very few leaves.'

The sentences in (25) contain *shi* 'be' marked focus items derived by movement. It is also the second clause that provides the focus of the first clause with a contrastive meaning.

(25) a. Shi [$_{Focus}$ ni-de taidu], [gongsi-de laoban bu xihuan];
       be   your manner company's boss not like
   bu-shi ni-de yi-zhuo.
   not-be your dressing
   'It is your way of doing things that the boss of the company doesn't appreciate; not your way of dressing.'

   b. Shi [$_{Focus}$ Mali de biaoyan], [dajia zuotian dou jiao-hao],
       be   Mary DE performance everyone yesterday all cry-good
   bushi Baoluo de.
   not Paul DE
   'It was (to) Mary's performance that everyone said "bravo!" yesterday; not to Paul's performance.'

In the following example, the original sentence does not contain any syntactically marked focus. Once we add a parallel clause, this clause gives a contrastive reading to the VP of the first clause. In this case, we can consider the whole VP *went to movie theater* as a contrastive focus.

(26) a. Wo [$_{VP}$ qu <u>kan-dianying</u> le], mei qu guang-shangdian.
       I   go see-movie   SFP not go shopping
   'I went to movie theater; not went out for shopping.'

Just like ordinary nominal topics and foci, *wh*-topics and *wh*-foci receive a prominent contrastive reading if another independent clause is added (cf. 27–28).

(27) [TopP Zuotian   na-yi-dao   cai, [TP ni   erzi zui   xihuan chi ___]];
         yesterday which-one-Cl dish   your son most like   eat

    [TopP na-yi-dao   cai, [TP ta   zui   bu-xihuan chi ___]]
          which-one-Cl dish   3SG most dislike   eat
    'Among all of the dishes yesterday, which one does your son like very much, which one doesn't he like at all?'

(28) [FocP Shi shei-de taidu,   [TP gongsi   de laoban zui   bu   xinshang ___]]?
           be whose   manner   company DE boss   most Neg appreciate

    [FocP Shi shei-de taidu,   [TP ta   zui   xihuan ___]]?
          be whose   manner   3SG most like
    'Whose manner is it that the boss of the company doesn't appreciate at all and whose manner is it that he likes most?'

Wh-topics and *wh*-foci behave exactly like ordinary nominal topics and foci with regard to the contrastiveness in that the contrastive reading always needs to be marked overtly.

2.2 Prosodic marking of contrastiveness

I begin by a brief clarification of some basic notions concerning tones, stress and intonation in spoken Chinese. Contrary to what is generally understood, tones, stress and intonation are clearly differentiated in Mandarin, all of which exist. On the one hand, every morpheme/character takes its own fixed lexical tone; on the other hand, a lexical tonal element (character) can be stressed and a whole sentence can be realized with different intonation patterns according to the requirement of the interpretation in different pragmatic contexts. Word-stress and sentence intonation exist independently from the lexical tonal system. Like many other languages, contrastiveness can also be marked by prosody. In this section, I will show how word-stress marks the contrastiveness in Information Structure in Mandarin.

First, let us consider an example of an in-situ focus. Without any overt prosodic marking, sentences like (29a) can hardly get a contrastive meaning. Once we put a word-stress on the focus item that we want to contrast, the contrastive reading becomes prominent, as shown in (29b).

(29) a. Wo   qu-nian   qu-le   Bolin.
        I   last-year go-Perf Berlin
        Ok 'I went to Berlin last year.'
        ??'I went to Berlin last year, (not other cities.)'

b. Wo qu-nian qu-le **BOLIN**.
   I   last-year go-Perf Berlin
   ??'I went to Berlin last year.'
   Ok 'I went to BERLIN last year! (not other cities.)'
   (*prosodically marked contrastive in-situ focus*)

Topic structures show similar effects. A topic sentence like (30a) does not really resist a contrastive reading; however, such a reading is not necessarily the prominent one. If we put a stress on the topic, the contrastive reading becomes prominent. (30b) shows an extracted contrastive topic, (30c) a base-generated contrastive topic marked by stress.

(30) a. Hali Bote, wo kan-guo.
        Harry Potter I read-Exp.
        Ok 'As for *Harry Potter*, I have read it'
        ?'*Harry Potter*, I have read it;
        (however, *The Lord of the Rings*, I have not read it yet.')
                                    (*extracted non-contrastive topic*)

   b. **HALI BOTE**, wo kan-guo.
      Harry Potter I read-Exp.
      '*Harry Potter*, I have (already) read it; (however, *The Lord of the Rings*, I have not read it yet.')
                            (*prosodically marked extracted contrastive topic*)

   c. **HALI BOTE** piaofang-shouru hen bucuo.
      Harry Potter box-office-returns very not-bad
      'As for *Harry Potter*, (its) box-office returns are good; as for other movies of the year, the box-office returns are not good.'
                        (*prosodically marked base-generated contrastive topic*)

To construct a contrastive topic, the stress must be put on the relevant topic item. (31a) illustrates that if we put the stress on the main verb, the contrastive reading will be realized on the predicate of the sentence, thus the whole predicate becomes a contrastive focus. (31b) shows that when the stress is put on the adverbial of location, the contrastiveness is realized on the adverbial of location.

(31) a. [$_{TopP}$ Songlu, [$_{FocP}$ wo **KAN**jian-guo]].
            truffle   1SG see-Exp
        'As for truffles, I have SEEN them (but never tasted...)'

b. [_TopP_ Hali Bote, [_FocP_ wo zai **DIANSHI**-shang kan-guo]].
   Harry Potter   1SG at TV-on   see-Exp
   'As for *Harry Potter*, I have seen it on TV (but never in a movie theater...)'

As for the in-situ foci that are syntactically marked by the copular *shi* 'be', the stress must be put on the foci to guarantee the contrastive reading (cf. 32).

(32) a. Wo shi [_Focus_ **QUNIAN**] qu faguo de.
       1SG be   last-year   go France DE
       'It was LAST YEAR that I went to France, (not this year.)'

   b. Shi [_Focus_ **WO**] bu xiang qu kan zhe-bu dianying.
      be   1SG Neg. want go see this-Cl movie
      'It is **I** that don't want to see this movie, (not my brother.)'

   c. Shi [_Focus_ xia **YU** le].
      be   fall rain PART
      'It is really the case that it is RAINING now, (not snowing.)'

If the stress is put on the focus marker *shi* 'be', then the contrastive reading is not available anymore. It reinforces the focus and it is translated by the adverbs like *indeed* and *really*.

(33) a. Wo **SHI** [_Focus_ qunian] qu faguo de.
       1SG be   last-year go France DE
       'It was indeed last year that I went to France.'

   b. **SHI** [_Focus_ wo] bu xiang qu kan zhe-bu dianying.
      be   1SG Neg. want go see this-Cl movie
      'It is indeed I that don't want to see this movie.'

   c. **SHI** [_Focus_ xia yu le], bu pian ni. (Lü 2000)
      be   fall rain PART Neg. trick 2SG
      'It is indeed raining now, and I am not kidding you.'

Word-stress marking of contrastiveness also applies to the ex-situ foci that are syntactically marked by the copular *shi* 'be'.

(34) a. Shi [_Focus_ **NI**-de taidu], [gongsi-de laoban bu xihuan].
       be   your manner   company's boss   not like
       'It is YOUR way of doing things that the boss of the company doesn't appreciate; (not Mary's.)'

b. Shi [Focus ni-de **TAIDU**], [gongsi-de laoban bu xihuan].
   be   your manner company's boss not like
   'It is your WAY OF DOING THINGS that the boss of the company doesn't appreciate; (not your way of dressing.)'

Wh-topics and *wh*-foci demonstrate similar contrastive readings under the stress marking. Generally, the tress is put on the nominal range specifier of the fronted *wh*-phrases to ensure that the relevant *wh*-phrase is interpreted as a contrastive topic. For instance, the nominal range specifier (i.e. the nominal restriction) of the *wh*-phrase *which movie* is the *movie* part, as shown in (35a). If we want to get a contrastive reading of the *wh*-topic *which movie*, the stress must be put on *movie*. Naturally, if the stress is realized on other elements in the sentence, it is those stressed elements that receive the contrastive reading, and in this case, the topic cannot be interpreted as a contrastive topic anymore (cf. (35b,c)).

(35) a. [TopP Na-yi-bu   **DIANYING**, [TP Zhangsan zui bu xihuan kan __]]?
         which-one-Cl film   Zhangsan most Neg like see
   'Which MOVIE (is the one that) Zhangsan doesn't like at all,
   (not which book) ?'

b. [TopP Na-yi-bu   dianying, [TP Zhangsan zui **BU** xihuan kan __]]?
        which-one-Cl film   Zhangsan most Neg like see
   Ok 'Which movie (is the one that) Zhangsan does NOT like at all,
   (not the one that he likes most) ?'
   #'Which MOVIE (is the one that) Zhangsan doesn't like at all,
   (not which book) ?'

c. [TopP Na-yi-bu   dianying, [TP **ZHANGSAN** zui bu xihuan kan __]]?
        which-one-Cl film   Zhangsan   most Neg like see
   Ok 'Which movie (is the one that) ZHANGSAN doesn't like at all,
   (not the one that Lisi doesn't like) ?'
   # 'Which MOVIE (is the one that) Zhangsan doesn't like at all,
   (not which book) ?'

This stress rule also applies to the base-generated *wh*-topics (cf. 36) or *wh*-foci (cf. 37).

(36) [TopP Na-ge **GUOJIA**, [TP ni xihuan de dachengshi buduo]]?
          which-Cl country   2SG like DE big-city   not-many
   'Which COUNTRY is the one that its big cities that you like are not many
   (not which continent) ?'

(37) Shi [Focus shei-de **TAIDU**], [gongsi-de laoban bu xihuan].
    be   whose manner   company's boss   not like
    'Whose MANNER is it that the boss of the company doesn't appreciate (not his/her way of dressing)?'

However, the stress cannot be put on the *wh*-portion of the relevant *wh*-phrase; such a stress pattern combined with unknown information does not give a contrastive reading. For instance, it is the *wh*-portion *which* that receives a tress in (38) and the whole *wh*-phrase *which movie* cannot get a contrastive reading.

(38) [TopP **NA**-yi-bu   dianying, [TP Zhangsan zui bu xihuan kan ___]]?
           which-one-Cl film   Zhangsan most Neg like   see
    'WHICH movie (is the one that) Zhangsan doesn't like at all?'
    (no contrastive reading)

2.3 Summary

We observe that contrastive elements can be marked either by syntax or by prosody in Mandarin and that a contrastively marked element can be either a topic or a focus (cf. Table 2).

Table 2

		Topics		Foci	
		Extracted topics	Base-generated topics	Ex-situ foci	In-situ foci
Contrastiveness	Syntactic marking	yes (8a)	yes (8b)	yes (9a)	yes (9a)
	Prosodic marking	yes (frequent in oral) (30b)	yes (frequent in oral) (30c)	yes (frequent in oral) (34a, b)	yes (frequent in oral) (29b)

3 Division of labor between syntax and prosody

In this section, I will discuss the **division of labor** between syntactic and prosodic marking of Information Structures in spoken Mandarin Chinese. Specifically, I will argue that prosodic marking of contrastiveness is only activated as the last resort at the interfaces in the computational system.

As what has been said, in spoken Chinese, independent from the fact that every morpheme (character) has its own fixed lexical tone, every tonal element can be stressed and a whole sentence can be realized by different intonation according to the requirement of the interpretation in different pragmatic contexts. Pan (2011a, 2012b) illustrates this point based on the prosodic licensing different readings of *wh*-words in Mandarin. According to the possible combination of the word-stress with the sentence intonation, a *wh*-word can get several different interpretations: interrogative, existential, polarity, exclamatives and rhetorical question readings.

The general idea is that a *wh*-word can receive several possible readings in certain special contexts that are called 'ambiguous *wh*-licensing contexts' in Pan (2011a, 2012b) and that only the prosodic contours can disambiguate these readings. (39) illustrates a progressive aspectual sentence containing a *wh*-word, and this sentence is four ways ambiguous in written form. However, in spoken form, these four readings can be distinguished clearly by four different prosodic patterns.

(39) a. Ta zai chi-zhe shenme ?
   he prog. eat-dur. what
   (no stress on the verb; no stress on the *wh*-word but a rising intonation at the end of the sentence)
   'What is he eating?'   (*Interrogative reading*)

b. Ta zai **CHI**-zhe shenme.
   he prog. eat-dur. what
   (stress on the verb *chi* 'eat' and a falling intonation or a neutral intonation at the end of the sentence)
   'He is eating something.'   (*Existential reading*)

c. Ta zai chi-zhe **SHENME!**
   he prog. eat-dur. what
   (Stress on the *wh*-word and falling intonation at the end of the sentence)
   'What he is eating! (It smells bad!)'   (*Exclamative reaing*)

d. **TA** zai chi-zhe shenme ?!
   he prog. eat-dur. what
   (Stress on the subject *he* and the falling/neutral intonation at the end of the sentence)
   'What is HE eating?! = He is eating nothing!)'   (*Rhetorical question*)

In the ambiguous contexts, the *wh*-word remains underspecified between two values: [+Q] (interrogative) and [-Q] (non-interrogative). The relevant contexts are not quantificationally 'strong' enough to provide such a sentence with a single operator to bind the *wh*-word as a variable. Thus, the prosodic elements play their roles as the last resort to disambiguate the sentence. The licensing relationship established between the corresponding prosodic forms and the relevant *wh*-words is called 'Prosodic Licensing of *wh*-in-situ'. Prosodic licensing is activated only when a single syntactic form is not sufficient to generate the different interpretations according to the different contexts. In this sense, Chinese data support the notion of 'repair system' proposed in Reinhart (2006). When a syntactic form is not sufficient to generate different semantic interpretations, some other mechanisms will be activated, and these mechanisms are treated as a 'repair system' in the sense of Reinhart. In her analysis on English focus structure, the mechanism called Main Stress Shift is an operation that creates different focus patterns. Each of these stress patterns corresponds to one and only one specific focus structure, and each focus structure corresponds to one and only one specific semantic reading. The mechanisms are costly in the sense of Economy Principle (Chomsky 1995); however, the computational system can tolerate them since they do not create any interpretation redundancy. The case of prosodic marking of *wh*-elements shows clearly that prosody intervenes quite often in the computational system in Mandarin. Our present case of the word-stress marking of contrastiveness further supports this observation.

Similarly, in the present case, if the contrastiveness is not marked overtly by syntax, it must be marked by word-stress. Take a topic structure for example. In (30a) (repeated below as (40a)), even if the contrastive reading is not the most prominent one, such a reading is still available. It is thus not unreasonable to think that without any overt syntactic marking, (40a) remains ambiguous between a non-contrastive reading and a contrastive reading. The only way to disambiguate the sentence is to put the stress on the relevant topic in order to bring out the contrastive reading, as shown in (30b) (repeated below as (40b)). In this situation, the prosodic intervention has exactly the same function as in the case of *wh*-questions discussed above. The stress in (40b) functions as a last resort in order to make the contrastive reading more prominent.

(40) a. Hali   Bote,   wo   kan-guo.
       Harry Potter   I   read-Exp.
       Ok 'As for *Harry Potter*, I have read it'
       ?'*Harry Potter*, I have read it; (however, *The Lord of the Rings*, I have not yet.')

b. **HALI BOTE**, wo kan-guo.
Harry Potter I   read-Exp.
'*Harry Potter*, I have (already) read it; (however, *The Lord of the Rings*, I have not yet.')

If the topic is already marked syntactically as a contrastive topic, then the stress is unnecessary (cf. Section 2.1). This means that the stress system functions as a "system repairing device" in the sense of Reinhart: the presence of the stress is only required when syntax fails to mark the topic as a contrastive topic.

Furthermore, we notice that when the stress is put on different elements in the sentence, the contrastiveness is thus realized on different components (cf. Section 2.2). The relationship between the word-stress pattern and the semantic interpretation of the contrastiveness is strictly 'one-to-one'. Therefore, there is no interpretation redundancy involved in the prosodic marking of the contrastiveness system. If the stress-marking pattern is regarded as a repair mechanism in the sense of Reinhart (2006), it is tolerated by the computational system.

In Chinese, topics and foci are only marked by syntax and contrastive elements can be marked either by syntax or by prosody. However, in spoken Chinese, it is much more frequent to mark a contrastive element by word-stress. Spoken Chinese data support the idea that the notion of "contrastiveness" should be kept as an independent component in the system of Information Structure. We also demonstrated that the prosodic intervention is only required when syntax fails to mark the contrastiveness. Therefore, prosodic marking of contrastiveness is activated as the last resort at the interfaces, and as any other system repairing mechanism, it is tolerated by the computational system.

References

Boeckx, Cedric & Kleanthes Grohmann. 2004. SubMove: Towards a unified account of scrambling and D-linking. In David Adger, Cécile de Cat & George Tsoulas, eds. *Peripheries*. Dodrecht: Kluwer, 241–257.
Chafe, Wallace. 1976. Givenness, contrastiveness, definiteness, subjects, topics, and point of view. In Charles N. Li (ed.), *Subject and topic*, New York: Academic Press: 25–55.
Chao, Yuen Ren. 1968. *A Grammar of Spoken Chinese*. Berkeley et alibi: California University Press.
Cheng, Lisa Lai-Shen. 2008. Deconstructing the *shi...de* construction. *The Linguistic Review 25*.
Chomsky, Noam. 1995. *The Minimalist Program*. Cambridge, Mass.: MIT Press.
Cinque, Guglielmo. 1990. *Types of A'-Dependencies*. Cambridge, Mass.: MIT Press.
É. Kiss, Katalin. 1998. Identificational focus versus information focus. *Language* 74: 245–73.
Erteschik-Shir, Nomi. 1997. *The dynamics of Focus Structure*. Cambridge: Cambridge University Press.
Erteschik-Shir, Nomi. 2007. *Information Structure*. Oxford University Press, New York.

Huang, C.-T. James. 1982. *Logical relations in Chinese and the theory of grammar*. Cambridge, MA: MIT dissertation.

Lambrecht, Knud. 1994. *Information structure and sentence form: Topic, focus, and the mental representation of discourse referents*. Cambridge University Press.

Li, Charles N. and Sandra A. Thompson. 1981. *Mandarin Chinese. A functional Reference Grammar*. University of California Press.

Lü, Shuxiang. 2000. *Xiandai hanyu babaici* [800 words of Modern Chinese]. Beijing: Shangwu yinshuguan.

Pan, Victor J. 2011a. *Interrogatives et quantification: une approche générative*. Presses Universitaires de Rennes.

Pan, Victor J. 2011b. ATB-topicalization in Mandarin Chinese and Intersection Operator, in 'Optionality of *wh*-movement', special issue of *Linguistic Analysis* 37.

Pan, Victor J. 2012a. When *Wh*-questions Interact With Information Structure. Handout given at the Workshop at the *34th Annual Meeting of the German Linguistic Society (DGfS)*, Frankfurt, Germany.

Pan, Victor J. 2012b. Interface Strategy in Mandarin : When Syntax Interacts With Prosody and Discourse. Handout given at *Joint Symposium on the Interfaces of Grammar*. Institute of Linguistics, Chinese Academy of Social Sciences (CASS) and the City University of Hong Kong, Beijing, China.

Pan, Victor J. 2014. *Wh*-ex-situ in Chinese: Mapping Between Information Structure and Split CP. *Linguistic Analysis*, Volume 39 (3–4). 271–413.

Paris, Marie-Claude. 1979. *Nominalization in Mandarin Chinese*. Paris: Département de Recherches linguistiques, Université Paris 7.

Paul, Waltraud and John Whitman. 2008. *Shi...de* focus clefts in Mandarin Chinese. *The Linguistic Review* 25. 413–451.

Paul, Waltraud. 2002. Sentence-internal topics in Mandarin Chinese: The case of object preposing. *Language and Linguistics* 3, 4. 695–714.

von Prince, Kilu. 2012. Predication and information structure in Mandarin Chinese. *Journal of East Asian Linguistics* 21:4. 329–366.

Reinhart, Tanya. 2006. *Interface Strategies : Optimal and Costly Computations*. MIT Press.

Rizzi, Luigi. 1997. The fine structure of the left periphery. In *Elements of Grammar: Handbook of Generative Syntax*, Liliane Haegeman (ed.), 281–337. Dordrecht: Kluwer.

Rizzi, Luigi. 1997. The fine structure of the left periphery. In Liliane Haegeman, ed., *Elements of grammar: A handbook in generative syntax*, 281–337. Dordrecht: Kluwer

Ross, John R. 1967. *Constraints on variables in syntax*. Doctoral dissertation, MIT.

Shyu, Shu-ing. 2014. Topic and Focus, Handbook of Chinese Linguistics, Blackwell Publishing Co.

Tang, C.-C. Jane. 1988. *Wh*-topicalization in Chinese. Ms, Cornell University, Ithaca.

Teng, Shou-Hsin. 1979. Remarks on Cleft sentences in Chinese. *Journal of Chinese Linguistics* 7, 1. 101–114.

Tsao, Feng-fu. 1979. *A Functional Study of Topic in Chinese: The First Step Towards Discourse Analysis*. Taipei: Stduent Book Co.

Wu, Jian-Xin. 1999. *Syntax and semantics of quantification in Chinese*, Doctoral Dissertation, University of Maryland at College Park.

Xu, Liejiong & Terence Langendoen. 1985. Topic structure in Chinese. *Language* 61. 1–27.

Zhang, Ning. 2002. Island Effects and Episodic Eventualities in Chinese Topicalization. In D. Hole, P. Law, and N. Zhang (eds.) *Linguistics by Heart: in honor of Horst-Dieter Gasde*. ZAS-Berlin.

Heete Sahkai
10 Demonstratives and Information Structure in Spoken Estonian

Abstract: The paper draws attention to the multifunctionality of adnominal demonstratives in spoken discourse: in addition to their primary demonstrative uses they can function as filler words, nominalisers, metalinguistic markers, affective markers. The present study confirms the previous findings that Spoken Estonian adnominal demonstratives are also used as an NP constructing device that helps to process NPs in marked syntactic positions, and that the Estonian anaphoric demonstratives are spreading to a wider range of previously mentioned referents, which is usually taken as evidence of their ongoing grammaticalisation into definite articles. The primary goal of the paper is to show that Spoken Estonian adnominal demonstratives also function as focus and (less clearly) topic markers, and to draw attention to a little-studied focus marking strategy that seems cross-linguistically characteristic of spoken language, namely the tendency to recruit existing particle-like elements for the purposes of focus marking. Finally, the paper suggests two hypotheses for further study: that the spreading of the identifiability marking function of demonstratives occurs primarily in topic and focus positions, and that the grammaticalisation of demonstratives into articles may be driven not only by their identifiability marking function but by the other functions as well.

Introduction

This paper contributes to the study of the signalling of Information Structure (IS) in spoken language[1]. The study is concerned with two aspects of IS: the marking of the identifiability and activation status of discourse referents, and the marking of the topic-focus structure of utterances[2] (the notions Information Structure,

---

[1] The study was supported by the grants ETF7998, SF0050023s09 and IUT35-1.
[2] These two dimensions have also been called referential vs. relational givenness/newness, cf. Gundel and Hedberg, this volume.

Heete Sahkai, Institute of the Estonian Language

topic, focus, etc. will be used in the sense of Lambrecht 1994), and how the two relate to the distribution of adnominal demonstratives. The functions of adnominal demonstratives are usually described in terms of the marking of referent identifiability, and the extension of this function to new classes of referents is assumed to drive their possible development into an obligatory element in the NP structure, the definite article. This paper draws attention to the fact that cross-linguistically, demonstratives have many other functions in spoken language, and pursues the hypothesis that at least in Spoken Estonian one of these functions is to signal another aspect of IS: the topic-focus structure. In addition, it will be discussed how the recognition of the multifunctionality of demonstratives affects the understanding of how they become an obligatory part of the NP.

Topic-focus structure can be expressed through prosody, word order, special syntactic constructions like clefts and dislocation, and morphological topic and focus markers. Adnominal demonstratives as potential topic/focus markers can be seen to instantiate a less discussed focus-marking strategy that seems to exist in spoken language independently of what are the primary means of signalling IS in the language, namely, the adoption of existing particle-like elements for the purposes of marking units of IS. This use has been attributed for instance to *like* in English and to *so* in German (Wiese 2011), although the primary grammatical means of expressing IS in these languages are prosodic and syntactic, not morphological. The exact nature of this strategy does not seem to be well understood, for instance, it is not clear whether it is motivated by factors related to the signalling or processing of IS or perhaps by prosodic factors (cf. Wiese 2011: 999). This paper will examine the distribution of an element that can be seen to have this function in Spoken Estonian, the temporal deictic *nüüd* 'now', and will test the hypothesis that the same function accounts for some otherwise unexpected facts of the distribution of Spoken Estonian adnominal demonstratives. This will be done by analysing their distribution in a subset of the corpus of Spoken Estonian and by verifying whether it correlates with topics and foci.

The paper is structured as follows: section 1 provides some background about Estonian adnominal demonstratives and the expression of IS in Estonian; section 2 gives a brief overview of the extended uses of adnominal demonstratives described in the literature, drawing attention to the fact that they are a multifunctional device of spoken language; section 3 motivates the hypothesis that one of the functions of adnominal demonstratives in Spoken Estonian is topic and/or focus marking, and discusses the implications of the multifunctionality of demonstratives for the understanding of how they grammaticalise into definite articles; section 4 describes the data and the method of analysis that were used to test the topic/focus marking hypothesis; section 5 presents the analysis and the discussion, concluding that the Spoken Estonian adnominal demonstratives indeed seem to mark foci and perhaps also topics, and section 6 summarises the paper.

1 Estonian adnominal demonstratives and the expression of Information Structure in Estonian

Standard Estonian has a very poor demonstrative system: it possesses a single adnominal and pronominal demonstrative, *see*, pl. *need*, ('this', 'that', 'it'), with no distal-proximal or strong form-weak form distinctions; in addition, the same form functions as a third person pronoun. However, nouns in the six local case forms may occur either with the local case forms of *see*, or with the locative demonstratives *siin* 'here', *siia* 'towards here', *siit* 'from here', and *seal* 'there', *sinna* 'towards there', *sealt* 'from there', which have the same uses as the adnominal *see* but which display the distal-proximal distinction (Pajusalu 1997: 166–171). Hence, the meaning 'in this house' can be expressed either as *selle-s maja-s* '*see*-iness.sg house-iness.sg'[3] or as *siin maja-s* 'here house-iness.sg' (literally 'here in (the) house'), and the meaning 'in that house' either as *selle-s maja-s* '*see*-iness.sg house-iness.sg' or as *seal maja-s* 'there house-iness.sg' (literally 'there in (the) house'). The present study will thus be concerned with the adnominal uses of *see* as well as of the locative demonstratives (for brevity, I will sometimes refer to all these forms as *see*).

Topic-focus structure is expressed in Estonian mainly through word order, which is described as free and as being shaped primarily by IS (Lindström 2005, Tael 1988). Possibly because of the free word order, Estonian seems to make relatively little use of special syntactic constructions like clefts and dislocations (cf. e.g. Amon 2009). Prosodic expression of IS in Estonian is only beginning to be studied, but the first results suggest (Sahkai, Kalvik, and Mihkla 2013, Salveste 2013) that Estonian may belong to the category of languages that possess both flexible or plastic syntax and flexible or plastic prosody (in terms of e.g. Vallduví and Engdahl 1996 and Van Valin 1999); however, the proportions and conditions of the use of these two strategies remain to be studied. Finally, Estonian does not possess morphological topic or focus markers but in spoken usage can be seen to make use of a number of particles that mark information-structural units. One of these particles will be examined in section 5.1, and the

---

3 Abbreviations used in the article: *adess* – adessive; *all* – allative; *cmpr* – comparative; *com* – comitative; COMP – complementiser; *cond* – conditional; *elat* – elative; EMPH – emphatic particle; *gen* – genitive; *ill* – illative; *impers* – impersonal; *iness* – inessive; *inf* – infinitive; *part* – partitive; PRTCL – particle; *prtcpl* – participle; *term* – terminative; *transl* – translative.

present paper will explore the hypothesis that the same function accounts partly for the distribution of adnominal demonstratives in Spoken Estonian. But before motivating and testing this hypothesis, I will give an overview of the non-demonstrative uses of adnominal demonstratives that have been described in the literature, both in Estonian and cross-linguistically.

2 Functions of demonstratives

The functions of demonstratives 'proper', in Estonian and cross-linguistically, are the deictic, anaphoric and recognitional function (Diessel 1999, Himmelmann 1996, Lyons 1999). In terms of the marking of the identifiability and activation status of referents (Lambrecht 1994: 74–116), the use of a demonstrative determiner signals, according to Gundel, Hedberg, and Zacharski (1993: 286–289), that the referent is at least familiar, i.e. the speaker assumes that the addressee can uniquely identify the referent because it is already represented in his or her memory; proximal demonstratives in particular may additionally require that the referent be activated, i.e. represented in the current short-term memory.

But demonstratives seem to have many additional functions in spoken language. In many languages, demonstratives have an affective function (cf. Potts and Schwartz 2010 and their references; Diessel (1999: 107) considers this function as part of the recognitional function). In spoken English, *this* has been described as an indefinite determiner that introduces new prominent referents (Prince 1981; some authors consider this use as part of the affective use (Potts and Schwartz 2010)). The function of introducing both identifiable and non-identifiable prominent referents has also been described as characteristic of demonstratives that are grammaticalising into articles (Epstein 1993). One typologically wide-spread use of demonstratives seems to be as filler words in situations where speakers encounter trouble formulating a word during spontaneous speech production (Hayashi and Yoon 2006).

In Spoken Estonian, a number of non-demonstrative uses of adnominal demonstratives have been described. As in many other languages, Spoken Estonian adnominal demonstratives can be used as filler words (Pajusalu 1997: 157), ex. (1)[4], and with an affective function (Sahkai 2002: 34), ex. (2). In addi-

---

4 Transcription marks: *(.)* – micropause (0,2 seconds or less); *(1.2)* – length of the pause in seconds; <u>word</u> – stress; >...< – accelerated speech; <...> – slow speech; : – lengthened syllable; @...@ – marked intonation; *(h)* – laughter; si- – interrupted word; = – pronounced as one word; *[...]* – overlapping.

tion, Pajusalu (1997: 152–155) notes that they are extensively used as metalinguistic markers of quotation, cf. ex. (3); this use may be seen as part of a more general function which is to indicate that an expression is being used markedly, e.g. figuratively or ironically, cf. ex. (4) (Sahkai 2002: 41). I have also found that adnominal demonstratives can be used grammatically to indicate the case of a phrase that cannot itself bear case, e.g. because it is a title or because it does not contain a noun (5), and that they also seem to mark phrases that are not in their canonical syntactic position, e.g. because they are dislocated (6) (Sahkai 2002, 2003).

(1) < aga **need**   > (0.5) **need**   sõidutunni-d   noh
    but see.NOM.PL   see.NOM.PL   driving.lesson-NOM.PL well
    need   (0.5) teoreetilise-d   tunni-d
    see.NOM.PL   theoretic-NOM.PL   lesson-NOM.PL
    'but what about those... those driving lessons, I mean those...
    theory lessons'   (Sahkai 2003: 128)

(2) *Jää-b   arusaamatu-ks,   kuhu   **need**   jalgratturi-d*
    remain-3SG   incomprehensible-TRANSL   where   see.NOM.PL   cyclist-NOM.PL
    veel   mahu-vad,   sest   nende   jaoks eraldi   teelõik-e
    still   have.room-3PL   because   3PL.GEN for   separately   road.part-PART.PL
    pole.
    be.NEG
    'It's incomprehensible where there's still room for the cyclists, because there are no separate lanes for them'   (Pajusalu 1997: 161)[5]

(3) *no   ütle-me   selle-s   maailma   osa-s   kus   me   asu-me*
    well say-1PL   see-INESS   world.GEN   part-INESS where   1PL   be.located-1PL
    on   võibolla   kõige   olulise-m   tõepoolest   see,   et   tõste-takse
    be.3   perhaps   most   important-CMPR   indeed   see   that   raise-IMPERS
    see *agressioon-i   lävi: kui   kasuta-da   termini-t   mida   me   siin*
    see   agression-GEN   treshold   if   use-INF   term-PART   that   1PL   here
    ole-me   kasuta-nud: niivõrd   kõrge-le,   et   mingi-t   agressioon-i   ei
    be-1PL   use-PRTCPL   so   high-ALL   that any-PART   agression-PART NEG
    tule-gi
    come-EMPH

---

[5] Cyclists have not been mentioned before in the conversation. Pajusalu analyses the demonstrative in this example as signalling that the NP is definite for the speaker; Sahkai (2002: 34) proposes however that it is used to express emotional involvement.

'well in this part of the world where we live the most important thing is perhaps indeed to raise this agression treshold – to use the term we have been using here – so high that there will be no agression'
(Pajusalu 1997:154)

(4) *et   kes   too-b   kõige   <u>odavam-a</u>:   retsept-i   onju, see*
    comp who   bring-3SG   most   cheaper-GEN   recipe-GEN   right see
    *saa-b   mingi   tasuta   <u>lõuna</u>   näiteks   **seal**   <u>kloaagi-s</u>*
    get-3SG some.GEN   free   lunch.GEN   for.example   *seal*   sewer-INESS
    'who brings the cheapest recipe gets a free lunch in that sewer'

(5) *siis   ma   käi-si-n   vaata-ma-s   veel   väikese-s   saali-s*
    then 1SG   go-PST-1SG   watch-INF-INESS also   small-INESS   hall-INESS
    seda   *"Fernando Kapp saat-is   mu-lle   kirja"*
    see-PART   Fernando Kapp send-PST.3SG   1SG-ALL   letter.GEN
    'then I went to see "Fernando Kapp sent me a letter" in the small hall'

(6) *taha-d   seda   ka   võt-ta   **seda**   (.) <u>salati-t</u>=vä.*
    want-2SG see.PART   too   take-INF   see.PART   salad-PART=Q
    'do you want it too, the salad?'

The latter two functions could be characterised in terms of Hawkins (2004: 87) as NP Construction uses driven by processing considerations: in the first case, the demonstrative permits the construction of a non-nominal expression as a NP and the indication of its role in the clause, and in the second case it helps to process a displaced NP by signalling its category and syntactic function. These NP Construction functions of Estonian demonstratives are restricted to spoken language, but both in written and spoken language they also perform the second function of determiners that Hawkins associates with processing, namely the NP Attachment function whereby the determiner attaches modifiers to the NP that it constructs (Hawkins 2004: 88); in Estonian, this function consists primarily in the occurrence of demonstratives with nouns that are modified by relative clauses.

But first and foremost, the extended usage of adnominal demonstratives in Spoken Estonian has been hypothesised to derive from their ongoing grammaticalisation into a definite article, since Estonian does not possess articles. The present study grew out of the conclusion that the Spoken Estonian adnominal demonstratives have uses that cannot be accounted for in terms of the grammaticalisation hypothesis, nor in terms of any other of the above-mentioned functions, and that a different explanation must be sought. The next section summarises the grammaticalisation hypothesis and the reasons why it was found not to account for the Spoken Estonian data, and formulates the hypothesis of the present study.

3 Information Structure and the grammaticalisation of demonstratives

According to the most common view, articles develop from the anaphoric use of demonstratives, which is gradually extended to all referents in the preceding discourse and visible situation, and further to all identifiable referents (Diessel 1999: 128, Greenberg 1978: 61–62, Hawkins 2004: 84–93). There also exist proposals according to which incipient articles may occur with new and unidentifiable referents: Himmelmann (1997: 90–101) proposes that articles develop from recognitional demonstratives, which mark new, but still identifiable referents, and Epstein (1993) proposes that a second function of developing articles besides identifiability marking is to mark prominent referents, including those that are new and unidentifiable. The marking of prominent referents as a function of incipient articles has also been proposed by Laury (1997), according to whom the Finnish incipient definite article *se* started out as a marker of referents that are prominent and accessible (usually through previous mention). In sum, the grammaticalisation of demonstratives into definite articles is taken to be driven primarily by the marking of one aspect of Information Structure, the identifiability status of discourse referents. More specifically, in the earliest stages of development a grammaticalising article is expected to mark previously mentioned and situationally given (and prominent) referents and to be difficult to distinguish from the deictic and anaphoric uses of demonstratives. Under alternative hypotheses, it can be expected to mark also new, but identifiable concrete referents (the marking of generic NPs is considered to appear in a later stage), or unidentifiable but prominent referents.

The hypothesis that Estonian adnominal demonstratives are developing into definite articles has been pursued by Hiietam and Börjars (2003), Pajusalu (1997, 2001), and Sahkai (2002). It has been found that they are clearly not grammaticalised articles: they are obligatory neither with identifiable referents in general nor with the more restricted class of previously mentioned referents. Still, Hiietam & Börjars and Pajusalu have concluded that the motivation behind their extended usage is identifiability/definiteness marking and that they can be considered to be developing into articles.

However, the demonstratives can be found in contexts that are not expected under the hypothesis that they are articles in a very early stage of grammaticalisation. Firstly, they can be found in contexts that are used to distinguish definite articles from demonstratives and where a developing article is expected to appear in a relatively advanced stage of grammaticalisation, after it has become obligatory with previously mentioned referents. Such uses may thus be seen to question the identifiability-marking hypothesis rather than to support it. These uses include (in the terminology of Hawkins 1978) associative anaphoric uses (e.g. I bought a house. The/*That roof was leaking, cf. ex. 30 in section 5.2.3), larger situation first-mention uses (the/*that sun, the/*that Prime Minister, cf. ex. 7), uses with superlatives and expressions like *first, last, only, same* etc., i.e. with expressions that presuppose the existence of no other possible referents (the/*that cleverest boy, cf. ex. 8) (Hiietam and Börjars 2003, Sahkai 2002, 2003); they are also found with generic referents (see section 5.2 for examples), which are expected to come to be marked in later stages of grammaticalisation.

(7) *ei no ma ütle-n et (.) et kui* **see** *vald ikka*
NEG PRTCL 1SG say-1SG that that if see municipality EMPH

maksa-ks nüüd ikka su-lle selle kool-i lõpu-ni
pay-COND now emph 2SG-ALL see.GEN school-GEN end-TERM

'no really I say that if the municipality would really pay you until the end of the school...'

(8) > *tända-b seal (on) nagu* < *kolm maja kokku*
mean-3SG there be.3 like three house.PART together

ehita-tud. kõigepealt on **see** *kõige vanem maja, siis*
build-IMPERS.PRTCPL first be.3 see most older house then

on mm=ee nõugu-d-e aja-l ehita-ti mingi: uus
be.3 uh soviet-PL-GEN time-ADESS build-PST.IMPERS some new

maja, (.) nüd=nüd hiljuti teh-ti mingi uus juurdeehitus.
house now now recently make-PST.IMPERS some new annex

'I mean there are three houses connected, first there is the oldest house, then a new house was built in the soviet era, and recently a new annex was built'

Secondly, Spoken Estonian adnominal demonstratives also occur in contexts from which definite determiners in general are excluded, e.g. with new non-identifiable referents (see 5.2 for examples), NPs marked explicitly as indefinite

(9), subjects of existential clauses (10) and even non-referential predicate nominals (11) (Sahkai 2002, 2003).

(9) *meie kooli-st võe-ti siis nagu kaks tükki onju*
our school-ELAT take-PST.IMPERS then like two piece.PART right

see *kaheteistkümnenda-st* **see üks** *Aivar onju ja siis nagu*
see twelfth-ELAT see one Aivar right and then like

mina onju.
1SG right

'from our school they took two people, from the twelfth class one Aivar and then me'

(10) *huvitav=e=seal ee:: et need vee-d on ikkagi*
interesting=that=there uh that see.NOM.PL water-NOM.PL be.3 still

nii puhtad et seal=on=nii=kohutavalt=palju
so clean-NOM.PL that there=be.3=so=terribly=much

*ikka=veel=**neid** kal-u=ja.*
EMPH=still=see.PART.PL fish-PART.PL=and

'it's curious that the waters are still so clean that there are still so many fish.'

(11) *mulle saade-ti siin notar-i juures: kinnita-tud*
1SG-ALL send-PST.IMPERS here notary-GEN at attest-IMPERS.PRTCPL

igasuguse-d dokumendi-d=ja tõesta-ti et ma
all.kind-NOM.PL document-NOM.PL=and prove-PST.IMPERS that 1SG

ikka **see** *eestlane ole-n.*
really see Estonian be-1SG

'they sent me all kinds of notarially attested documents and proved that I really am an Estonian.'

In sum, a large part of the distribution of Estonian adnominal demonstratives does not seem to be compatible with the identifiability-marking hypothesis and calls for an alternative explanation.

This study will try to verify the alternative hypothesis that, in addition to or instead of referent identifiability, the adnominal demonstratives are used to signal another dimension of IS, namely the topic-focus structure of utterances. The two dimensions are independent from each other (Lambrecht 1994: 113–116), but they correlate to some extent. In particular, the referent of a topic expression must be active or accessible (given that topic is defined in terms of pragmatic aboutness and relevance), but active and accessible referents may equally well appear as focus expressions (Lambrecht 1994: 164). This hypothesis grew out from the study summarised in the previous paragraphs (Sahkai 2003) and a preliminary analysis suggested that it seems to account for some of the cases that are problematic for the identifiability-marking hypothesis.

As was mentioned in the introduction, there seems to be a tendency in spoken language to recruit existing elements for the purposes of marking the units of IS. In Spoken Estonian, several particles seem to be used in this function, including the temporal deictics *nüüd* 'now' and *siis* 'then', which suggests that deictics can in principle be recruited for this function. Similar uses were also proposed in Sahkai (2002, 2003) for the demonstrative proadverb *niimoodi* 'in this/that way', which seems to introduce focal manner adjuncts, and for the demonstrative proadjective *selline* 'such' preceding focal predicate adjectives; however, it is possible that these forms are more accurately analysed as hedges. Section 5.1 will describe the distribution of one of such elements, the temporal deictic *nüüd* 'now', showing that it indeed correlates with IS, in particular narrow focus.

The hypothesis that adnominal demonstratives are used as topic or focus markers does not exclude that, as a parallel process, anaphoric demonstratives are gradually extending to new classes of identifiable referents, since it is by now established that demonstratives are highly multifunctional. This possibility will be tested together with the topic/focus-marking hypothesis in section 5.

The recognition of the multifunctionality of demonstratives also suggests the need to reconsider the traditional understanding according to which it is solely the identifiability marking function of demonstratives that drives their development into obligatory elements in the NP: it seems possible that their other functions play a role in this process as well. This is supported by the fact that the functions of definite articles vary from language to language and are not always definable in terms of the pragmatic notion of identifiability (cf. Lambrecht 1994: 79–87, Lyons 1999: 278). That identifiability marking does not contribute to the development of articles at all has been suggested by Hawkins (2004: 82–93), who proposes that the grammaticalisation process is driven by the processing-related functions of NP Construction and NP Attachment and that the same functions account for certain uses of definite articles that cannot be described in terms of definiteness marking. Alternatively, the grammaticalisation of demonstratives could result precisely from the multiplicity of their functions. The present study however is synchronic and will not permit to establish whether or in which functions the usage of adnominal demonstratives in Spoken Estonian is spreading.

In the next section, I will describe the data and the procedure by which I tried to establish whether the distribution of adnominal demonstratives correlates with topic-focus structure.

4 Data and procedure

The data come from the Corpus of Spoken Estonian assembled and transcribed at the Institute of Estonian and General Linguistics of the University of Tartu[6]. The corpus consists of formal and informal face-to-face conversations and telephone conversations, but also monologues and TV and radio shows. The corpus is not tagged or automatically searchable. For the present study I chose and analysed manually 12 conversations between travel agents and customers, 2 face-to-face conversations and 10 telephone conversations. I chose customer service dialogues because they consist in giving information and contain many question-answer pairs, being thus easier to analyse for IS than informal everyday conversations. They are also easier to analyse in terms of the identifiability of referents since the whole relevant discourse context is contained in the dialogue. From customer service dialogues, I chose travel agency dialogues because they were longer than the others. Travel agency conversations constitute a large subgroup in the corpus and the individual dialogues were chosen randomly.

I extracted from the dialogues all the utterances that contained non-demonstrative uses of *see* and the locative demonstratives in adnominal position, i.e. uses where the demonstrative was not interpretable as deictic, anaphoric or recognitional.

To test whether the distribution of the adnominal demonstratives correlates with the topic-focus structure, I analysed the extracted instances into three categories according to whether the constituent introduced by the demonstrative was (i) narrowly focused, (ii) contained in a focal VP, or (iii) a topic (no sentences in the data were analysed as being all-focus). I did not calculate the proportion of the NPs marked with a demonstrative as compared to the proportion of bare NPs or NPs marked with other determiners or focus signalling elements in information-structurally identical contexts: it is clear that in none of these contexts are the adnominal demonstratives or any other determiners or focus marking particles obligatory.

---

[6] http://test.cl.ut.ee/suuline/Korpus.php?lang=en

The multifunctionality of demonstratives and the existence of alternative hypotheses makes it difficult to establish their function in any particular instance. In the course of the analysis, I attempted to test or to control for possible alternative functions and hypotheses: the metalinguistic, NP Construction, NP Attachment, filler word and affective functions, and the identifiability marking and prominent referent marking hypotheses.

In order to control for the other possible functions of the demonstratives, I excluded from the data instances (i) where the demonstrative seemed to be used as a filler word, (ii) where the noun introduced by the demonstrative was followed by a relative clause, (iii) where the phrase introduced by the demonstrative was not headed by a noun (and hence the demonstrative functioned probably as a nominaliser), (iv) and where the demonstrative was used metalinguistically to mark a quotation or some other kind of marked use of the noun. I included sentences with marked syntax, but I categorised them separately. Although the demonstratives in these sentences can be seen to serve the function of NP Construction, the marked syntax itself often signals IS and thus indirectly, this function relates the demonstratives to the signalling of topic-focus structure. As for the affective function, I assumed that it was excluded by the nature of the data: formal dialogues between service attendants and customers are not expected to contain many affective elements.

In order to control for the identifiability marking hypothesis, I categorised separately previously mentioned, new and indefinite referents as well as generic referents, which are expected to become marked in later stages of grammaticalisation. As for the prominence marking hypothesis, I assumed that the criterion of prominence is the repeated mention of a referent and paid attention to whether a new referent marked by a demonstrative was mentioned more than once. To control for the hypothesis that articles develop from recognitional demonstratives, which predicts that they may also occur with new but identifiable concrete referents, I also paid attention to whether a new referent introduced with a demonstrative could be considered as identifiable.

In sum, the analysis will (i) compare the identifiability marking and the topic or focus marking hypotheses and (ii) examine the extent to which adnominal demonstratives occur in marked syntactic contexts.

As the first step however, in order to get an idea of the distribution of a focus marker, I analysed, in terms of the same categories and in the same dataset, the distribution of an element that is not as multifunctional and that can more straightforwardly be taken to mark focus, namely the temporal demonstrative *nüüd* 'now' in its particle-like uses. In the next section, I will present first the analysis of *nüüd* and then the analysis of *see* and the adnominal locative demonstratives.

5 Analysis and discussion

5.1 Distribution of *nüüd*

The data contained altogether 47 particle-like uses of *nüüd*. It has been previously found that *nüüd* introduces in particular (focal) temporal adjuncts (Sahkai 2002, 2003). However, in the present data only 7 instances of *nüüd* occurred with temporal adjuncts. 5 of these were narrowly focused, e.g. (12) (note that in this example another temporal adjunct which functions as a setting topic is introduced with another temporal deictic, *siis* 'then'), one was a setting topic and one a sentence-final setting topic in a focus-initial sentence.

(12) ja=see   lõpe-b=mei-l=**nüd**   *homme*   ja:=ja   sis
    and= see end-3SG=1PL-ADESS=*nüüd* tomorrow and=and then

   järgmise-st nädala-st me pane-me=noh *uue-d*   kuupäeva-d
    next-ELAT   week-ELAT 1PL put-1PL=well new-NOM.PL date-NOM.PL

   paika
    place.ILL
    'and this will end tomorrow and next week we will set the new dates'

From the remaining 40 cases 28 involved narrowly focused constituents. All introduced new (and also mostly indefinite, generic or non-referential) information, except for two contrastive foci. Syntactically, the marked constituents are in an equal proportion arguments and adjuncts (13), predicate nouns or adjectives (14), and existential subjects (15):

(13) *Austria-s*   on   ned   kuskil   ütle-me kaks=tuhat=*viissada*
     Austria-INESS be.3   see.NOM.PL somewhere say-1PL 2500

   kaks=tuhat=*seitsesada*, olene-b   **nüd** *piirkonna-st* ja   oleneb
    2700   depend-3SG *nüüd* region-ELAT and depend-3SG

   selle-st   *aja-st*
    see-ELAT time-ELAT
    'in Austria they cost about let's say 2500–2700, it depends on the region and it depends on the period'

(14) ee *otell*   tule-b   **nüd**   *kõige* kalli-m
     uh   hotel   come-3SG *nüüd* most   expensive-CMPR
     'the hotel will be the most expensive [option]'

(15) *seal on* **nüd** *kolgend kohta*
    there be.3 *nüüd* 30   place.PART
    'there are thirty places'

Example (13) illustrates a verb which occurs several times in the data with a marked argument, namely *olenema* 'depend'. The example also contains a second instance of the verb, with a generic argument that is introduced with *see*, suggesting that *see* and *nüüd* can indeed be used in the same function and supporting the hypothesis that *see* can be used to mark focus.

In 4 cases *nüüd* introduces a focal VP or an argument contained in a focal VP (16), and in 4 cases an all-focus sentence (17).

(16) *Kanaaride-l*   **nüüd** *sellis-t   ajalugu   kui sellis-t*
    Canaries-ADESS *nüüd* such-PART history.PART as such-PART

    eriti   ei   ole
    particularly NEG be
    'on the Canaries there's not so much history as such [i.e. historical sights]'

(17) *kui* **nüüd** *kõht   lähe-b tühja-ks   et   **nüüd** mei-l*
    if   *nüüd* stomach go-3SG empty-TRANSL COMP *nüüd* 1PL-ADESS

    ei   ole siin enam   õhtusöök-i   hinna   sees
    NEG be here anymore supper-PART price.GEN inside
    'if you get hungry well there's no supper anymore included in the price'

In 5 cases *nüüd* introduces a contrastive topic (18) (note that while *nüüd* introduces the contrastive topic in this example, the contrastive focus in the same sentence is introduced by *siis* 'then'):

(18) *Soome   reisikorraldaja-d   lähe-vad neljappäev ... ja   **nüüd***
    Finnish tour.operator-NOM.PL go-3PL   Thursday   and *nüüd*

    Eesti   oma-d=ee   välju-vad   sis   reedeti
    Estonian one-NOM.PL=uh depart-3PL then on.Fridays
    'Finnish tour operators go on Thursdays ... and the Estonian ones depart on Fridays'

In conclusion, *nüüd* indeed correlates with the topic-focus structure. In 70% of the cases it introduces narrow foci and new information, but it also occurs with topics, especially contrastive topics. It also seems to mark arguments rather than whole VPs or clauses (in 2 of the 4 predicate-focus cases it marks the argument, and in one (ex. 16) it is ambiguous between argument marking and VP marking since the argument precedes the verb) – this suggests that adnominal demonstratives, which can only mark arguments or adjuncts, are in principle suitable for this function. As to the question of whether *nüüd* directly signals an information structural category or rather helps to organise the temporal and rhythmic structure of the utterance in a way that facilitates the processing of IS, the latter seems to be the case rather than the former, given that different elements – *nüüd, siis* 'then', *see* – are used interchangeably in the same function. It does seem possible however that over time these elements will become more conventionalised and semantically or pragmatically differentiated.

5.2 Distribution of *see, siin, seal*

The analysed data contained altogether 230 instances of non-demonstrative adnominal uses of *see* and the locative demonstratives. They were analysed into the three categories introduced in the previous section. 3 of the instances were not analysable in terms of these categories because they involved NP-internal modifiers (with previously mentioned referents). Next, I will analyse each category in turn.

5.2.1 Narrow focus

This category includes instances where the demonstratives introduce narrowly focused arguments and adjuncts, predicate nominals, and constituents introduced in presentational sentences. *See* co-occurred with narrow focus in a smaller proportion of cases than *nüüd*: in 70 cases. 10 of these involve marked syntax, including 5 NPs that are not embedded in syntactic structure, 4 topicalised foci, and 1 cleft construction. From the remaining 60 cases 34 introduced new information, including 6 generic (19) and 10 indefinite referents (20). At least in 9 instances the new referent is a place or a sight that is not necessarily identifiable by the addressee, and most of the new referents are mentioned only once, suggesting that they are not prominent either, e.g. (21) (the place names in this example are mentioned only once during the conversation and they are not part of general knowledge, for example they are new for me; in the dialogue, the travel agent is telling the client about South-Estonia and the client has explicitly said that he is not familiar with the region).

(19) st=noh jalgratta-ga sõitmise-l   pea-b   vaata-ma **seda**
     well bike-COM   riding-ADESS must-3SG watch-INF see.PART
     <u>liiklus-t</u>
     traffic-PART
     'but with the bike you have to watch out for the traffic'

(20) a:ga <u>Kanaarid</u> on   jah <u>rohkem</u> ikka   selline (0.6) <u>päevitamis</u>=[ja]
     but Canaries be.3 yes more   PRTCL such   sunning.GEN=and
     ja   ja   kui on   noh <u>tõesti</u> see <u>loodus-e</u>   <u>huvi</u>
     and and if   be.3 well really see nature-GEN interest
     'but the Canaries are more for sunning and if you really have an interest in nature'

(21) noh isegi on   käi-dud   **selle-s**   <u>Varnja-s</u>   ja
     well even be.3 go-IMPERS.PRTCPL see-INESS Varnja-INESS and
     <u>Kolkja-s</u>
     Kolkja-INESS
     'some have even been to Varnja and Kolkja'

These 34 instances thus seem to be better accounted for by the focus-marking hypothesis than the identifiability (or prominent referent) marking hypothesis. As for the 26 narrow focus constituents with previously mentioned referents (e.g. (22); tickets and accommodation have been mentioned before), these could be equally well accounted for both by the identifiability-marking and focus-marking hypothesis. It is also worth mentioning that 9 of these 26 instances are contrastive foci (e.g. (23); price differences for adults and children have been previously mentioned): contrasted referents constitute a relatively large category in the data and seem to be an independent factor that favours the use of adnominal demonstratives.

(22) (h) meie organiseeri-me tei-le=**ned**   (h) .hh
         1PL   arrange-1PL   2PL-all=see.NOM.PL
     <u>laevapileti-d</u>=ja=ja   <u>majutuse-d</u>=ja: ja=n- (.) ja
     boat.ticket-NOM.PL=and=and accommodation-NOM.PL=and and   and
     ned=e   noh (.) <u>sellise-d</u>   asja-d
     see.NOM.PL=uh well   such-NOM.PL thing-NOM.PL
     'we will arrange you the boat tickets and accommodations and that kind of things'

(23) ma ütle-n **need** täishinna-d praegu
    1SG tell-1SG *see*.NOM.PL full.price-NOM.PL now
    'I will tell you the full prices now'

5.2.2 Predicate focus

This category contains 38 instances where *see* marked a complement or adjunct NP contained in a focal VP. 4 of these involved marked order. From the remaining 34 instances 26 occur sentence-finally and bear the sentence accent, being very similar to the narrow focus cases (in the remaining 8 cases sentence accent falls on a sentence-final non-finite verb or predicate complement which follows the marked argument). Such cases could be considered as instances of focus marking, as is suggested by the fact that *nüüd*, too, was found to mark arguments rather than whole focused predicates.

From these 34 cases, 14 introduce new information, including generic and indefinite referents, and are thus not best accounted for in terms of identifiability marking (24) (this example also contains the locative demonstrative *seal* 'there' introducing a contrastive focus).

(24) ja kui on nagu <u>soov</u>=õ (0.7) rohkem tutvu-da **nende**
    and if be.3 like wish=uh more visit-INF *see*.GEN.PL

<u>vaatamisväärsuste-ga</u> siis on parem olla seal <u>Hurgadaa</u>
sight.PL-COM then be.3 better be.INF *seal* Hurghada.GEN

piirkonna-s
region-INESS
'and if you prefer to go sightseeing then it's better to be in the Hurghada region'

The remaining 20 instances introduce previously mentioned information (25). These 20 instances also include the 8 cases where the marked constituent does not bear the sentence accent. They also include 2 contrastive referents. Again, since these 20 instances have previously mentioned referents, they are equally well or even better accounted for in terms of identifiability marking.

(25) ta=n ikkagi <u>orienteeri-tud</u> **selle-le:** <u>suusategevuse-le</u>=ja
    3SG=be.3 still orient-IMPERS.PRTCPL *see*-ALL skiing-ALL=and
    'it is still primarily oriented at skiing'

5.2.3 Topics

In 120 instances the *see*-marked NP was analysed as a topic. In one case the NP introduced with *see* is in fact the subject of an adverbial clause that is itself a setting topic. From the remaining 119 cases, a total of 76 can be analysed as being syntactically induced. In 38 cases the demonstrative introduces a NP in a marked syntactic position, including 13 left dislocations, 8 right dislocations and 7 sentence-final topics; these NPs introduce both new and given information. The remaining 38 instances were topics of questions (26) and involved again in an equal proportion new and given referents. It seems that the presence of the demonstrative is a fixed constructional property of questions. It could be hypothesised to originate in contexts where the topic is a pronominal *see*, e.g. *Mis see on?* 'What is this?' In spoken language, the pronominal *see* has been described as having cliticised to or contracted with the interrogative word (e.g. *Misse on?*, cf. Erelt 1996: 16). As a result, *see* has perhaps been reanalysed as part of the interrogative word and has spread to contexts where the topic is not a pronoun but a NP.

(26) mis **see** teenustasu tei-l   nagu siis ole[-ks   või]
     what see service.fee 2PL-ADESS like   then be-COND.3SG Q
     'what would be your service fee?'

Consequently, from the 119 instances where the demonstrative introduces a topic more than 60% can be seen to be due to syntactic factors. From the remaining 43 instances two larger categories stand out: 9 immediate anaphoric uses and 11 contrastive topics[7].

Immediate anaphora after first mention is considered to be a typical use of anaphoric demonstratives (Himmelmann 1996: 229) and can be illustrated with example (27). However, whereas (27) would sound ungrammatical without the demonstrative, in the above-mentioned 9 instances, exemplified in (28), the demonstrative could be omitted without rendering the sentence ungrammatical. It is thus possible that these uses are precisely the kind of borderline case where the use of the anaphoric demonstrative is beginning to extend to new kinds of referents. It is interesting though that such immediate anaphoric uses are found only in topic position in the present data: in the narrow focus and predicate

---

[7] There exist finer divisions of information structural categories than the one used in the present study. For instance, Vallduví and Engdahl (1996) combine the divisions topic-comment and focus-ground into a tripartite system consisting of focus, link and tail; in terms of this system, the elements analysed as topics in the present study qualify as links rather than tails.

focus categories, the NPs with previously mentioned referents all have more distant antecedents. It is thus possible that this particular use of anaphoric demonstratives, and its possible extension, is related to topic position.

(27) sis   käia-kse   Sürakuusa   linna-s,   **see** linn on
     then go-IMPERS Syracuse.GEN city-INESS see city be.3

   kaks ja <u>pool</u> tuhat aasta-t   <u>vana</u>?
   2500   year-PART old
   'then you will visit the city of Syracuse. This city is 2500 years old.'

(28) olenevalt   <u>pansionaadi-st</u>   saa-b   võt-ta   <u>poolpansion-i</u>
     depending boarding.house-ELAT can-3SG take-INF half-board-GEN

   <u>teenus-e</u>.   **see** <u>poolpansion</u> tähenda-b <u>seda</u>   et   tei-l
   service-GEN see half-board   mean-3SG see.PART COMP 2PL-ADESS

   on   võimalus   telli-da   <u>juurde</u>   majutuse-le   <u>õhtusöök</u>
   be.3 possibility order-INF in.addition accommodation-ALL supper
   'depending on the boarding house you can have the half-board service. Half-board means that you can order supper in addition to the accommodation'

Contrastive topics marked with *see* are illustrated in (29) (this example also contains a contrastive focus marked with *nüüd*). Marking contrasted referents is another typical use of anaphoric demonstratives (Diessel 1999: 128), thus again, the use of demonstratives with contrastive topics is closely related to their anaphoric demonstrative use. Unlike the immediate anaphoric uses, contrastive uses are also found in the previous categories (there are altogether 33 instances in the data) and hence do not seem to be related to the topic position. The use of demonstratives with contrastive referents could thus be another context where the anaphoric demonstrative is spreading to previously mentioned referents. On the other hand, *nüüd* was similarly found to mark contrastive topics, suggesting that the marking of contrasted referents may be a typical function of focus markers as well.

(29) ää   <u>majutuse-ks</u>   on   mei-l: ä   **se**=<u>odavam</u> variant
     uh   accommodation-TRANSL be.3 1PL-ADESS uh see=cheaper option

   on=nüd   kolmetärnihotell koos <u>ommikusöögi-ga</u>.
   be.3=nüüd three.star.hotel with breakfast-COM
   'for accommodation we have uh the cheaper option is a three star hotel with breakfast'

From the remaining 22 instances where the constituent introduced by a demonstrative was analysed as a topic, 7 involve associative anaphoric uses (in terms of Hawkins 1978), i.e. referents that have not been mentioned before but are activated as part of a frame; for instance in (30) planes have not been mentioned before, but are activated by the mention of flights. Such uses are considered as characteristic of definite articles and as one type of context that permits to distinguish articles from demonstratives. It is thus not a context where an identifiability marker in the first stage of grammaticalisation is expected to appear, and the demonstratives there could be analysed as introducing the topic rather than signalling the identifiability of the referent. This would mean that they differ from *nüüd* which did not occur with topics, except contrastive ones.

(30) ää tšarterlend tähenda-b seda=et   see: (.) l-lennuk=lähe-b
     uh charter.flight mean-3SG see-1.PART=COMP see   plane=go-3SG

     otse: (.) Tallinna-st   sihtkohta
     straight   Tallinn-ELAT   destination.ILL

     'charter flight means that the plane goes straight from Tallinn to the destination'

The remaining 15 cases involve previously mentioned referents, but unlike in the immediate anaphoric uses the previous mentions occurred a longer time ago (31). In these cases the identifiability-marking and topic-marking hypotheses seem equally possible.

(31) **selle**   inna   puhul kahjuks   üliõpilaste-le   nagu: (.)
     see.GEN   price.GEN for   unfortunately student.PL-ALL   like

     {ka=erandi-t}   ei   tehta.   (0.3) et   see paket-i
     PRTCL=exception-PART   NEG make.IMPERS   comp see package-GEN

     hind=õõ   (0.5) ikkagi on   see mis   on.
     price=uh   still   be.3 see what   be.3

     'for the price unfortunately no exception is made for students. the package price is what it is'

5.3 Summary and discussion

In conclusion, the data does contain syntactically unmarked uses of adnominal demonstratives that seem to be better accounted for in terms of focus marking than in terms of identifiability marking: these are primarily the 34 instances where the demonstratives precede narrowly focused constituents with new, including indefinite, generic, non-identifiable and non-prominent referents, and also the 14 cases where the demonstratives introduce a new referent expressed by a sentence accent-bearing constituent in a focal VP. This could be considered as evidence that one of the functions of Spoken Estonian adnominal demonstratives is focus marking. Of course, they are not grammaticalised focus markers, just like they have not been assumed to be grammaticalised articles; there exist a number of other forms that are used in the same function (e.g. the temporal deictic *nüüd*) and the data also contains focal NPs with no marking. There are 38 more instances where the demonstrative correlates with a narrow focus or with a sentence accent-bearing argument in a predicate-focus structure, but these instances involve previously mentioned referents and could thus equally well be accounted for in terms of identifiability marking (they also include 11 contrasted referents which may independently induce the use of demonstratives).

In 43 cases, the demonstratives introduce syntactically non-marked topic constituents. Since topics have to be accessible (Lambrecht 1994: 165–171) most of these can be accounted for in terms of identifiability marking. However, some uses are less amenable to this explanation than others: in 7 cases, the demonstratives occurred in associative anaphoric uses which are expected to be marked by a developing identifiability marker only after it has become obligatory with previously mentioned referents. On the other hand, some uses are more plausibly accounted for in terms of the extension of anaphoric demonstratives: these are primarily the 9 immediate anaphoric uses (although such uses seem to be related to the topic position) and the 11 uses with contrasted referents (although focus markers occur with contrasted referents too, as suggested by the distribution of *nüüd*). In 15 cases involving referents that have been mentioned some time ago, both hypotheses seem equally plausible.

Altogether, 54 instances seem better accounted for in terms of identifiability marking: the 33 instances involving contrastive referents, the 9 immediate anaphoric uses, and the 12 instances where the use of the demonstrative does not correlate with IS (8 arguments in focal VPs, 3 NP-internal modifiers, and one subject in a topical adverbial clause). The fact that both hypotheses are favoured by a more or less equal number of instances suggests that both functions are present. This is supported by the comparison with *nüüd*, which correlates much more strongly with narrow foci and with new information than *see*, suggesting that the distribution of *see* reflects more than one function. Given that there is no doubt about the multifunctionality of demonstratives, it seems plausible that the identifiability marking use and the focus and topic marking functions occur in parallel (together with the other functions mentioned in section 2).

In a total of 42 instances the two hypotheses seem equally plausible: these are the topic and focus constituents with non-contrastive referents that have been mentioned some time ago in the previous discourse. This overlap together with the fact that 42 (or 78%) of the instances that seem to prefer the identifiability marking interpretation occur in a topic or focus position suggests that identifiability marking may occur primarily in topic and focus positions. After all, the data contained only 12 instances where the constituent marked with *see* did not correlate with the topic-focus structure; of course, I have not calculated the overall proportion of NPs that do not correlate with topic-focus structure: it may well be that it is equally small.

The data also confirms the previous finding that marked syntax favours the use of *see*: altogether 52 instances involved NPs in a marked syntactic position or outside syntactic structure. Finally, the analysis revealed a construction-specific use of Estonian demonstratives that has not been described before: they seem to be a fixed part of the question construction, in which they occur 38 times in the data. Hence, a total of 90 uses in the data can be seen to be syntactically induced.

6 Conclusion

The study demonstrated that, in addition to their other functions, Spoken Estonian adnominal demonstratives serve to signal foci and possibly topics. As such, they instantiate a little-studied focus marking strategy that seems to be characteristic of spoken language, namely the tendency to recruit existing particle-like elements for the purposes of focus marking. This strategy was explored by analysing the distribution of the particle *nüüd* 'now', which was found to signal primarily narrow foci, but also contrastive topics, and, more rarely, focal predicates (or arguments contained in focal predicates) and all-focus sentences. The exact nature of this strategy, e.g. whether it is induced by semantic/pragmatic, processing-related or prosodic factors, requires further study. However, the fact that different elements – e.g. *see* and the temporal deictics *nüüd* 'now' and *siis* 'then' – seem to be used interchangeably in the same function without an easily identifiable semantic or pragmatic import suggests that their role is to facilitate the processing of IS by allowing a flexible temporal and rhythmic organisation of the utterance.

It was also confirmed that Estonian adnominal demonstratives occur in contexts that may reflect the spreading of anaphoric demonstratives to a wider range of previously mentioned referents, a process that is assumed to drive the grammaticalisation of demonstratives into definite articles. These contexts were primarily uses with contrasted referents and immediate anaphoric uses. Interestingly, such uses tended to coincide with topic and focus positions, suggesting that the extension of the use of anaphoric demonstratives occurs primarily in topic and focus position. However, this hypothesis requires further study.

More generally, the study draw attention to the multifunctionality of demonstratives in spoken language: e.g. in Spoken Estonian they have been described as metalinguistic markers, filler words, affective markers, nominalisers, relative clause markers. The present study confirmed the previous finding that they are also used to mark NPs in marked syntactic position, a function that can be characterised in terms of NP Construction (Hawkins 2004) but is indirectly related to the expression of IS since marked syntax usually signals IS. It was also found that Estonian adnominal demonstratives occur as a fixed part of questions.

In the light of this multifunctionality, this paper suggested the need to rethink the view according to which it is solely the spreading of the identifiability marking function of demonstratives that drives their grammaticalisation into definite articles: given the multiplicity of their functions in spoken discourse, it seems likely that the development of demonstratives into an obligatory element in the NP is not driven by just one of these functions.

References

Amon, Marri. 2009. Les détachements finaux en estonien oral: productivité et fonctionnement. In M. M. J. Fernandez-Vest (ed.), *Plurilinguisme et traduction – des enjeux pour l'Europe*, 151–164. Paris: l'Harmattan.

Diessel, Holger. 1999. *Demonstratives: form, function and grammaticalization*. Amsterdam & Philadelphia: John Benjamins.

Epstein, Richard. 1993. The definite article: early stages of development. In Jaap van Marle (ed.), *Historical Linguistics 1991. Papers from the 10th international conference on historical linguistics. Amsterdam, 12–16 august 1991*, 111–134. Amsterdam & Philadelphia: John Benjamins.

Erelt, Mati. 1996. Relative Words in Estonian Relative Clauses. In Mati Erelt (ed.), *Estonian: Typological Studies I*, 9–23. Tartu: Tartu Ülikooli Kirjastus.

Greenberg, Joseph H. 1978. How Does a Language Acquire Gender Markers? In Joseph H. Greenberg (ed.), *Universals of Human Language. Vol. 3, Word Structure*, 47–82. Stanford: Stanford University Press.

Gundel, Jeanette K., Nancy Hedberg & Ron Zacharski. 1993. Cognitive Status and the Form of Referring Expressions in Discourse. *Language* 69. 274–307.

Hawkins, John A. 1978. *Definiteness and indefiniteness: a study in reference and grammaticality prediction*. London: Croom Helm.

Hawkins, John A. 2004. *Efficiency and complexity in grammars*. Oxford & New York: Oxford University Press.

Hayashi, Makoto & Kyung-eun Yoon. 2006. A cross-linguistic exploration of demonstratives in interaction. With particular reference to the context of word-formation trouble. *Studies in Language* 30. 485–540.

Hiietam, Katrin & Kersti Börjars. 2003. The emergence of a definite article in Estonian. In Diane C. Nelson & Satu Manninen (eds.), *Generative approaches to Finnic and Saami Linguistics*, 1–39. Stanford: CSLI Publications.

Himmelmann, Nikolaus P. 1996. Demonstratives in Narrative Discourse: A taxonomy of universal uses. In Barbara A. Fox (ed.), *Studies in Anaphora*, 205–254. Amsterdam & Philadelphia: John Benjamins.

Himmelmann, Nikolaus P. 1997. *Deiktikon, Artikel, Nominalphrase: Zur Emergenz syntaktischer Struktur*. Tübingen: Niemeyer.

Lambrecht, Knud. 1994. *Information structure and sentence form*. Cambridge: Cambridge University Press.

Laury, Ritva. 1997. *Demonstratives in Interaction. The emergence of a definite article in Finnish*. Amsterdam & Philadelphia: John Benjamins.

Lindström, Liina. 2005. *Finiitverbi asend lauses. Sõnajärg ja seda mõjutavad tegurid suulises eesti keeles* [The position of the finite verb in a clause: word order and the factors affecting it in Spoken Estonian]. Tartu: Tartu Ülikooli Kirjastus.

Lyons, Christopher. 1999. *Definiteness*. Cambridge: Cambridge University Press.

Pajusalu, Renate. 1997. Is there an article in (Spoken) Estonian? In Mati Erelt (ed.), *Estonian typological studies II*, 146–177. Tartu: Tartu Ülikooli Kirjastus.

Pajusalu, Renate. 2001. Definite and indefinite determiners in Estonian. In Enikő Németh (ed.), *Pragmatics in 2000. Selected Papers from the 7th International Pragmatics Conference*, 458–469. Antwerp: International Pragmatics Association.

Potts, Christopher & Florian Schwarz. 2010. Affective 'this'. *Linguistic Issues in Language Technology* 3(5). 1–30.

Prince, Ellen. 1981. On the inferencing of indefinite 'this' NPs. In Aravind K. Joshi, Bonnie L. Webber & Ivan A. Sag (eds.), *Elements of Discourse Understanding*, 231–250. Cambridge & New York: Cambridge University Press.

Sahkai, Heete. 2002. *Demonstrative Doubling in Spoken Estonian*. Unpublished MA Thesis, University of Tartu.

Sahkai, Heete. 2003. Demonstrative Doubling in Spoken Estonian. *Trames: Journal of the Humanities and Social Sciences* 7(2). 120–144.

Sahkai, Heete, Mari-Liis Kalvik & Meelis Mihkla. 2013. Prosodic effects of Information Structure in Estonian. In, *Nordic Prosody. Proceedings of the XIth Conference, Tartu 2012*, 323–332. Frankfurt am Main: Peter Lang Edition.

Salveste, Nele. 2013. Focus perception in Estonian: is it governed by syntax or prosody? In Eva Liina Asu, Pärtel Lippus (eds.), *Nordic Prosody. Proceedings of the XIth Conference, Tartu 2012*, 333–342. Frankfurt am Main: Peter Lang Edition.

Tael, Kaja 1988. *Sõnajärjemallid eesti keeles (võrrelduna soome keelega)* [Word order patterns in Estonian (in comparison with Finnish)]. Preprint KKI-53. Tallinn: Eesti NSV Teaduste Akadeemia Keele ja Kirjanduse Instituut.

Vallduví, Enric & Elisabet Engdahl. 1996. The linguistic realization of information packaging. *Linguistics* 34. 459–519.

Van Valin, Robert D. Jr. 1999. A Typology of the Interaction of Focus Structure and Syntax. In E. Raxilina, J. Testelec (eds.), *Typology and the Theory of Language: From Description to Explanation*, 511–524. Moscow: Languages of Russian Culture.

Wiese, Heike. 2011. *So* as a focus marker in German. *Linguistics* 49. 991–1039.

III IS and Discourse Particles

Diana Forker and Oleg Belyaev
11 Word order and focus particles in Nakh-Daghestanian languages

1 Introduction

This paper offers an account of how information structure is expressed in the Nakh-Daghestanian languages. The focus of this paper is on word order and focus particles which can be regarded as the most important means of manipulating the information structure because they are to varying degrees employed in all languages of the family. Other means such as a special cleft-like focus construction (cf. Xaidakov 1986, Kazenin 2002), the opposition between certain verb forms (cf. Sumbatova 2004), the use of so-called 'predicative particles' (Kalinina & Sumbatova 2007), or intonation are either not very prominent or restricted to a subset of the languages.

Nakh-Daghestanian languages are located in the eastern part of the Caucasian mountains. Most of the languages are found in Russia, but some speech communities live in Azerbaijan and Georgia. Only the larger languages (e.g. Chechen, Ingush, Avar, Lezgian) are regularly written. The majority of the Nakh-Daghestanian languages are oral languages used as primary means of everyday communication. Much of the data on which this paper is based comes from originally oral texts that have been collected and/or analyzed by the authors and thus lack references. All remaining examples originate from texts that have been published by other researchers.

The aim of this paper is to present a typologically oriented study of the expression of topic and focus via word order and the use of particles. We employ the standard information structure-related terms – topic, focus[1], contrast, pragmatic presupposition and assertion – that are widely accepted in typological and theoretical literature on information structure (cf. Vallduví 1992, Erteschik-Shir 1997, Krifka & Musan 2012 and many other works). Our specific understand-

---

[1] An important issue that has been debated in recent literature is whether "focus" can be defined as a cross-linguistically valid notion at all (Matić & Wedgwood 2013). However, whatever conclusion on this question is reached, it does not directly affect our use of the term in this paper, as we are dealing with a group of closely related languages, within which all of the IS terms we use are easily identifiable with particular pragmatic and structural configurations.

Diana Forker, University of Bamberg and James Cook University
Oleg Belyaev, Lomonosov Moscow State University and Sholokhov Moscow State University for the Humanities

ing of these terms is following Lambrecht (1994). We show that topics are placed at the edges of clauses, often depending on the activation status of the topical referent. Focus is usually verb-adjacent and can precede or occasionally follow the verb. Focus particles express narrow focus, which precedes the verb. They represent additional means of emphasizing single words within focused phrases.

The paper is organized as follows. In Section 2, we present a description of topic and focus positions and the impact of different words orders on the information structure of clauses. In Section 3 we give an account of the major focus particles. Section 4 analyzes the interaction of focus particles and focus marking by means of word order and Section 5 contains the conclusion.

2 Word order

Nakh-Daghestanian languages are usually assumed to possess an unmarked SOV word order. While this order of constituents is indeed most frequently used, the ordering of constituents is not determined by grammatical relations, but by information structure. The reason why SOV word order is most common is that objects are typically focused and subjects are typically topics. When the situation is reversed, the object is placed before the subject (1).

(1) Lezgian (Lezgic) (Haspelmath 1993: 301)
 rak č'exi xei-n swas [ajnise-di]^{FOC} aqʰaj-na
 door big son-GEN bride Ajnise-ERG open-AOR
 'The door was opened by his older son's wife Ajnise.'

The final position of the verb is a more strongly observed rule. However, there are no Nakh-Daghestanian languages where this is a strict rule; most languages allow postverbal placement of noun phrases at least in certain contexts (e.g., in direct speech), while some rather consistently place "old" topics postverbally (see Section 2.1). Word order is used to mark topic and focus; thetic ("all-new") sentences are also characterized by a special word order. Predicate focus is marked by a special construction. Finally, left and right-dislocation with pronominal doubling is also available.

2.1 Topic

In all Nakh-Daghestanian languages, topic constituents are positioned at the edges of the clause. Clause-initial topics are common, though clause-final topics are also found. The distribution appears to be the following: highly activated

NPs (that represent "old" information, or protagonists) are placed at the right edge of the clause, while NPs with lesser degrees of activation are placed at the beginning of the clause (2).

(2) Hinuq (Tsezic)
[A story about a man whose wife died because of his fault.]
hagoƛ'o-šid   [hado rek'we]^TOP ƛexwe-n   Ø-a:-ho.
at.that.time-ON this man(I)   remain-UWPST   I-cry-IPFV
t'ok'aw cingi aqili=n   y-iq'e-n   gom   [haɬoy]^TOP
more   then woman=ADD   II-bring-UWPST   be.NEG   he.ERG
'From that time on **this man** remained (alone) crying. **He** did not marry another woman.'

The same correlation is observed in Dargwa languages (3a, b). Sentence (3a) is the beginning of the text, where mother Khadizha and Arbakh are not activated (although they are assumed to be known to the speaker) and thus the coordinate NP referring to them stands at the beginning. In (3b), which directly follows (3a) in the text, the numeral $k^{w}e{:}l$ 'two' referring to the topic is positioned at the right boundary of the clause (in both (3a) and (3b), the predicate is nominal and marked by the predicative enclitic =di, thus in (3b) the right boundary is everything after the first prosodic word). The fact that $k^{w}e{:}l$ in (3b) is a topic follows from the fact that Khadizha and Arbakh are protagonists of the text and were also topics in the preceding sentence, thus in any conceivable sense of aboutness, (3b) is "about" them (the discourse continues describing their actions).

(3) Icari (Dargwa) (Sumbatova & Mutalov 2003: 209)
a. [di-la   xadiža   waba=ra   hejk' arbax=ra]^TOP
   1sg-GEN   Khadizha   mother=ADD dem   Arbakh=ADD
   s:ingli-la   q:at:a-b   diči-b=di
   Singli-GEN   canyon-HPL[ESS]   pasture-HPL[ESS]=PST
   '**My mother Khadizha** and **Arbakh** were at the pasture in the canyon of Singli.'

b. dukluš:-i=di   [k'ʷe:l=ra²]^TOP   ha⁽jwant-a-lla   kalxuz-la
   shepherd-PL=PST   two=ADD   cattle-OBL.PL-GEN   kolkhoz-GEN
   '**The two** were shepherds of the kolkhoz cattle'

---

2 The additive clitic =ra is typically used with numerals and quantifiers in Icari and in other Dargwa varieties, and is not in this case related to topicality or other information structure notions.

Other languages that observe this distribution of old and new topics include Archi and Avar (Testelec 1998: 260). However, the placement of old topics at the right edge is hardly a strict rule. Each of the languages cited above allows old topics to also appear clause-initially (4). The placement of old topics is probably motivated by discourse prominence, protagonism or the degree of activation. The earlier a participant has been introduced as a topic, the higher the probability that it will be placed postverbally.

(4) Archi (Lezgic)
(http://www.philol.msu.ru/~languedoc/rus/archi/corpus.php, ex. 25.002)
[Once upon a time there was a poor man.]

[jamum-mi-n]^TOP kummu-s c'abu-s nac' eχ:u-li
he-OBL-ERG eat.IV-INF drink-INF nothing IV.stay.PFV-CVB
edi-li i-t'u
IV.AUX.PFV-CVB IV.AUX-NEG

'**He** had nothing to eat or drink.'

It still needs to be clarified whether all Nakh-Daghestanian languages allow for postverbal topics. Judging from the available texts and grammars it seems that a few languages (e.g. Lezgian, Lak, Ingush in the verb-final construction, eventually Bagvalal, Tsakhur) do not generally admit clause-final topics, or, for that matter, postverbal constituents in general. However, in these languages, as well as in other Nakh-Daghestanian languages, postverbal constituents, regardless of their information structure status, occur for other reasons: in direct speech constructions where the verb of speech follows the quote (5a), in "emphatic or emotional speech" (5b) (Haspelmath 1993: 300), or when the postverbal NP is heavy.

(5) a. Bagvalal (Andic) (Kibrik et al. 2001: 775)

"čo=ʁala tak mala=di?" heƛ'i gaʔišnik-š:u-r
what=PRT so little=PRT say road.policeman-OBL.I-ERG

'"Why so little (money)?" said the road policeman.'

b. Lezgian (Lezgic) (Haspelmath 1993: 300)

paka hat-da kun či ğil-e!
tomorrow get-FUT 2pl 1pl.GEN hand-IN.ESS

'Tomorrow you will fall into my hands!'

Even though examples with postverbal topics are occasionally encountered in these languages, this is due to independent factors that are hardly related to information structure; in addition, the frequency of postverbal topics in these languages is in any case incomparable to their frequency in such languages as Dargwa and Archi.

2.2 Focus

Nakh-Daghestanian languages allow placing the focus both before and after the verb. In most languages, the distribution between the preverbal and postverbal positions correlates with the distinction between narrow and wide focus. Narrow focus is marked by placing the focused constituent preverbally (6a, b). This includes WH-questions and the answers (6b) to them.

(6) a. Tabasaran (Lezgic) (Uslar 1979: 491)

sul-u   kʷ-ap-ir,   diriz   žiwab   [izu]ᶠᴼᶜ lic'-an-z-a
fox-ERG PST-say-PST.3 3sg.N.DAT answer   1sg.ERG   give-FUT-1-SG

'The fox said: it is **me** who will answer him.'

b. Qunqi (Dargwa) (Dmitry Ganenkov, p.c.)

"he‹b›a   [murt]ᶠᴼᶜ b-ik'-an-ce=ji"   ikʲʷ-le   ca‹w›i il
then‹HPL› when   HPL-come-POT-ATTR=Q   say-CVB COP‹M› DEM

w-iqna-c:e.   w-iqna ikʲʷ-le   ca‹w›i, "he‹b›a   [dus:-li-j
M-old-INTER[LAT] M-old   say-CVB cop‹m›   then‹HPL› year-OBL-DAT

ji   zamana, ji   bari]ᶠᴼᶜ b-ik'-an-ce   ca‹w›i
dem time   dem day   HPL-come-POT-ATTR COP‹M›

'"**When** will they come?" (he) says to the old man. The old man answers, "**Next year at this time, on this day** (they) will come".'

This generalization seems to be quite robust. It is confirmed by the fact that in elicitation speakers often reject narrow focus occurring after the verb, as it is apparently the case in Tsakhur (cf. Testelec 1999: 294–295). However, judging from the available spoken texts, preverbal placement is only strictly necessary for interrogatives (7a). Answers to WH-questions can also contain the narrow focus in the postverbal position (7b), although such examples are much less frequent than those with preverbal narrow focus. This demonstrates that generalizations about information structure obtained through elicitation can represent mere tendencies rather than strict rules.

(7) a. Tsakhur (Lezgic) (Kibrik et al. 1999: 833)
wuš-da   gaʕmra   [njaː=niː]ᶠᴼᶜ wo-b-na?
2pl.POSS-AA sheep.shed(III) where=Q   be-II-AA
'Where was your sheep shed?'

b. ši   wo-b=niː   [centr-eː a-b]ᶠᴼᶜ
   1pl be-HPL=EMPH center-IN inside-HPL
   'We were in the center.'

Wide focus can be marked by placing the constituents that are part of the focus either preverbally (8a, b) or postverbally (9a, b).

(8) a. Agul (Lezgic) (Dmitry Ganenkov, p.c.)
[The speaker promises another man a gift for accompanying him.]
[sa   dewe   ic'.a-s-e]ᶠᴼᶜ
one camel give.IPFV-INF-COP

'(I) will **give** (you) **one camel**.'

b. Tabasaran (Lezgic) (Uslar 1979: 510)
[The speaker (a fox) tells about its preceding activities]
izu   [simč'ur jisː-an   taʕhmim-ar-iz   dars   gʷu-nu-z-a]ᶠᴼᶜ
1sg.ERG thirty   year-GEN   student-PL-DAT   lesson give-PFT-1-SG

'**For thirty years I have been giving lessons to students.**'

(9) a. Agul (Lezgic) (Dmitry Ganenkov, p.c.)
[The protagonist wanted to go outside and asked his mother to prepare his clothes]
bagajmi   [ʕučːu-na   uči-n   kan]ᶠᴼᶜ
in.the.morning wash.PFV-CVB   REFL-GEN   clothes

'In the morning (she) **washed his clothes**.'

b. Bagvalal (Andic) (Kibrik et al. 2001: 733)
[The text describes the history of Kwanada]
haddiłːir raʁiri-r-o   [q'abul   že:-b-o   ek'ʷa   busːurman din]ᶠᴼᶜ
long   fight-HPL-CVB   acceptance   do-N-CVB   cop   Muslim   religion

'After long fighting, (the people of Kwanada) **accepted the Muslim religion**.'

It is also possible to have simultaneously pre- and postverbal wide focus (10).

(10) Archi (Lezgic)
(http://www.philol.msu.ru/~languedoc/rus/archi/corpus.php, text 11, 6)

χit:a jemim-mij [q'ˁʷet'u lo aq:'u-li noλ'a]ᶠᴼᶜ
then they-OBL.PL[ERG] two child IV.abandon.PFV-EVID house.IN[ESS]
'Once they **left both children at home**.'

An important feature of preverbal focus marking is that in some languages, only the head of a noun phrase occupies the immediately preverbal position, while the rest is displaced postverbally; for example, this is the case in Icari (Sumbatova & Mutalov 2003: 160) and in Hinuq (examples (11a, b), the phrasal constituents that belong together are underlined). Presumably, this is due to prosodic reasons. In these languages genitive phrases can be split up with the phrasal head occurring immediately before the verb and the genitive modifier following the verb.

(11) a. Icari (Dargwa) (Sumbatova & Mutalov 2003: 160)

č'ug q:at:a-d [haˁjwan-ti d-ir-iri]ᶠᴼᶜ niš:a-la
down canyon-NPL[IN.ESS] cattle-PL NPL-become-HAB.PST 1pl-GEN
'And down in the canyon used to be **our cattle**.'

b. Hinuq (Tsezic)

haze oλra=n essu-y haw [ɬad-i teɬ]ᶠᴼᶜ
those.OBL seven.OBL=ADD brother-ERG she rock-IN inside
[raλ'-mo-ɬ]ᶠᴼᶜ [yašik'-ma gor-no ker-u-zo]ᶠᴼᶜ
earth-OBL-CONT box-OBL-IN put-UWPST iron-OBL-GEN
'The seven brothers put her **into a rock, into the earth, into an iron box** (i.e. coffin).'

It should be noted that when wide focus is expressed postverbally, it is especially common with goals, including spatial goals, addressees, recipients, etc. (12).

(12) Qunqi (Dargwa) (Dmitry Ganenkov, p.c)

w-ax-le [w-et-aʁ-ib-le ca‹w›i ca žuhut' šahar-li-c:e]ᶠᴼᶜ
M-go-CVB M-THITHER-reach-PRET-CVB COP‹M› one Jewish city-OBL-INTER[LAT]
'Going, (he) **came to some Jewish city**.' {from a story about a prince called Žanšah, which describes his consequent actions}

Another type of focus that tends to be expressed postverbally is contrastive focus (13). In fact, this extends also to modifiers in NPs, which also occur postnominally if they are contrastive and/or in focus (cf. Testelec 1998: 274).

(13) Budukh (Lezgic) (Talibov 2007: 273)
q'ažir-a suʕre-rber č-aʁ-ar [qːiʕšːlaχ-ǯ-e]^FOC, jaz-ǯ-e
winter-LOC herd-PL SUB-go-MSD qishlaq-OBL-LOC autumn-OBL-LOC
ʕoʕšχ-ar-i [daʁ-ǯ-a]^FOC
return-MSD-PRS mountain-OBL-LOC
'In winter the herds go **to the qishlaqs**, in autumn they return **to the mountains**.'

Verb fronting is a typical way of marking predicate focus. In (14), the verb is located in the clause-initial position while the argument NPs retain their unmarked SO order.

(14) Qunqi (Dargwa)
[ka-d-čː-ib-le]^FOC, [atrezat-d-arq'-ib-le]^FOC [gu-r-he-b-ertː-ib-le]^FOC
down-NPL-cut-PRET-CVB cut-NPL-do-PRET-CVB SUB-EL-up-III-cut-PRET-CVB
qːačaʁ-a-d bandit-a-d tilipunnij svʲaz, tilipun
brigand-OBL.PL-ERG bandit-OBL.PL-ERG telephone connection telephone
'The bandits **cut off, cut away, undercut** the telephone connection.'
{the speaker had already stated in the preceding context that bandits had ruined the telephone connection; in this sentence he underlines the specific action that they have commited}

2.3 Thetic sentences

In thetic sentences standing at the beginning of texts, unmarked (SOV) word order is normally used. However, other orders, including SVO, are also quite frequent, so it cannot be said that a certain word order strategy is definitely preferred for these contexts. Intransitive thetic sentences show very clear word order preferences. Presentational sentences that introduce new referents (usually human, but sometimes also non-human, e.g. in fairy tales) are verb-initial (15a); an interesting feature for SOV languages that has also been reported for Georgian in Asatiani & Skopeteas (2012: 134). This generalization is quite robust and attested not only with existential verbs, but also with other intransitive predicates such as 'come', 'arrive', etc. Other kinds of intransitive thetic sentences are verb-final ((15b), see also (23) below).

(15) a. Shiri (Dargwa)

[le-b-li ca‹b›i le-b-ak:ʷar-ri ca‹b›i ca hämhä]^FOC
exist-N-CVB COP‹N› exist-N-NEG-CVB COP‹N› one donkey
'Once upon a time there lived a donkey.'

b. [dirix^w če-b-äʁ-ib-li ca‹b›i]^FOC
fog SUPER[LAT]-N-reach-PRET-CVB COP‹N›
'Fog came down.'

2.4 Co-occurrence of postverbal topic and focus

Focus placed before the verb is strictly preverbal, i.e. no material that is not part of the focus may stand between the focused NP and the verb. Postverbal focus, however, is not strictly verb-adjacent: when both a postverbal topic and a postverbal focus are present, they can be ordered in any way. This is exemplified by the following two examples from Khuduts Dargwa, both taken from the same text and with the same character (the protagonist) as the topic:

(16) a. Khuduts (Dargwa) (Natalia Serdobolskaya, p.c.)

na q'ˤʷal=ra sač-ib-li, [sa:č'-ib-li ca-w]^FOC
now cow=ADD HITHER:bring-PRET-CVB HITHER:come-PRET-CVB COP-M
[il]^TOP [qili]^FOC
he home.IN[LAT]
'Now, having brought the cow, he went home.'

b. Khuduts (Dargwa) (Natalia Serdobolskaya, p.c.)

ag-ur-ri ʁaj-la q:anta, [b-arč:-ib-li ca-b
go-PRET-CVB speech-GEN short N-find-PRET-CVB COP-N
nerx-la c'iq'a]^FOC [il-ij]^TOP
butter-GEN jug he-DAT
'In short, he went and found a jug of butter.'

In other languages such as Hinuq it seems that it is far more common to have first postverbal topic and then focus (i.e. V-TOP-FOC) as in example (17) rather than the other way around (V-FOC-TOP). However, apart from those sentences in which one of the NPs is a goal, two NPs following the verb are not frequently found.

(17) Hinuq (Tsezic)

Ø-ežinnu uži-ž   r-aš-a   goł [hayłoz]ᵀᴼᴾ [nasibaw   žo]ᶠᴼᶜ
I-old   son-DAT V-find-INF be he.DAT   predestined thing(v)
'The oldest son will find **the thing predestined for him**.'

Characterizing the postverbal focus as either verb-adjacent or clause-final has important typological implications. In recent work it has been argued, e.g. in Büring (2010), that a specialized syntactic focus position (such as a preverbal position) must necessarily coexist with either an *in situ* focus position ("boundary focus", indicated by intonation) or an edge focus position (defined as occurring at the edge of some prosodic domain). Daghestanian languages, however, mostly express focus structurally, not purely intonationally, and therefore could be analyzed as having two dedicated structural focus positions. Similarly, van der Wal (2012) maintains that in languages where focus is verb-adjacent, focus can either be preverbal or postverbal. That is, a given language cannot have both immediately preverbal and immediately postverbal focus.

Due to the paucity of examples containing both topic and focus postverbally, the evidence that we have concerning the nature of postverbal focus in Nakh-Daghestanian languages is, unfortunately, too scarce at the moment. More work based on textual evidence is required in order to have a clear understanding of the nature of the focus positions in these languages. However, examples like (16a) and (17) may be taken to suggest that postverbal topics and foci do not occupy specific syntactic positions, but are rather in general associated with the postverbal part of the clause (whether for prosodic reasons or due to the fact that the postverbal area in general admits both topics and foci).

3 Focus and focus-sensitive particles

Nakh-Daghestanian languages have a rich inventory of discourse particles with emphatic and intensifying meaning. They also have a number of particles and enclitics serving more specific information-structural and partially grammatical purposes. The most important of these items are (i) additive, (ii) interrogative, and (iii) intensifying particles.

3.1 Additive particles

Most (if not all) Nakh-Daghestanian languages have an enclitic with the meaning 'and, also, even'. We will call these particles 'additive' particles and we assume that their basic meaning is 'and, also'. They fulfill grammatical and semanto-pragmatic functions, and in most of the languages they are also used for derivation (e.g. formation of indefinite pronouns). One major function of additive particles is the conjunction of various types of phrases (NPs, clauses, adjectival phrases, etc.). In case of NP conjunction the additives mostly occur on each conjunct (3a). In case of clauses it is typical for additives to occur in all but the last clause, in order to reinforce the fact that the events in the clauses are tightly connected. Various words can function as hosts regardless of their contribution to the information structure (18).

(18) Qunqi (Dargwa) (Dmitry Ganenkov, p.c.)
c'it:ar čuja=**ra** luχ-un-ce ca‹b›i, c'it:ar ʔirʔ-le=**ra**
black ram=ADD slaughter-PRET-ATTR COP‹N› black hen-PL=ADD

luχ-un-ce ca‹d›i, it:i=**ra** d-urt'-ib-ce ca‹d›i
slaughter-PRET-ATTR COP‹NPL› DEM.PL=ADD NPL-give-PRET-ATTR COP‹NPL›

'Then they slaughtered a black ram, they slaughtered black hens and they gave them (=the slaughtered animals) away.'

In (18), the additive particle =ra is attached to all the NPs functioning as objects. Here the semantic/pragmatic contribution of the particle is to produce a narrative chain of subsequent conjoined actions. The particle is attached to the first constituent but has the whole clause in its scope. Similar additive particles are encountered in other languages; a well-known case is Latin =que, which attaches to the first word of the following sentence when conjoining sentences (Zwicky 1977: 6).

Additives also function as focus sensitive particles. Such particles entail the corresponding sentence without the particle and presuppose the existence of a set of alternatives and that at least for one alternative the corresponding sentence is true (König 1991: 62 see also Sæbø 2004 and Winterstein & Zeevat 2012 for more recent accounts). If the alternatives can be ordered along a scale we have the scalar additive meaning 'even' (19) (cf. Gast & van der Auwera 2011 for scalar additives in European languages). Sometimes it is hard to tell from the context alone whether 'also' or 'even' is the best translation.

(19) Bagvalal (Andic) (Kibrik 2001: 828)
in-š:u-b=da ʕormi qʷas:ar ʒ-a:la, o-š:u-r
REFL-OBL.M-GEN.N=INT life salvation do-POT.INF this-OBL.M-ERG

b-uq'u-b-o ekʷa hʷaj=**la**
N-cut-N-CVB be dog=ADD

'In order to save his life he even slaughtered a DOG.'

Some Nakh-Daghestanian languages have an additional dedicated scalar additive, which can usually co-occur with the simple additive (20a). Occasionally, additives merely emphasize elements in the clause (20b).

(20) a. Archi (Lezgic)
(http://www.philol.msu.ru/~languedoc/rus/archi/corpus.php, ex. 30.010)

tuχt'ur-til=**u**=jaš:i   b-i   la-t:i-š,   b-olo   ʕeležu-b
doctor-PL=ADD=EVEN HPL-be 1pl.OBL-SPR-EL III-1pl.GEN ugly-III

porma-li-t:i-š   tama:ša bu-š:u-r-ši
clothes-OBL-SPR-EL surprise III-take-IPFV-CVB

'It was even the DOCTORS who were wondering about us, about our ugly clothes.'

b. Lak (Schulze 2011)
ut:i na   qun-ma=**gu** qan-na   b-i‹w›k'u-n   b-u-ra
now 1sg old-III=ADD   become-INF III-be‹III›-PST III-COP-1SG
'Now I am getting OLD.'

Apart from the just illustrated functions, it has been claimed that additives also have a genuine IS-related function. In this respect, two opposing approaches can be identified: the topic approach and the focus approach. The first has been advanced by Polinsky & Potsdam (2001) for Tsez =*n*. They argue that the Tsez additive is a topic particle by showing that it cannot be attached to WH-words in questions, not to those words that are answers to WH-questions, not to constituents in thetic sentences and not to non-referring words such as negative indefinite pronouns.

For the majority of Nakh-Daghestanian languages the argumentation of Polinsky & Potsdam (2001) is doubtful. One of their arguments is that Tsez =*n* cannot be added to the focused item in an answer to a WH-question. However, since the examples are elicited, it is hard to tell whether their unacceptability is due to ungrammaticality or simply to lack of an appropriate context. In natural texts from other Nakh-Daghestanian languages, additive enclitics are possible in unambiguously focal contexts such as the answer to a WH-question (21).

(21) a. Tsakhur (Lezgic) (Kibrik 2001: 805)
xule-l-le   nafas=ne wa-qa=d   wo-d-un?
how.many-IV-CARD soul(IV)=Q 2sg.OBL-POSS=ADD be-IV-A
'How many souls do you have?' [~ 'How numerous is your family?']

b. jic'ɨ-l-e=**d** nafas wo-d-un
   ten-IV-CARD=ADD soul(IV) be-IV-A
   '(I have) TEN souls.' [~ 'I have a large family']

Second, conjunction enclitics may occur on words in thetic (i.e. fully-focused) sentences as example (22) from Lak shows. The NP 'small box' is newly introduced into the discourse in a thetic sentence. It is therefore part of the focus while bearing the additive enclitic.

(22) Lak (Victor Friedman, p.c.)
   ga-na-l k'u-siw-ru-l uːtuːsːa ǧa‹ɾ›ǧ-unu d-ur wa
   this-OBL-GEN weight-MSD-OBL-GEN beam(IV) break‹IV›-CVB IV-COP and
   k'ičːa ca č'i-w-isːa qːurši=**gu** b-ah-nu b-ur
   up.there one small-III-ATTR box(III)=ADD III-fall-CVB III-COP
   'His weight broke the beam, and from up there A SMALL BOX fell.'

Third, other types of thetic sentences containing additives that are apparently ungrammatical in Tsez are admissible in other Nakh-Daghestanian languages such as Hinuq, the closest relative of Tsez (23).

(23) Hinuq (Tsezic)
   qema=**n** r-aq'-o
   rain(V)=ADD V-come-PRS
   'It is also/even raining.'

Furthermore, the cleft construction, which is a focus strategy (Kalinina & Sumbatova 2007), can be combined with additive particles on focused constituents. In example (20a) from Archi the noun *tuχt'urtil* 'doctor-PL' bears the simple additive (and the scalar additive) and is focused by means of the following copula.

The second approach (focus) has several followers. Nichols & Peterson (2010) do not give an explicit analysis of additive enclitics in information-structural terms, but they list emphatic and/or contrastive focus as one of the possible functions. In fact, additive enclitics can co-occur with intensifying particles (e.g. Bezhta =*zu*, Hinuq and Tsez =*tow*, Godoberi =*da*, Avar =*go*), which are also focus markers (Section 3.3), and with other focus-sensitive particles such as Tsez =*kin* 'even', Archi =*jašːi* 'even' (20a).

However, there is no reason to believe that the additives are grammaticalized focus markers. It is possible to find examples where additive particles occur on topical items, which is unexpected if part of their meaning is the expression of focus (24).

(24) Shiri (Dargwa)
[There used to be friends who knew how to read Injil, says the donkey.]
na   hel-t:i   juldaš:-i=**ra**   le-b-ak:u   b-ik'-u-l   ca‹b›i
now   DEM-PL friend-PL=ADD exist-HPL-NEG N-say-PRS-CVB COP‹N›
'Now **even/also** these friends are gone, says (the donkey).'

In (24), the noun phrase 'these friends' is a topic in the sense of aboutness, and yet bears an additive particle. The function of the particle in this example is to convey (scalar) additivity. Hence, when additives particles are used with the meanings 'also' or 'even' they can occur on topics and foci and there is no sensitivity to the IS status of the constituent that hosts the particle.

Apart from additivity, the particles have a function that is directly relevant for information structure, namely the marking of contrastive topics (25). Contrastive topics are special types of topics: they need not be topics in the narrow aboutness sense (Repp 2010). Since they presuppose the existence of relevant alternatives (Sudhoff 2008), the function of the additive in examples like (25) is related to the (scalar) additive function.

(25) Godoberi (Andic) (Kibrik 1996: 269)
ho-b   zamana-ɬi   den   kalxoz-u-ɬi   uns-e:-x=da-bu-q'aɬi
DEM-N time-INTER 1sg kolkhoz-OBL-GEN bull.OBL.PL-APUD=be-PTCP-WHEN
rix-u-ɬi   xaraš-i=**la**   b-ak'-uda b-ak'wa rix-u-xa
sheep-OBL-GEN shepherd-PL=ADD N-be-HAB   N-be.PST flock-OBL-APUD
'While I was with the kolkhoz bulls, the shepherds were with their sheep.'

In sum, except for derivational uses, the following functions of additive particles can be identified: (i) conjunction of various types of constituents; (ii) additive 'also' and scalar additive 'even' (presupposes a set of alternatives to which the constituent marked by the particle belongs); (iii) emphasis (22b); and (iv) contrastive topic. Of these four functions, only the last is related to information structure proper. The use of additives in other functions is insensitive to the topical or focal status of the constituent to which they attach. The analysis of Tsez =*n* by Polinsky & Potsdam (2001) as a topic particle is not applicable to most Nakh-Daghestanian languages including other Tsezic languages such as Hinuq. Even though additive particles can mark contrastive topics, they have a wide range of other functions in which they can appear on topics and foci. The characterization of these enclitics in Nichols & Peterson (2010) as marking emphatic and/or contrastive focus is also hardly correct. As we have shown, additive particles encliticize to topical constituents and we have not been able to find examples that clearly illustrate the use of them as markers of contrastive focus.

3.2 Interrogative particles

Nakh-Daghestanian languages have between one and five enclitic particles that express interrogative illocutionary force (see Forker 2013 for an overview). All languages mark at least simple polar questions and disjunctive polar questions, but some languages also mark WH-questions.

Interrogative particles have two functions: (i) they mark interrogative illocutionary force, and (ii) they express focus. The occurrence of interrogative particles in questions is often optional though preferred, and they have scope over the whole sentence. In Hinuq and Tsez the particles obligatorily replace the affirmative witnessed past suffix (26a). This is a purely morphological phenomenon concerning all questions in the witnessed past and does not lead to an automatic focus on the verb.

When being employed as focus markers the interrogative particles occur on the focused constituent. In simple polar questions this is commonly the verb (26b), but Tsez, Hinuq, Bagvalal and Tsakhur also allow interrogative particles to attach to other constituents if these represent the focus of the question. These constituents must precede the verb. This amounts to a general rule on the placement of interrogative particles: they are either added to the verb or to another item obligatorily preceding the verb.

(26) a. Tsez (Tsezic) (Abdulaev & Abdullaev 2010: 192)
   mi=**yä** daz čan-ya-za-ƛ' č'aq'ˤ=**a**=ƛin
   2sg=Q 1sg.GEN she.goat-OBL-OBL.PL-SPR fall.down=Q=QUOT
   'Did YOU assault my goats?'

 b. Archi (Lezgic)
   (http://www.philol.msu.ru/~languedoc/rus/archi/corpus.php)
   "ha lo" bo-li "inžit i‹w›t:i=**ra**?"
   well boy(I) say.PFV-EVID suffer ‹I›COP.PFV=Q
   "Well boy, did you suffer?"

In disjunctive polar questions, the constituents that are in focus take the particles. If the disjuncts are fully-fledged clauses, then the particles occur on the verbs, but in case of nominal or other disjuncts the particles are attached to the respective words (27).

(27) Tsakhur (Lezgic) (Kibrik 2001: 830)
 [How do you see it (i.e. the fact that the Tsakhur language has gained attention)?]
 jug-un=**e:** kar pis-in=**e:**?
 good-A=Q thing(IV) bad-A=Q
 'Is it a GOOD or a BAD thing?'

In WH-questions the particles are usually encliticized to the head of the interrogative phrase, which can be a WH-word (7a), (28) or another word (21a), or occasionally to the verb.

(28) Bezhta[3] (Tsezic)
 ło-qa=**d** wodi-? sid=zu zamalli-? giyač'e-š=ƛo
 who.OBL-AT=Q day.OBL-IN one=INT.PRT time.OBL-IN look.II-PRS=QUOT
 'At whom do you look daily at ONE AND THE SAME time?'

Interrogative particles may co-occur with other particles. In Bezhta and Tsez, the intensifying particle =*zu* (Section 3.3) and the focus-sensitive enclitic =*kin* ('even') have three possibilities for appearing together with the interrogative particle: (i) both enclitics are attached to the same item in the order =PRT=Q, (ii) the interrogative particle is attached to a WH-word, which represents the focus of the question, and the focus particle is attached to a different item which is emphasized (28), and (iii) the interrogative particle appears on the verb, and the focus particle on a different item. The last possibility is also attested for Ingush.

3.3 Intensifying particles

Avar, the Andic and the Tsezic languages have a type of intensifiers that is not found in the other Nakh-Daghestanian languages. These particles are found on

---

[3] All Bezhta examples are from an autobiographical text written by Šeyx Ramazan at the end of the last century, translated and edited by Madžid Xalilov and glossed by Diana Forker.

pronouns in reflexive constructions (29). In some languages their use is obligatory and ensures that the interpretation as clause-bound reflexive construction.

(29) Akhvakh (Andic) (Indira Abdulaeva, p.c.)
 Madina-La   iɬiLa=**da**   žije=**da**   kwini
 Madina-DAT REFL.SG.F.DAT=INT REFL.SG.F.ABS=INT loves
 'Madina$_i$ loves herself$_i$.'

They also occur in emphatic reflexive constructions together with a reflexive pronoun or as the only marker of the emphatic reflexive meaning (Testelec & Toldova 1998). Their occurrence indicates that the speaker corrects the incongruous, inadequate expectations of the hearer (30a, b).

(30) a. Bezhta (Tsezic)
  allah-li=**zu**   gey die   hari   q'abul.b.oh-na
  Allah-ERG=INT.PRT be   1sg.GEN request accept.III-UWPST
  'It was Allah himself who accepted my request.'

 b. žek'u-z   raλ'-ma   xanɬi=n   Ø-iči-zaλ'or, daz=**tow**
  man-GEN land-IN khanship=ADD I-be-POST   1sg.GEN=INT
  raλ'-ma laɣ=ɬun   r-igu   dar=λin
  land-IN slave=AS IV-good 1sg.LAT=QUOT
  'Before I become king over a someone's land, I would rather be like a slave in MY land.'

The second function of intensifying particles is the expression of identity. This concerns the identity of whole situations as well as the identity of participants, spatial, temporal and other circumstances. The use of the particles in this function presupposes that the situation, the participant or the place whose identity is asserted has already been mentioned in the preceding discourse. For instance, example (31) is preceded by the description of a cave, in which the people of the village keep their sheep, such that the following sentence (31) can directly refer back to that cave.

(31) Bagvalal (Andic) (Kibrik 2001: 827)
 [Once upon a time there was a big cave where the sheep were kept.]
 ongi=**da**   w-uk'-ur-oː-w   w-uk'a-w-o   ekʷa   eχʷːa=la
 there=INT I-be-IPFV-PTCP-M M-be-M-CVB COP   shepherd=ADD
 'In that very same place was also a shepherd.'

Third, intensifying particles are used to mark emphasis and to call attention to the host expression. This is a very broad characterization and in fact this function is quite heterogeneous among the various languages. Depending on the context, the particles can be translated with 'even', 'completely', 'only' or 'yet'. They are often found on clause-initial adverbs (32), on words or phrases that bear contrastive focus, or on temporal converb clauses. In some of the languages (e.g. Bagvalal, Hinuq, Tsez and Bezhta) these particles occur in reduplication with verbs, nouns, numerals and adverbs and convey an iterative and/or intensifying meaning.

(32) Avar (from the song *T'uhdul* 'flowers' by Gadzhilav Gadzhilaev)
bison=**go** bercina-b ƛ'er ƛ'er.ƛ'era-l ha-l t'uhduzul
most=INT beautiful-III color(III) colorful-PL this-PL flower.PL.OBL.GEN
'The MOST beautiful color (is) the color of these flowers.'

In short, the overall function of the intensifying particles is the expression of emphasis and contrast. They stress linguistic items that contradict the expectations of the hearer. The term *contrast* implies that at least two items must be contrasted (the marked items and another one), and often the other item has explicitly been mentioned or is implicitly present. For instance, in most situations agent and patient are not identical, thus agent ≠ patient can be taken as a default expectation of speakers. If, as in reflexive constructions, the agent and the patient are identical, then the default expectation is contradicted. Therefore, the patient, especially in those cases where there are no specialized reflexive pronouns (i.e. first and second person), is marked with the intensifying particle.

Similarly, the emphatic use of reflexive particles implies that the marked item contradicts expectations. The host of the particle is contrasted with other items in the preceding context. The identity function ('this very same X, and not any other') is also used to correct hearer expectations. From the contrastive function the particles have developed a general emphatic and intensifying meaning. They can be encliticized to focalized items, e.g. WH-pronouns, follow interrogative enclitics (which are also focus markers, see Section 3.2) and occur together with focus-sensitive additives (Section 3.1).

Nakh-Daghestanian languages are not the only language where reflexive expressions can convey emphasis and identity. Similar multifunctional reflexive words exist in many other languages such as English *x-self* and Turkish *kendi* (König & Siemund 2005).

4 The interplay of word order and focus particles

Focus particles far more often mark preverbal focus than postverbal focus. This corresponds to the different focus types: focus particles are used to mark narrow focus occurring before the verb (Section 2.2). The clitic hosts may be the only bearers of the focus (26a), (30a), or they may be part of larger focus phrases (e.g. (21a), (22), (28), (32)). In the latter case the particles are attached to the head if the whole phrase is in focus (22). Or they appear on the emphasized word, in which case the particles have scope over the whole phrase, but the host is especially emphasized (21a). In content questions like (21a) and (28) the WH-phrases marked with interrogative particles are in clause-initial position, and another particle attaches to a phrase immediately before the verb.

As mentioned in the introduction, Nakh-Daghestanian languages have a cleft construction that expresses narrow focus. In this construction the copula immediately follows the focus, which may be additionally marked with a particle ((20a), (30a)). Since the copula counts as the finite verb in periphrastic verb forms, this is another instance of preverbal focus.

Focus particles are also found on hosts following the verb. This is the case with wide focus. For instance, in (19) the whole verbal complex and the direct object are in focus, and the focus-sensitive particle is encliticized to the direct object.

5 Conclusion

Word order is one of the basic means of marking information structure in Nakh-Daghestanian, but the situation is rather complex and far from a clear mapping from information structure functions to certain syntactic positions. Topics are positioned in clause-initial and in clause-final position, whereby we observed a tendency for placing newly introduced topics at the left boundary, and highly-activated topics at the right boundary of the clause. The placement of focus is somewhat more rigid: narrow focus occurs immediately before the verb, whereas wide focus can include both pre- and postverbal elements. Though it is not very common, it is nevertheless possible for the topic and the focus to follow the verb at the same time. In such a case both orderings (i.e. V-TOP-FOC and V-FOC-TOP) are found, with varying frequencies across languages. Therefore, neither postverbal topic nor focus have dedicated positions in the structure of the clause, but can both be characterized as "clause-final". This conforms to the statement in Büring (2010) that there are no languages with only a purely syntactic position for focus, but that such a position must coexist with either prosodic means of focus marking ("boundary" languages) or with so-called "edge" focus (related to the focused phrase being peripheral to some prosodic domain). Nakh-Daghestanian languages provide the latter possibility.

However, the preverbal and postverbal focus positions in Nakh-Daghestanian languages appear to be functionally differentiated: the postverbal position is only possible for elements belonging to wide focus, while the preverbal position is available for both wide and narrow foci (e.g. WH-words). The preverbal position is also much more frequent in spoken texts. Therefore, while Nakh-Daghestanian languages do have a "prosodically motivated" means of focus marking, it appears to be secondary compared to purely syntactic preverbal focus marking.

In addition to word order, Nakh-Daghestanian languages also make use of particles for marking information structure. Most widespread are additives and interrogative particles. The central functions of additive particles are marking conjunction and expressing (scalar) additivity ('also', 'even'). It has been argued that these particles express topic (Polinsky & Potsdam 2001) or focus (Nichols & Peterson 2010). From our data, we can conclude that both viewpoints are not supported for the majority of Nakh-Daghestanian languages. Most of the functions of additive particles are equally compatible with both topical and focal interpretations of their hosts. The only dedicated information structure-related function of additives is the marking contrastive topics, but in light of the other, more frequent uses of the additive enclitics, this particular specialized function is hardly sufficient for classifying them as topic or focus markers.

Interrogative particles serve a double function. They mark illocutionary force and focus. Thus, they have scope over the whole clause and over a particular constituent. In polar questions, interrogative particles attach to the focus of the question, which is either the verb (if the whole proposition is in focus) or the immediate preverbal constituent (narrow focus). In WH-questions, interrogative particles are placed on either WH-phrases or on the verb.

A minority of Nakh-Daghestanian languages also have intensifying particles whose functions are related to information structure. The meanings they convey are quite diverse. They can be used in emphatic and non-emphatic reflexive constructions, to express identity or to mark contrast or contradiction with the hearer's expectations. Particles are often combined with each other, and serve to clearly indicate the IS function of constituents in those languages where topic and focus can be expressed in the same position.

Abbreviations

I-V gender markers, A attributive gender IV, AA attributive, other genders, ABL ablative, ABS absolutive, ADD additive, AFF affective, ALL allative, ANT anterior, AOR aorist, APUD apudessive, AT localization 'near, at, by', ATTR attributive, AUX auxiliary, CARD cardinal, CONT localization with contact, COP copula, CVB converb, DAT dative, DEM demonstrative, EL elative, ERG ergative, ESS essive, EVI evidential, FUT future, GEN genitive, HAB habitual, HPL human plural, IN localization 'in', INF infinitive, INT intensifier, INTER localization 'INTER', IPFV imperfective, IS information structure, LAT lative, LOC locative, M masculine, MSD masdar, N neuter, NEG negation, OBL oblique stem, OPT optative, PFT perfect, PFV perfective, PL plural, POSS possessive, POST posterior, POT potentialis, PRET preterite, PRS present, PRT particle, PST past, PTCP participle, Q question, QUOT quotative, REFL reflexive, SG singular, SPR localization 'on', SUB localization 'under', UWPST unwitnessed past

References

Abdulaev, Arsen K. & Isa K. Abdullaev. 2010. *Didojskij (cezskij) fol'klor* [Tsez folklore]. Makhachkala: Lotos.

Asatiani, Rusudan & Stavros Skopeteas. 2012. The information structure of Georgian. In Manfred Krifka & Renate Musan (eds.), *The expression of information structure*. Berlin: Mouton de Gruyter.

Büring, Daniel. 2010. Towards a typology of focus realization. In Malte Zimmerman & Caroline Fery (eds.), *Information structure. Theoretical, typological, and experimental perspectives*, 177–205. Oxford: Oxford University Press.

Erteschik-Shir, Nomi. 2007. *Information structure: The syntax-discourse interface*. Oxford: Oxford University Press.

Forker, Diana. 2013. Interrogative particles in Nakh-Daghestanian languages. *Rice Working Papers in Linguistics* 4.

Gast, Volker & Johan van der Auwera. 2011. Scalar additive operators in the languages of Europe. *Language* 87. 2–54.

Haspelmath, Martin. 1993. *A grammar of Lezgian*. Berlin: Mouton de Gruyter.

Kalinina, Elena & Nina R. Sumbatova. 2007. Clause structure and verbal forms in Nakh-Daghestanian. In Irina Nikolaeva (ed.), *Finiteness*, 183–249. Oxford: Oxford University Press.

Kazenin, Konstantin. 2002. Focus in Daghestanian and word order typology. *Linguistic Typology* 6. 289–316.

Kibrik, Aleksandr E. (ed.). 1996. *Godoberi*. Munich: Lincom.

Kibrik, Aleksandr E. (ed.). 1999. *Èlementy caxurskogo jazyka v tipologičeskom osveščenii* [Elements of Tsakhur in typological perspective]. Moscow: Nasledie.

Kibrik, Aleksandr E. (ed.). 2001. *Bagvalinskij jazyk* [The Bagvalal language]. Moscow: Nasledie.
König, Ekkehard. 1991. *The meaning of focus particles: A comparative perspective.* London: Routledge.
König, Ekkehard & Peter Siemund. 2005. Intensifiers and reflexive pronouns. In Martin Haspelmath, Matthew S. Dryer, David Gil & Bernard Comrie (eds.), *The world atlas of language structures*, 194–197. Oxford: Oxford University Press.
Krifka, Manfred & Renate Musan. 2012. Information structure: Overview and linguistic issues. In Manfred Krifka & Renate Musan (eds.), *The expression of information structure*, 1–44. Berlin: Mouton de Gruyter.
Lambrecht, Knud. 1994. *Information structure and sentence form.* Cambridge: Cambridge University Press.
Maisak, Timur & Marina Chumakina. 2001. Diskursivnye časticy [Discourse particles]. In Aleksandr E. Kibrik (ed.), 702–724. Moscow: Nasledie.
Matić, Dejan & Daniel Wedgwood. 2013. The meaning of focus: The significance of an interpretation-based category in cross-linguistic analysis. *Journal of Linguistics* 49 (1). 127–163.
Nichols, Johanna & David A. Peterson. 2010. *Contact-induced spread of the rare Type 5 clitic.* Paper presented at the LSA annual meeting, Baltimore, 7th January.
Polinsky, Maria & Eric Potsdam. 2001. Long-distance agreement and topic in Tsez. *Natural Language and Linguistic Theory* 19. 583–646.
Repp, Sophie. 2010. Defining 'contrast' as an information-structural notion in grammar. *Lingua* 120. 1333–1345.
Saebo, Kjell Johan. 2004. Conversational contrast and conventional parallel: Topic implicatures and additive presuppositions. *Journal of Semantics* 21. 199–217.
Schulze, Wolfgang. 2011. The Lak language. *Nová fiilologiická revue* 3. 11-36.
Sudhoff, Stefan. 2008. Focus particles in the German middlefield. In Anita Steube (ed.), *The discourse potential of underspecified structures*, 439–459. Berlin: de Gruyter.
Sumbatova, Nina R. 2004. Kommunikativnye kategorii i sistema glagola (o nekotoryx tipologičeskix osobennostjax dagestanskogo glagola) [Information structure and the verbal system (on some typological features of the Daghestanian verb)]. In Victor S. Xrakovskij, Andrej Malchukov & Sergej J. Dimitrenko (eds.), *40 let Sankt-Peterburgskoj tipologičeskoj škole* [40 years of the Saint Petersburg Typology Group], 487–504. Moscow: Znak.
Sumbatova, Nina R. & Rasul O. Mutalov. 2003. *A grammar of Icari Dargwa.* Munich: Lincom.
Talibov, Bukar B. 2007. *Buduxskij jazyk.* Moscow: Academia.
Testelec, Jakov G. 1998. Word order in Daghestanian languages. In Anna Siewierska (ed.), *Constituent order in the languages of Europe*, 257–280. Berlin: Mouton de Gruyter.
Testelec, Jakov G. 1999. Porjadok slov [Word order]. In Aleksandr E. Kibrik (ed.), 293–313. Moscow: Nasledie.
Testelec, Jakov G. & Svetlana Ju. Toldova. 1998. Refleksivnye mestoimenija v dagestanskix jazykax i tipologija refleksiva [Reflexive pronouns in Daghestanian languages and the typology of reflexives]. *Voprosy jazykoznanija* 4. 35–57.
Uslar, Petr K. 1979. *Tabasaranskij jazyk* [The Tabasaran language]. Tbilisi: Mecniereba.
Vallduví, Enric. 1992. *The informational component.* New York: Garland.
van der Wal, Jenneke. 2012. *Why does focus want to be adjacent to the verb?* Talk given at the 45th Annual Meeting of the SLE, 29 August 2012, Stockholm.

Winterstein, Grégoire & Henk Zeevat. 2012. Empirical constraints on accounts of *Too*. *Lingua* 122. 1787–1800.

Xajdakov, Said M. 1986. Logičeskoe udarenie i členenie predloženij (dagestanskie dannye) [Logical stress and the segmentation of sentences (Daghestanian data)]. In Georgij A. Klimov (ed.), *Aktual'nye problemy dagestansko-naxskogo jazykoznanija* [Current problems of Nakh-Daghestanian linguistics], 79–96. Makhachkala: IJa AN SSSR.

Annie Montaut
12 The discourse particle *to* and word ordering in Hindi: From grammar to discourse

Introduction

The Hindi word *to* is both a conjunction ('so', 'then'), and a discourse clitic particle, both of which have usually been considered as different (homonymous) units. The discourse particle itself, described as intensive, vaguely contrastive (McGregor 1972: 141), or emphatic (Kellogg [1856] 1938 : 490), covers such a collection of highly distinct meanings ('sure, well, at least, finally, will you, but', etc.) that it too has been assumed to represent homonymous words (Shapiro 1999; Lakshmi Bai 1977). This study aims to show that the diversity of the surface meanings and functions of the latter (clitic particle) may be accounted for by a common abstract operation, implemented according to the various specific contexts of occurrence, both syntactic and enunciative (discursive). After a brief presentation of the grammatical *to*, always clause initial, in section 1, I will attempt in the following sections to disentangle the various factors (position and scope, intonation) at play in the scope of the discourse particle *to*, and show that the operation underlying all surface meanings, as a topic marker (section 2) and as the so-called contrastive marker (section 3), involves intersubjectivity. By connecting this abstract operation with the meaning of conjunctive *to*, we assume polysemy rather than homonymy as the more effective explanation of the various readings of *to*.

1 From the conjunction to the theme marker

1.1 The conjunction *to*: Discourse paragraph, sentence or clause initial

The non-clitic *to*, strongly stressed, essentially behaves as a coordinative conjunction ('so', 'then'), and as a correlative, particularly in conditionals.

Annie Montaut, INALCO-USPC, SeDyL UMR 8202, Labex EFL

In the first case, *to* mostly operates as a linker between two discourse paragraphs, the second one still remaining in the logical sequence of the first one but adding to it a new element instead of a simple relation of cause-effect or of temporal sequence[1]: it introduces a new turn or phase of the story in narrative contexts. It may also introduce a new idea or argument in an argumentative sequence, in the same way as its English equivalent 'then/so'.

Given the fact that *to* occurs at cardinal moments in a narration, for chaining a distinct episode or for shifting the frame or scenario or viewpoint, when a story teller interrupts his tale after a non-final event, the hearer who wishes to know what happens next (and is not predictable) usually maps his expectation by somewhat providing the empty frame for further instantiation, and he does so by using *to* (1a), a *to* which may even behave as sentential (1b):

(1) a. **to** kyā huā?   b. *to* ?
       to interr be.PFV   to
       'And then what happened?'   'And then ?'

Using this *to*-sentence in interrogative contexts which do not convey interrogation regarding some following event as in (1b) is potentially polemical (*cf* English "so what?") with underlying aggressive denegation ("what does it prove? what does it amount to?"): such rhetorical interrogations indeed question the potential of the previous statement to provide a step for further innovative developments in a logical argument. Hence the polemical meaning, since it dismisses the relevance of what has just been said: the speaker A who uses this rhetorical *to* means that there is nothing to make out of what has been said, and that the information or argument given by the speaker B is nil. With *to*, A pretends to provide a frame to further instantiate, in order to mean that it has not been instantiated yet and cannot be:

(1) c. A – abhī   tak   merā   kām   kiyā   nahīn ?
            now.just till POSS.1SG work.MSG do.PFV.MSG   NEG
       A – 'You still have not done my work (what I asked you to do)?'

       B – Sir, mere-pās das aur chiTThiyān āyīn...   A – **To** ?
           Sir 1SG-near ten more letter.FPL come.PFV.FPL   to
       B – 'Sir, ten other letters came [I got much work]... A – **So what** ?'

---

[1] Two relations which can also be lexically expressed respectively by *islie* 'therefore' and *phir* 'after that', 'then'.

The other main use of the non-clitic *to* is to introduce the apodosis after a conditional clause (*agar/yadi*: 'if'), in a correlative system typical of Indo-Aryan languages.²

(2) a. *agar tum merī madad karte* **to** *main saphal ho-jātā*
if 2 my help do.CTF to 1SG successful become.CFT
'If you helped me [had helped me] I would succeed [would have succeeded]'

The term introducing the first element of the correlative dyptich is often omitted in Hindi but never is *to*, required in the hypothetic system even when the protasis is left unexpressed:³

(2) b. *yah pahle hī jāgī huī* **to**...?
this.one already just awake be.PFV.PL to
'And if she is already awake?'

The correlative *to* in the conditional system is then a marker of entailment which chains the protasis p to the apodosis q in the way $p > q$ (you help me $> I$ succeed), but in such a situation where two divergent paths are available: p' (you do not help me) would entail q' (I do not succeed). The speaker presents an alternative, and the apodosis is constructed in leaving aside one of the possible scenarii. *To* corresponds to the selection of one of these two scenarii in contrast with the other one in a given situation where the speaker has constructed what Culioli (1999) calls a fictive landmark, that is, a point of localisation for the predication q which is not real (not asserted) but virtual ("if": if

---

2 Cf. Montaut (1999, 2012). The correlative *to* can also correlate temporal dependent clauses (protasis introduced by *jab* 'when'), adding a nuance of cause-effect in contrast with the simply temporal *tab*. It is also more frequent in iterative contexts, where a whole series is occurrence is scanned.

jab āp log cale gae **to/tab** *mainne usko bulā liyā*
when 2H people leave go.PFV to/tab 1S.ERG 3S.ACC call take.PFV
'When you left I called him'

Abbreviations : ERG (ergative), ACC (accusative), DAT (dative), PFV (perfective: simple anterior), PFT (perfect), PRES (present), CTF (counterfactual), H (honorific), PPFT (pluperfect).

3 Whether *to* belongs to the protasis or to the apodosis is a real question: it is traditionally considered to belong to the protasis (as correlatives in general), yet it cannot be omitted if the protasis is suspended.

we admit, let us imagine).[4] It behaves as an indicator of contrastive selection triggering q by contrast with q'.

1.2 A continuity from coordination and correlative to thematic particle?

Whereas, as a correlative in conditional constructions, *to* involves the selection of one path in contrast with another one, as a coordinative conjunction, it opens a new sequence which re-sets the narrative flow on the basis of the previous statement, by shifting the scenery or the viewpoint, which makes the sequence following to distinctively salient.

The word etymologically stems from an ancient pronominal basis (Sanskrit *ta-*) referring to third person ('that', 'he'), which is still used as such in certain Indo-Aryan languages such as Marathi (*to* 'he') although not in Hindi.[5] This basis is typically used throughout Sanskrit, Prakrits and modern Indo-Aryan in the correlative system, as a linker between a relative clause (Sanskrit *ya-* 'wh-') and its correlated clause. It is well known that anaphoric devices have often provided for coordinators in many languages (Brill & Rebuschi 2006, Haspelmath 2004: 3–39), and their use as correlators results from the same logic.

As for the shift from correlative to discourse particle, the evolution from conditional markers into theme markers has also been well described (Haiman 1978, Haspelmath 2008: 1005 sq): the conditional clause (protasis) behaves as the frame for the following predication in the apodosis. Since in Hindi the correlator which introduces the apodosis, represents the end part (right position) of the protasis in truncated systems (*cf.* ex 2d), it is all the more understandable that it came to be used as a topic marker, cliticized at the right of the topicalized term (Montaut 2012). The non-thematizing functions of the clitic, depending on its scope in the sentence, will be described in section 3.

2 *To* as a thematic particle

When the particle *to* is a clitic which forms a single accentual word with the term at its left, a word which can always be followed by a brief pause, it behaves mostly as a topic marker.

---

[4] The notions of fictive landmark ("repère fictive"), entailment ("entraînement"), scanning ("parcours") and access path ("chemin d'accès") are borrowed from Culioli (1999). Conditionals are considered in Culioli's model as involving "bifurcation" from one possible path to the other.
[5] The Sanskrit pronominal basis *ta-* displays in certain flexions and genders a form in *sa-* (*sah* 'he', *tat* 'it'), a form (Hindi *so*) which is still used in Hindi as an adverbial coordinator ('then', 'so') and has long been used as a correlator for relative clauses (Montaut 2012).

(3) *ājkal*   ***to*** *āp akele hain*
    nowadays *to* 2H alone be.PRES.PL
    'These days, you are alone'

In (3), the intonation shows an ascending tone on *to* which bears the accent in the "word" *ājkal* to which is the topic, while the remaining of the clause (comment) is intoned in lower pitch

2.1 Theme, rheme and focus in Hindi

Whether according to Chafe (1976)'s more cognitive definition based on the "given" and "known", then Gundel & al. (1993)'s finer definition of "givenness", including "semi-activated" and "inferred", or to Bonnot (1990, 2006) and Guimier (1999)'s more formal definition based on the position and intonation, the topic or theme comes first in the sequence. Although significant research has been carried out during the last decades on focus and focalization in Hindi, mainly within the generative frame, practically none is available on the theme. I am using the term "focus" in its restricted meaning, and not in reference to the part of the sentence which comments the theme, which I will label rheme or rhematic content. A focalized constituent within the rheme is marked by its linguistic prominence (emphasis) by means of intonational or accentual marking, specific word ordering or morpho-syntactic devices such as cleft sentence or focus particles (Wlodarczik 2006, François & Lacher-Dutour 2003).[6]

A statement may have no theme nor focus, and be an entirely rhematic content, what is currently designed as a thetic sentence ("it is two o' clock").[7] In Hindi, an ergative head final language usually considered with SOV order,[8] the equivalent entirely rhematic statement (*do baj gae*, two strike went) shows no

---

[6] This restricted meaning is distinguished from the "general" or psychological meaning of focus of attention by Gundel & al. (1993: 279, note 1, after Hajičova). Focus in the psychological/cognitive meaning (focus of attention) is equivalent to the rhematic content, but not in its restricted meaning (linguistic focus).

[7] As clearly stated by Gutierrez-Alvares (2003: 17): "Rheme is present in all statements. Focus is not, and it requires a specific marking: it is always a marked function".

[8] It has postpositions and no prepositions, goal complements always precede the verb, and only the SOV order allows all syntactic transformations are available. Some scholars (Mohanan 1994) consider Hindi as a free order language because all constituents can shift position without morpho-syntactic restructuration. but they mention "scrambling", which implicitly refers to some basic or dominant order.

pause and no accentual pitch. Similarly in (4a), uttered in answer to a medical inquiry, is entirely rhematic:

(4) a. *mainne bacpan se ainak rakhī hai*
 1SG.ERG childhood from glasses put PFT
 'I wear glasses since my childhood'

Although the theme is essentially marked by its position, always initial, and by the possibility of marking a pause after the thematized expression, not all fronted constituents are thematic, since a subject placed between the object and the verb is in the focus position without necessarily the first constituent being a theme. In (4b), uttered as a polemical answer to the previous statement "I don't see any woman around", the object *ainak* "glasses" is not a theme although first in the sequence, with the subject in the second place as a contrastive focus. But it is in (4c), in answer to "where are my glasses, everything gets lost in this house", the object *ainak*, with the same position, is a theme:

(4) b. *ainak* **tūne** *lagā rakhī hai yā mainne?*
 glasses 2S.ERG place put PFT or 1SG.ERG
 'Is it you who is wearing glasses or I?'

(4) c. **ainak** *kal rāt mez par rakhī thī*
 glasses yesterday night table on put PPFT
 'The glasses, you had put them on the table yesterday night'

Detached after the verb, the same object behaves as a delayed theme or post rheme ("antitopic" in Chafe 1976, "mneme" in Fernandez-Vest 2004 and in this volume) in the same context as (4c):

(4) d. *kal rāt tumne xud mez par rakhī thī* <u>ainak</u>
 yesterday night you.ERG REFL table on put PPFT glasses
 'You had put them on the table yesterday night, the glasses'

Regarding the intonation pattern, sentences with a focalized constituent does not make a significant difference, as opposed to better studied languages such as English or French. The constituents in Hindi or Bengali are in a strict down step relationship regardless of word order (Lahiri 1999), probably because of the prominence of lexical stress (Ohala 1986). The only difference observed by Patil et al. (2008) is that pitch excursion and duration are higher in OSV sentences where the subject is focused compared to SOV sentences, and focus constituents show greater pitch excursion and longer duration. But no acoustic study is available for OSV sentences where the object is thematized.

It is often considered that "scrambling" results in adding definiteness to all constituents in Hindi,[9] but the reason why the object is always definite in (5b) is that a term shifted to the initial position is potentially a theme and a theme is necessarily definite (on the other hand, a term shifted to the preverbal position is focalized and potentially definite):

(5) a. *sunār   ne   laRkī ko   hār   bhejā*
       jeweller ERG girl DAT necklace send.PFV.MSG
       'The/?a jeweller sent the/a necklace to the/a girl'

(5) b. *hār   sunār   ne   laRkī ko   bhejā*
       necklace jeweller ERG girl DAT sent
       'The jeweller sent the/*a necklace to the girl'[10]

2.2 Constructing a theme as contrastive

Practically all lexical categories (noun, adjective, adverb, verb) may be thematized by the particle *to* in all syntactic functions (subject, object, beneficiary, oblique, attribute, predicate). Since a topic does not require *to* for behaving as such – position and accent are sufficient indicators of thematization –, it must be hypothesized that *to* constructs a particular kind of theme, intuitively perceived as "contrastive" or "emphatic" (McGregor 1972: 141). This section shows that this operation involves either a contrast with another term belonging to the same paradigm, or a contrast in judgements on the same term.

2.2.1 Contrast with other elements belonging to the same paradigm

Example (3) above makes the temporal frame (*ājkal* 'nowadays') a contrastive theme, implicitly suggesting that before or after, the situation was/will be different: in the narrative, it corresponds to the moment when the addressee gets up to take leave and the speaker gives the answer in (3), suggesting that

---

9 Dvivedi (1994) however shows that contrastive focuses may, exceptionally, remain indefinite.
10 Example from Mohanan & Mohanan (1994 : 169). In fact, *hār* 'necklace' is thematized in (5b) with a possible pause after *hār*, and the literal translation would rather be 'the necklace, the jeweller sent it to the girl' ('to a girl' would correspond to Hindi *kisī laRkī ko*, INDEF girl DAT).

he should stay some more since "he is alone", and implicitly there is nobody home waiting for him these days, as opposed to last week or next week for instance. *To* makes the adverb a theme by actualizing the relation which the other terms of the same paradigm could have had with the implicit meaning: usually you are not free, the fact that you are alone *nowadays* is a good occasion not to miss. The answer given ("I am alone/alone, sure, but I still must absolutely be back home" in example (13) below) makes this intended meaning ("you should stay longer as usual") clear. In (6), the elements of the paradigm contrasting with the *to*-topic are explicit in the previous context: "give me your school books for a few hours, I forgot mine". The particle *to* here builds the item as contrasting with the other items (available now) of the paradigm of school books:

(6) *ye   lo!   hindī kī kitāb **to** tumhen kal   dūngī*
    these take Hindi of book *to* 2.DAT tomorrow give.FUT.1SG
    'Take these! The Hindi book, I will give it to you tomorrow'

In (7), the possible substitutable terms in the paradigm out of which *mujhe* "to me" is contrastively selected are implicit:

(7) *mujhe   **to** usne   kuch   nahīn diyā*
    1SG.DAT *to* 3SG.ERG something NEG   gave
    '(But) to me (I, as far as I am concerned) she has not given me anything'

(7) occurs as an answer to the description of X as extremely generous. The speaker reacts by representing himself (theme), as somebody who, contrary to the others, has never benefited from it. The operation consists in constructing the topic in contrast with the implicit paradigm of the other terms which could illustrate the generosity of X, and thus amounts to contest the previous representation of a supposedly universal giver. Its argumentative meaning derives from its basic function, which consists in making its scope as a contrastive theme.

Example (8), displaying an even more polemical meaning, appears in (8) where the thematized numeral *tīn* "three" is followed by *to*. The speaker B, a Muslim, in a train, answers a question from A, a Hindu, which does not really aim at getting an information, since A only seeks to blame his own wife for her stupidity in not going and sit in the "ladies compartment". A's rhetorical question aims at having his judgment on his wife cautioned by the other travellers.

(8) a. A – *koī   aur   aurat   bhī   hai baiThī huī   mardāne Dabbe   men*
         INDEF other woman   even   is seated being   male   compartment in
   A – 'Is there any another woman sitting in the men compartment ?'

   B – *tīn   **to** mujhe   nazar ā   rahī hain*
         three to   1SG.DAT look come   PROG PRES
   B – 'There are three (you can't deny) I can see'

The term *tīn* 'three' is constructed by *to* as contrasting with the number presupposed by A's rhetoric, zero (none would be so stupid as not to travel in the ladies compartment). When A answers that he sees three of them, he emphasizes the dishonesty of B in the count (you want us to believe that there are none but there are three I can see), and so dismisses his rhetoric: hence the polemical interpretation of *to* here, followed by a hot discussion between both A and B. If A had answered by a thematic "I"-*to*, contrasting then his own vision to B's vision, he would simply have opposed his own count to B's count, with a milder polemical impact:

(8) b. *mujhe   **to** tīn   nazar ā   rahī hain*
        1SG.DAT to   three look come   PROG PRES
   'As for me I (But if you ask me) I can see three of them'

And if he had simply uttered (8c) without the particle *to*, the statement would have meant that B interprets A's question as a real question, devoid of polemic undertones, to which B could give a factual answer. Such an answer, at least strange in the above context, is natural after a real question like "how many of them do you see?"

(8) c. *mujhe   tīn   nazar ā   rahī hain*
        1SG.DAT three look come   PROG PRES
   'I can see three of them'

In the context of a quite aggressive discussion between Hindu and Muslim travellers just before the Partition of India, (8a) has the expected impact of a very polemic statement: it discards the Hindu husband's rhetoric about the stupidity of his wife.[11] And indeed the further context shows that B has only

---

11 The wife (C) consequently gets over her own shyness to protest and then the husband (A) overtly insults her, finding no longer escape in pseudo-rhetorical arguments since they have been torn out by (8a):
C – *zanāne Dabbe men koī bandā na pardā! main kaise baiTh jātī?*
A – *tū chup karegī ki nahīn? Bevakūf !*
'C– There is not a soul in the ladies compartment! How could I sit there?
A – Will you shut up (or not)? Idiot!'

wished to contest the Hindu husband's tyranny over his wife, a tyranny he wants to emphasize because he is a Muslim and the Muslims are generally the ones blamed for depriving their women of freedom. This polemical use of *to*, whose efficiency is immediately perceptible in the dialogue following this sequence (violent quarrel about women's freedom in both communities), is in conformity with the logic of the particle's meaning, always more or less argumentative.

2.2.2 To as a re-qualification of an already mentioned term

When *to* has scope over a term which repeats an already mentioned term (either or not a previous theme), it re-qualifies it. Shapiro (1999: 182–3) interprets this "reiteration" as "sustaining" a previous interpretation, or "in contradistinction to a parallel form that is operative in the discourse at hand". Yet this "sustaining", echoing of McGregor "emphasis", always implies a re-qualification. In (9) for instance, the attribute "shameless", part of the previous statement by A in a non topical position (attribute), is repeated in B's statement:

(9) a. ye   log   besharam hain.   b. besharam **to** āp hain!
      these people shameless are   shameless *to* you are
      'These people are shameless'.   'Shamelessness is rather yours!'

The term *besharam* "shameless", formerly part of the comment, is promoted by B in the theme position, but a theme re-qualified in its relation with its referent since the referent is now the opposite group (it is you, not us, who are shameless): the already given term, when thematized with *to*, is redefined as a different type of shamelessness in relation to the new subject.

In (10), *to* occurs three times, and is used each time in order to re-qualify a term which has been previously introduced by another speaker with a different viewpoint. Two parents are complaining about the Hindi teacher of their daughter and the stupid homework she has required, an essay on hunger:

(10) MOTHER – *itnā sārā homework, vah bhī hindī men ! Ab hindī bhī koī sabjekt rah gayā hai, ājkal ke zamāne men ! islie main kahtī hūn iskī hindī kī Madam ko haTvā do !*
'So much of homework! And in Hindi on top of that! As if Hindi was still a real subject nowadays! That's why I am asking you to have this Hindi Madam (teacher) fired!'

DAUGHTER – *nahīn Pāpā, please aisā mat karnā ! merī hindī kī Madam bahut kyūT hai.* 'No, daddy, please, don't do that! My Hindi teacher is very cute'

Vah to hindī kī lagtī hī nahīn, bahut smart hai, ekdam !
3SG *to* hindi of seem just NEG much smart be.PRES.3SG totally

She (you know) just does not look like a Hindi (teacher) at all, she is very smart, absolutely!

[Both parents discuss the question of homework between themselves]

FATHER – *ham apnī biTiyā ke lie ek aisā tutor rakh lenge jo sārā homwork phaTā-phaT kar diyā karegā*
Well, we will find a tutor for our daughter who will get the homework done in a minute.

MOTHER – **Tutor se to** *computer behter. (...) Computer yes, tutor no. Never ! Tutor badmāsh hote hain. Always! Merā ek tutor hotā thā, very bad.*
A tutor [do you realize what a tutor means ?], a computer would do better (...). Computor yes, tutor no. Never ! All tutors are wrecks.
I used to have a tutor, very bad.

FATHER – *(...) khair, is māmle ke bāre men main pūchtāch phir kabhī karūngā.* **Apnī bīTīyā ke lie to** *ham lady tutor hī rakhenge*
(...) Well, I will look in that matter some other time. [But] **For our daughter** [at any rate] we will find a lady tutor [not a man])

In the first sequence, the requalification of the same referent (*vah to* thematize a previous subject "my Hindi teacher" which itself requalifies a previous object "her Hindi Madam") amounts to construct the theme as contrastive in relation to its occurrence in the mother's statement. The occurrence of the referent in the daughter's talk without *to* ("my Hindi teacher"), already associated with a positive evaluation contrary to the mother's viewpoint, only serves as an argument given by the daughter for not firing her Hindi teacher. The next sentence with *to* presents the positive qualification as relevant *per se*, in total opposition with the other speaker's viewpoint. *To* expresses the discrepancy between an initial viewpoint on a class (the type: Hindi teacher, generally considered as dull) and an individual (who gives too much work) as well as a different viewpoint on a particular individual belonging to the class but not fitting the usual qualification.

The second sequence of the dialogue opens with a proposal by the father to substitute a tutor for school classes in Hindi: what he emphasizes is the competence of the tutor in helping for homework, the idea of having a tutor is itself taken for granted. And it is this very idea (presupposition) which the mother opposes, by shifting the debate to tutors in general and then to one in particular, her former tutor. Attached to "tutor" in the mother's discourse, *to* makes it a theme which negatively contrasts with the implicitly positive opinion on tutors expressed by the other speaker, the father. Without *to*, the statement would have only expressed a mere comparison between various school props. *To* gets the class of tutors questioned, hence the following shift towards personal (bad) memories.

And when the father tries to come back to the initial question, it is again *to* (third occurrence) that brings back to the foreground the main theme ("our daughter"). Thematizing "daughter" is a device used for going on with the initial problem – how to help the girl – while contrasting the relation girl-tutor with the relation mother-tutor previously commented by the mother: contrary to the previous relation, bad because of male tutors, father's statement qualifies positively the relation daughter-tutor (lady tutor): *to* does not contrast a distinct viewpoint on the daughter, but the relation 'daughter-tutor' with the parallel relation 'pupil-tutor' represented in the viewpoint of previous speaker (mother).

Example (11), also exhibits a conflict in viewpoints, on the predicative notion this time: B and C have just expressed that they do not understand what C means (hence asking for more information), whereas C questions his own statement as potentially dubious (regarding his own understanding).

(11) *A – main nahīn samajhtī   B – main bhī nahīn samajhtī*
    'I don't understand'   'I too don't understand /neither I'

  *C – samajhtā   **to** shāyad main bhī nahīn*
    understand *to* may-be1SG   too NEG
    'Understand, may-be I don't neither/ I also don't think I understand myself"

But it frequently happens that the particle, although placed after the first segment of the statement, has scope on the whole sentence: in this case *to* re-qualifies the statement as a whole, most of the time with polemic intentions.

3 The argumentative particle

The formal difference between thematizing and non thematizing uses of discourse particle *to* relies not so much on the position of *to* than on the unavailability of any pause after the term on which the particle cliticizes. The position however may be relevant in certain cases: when *to* is clause final, it is always strongly argumentative.

3.1 Denying or shifting the relevance of a previous argument

The particle *to*, with scope on the whole statement, usually consists in limiting the relevance of an argument previously proposed by the other speaker, while pretending *to* confirm it. To rephrase the argument with *to* amounts to giving this argument a limited or factual confirmation, in order to better deny its wider or real relevance. In (12) for instance, a statement by B, *to* has scope over a clause P which rephrases the clause P' previously stated by speaker A, "speak the truth": no segmentation is possible and *to* receives a light stress (stronger stress on *hī*), the meaning intended by B amounts to agree with A but only in order to relativize the relevance of A's argument (sure you are right, but it is not the point).

(12) A – *shaharī log baRe beīmān hote hain. Marad kyā aur aurat kyā. Hindū kyā aur musalmān kyā. Sāre fitne-fasād shaharon se hī shurū hote hain. kyon bābājīī main jhūTh bol rahā hūn yā sac ?*
'The city folk is all very dishonest. Men and women alike. Hindus and Muslims alike. All communal riots start in cities. Right, Baba-JI ? Do I speak lie or truth ?'

B – bol **to** tū sac hī rahā hai,
speak *to* you true just PROG PRES
'You (indeed) speak true (Sure you are right),
par isse bhī baRā sac yah hai ki insāf na shahar men na gānv men. Insāf to[12] tum dekh lenā Pakistān men bhī nahīn hogā.
but there is a bigger truth than that, and this is that justice is neither in cities or villages. Justice, you will see, you won't find it either in Pakistan'

The fronted thematized verb (*bol* 'tell'), in the strongly marked order V-*to*-S-O-aux, is not the simple quote of A's utterance, which is unmarked in its ordering (SOV) with the same object (*sac* 'truth'). The new mapping within *to*... *hī* does not simply discard the alternative ("or wrong") nor does it bring a different viewpoint on the predicate or the clause P, whose validity is not questioned. But if B

---

[12] *To* here is a topic particle which backs the topic of justice (in contrast to previously mentioned: justice in God's realm =Pakistan) after the digression about cities/villages.

agrees with A on the initial location of communal violence, he does so in order to signal that this "truth" has little relevance (*to*) in the present discussion. B implicitly disqualifies A's interpretation of facts, while granting him the confirmation he rhetorically asked for ("right or wrong": you can't say I am not right). But he grants him such a confirmation ("sure you are right") only for the sake of shifting from P1 to P2: the real problem is not your being right on the initiation of violence (P1) but to deal with justice (P2). B does not enter in A's rhetoric and *to* marks this refusal to accept A's premises while accepting only the conclusions.

Similarly, in (13), the continuation of (3) *supra*, B in the first clause, with the same structure as (12), qualifies A's argument as weakly relevant, and in the second adversative clause provides another argument as crucially relevant, in contradiction to A's request:

(13) A – ājkal   to āp akele hain…
       nowadays *to* 2H alone are

    B – akelā **to** hūn, lekin ghar   to jānā hī hai
       alone *to* am   but   house *to* go   *hi* is
    '– These days you are alone… – Sure I am alone, but I really must go home'

In the first (underlined) clause of B's answer, the absence of *to* would result in a rather strange meaning in this context, since A was not asking for a confirmation but was using the argument to convince B to stay longer. In B's second sentence, *to… hī* in an adversative clause makes the clause a crucially relevant argument in countering A's offer.

3.2 Making the clause a crucial discursive argument

Discursive cruciality is involved in the last clause of last example (13) *ghar to jânâ hî hai* 'I really have to go home'. Although apparently opposed to the meaning of *to* in the first clause of the same example (denial of relevance), it nonetheless participates in a similar operation: speaker A provides a new element in the discussion, something that the addressee had either not thought of or had not wished to consider. What is at stake is the promotion of the propositional content within a perspective opposed to the addressee's view, for which the proposal is either not relevant or not conceivable. Such an operation is then symmetrical to the denial of relevance, where P was relevant for speaker A and not for speaker B. When this operation occurs in non adversative contexts (of the type 'sure, but'), the salience intuitively perceived in *to*-statements is due to the fact that such statements are constructed in opposition to a previous implicit assumption of speaker A. Hence their objection-like character instead of simple assertions. The series of answers to the suggestion 'let us go and have some tea' given by Lakshmi Bai (1977) as examples of "assertive particle" can be explained in this way:

(14) a. *mere   pās **to** bas   das paise hain*
       1SG.GEN at   to   only ten paise are
       'I have only ten pence with me [not enough]'

(14) b. *kanTīn **to** band ho gayā   hogā   abhī*
       cantine to   closed be go.PFV PRESUMPTIVE right.now
       'The cantine must be closed by now'

(14) c. *abhī   **to** tīn   nahīn baje hain*
       right.now to   three NEG   ring PFT
       'It is not yet three o'clock [too early]'

(14) d. *das minaT **to** kām   karne do bhāī*
       ten minutes to   work do   let brother
       'Let us work ten minutes more, brother'

Each of the answers (14a–d) represents according to Lakshmi Bai the choice of the speaker among various alternatives, and *to* asserts this choice. However, a single speaker does not really select one by dismissing the other alternatives, and the 'assertive force' is the result of the inter-subjective relation involved in the whole series as an answer to a proposal which the speaker wishes to discard. Speaker A in (14a) signals to speaker B (let us have some tea) something of which B was not aware (not enough money, closing time, unfinished work), which makes it difficult to obey the request and therefore acts as an indirect objection or refusal. *To* here behaves as a request for taking into account what the speaker valuates as a crucial argument that has been neglected by the addressee. Hence the possible translations opening with "but you know", "the problem is", "but"...

When the discourse particle *to* has scope on a proposal already stated by a previous speaker, it denies it full (or any) relevance. When it has scope on a proposal which is new, it builds the relevance of this new P in contradiction with what the speaker thinks is the viewpoint of the other speaker.

3.3 Final *to*: winning over the other's reluctance

I have shown elsewhere that preverbal *to* in the last syntagm of questions amounts to checking if the proposition has been successfully realized (in conformity with the speaker's expectations and against the obvious difficulties barring access to that realization ("let us hope that P").[13]

In a postverbal position, mostly after a verb in the imperative, the particle *to* acquires such a specific meaning that it is often deemed a quasi homonym of the "assertive" particle (Lakshmi Bai 1977: 73; Shapiro 1999: 186).

(15) *batāo* **to** !
 tell   to
 'But tell it (now)! Come on, why don't you tell? Will you finally tell it?'

Statement (15) strongly differs from its counterpart without *to* and requires a specific context: it echoes a strong reluctance on the part of the addressee, or at least the speaker's anticipation of such reluctance.[14] Example (16) shows concrete evidence of B's reluctance:

(26) A – *ā* !   B – *hān*... A – *idhar ā!*   B – *ū hūn*...
 come   yes   here come   ok ok

 C – *is   buddhū ko   ek   bār men bāt   mān   lene kī ādat nahīn.*
  this idiot   DAT one time in   thing accept take of habit NEG

 A – *are! ā*   **to**!
  hey come to

 'A – Come! B – Ya... A – Come here ! B – Ok ok... C – This idiot is not used to obey at the first time. A – Hey you! **you do come!**
 [what are you waiting for!/ will you move your ass?]'

When A utters the last sentence (with *to*), he has already ordered B twice to come, without *to*, and this order has not yet been fulfilled. Only in the third utterance of the same order, once fully aware of B's reluctant behaviour, A uses

---

[13] Montaut (2002). Such a use is idiomatized in the expression *āp acche to hain*? 'How are you/ hope you are fine?' [you well *to* are] but still differs from the same statement uttered without *to* by its contextual constraints: it is natural only when the speaker has not seen the person he greets since a long time, or has got bad news, or thinks he may not be so well... example of the meaning "insistence" in McGregor.

[14] A weaker (because idiomatized) expression of the same meaning is still associated to the common polite way of welcoming a visitor *baiThie to* (sit-down *to*) 'why don't you sit down'.

to after the order verb. The intuitive perception of insistence results in reality from the feature "unwillingness" imputed by A to B.

Far from a mere emphasis, stylistically optional, such examples show that the particle *to* operates systematically in constructing P as countering a non-P imputed to the addressee. With *to*, an order then conjures up the risk of not reaching its goal, and at the same time emphasizes the addressee's reluctant behaviour. Here again, the meaning of *to* stems from contrastive and even conflicting attitudes of both partners. Similarly, phrasal *nahīn* ('no') in answers to P, when followed by *to* (*nahīn to*) acquires its "emphasis" from the fact that the speaker refutes an assumption he imputes to the addressee.

Conclusions

The very high frequency of the occurrences of *to*, particularly remarkable in oral interaction, as well as the variety of its meanings and functions, may be correlated to the limited number of words behaving as discourse particles in Hindi.[15] This contrasts with the situation in Germanic languages which display far more numerous discourse particles, a dozen in German (Weydt 1969) with more than one equivalent for each in Serbo-croatian (Diewald and Krescic 2010), in which each particle has consequently a more restricted usage.

In spite of the apparent heterogeneity of the meanings involved in the data studied, one can argue that the multiple surface meanings and functions of the discourse particle *to* obey a single basic meaning, although not concretely semantic but rather pertaining to an abstract operation. This basic meaning consists in triggering an operation which deals with alterity ("altérité": 'otherness'), at various levels: *to* seems to convey the speaker's judgment on a term or sequence on which it has scope, in such a way that *to*-P triggers the implicit or explicit representation of P' (P': non P or other than P).

When *to* is a thematic particle, P is the thematized term and P' either refers to other members of the same paradigm where P belongs, or it constructs a different relation between P and its rheme, or a viewpoint on P differing from

---

15 As evidenced by the various examples: (13), (20), (21), (22), (27) are from *Bhūkh āg hai* (KB Vaid, Hunger is fire), contemporary theatre, or (11), (14), (15), (16), from *Guzrā huā zamānā* (KB Vaid, *The broken Mirror* [lit. Time past]), a contemporary Partition novel, or from recorded conversations (Standard Hindi, middle class, 40-60 years old informants, Delhi). The other two commonly used discourse particles are *hī* (focus particle, particularly in restricted focus) and *bhī* 'even'.

the viewpoint previously expressed by (or attributed to) the other speaker (requalification). This thematic function has no parallel in the Germanic discourse particles (more often called modal particles or Abtönungspartikel), since their common characteristic is to have for "focus the relational category of discourse rheme in a sentence", and to have "scope over the whole VP" (Abraham 1991: 356). In Hindi the non-thematic *to* only has scope over the whole sentence.

In such cases, that is, in Hindi, in sentences entirely rhematic, structured as thetic or focus sentences, *to* presents the whole statement on which it has scope as a correction of another distinct viewpoint: either a new argument is presented as countering an initial proposal, or a proposal already voiced is presented with weaker relevance or no relevance, or (in pre- or postverbal positions) *to* aims at rejecting an opposite eventuality (conjuring a fear, dismissing a fictive assumption, winning over an anticipated reluctance from the other speaker). The operation triggered by the discourse particle *to* always involves inter-subjectivity, since it negotiates with the other's viewpoint, distinct from and often conflicting with the utterer's viewpoint.[16] This prerequisite of inter-subjectivity is paralleled by the behaviour of Germanic modal particles as described in terms of dialogic interaction in Weydt (2006) or grounding and common grounds in Fischer (2007), Diewald and Krescic (2010) or Bross (2012): the speaker acknowledges what the hearer thinks as a common ground for anchoring his/her proposal. The specificity of Hindi *to* is that this inter-subjective interaction rarely fosters conviviality or connivance since it basically involves conflicting or at least diverging view-points.

This orientation is compatible with the origin of the word, initially a pronominal basis related to the sphere of non-ego. As for the conjunction *to*, when it is a correlative, *to*, which is directly related to the anaphoric pronoun, correlates the apodosis to a conditional, acting both as an anaphoric device and as a selecting a given path among others; when it coordinates two discourse sequences ('then'), it opens a new scenario resulting yet distinct from the previous discourse sequence.

The behaviour and meaning of *to* as a discourse particle certainly differ from its syntactic meanings: they are highly diversified and often involve polemical values. Yet they form a constellation of meanings and uses whose consistency becomes clear as soon as the operation at stake is analyzed on the basis of

---

[16] As opposed to the uncontroversial meaning of the focus marker derived from the tag question marker in Even (Matic, this volume, example 26b). There is probably a logical correlation between the fact that the focus marking element produces uncontroversial common ground in the inter-subjective relation of speaker A and B, whereas the topic marking element emphasizes diverging view points in the interaction.

interactive contexts; besides, they are not totally disconnected from the grammatical word.[17] But the discourse particle always involves inter-subjectivity, whereas the conjunction is not sensitive to it. The above study is of course only a fist attempt to disentangle the meanings and functions of *to* in interactive situations, and finer grain studies are still awaited, particularly regarding the exact intonational contours in the various scopes (thematizing *vs* non-thematizing) of the particle.

References

Abraham, Werner. 1991. The Grammaticization of the German Modal Particles. In Edith Traugott & Berndt Heine (eds.). *Approaches to Grammaticalization II*, 331–80. Amsterdam: Benjamins.
Bonnot, Christine. 1990. La Particule *to* et la polémique cachée en russe moderne. A propos du statut énonciatif du thème. *Revue des Etudes Slaves* LXII-2: 67–75.
Bonnot, Christine. 2006. Lorsque la focalisation porte sur l'ensemble de la relation prédicative : les énoncés à accent non final en russe moderne. In Wlodarczik Hélène & André (eds.). *La focalisation dans les langues*, 135–148. Paris : L'Harmattan.
Bril, Isabelle & Rebuschi, Georges. 2006. *Coordination et subordination, Typologie et modélisation*. Gap: Ophrys.
Bross, Fabian. 2012. German modal particles and the common ground. *Helikon. A Multidisciplinary Online Journal*, 2: 182–209.
Culioli, Antoine. 1999. *Pour une linguistique de l'énonciation 2. Formalisation et opérations de repérage*. Gap: Ophrys.
Diewald, Gabriele & Marijana Kresic. 2010. Ein übereinzelsprachliches kontrastives Beschreibungsmodell für Partikelbedeutungen. *Linguistik Online* 44-4/2010.
Fischer, Kerstin. 2007. Grounding and common ground: modal particles and their translation equivalents, in Anita Fletzer & Kirsten Fischer (eds.). *Lexical Markers of common ground, Studies in Pragmatics 3*, 44–66. Amsterdam: Elsevier.
Dvivedi, Veenita. 1994. Topicalization in Hindi and the Correlative Construction. In Butt, M., T.H. King & G. Ramchand (eds.). *Theoretical Perspectives on Word Order in South Asian Languages*, 91–118. Stanford: CSLI Publications.
Guimier, Claude (ed.). 1999. *La Thématisation dans les langues*. Bern: Peter Lang.
Fernandez-Vest, M.M. Jocelyne. 2004. Mnémème, Antitopic : Le post-rhème, de l'énoncé au texte. In Fernandez-Vest, M.M. J. & Sh. Carter-Thomas (eds.). *Structure informationnelle et particules énonciatives: Essai de Typologie*, 65–104. Paris: L'Harmattan.
Fernandez-Vest, M. M. Jocelyne. Detachment linguistics and information grammar of oral languages. In this volume.
François, Jacques & Lacher-Dutour, Anne. 2003. *Fonction et moyens de la focalisation à travers les langues*. Mémoires de la Société de Linguistique de Paris. Leuven : Peeters.

---

17 Which is also true of the Russian particle *to*, analyzed by Bonnot (1990), equally issued from the same Indo-European pronominal basis. Russian *to* has numerous uses comparable to those of Hindi *to*, but not the correlative one nor the meanings observed in section 3.2.

Gundel, Jeanette K., Helberg, Nancy & Zadarsk, Ron. 1993. Cognitive Status and the Form of Referring Expressions in Discourse. *Language* 69-2: 274–307.

Gutierres-Ordonez, Salvador. 2006. Focalisation, Thématisation, Topicalisation. In Wlodarczik, Hélène & André (eds.). *La focalisation dans les langues*, 11–26. Paris : L'Harmattan.

Haiman, John. 1978. Conditional are Topics. *Language* 54-3: 564–89.

Haspelmath, Martin (ed.). 2008. *Language Typology and Language Universals*. Berlin/Amsterdam: de Gruyter.

Haspelmath, Martin (ed.). 2004. *Coordinating Constructions*. Typological Studies in Language. Amsterdam: John Benjamins.

Kellogg, Rev. S.H. 1938 [1856]. *A Grammar of the Hindi Language*. London: Paul Kegan.

Lahiri, Aditi & Jennifer Fitzpatrick-Cole. 1999. Emphatic clitics and focus intonation in Bengali. In R. Kager & W. Zonneveld (eds.). *Phrasal Phonology*, 119–144. Nijmegen: University of Nijmegen Press.

Lakshmi Bai B. 1977. Syntax and Semantics of the Particle *To* in Hindi. *Osmania Papers in Linguistics* 3: 64–75.

Matic, Dejan. Tag questions and focus markers. In this volume.

McGregor, R. S. 1972. *An Outline of Hindi Grammar*. Delhi: Oxford University Press.

Mohanan, Tara & K. P. Mohanan. 1994. Issues in Word Order. In Mariam Butt, Tracy H. King & Gillian Ramchand (eds.). *Theoretical Perspectives on Word Order in South Asian Languages*, 153–184. Stanford: CSLI Publications:.

Montaut, Annie. 2002. La particule énonciative to en hindi/ourdou. *Cahiers de Linguistique de l'INALCO* 4 : 111–134.

Montaut, Annie. 2004. *Hindi Grammar*. Munchen : Lincom Europa.

Montaut, Annie. 2012. De l'anaphore à la subordination en passant par la corrélation, In Olga Inkova & Pascale Haderman (eds.). *La Corrélation*, 193–213. Paris : Champion.

Ohala, Manjari. 1986. A Search for Acoustic Correlates in Hindi Stress. In Bh. Krishnamurti (ed.), *South Asian Languages: Structure, Convergence and Diglossia*, 81–90. Delhi: Motilal Banarsidass.

Patil, Umesh, Gerrit Kentner, Anja Gollrad, Frank Kügler, Caroline Féry & Shravan Vasishth. 2008. Focus, Word Order and Intonation in Hindi. *JSAL* 1: 55–72.

Shapiro, Michael. 1999. Hindi *to* as discourse marker. In P. J. Mistry and Bharati Modi (eds.). *Vidyopaasanaa: Studies in Honor of Harivallabh C. Bhayani*, 179–89. Mumbai and Ahmedabad: Image Publications Pvt. Ltd.

Weydt, Harald. 1969. *Abtönungspartikel. Die deutschen Modalwörter und ihre französischen Entsprechungen*. Berlin West & Zürich : Bad Homburg.

Weydt, Harald. 2006. What are particles good for? In Kirsten Fischer (ed.). *Approaches to Discourse Particles*. Amsterdam: Elsevier.

Wlodarczik, Hélène & André Wlodarczik (eds.). 2006. *La focalisation dans les langues*. Paris: L'Harmattan.

IV IS and Language Contacts

Fida Bizri
13 Discourse Regulating Strategies in Pidgin Madam

1 Introduction

Due to their prominently oral nature, pidgins are of particular value to the study of discourse strategies. Pidgin Madam (PM) is related to a number of contemporary Arabic-based pidgins that developed in the last forty years within the context of cheap labour migration from Asia to the Middle East. Its incipient character, and a rich recorded corpus of spontaneous speech and interactions, allow us to follow the development of linguistic change *ab ovo* and to question the interaction between the purely syntactic and the pragmatic. This paper discusses three devices developed in PM to structure discourse and achieve constituent emphasis: First, a theme marking device consisting of a specific intonational pattern following an initially-detached constituent (the theme). Second, a contrastive prosodic device, formally related to the theme marking intonation pattern. And third, a verum focus particle, derived from the superstrate's lexical stock but endowed with a new function. In fact, the functions attributed to all these three devices are very innovative in regard to Arabic. They may be internal developments triggered by the communicative necessity. However, a look at the substrate language (here Sinhala) shows similarities in many regards. Examples from Colloquial Sinhala are therefore discussed at the end of the paper, in an attempt to assess its possible impact.

The data presented in this paper are extracted from the PM corpus (an important part of which has been published in Bizri 2004, 2005, 2010, and 2013), consisting of long narratives, discussions, question-answer interactions between Lebanese employers and Sri Lankan housemaids, as well as amongst (Sinhala native speaking) Sri Lankans. Considering that all the examples presented here are largely drawn from recorded spontaneous dialogues, the analysis is based on a minute examination of the conversational logic of the interactions. It is structured around a bipartite division distinguishing between: theme and rheme (respectively topic and focus) following the framework set in the present volume.

Fida Bizri, SeDyL (INALCO, CNRS umr 8202, IRD umr 135)

2 The Case of Pidgin Madam[1]

PM is linguistically and culturally related to other varieties of contemporary Arabic-based pidgins attested in various countries of the Gulf area and the modern Arabic world, and best referred to as Asian Migrant Pidgin Arabic (AMAP, cf. Bizri 2014 for more). Such varieties include: Gulf Arabic Pidgin in the UAE, Oman and Kuwait (Smart 1990; Wiswall 2002 ; Næss 2008; Bakir 2010; Veersteegh 2010, Avram 2012), Urdu Pidgin Arabic (Al-Moaily 2008 and 2013), Saudi Asian Pidgin (Al-Azraqi 2010), and Jordanian Pidgin Arabic (Al-Salman 2013).

PM, recorded in Lebanon, is however distinguishable from other AMAP varieties to which it is related by the fact that it is spoken only by Sinhala-speaking female housemaids and their Lebanese Arabic-speaking employers. Most of the Sinhala housemaids recorded in Lebanon within the scope of the research on PM (Bizri 2004, 2005, 2010, and 2013) had already been to another Arabic-speaking country where AMAP varieties are attested, or had headed towards one of these countries after completing their contract in Lebanon. This results in a cross-fertilization of the pidgin due to the constant but always temporary migration of labour workers in the area (Bizri 2014a, 2014b).

However, although this is the common trend, in reality not all migrants travel from one Arab country to the other during their often decade-long migration. Some spend more than thirty years in the same country, either accumulating several temporary contracts, or working on their own account. This results in a set of distinctive features characterizing PM from other varieties to which it is nonetheless related: PM has a unique Sinhala substratum whereas, in the case of other varieties of AMAP spoken elsewhere in the Arab world, many substratal languages are involved (mainly South Asian: Hindi, Urdu, Bengali, Sinhala, Tamil, but also South East Asian: Tagalog, Malay, Javanese). Furthermore, since PM is mainly spoken by live-in housemaids and their female employers (unlike the situation in the Gulf area, for instance, where male non live-in migrant workers are as important in number as female housemaids), its lexical stock derives, mainly, from Arabic feminine forms: Arabic feminine imperatives are

---

[1] Throughout the paper, the migrants' native language is referred to as "substrate" although, here, we are clearly not in the traditionally described situation where a pidgin develops out of the contact between autochtonous substratal languages and an outsider linguistic variety. Besides, all the examples presented here are numbered and have one of the two signs: "PM" indicating that the utterance is spoken in Pidgin Madam, and "SIN" indicating that it is spoken in (Colloquial) Sinhala. Unless otherwise mentioned, all PM and SIN examples come from my own recorded data during fieldwork in Lebanon and in Sri Lanka from 1999 onwards.

interpreted in PM as basic verbal forms; Arabic feminine adjectives are treated as non-gendered basic forms; Arabic nouns which often appear with relational referents in discourse have been adopted in the pidgin along with a feminine Arabic suffixed pronoun that has become an integral part of the noun losing, thus, the original semantic value it indexes.

PM also developed the set of three devices exposed below. Judging by the publications so far available on other varieties of AMAP, nothing similar had been reported from the Gulf area, Arabic Peninsula or Jordan. This could point out that such devices are absent in other varieties, but it may also be indicative of the type of data collected in each case (elicitation vs. *impromptu* speech), and of the way it is retrieved and presented.

3 A Theme Marking Device

A specific intonational pattern occurs with high frequency in the recorded corpus of PM. It is characterized by a melodic height followed by a short pause before the main clause, similar to what has been called "comma intonation" (Chafe 1988), creating a separate pitch contour boundary between the main clause, and the preposed clause. It is referred to, here, as intoneme because, although prosodic, it covers complex and well-defined functions, both at the semantic and morphosyntactic levels. Since it is, here, discussed more in terms of its prosodic function (its semantic interpretation by listeners), than of its prosodic form (its sound), I have chosen to annotate it through a simplified manual transcription, where ↑ indicates an ascending intonation, ↓ a descending intonation, / a short pause marking non-completion, and // a final pause marking completion. In spite of their technical oversimplification, these signs do have an acoustic (therefore, unequivocal semantic) reality to the speakers of the linguistic system here described, a reality that is, *de facto*, very extensively used in communication.

This intonation pattern, together with the initial detachment of one of the utterance's constituents, has one main purpose: it limits the boundary of the theme, the old information shared by hearer and speaker, that which is considered to be given, and which is usually followed by the complementary new information in the main clause. The model can be schematized as follows: //Theme-Given↑/ Rheme-New Information↓//. As such, the theme is not limited to one syntactic role in the utterance, it can be a subject (1), a verb (2), an object (3) or any other argument. Examples (1–3), therefore, typically illustrate this situation where the theme is initially-detached, followed by an ascending intonation separating it from the rheme that is executed with a descending intonation.

(1) bēbi ↑/ ana māma bēt↓
PM baby↑/ 1SG mother house↓
'As for [my] *baby*, [well,] he's at my mother's house.'

(2) mūti harep ↑/ ana hibbīni kayyik↓
PM die war↑/ 1SG love brother
'The one [brother] who died at war, he was my favourite brother.'

(3) masāre ↑/ kullu kodi hasbent ↓
PM money↑/ all take husband↓
'As for the *money*, [well, my] husband took it all [from me].'

Along the same lines, this intoneme achieves intra-clausal semantic linkages, where the subordinate clause is itself treated as a theme, a given on which new information could be built, a framework to which the following clause will refer. Four types of semantic linkages in PM are considered here, namely: conditional, contrastive, causal, and temporal linkages. What they have in common is the presence of this intoneme that acts as a syntactic element correlating the highest clause to the lowest one. In all these types of linkages in PM, the preposed clause sets a prerequisite (like an environment, or a parameter) for the event in the highest clause to occur. Structurally, the preposed clause is treated as themes are (initially-detached; immediately followed by the ↑ ascending intonation and a short pause before the descending intonation accompanying the rheme; ant it cannot occur as the only element of a sentence). Semantically, it is presented as a given, a known, a presupposed, subject to neither interrogation nor denial, linking the antecedent to the consequent.

In the examples below from PM, the thematic protasis indexes one of the semantic linkages: conditionals as in *if*-clauses (4); conditional-temporal as in *it's only when*-clauses (5); temporal as in *as soon as*-clauses and *when*-clauses (6, 7, 8b); and causal as in *since/considering that/because*-clauses (9, 10, 11).

(4) pi dam wāhad ↑/ mannūh ↓
PM there is blood one↑/ forbidden↓
'*If* [they are of the] same blood, *then* it [marriage] is forbidden.'

(5) hēk musækel kallasit ↑/ ana dallit hōn ↓
PM such problem finish↑/ 1SG stay here↓
'*It's only when* such problems are over, *that* I would [accept to] stay here.'

(6) *ana supta hiyi ↑/ ana tarip hiyi no gūḍ ↓*
PM 1SG see 3SG↑/ 1SG know 3SG no good↓
'*As soon as* I saw her, I knew she was a bad [person].'

(7) *nēmit opīs, bas nēmi. payīni ↑/ rūhit mahal ↓*
PM sleep office, only sleep wake up↑/ go shop↓
'They sleep at the office. They only sleep [there]. *When* they wake up, it is to the shop that they go.'

(8a) *sirlanka pi budda. sirlanka*
PM Sri Lanka there is Buddha/Buddhist Sri Lanka
'In Sri Lanka I am Buddhist. [But that's] in Sri Lanka.'

(8b) *tīji sawiya walla lebanan, honīk tījī ↑/ læsem pi alla↓*
PM come Saudi or Lebanon there come↑/ must there is Allah↓
'*When* one goes to Saudi Arabia, or Lebanon, or any other place over there, *then* one must [pray] for Allah.'

(9) *ana ultelli: ana sitti nos payīni ↑/ ana nēmit badde ↓*
PM 1SG say 1SG six half wake up↑/ 1SG sleep want/must↓
'I said: *Since* I have to wake up at 6.30, I must get some sleep.'

(10) *pi māma ↑/ no nār↓*
PM there is mother↑/ no fire ↓
'*Because/when/if* the mother is alive, there [can be] no incineration.'

The linkages obtained by this strategy hierarchically range from the "closest" (facets of a single event or action, as shown above) to the "loosest" (link between distinct events or actions) (Van Valin 2007). The "loosest" are achieved through the resort to tail-head linkage mechanisms, whereby the main verbal predicate of the last clause finds itself as an initially-detached theme at the beginning of the new clause. Tail-head linkages, widely attested in Oceanic and Papuan languages as an areal feature (De Vries 2005), are event-sequencing mechanisms which allow for greater discourse processing ease in long narratives. They are usually executed with a specific intonational pattern: slowly pronounced, rising intonation, pause phenomena.

In PM, tail-head linkages (THL) are immediately followed by the typical theme marking intonational pattern described above. And this is not surprising, since they participate of the same dynamics of discourse anchoring and reinforcement: selection of a prominent element or event, and its reuse in the following sequence as an echo, preparing thus the next event. This mechanism is shown in the following long excerpt (11a–h) taken from a PM narrative, where the Sri Lankan speaker relates a problematic cohabitation with two Ethiopian domestic workers at her Lebanese employers' house. The narrative is not presented in its entirety, the sign [...] indicating the cuts (for the full narrative, cf. Bizri 2010).

(11a) *ana sēya nās pūti juwwa*
PM   1SG hour twelve enter inside
    'I go inside at midnight.'

(11b) *ana nās pūti juwwa↑/ ana ma pi dogre nēmit↓,*
PM   1SG 12 enter inside↑/ 1SG no there is immediately sleep↓
    ana sūpa sarīde
    1SG see newspaper
    '*Having gone inside at midnight,* I don't sleep right after, I read the newspaper.'

(11c) *hiyyi badde tekkīni ṭīr nēmi*
PM   3SG/PL VF[2] talk much sleep
    'They[3] do chatter a whole lot while sleeping' [...]

(11d) *madam aletli rūhi ulīli badde nēmi*
PM   Madam say[4] go say VF sleep
    'Madam told me to go tell them to sleep'

(11e) *ana rūhit ↑/ ana ma ulīli uskote ↓*
PM   1SG go↑/ 1SG no say shut up↓
    '*Having gone* there, I didn't tell them to shut up' [...]

(11f) *hēk aletli mister ↑/ hiyi salēni↓*
PM   thus say Mister↑/ 3SG angry↓
    'Mister having spoken thus, she got angry'

---

2 VF Verum Focus. The function of this particle will be discussed under section 5.
3 *hiyi* is a third singular feminine Lebanese Arabic pronoun "she", but in PM it is used to denote both singular "she" and plural "they", sometimes followed by Arabic *kullu* "all", but not necessarily.
4 Due to the incipient character of PM, and to the migrants' language acquisition by "mimesis", i.e. scaffolding on their employers' Arabic (discussed in length in Bizri 2010), verbs in PM have several equivalent Arabic forms.

(11g) *hiyi salēni* ↑/ *payīni   no tekkini ana*↓
PM   3SG angry↑/ wake up no talk   1SG↓
'*Being angry,* she would not talk to me upon waking up' [...]

(11h) *badēn dohor asa   hiye. dohor asa*↑/   *ana tahe bēb*↓
PM   then   noon come 3SG   noon come↑/ 1SG open door↓
'Then she came at noon. *Her having come at noon*, I opened the door...' [...]

The THL occurrences in (11a–h) all belong to the so-called "chained type" of THL identified by de Vries (2005), a bridging device ensuring thematic continuity, different from the so-called "thematic THL" that highlights discontinuity.

4 A Contrasting Device

To highlight contrast between two situations in PM, the strategy is to double use the same intonation pattern described in the previous section. When doubled, this intoneme can be translated into English by "whereas", or "while", as shown by the subsequent examples.

(12) *hayda abel   asa* ↑/   *no gūḍ* ↓//   *tēni* ↑/   *ṭīr   gūḍ* ↓//
    this   before come↑/ no good↓// second↑/ very good↓//
    'The one that came before is no good, *whereas* the second one is very good'

(13) *hiyi   pæyīni* ↑/   *sēya mēni nōs* ↓//   *ana* ↑/ *sitti nōs* ↓//
    3SG/PL wake up↑/ hour eight half↓// 1SG↑/ six half↓//
    'They wake up at 8.30, *whereas* I wake up at 6.30'

The presence or absence of this double intonational token corresponds to two different semantic readings. Consider the following two examples, where (14) shows contrast, while (15) is a simple enumeration, and the distinction between the two is enacted through intonation:

(14) *wehde*↑/ *nēmit opīs*↓// *wehde*↑/ *kalli   bil   bēt*↓//
PM one↑/   sleep office↓// one↑/   remain inside house↓//
    'One [of them] sleeps at the office, *while* the other sleeps at home'

(15) *ana nēmi ūda, hiyi nēmi salōn.   ma pi   muskal, kullu massūta*
PM 1SG sleep room 3SG sleep living-room no there is problem all   happy
'I sleep in the room, and she sleeps in the living-room. There's no problem [whatsoever], everyone is happy'

The excerpt shown below (16a–g) comes from a conversation between a Sri Lankan worker (SLW), trying to explain to her Lebanese Madam (MAD) funerary customs of her village in Sri Lanka. She's trying to make a distinction between: situation a) when the corpse is inside the house; and situation b) when the corpse does not (or cannot) enter the house. Different mourning attitudes are adopted accordingly. She takes the example of her father's recent death, at home, distinct from the earlier death of her brother, at the war front.

(16a) SLW: *bil   bēt   mūti↑/ bil   bēt   ma pi   ēkol↓//*
　　　　　 inside house die ↑/ inside house no   there is eating↓//
　　　　　 'If one has died inside the house, then there shall be no eating inside the house.'

(16b) MAD: *ilīle lē.   lē   no ēkol ?*
　　　　　 tell why why no eating
　　　　　 'Tell me why so? Why should there be no eating?'

(16c) SLW: *hēki,   soma wahad ma pi   ēkol*
　　　　　 like this, week one   no there is eating
　　　　　 'This is how it is. For one whole week, there is no eating'

(16d) SLW: *klētīn yōm, killu bēt   ana same, killu ma tēkol, ana bil*
　　　　　 3 (30?) day all   house 1SG fast   all   no eat   1SG inside
　　　　　 bēt   bas
　　　　　 house only
　　　　　 'For 3 (30) days. All my family [should] be fasting. No one eats. Only my family [does not eat].'

(16e) SLW: *bāba   bil   bēt   mūti. bas   bil   bēt   hēki.*
　　　　　 father inside house die only inside house like this
　　　　　 '[Because you see,] my father died at home. Only [at] home, is it like this.'

(16f) SLW: *ana kaya   bil   bēt   la, harep↑/ ēkol↓//*
　　　　　 1SG brother inside house no war ↑/ eating↓//
　　　　　 '[For instance,] my brother was not at home [did not die at home], at the war front, so we ate [at home].'

The conversation culminates in a conclusive statement, putting in contrast the two situations with the help of the double use of the intoneme.

(16g) SLW: *bil   bēt   ma pi↑/   ēkol↓//   bil   bēt   mūti↑/*
inside house no there is↑/ eating↓// inside house die↑/
bil   bēt   ma pi   ēkol↓//
inside house no there is eating↓//
'If [the dead] is not at home, [there could be] eating [inside the house]. *Whereas*, if you die at home, there should be no eating inside the house.'

5 A Verum Focus Device

PM achieves verum focus (VF) through the particle *badde*. Originally, *badd-e* (or *badd-i*) is a Levantine Arabic pseudo-verb that literally means "I want". It is etymologically related to *bi-wedd-e*, whereby *bi* is a preposition meaning "in", *wedd* a noun meaning "intention", and *–e* a personal suffix designating first person singular, "I". The personal suffix can be conjugated[5], giving thus the Arabic pseudo-verbal paradigm "I want, you want, etc...". As discussed elsewhere (Bizri 2004, 2005, 2009, and 2010), Arabic personal clitics find themselves in the pidgin totally demotivated semantically and grammatically, becoming part of the element they are attached to, hence their extremely high occurrence in the PM corpus. The main two forms retained in the pidgin of the Arabic "want" paradigm are: *badd-e* "I want", and *badd-ik* "you (feminine) want", *–ik* being a second feminine singular pronoun[6]. Both forms denote desire in PM, irrespectively of number and gender: *badde* and *baddik* alike may mean "I want", "he wants", "we want", etc... They may also occasionally express participant internal-necessity "need to..." as it is the case in Arabic itself. Unlike Arabic, however, in PM *badde* can also occur in redundant complementation of the Arabic deontic marker *lēzim* (17).

(17) *badde lēsim ulīla maḍam*
PM   badde   must   tell   Madam
    'You have to tell Madam'

---

[5] Personal pronouns in their clitic form can be suffixed in Arabic either to a noun, or to a preposition, or to a verb (denoting direct or indirect objects).
[6] Different clitics (other than 2SGF *–ik*, and 1SG *–e*) appear in PM, but these two forms are statistically most frequent.

Of both forms (*badde* and *baddik*), only *badde* has taken on a new role (not attested in Arabic) as a VF. In such cases, *badde* is often used in a semantically empty guise in marked environments as a verum focus. The two following constructions (18-19) differ in terms of markedness.

(18) *ana māma mūti aprel*
PM 1SG mother die April
  'My mother died in April'

(19) *ana bāba badde mūti, ana ma hada ulīla*
PM 1SG father badde died 1SG no one say
  'My father *died/ did in fact die*, and no one has told me'

Verum focus, a term coined by Höhle (1988 and 1992) for German, is broadly associated with emphasis of propositional truth. It highlights evidence relevant to the speaker's claim or updates the addressee's beliefs. This function is better captured in conversations than in decontextualized statements. Below are two different extracts (20a–c, and 21a–c) of an interaction in PM, showing how *badde* occurs at the discourse level. Example (20) is a fragment from a conversation between a Sri Lankan housemaid and a Lebanese neighbour, friend of 'Madam' (therefore herself a 'Madam', the term usually referring to the female employer).

(20a) SLW: *tayi bukra*
PM   come tomorrow
         'Come tomorrow'

(20b) MAD: *nšalla*
PM   loc. (if God wills)
          'Hopefully [I will]'

(20c) SLW: *plīs,   baddi tayi*
PM   please VF   come
          'Please, *do come*'

Example (21) is an exchange between two Sri Lankan maids discussing their future projects. In the full exchange, SLW1 claims she knows from her own sister back home that SLW2's husband is officially dating another woman in Sri Lanka, and squandering SLW2's money. SLW2, however, refuses to believe her.

(21a) SLW1: *hasband dhakelayke*
PM   husband make fun/lead on
           '[Your] husband is leading [you] on'

(21b) SLW2: *la ma   pi.   ma   pi   hēk.   ma   pi*
PM   no NEG there is NEG there is like this NEG there is
            dhakelayke
            make fun/lead on
            'No he's not. He's not like this. He's not leading [me] on'

(21a) SLW1: *hasband pi   wehde tēne. badde dhakelayke*
PM   husband there is one   other.   VF   make fun/lead on
            '[Your] husband has [taken] another [woman]. [Now, believe me]
            he is leading you on.'

In example (22), we have in the same statement two different occurrences of this Arabic form *badd-*. In the first instance, under the format *baddik*, it takes on the Arabic meaning of the token (that of desire, internal-necessity), while in the second instance (as well as in examples 22–23), under the form *badde*, it is emancipated from its primary motivation, and ritualized into a VF. All three examples (22–24), come from the same narrative, in which the sequence of events (of the highest importance to the locutor/narrator) is carefully emphasized due to the unexpected character of such events.

(22) *ana abel   ana aytilayki ma baddik, ana badde ulla ōkē, tayb*
PM   1SG before 1SG shout   no   want   1SG VF   say OK   fine
     'At first, I didn't want him to scold me. [So] *I did say* okay, fine'

(23) *hiyi dogre   badde droba*
PM   3SG immediately   VF   hit
     '*What she* immediately *did* was to *hit* me'

(24) *madam hottīlo barra   badde sakkere bēb*
PM   Madam put   outside   VF   close   door
     'Madam put her out, and she *did shut* the door'

The particle *badde*, as a VF, is also similar to the *Do*-support in English implying a focus reading on the main verb (Denison 1985; Stein 1990, amongst others), as is shown by the English translations proposed. It also displays a mechanism comparable to that of the French assertion marker "*je veux*" with the same meaning "I want" (Culioli 2002), whereby the demotivated expression marks assertive and subjective commitment, implying a reinforcing of the argument (here: the verb), an increase of the intensity of that argument, thus, its foregrounding. Consequently, the repertoire of values of *badde* in PM is further extended to that of intensifying the quality/action of the verb by putting focus on it, such as shown in (25-26). It is particularly frequent in surprise-event narratives, where the speakers gradually prepare the addresee to reach the climax of the narrative. Here, they are often combined with the prosodic discourse regulating strategies discussed under section 3. *Badde* can also occur with a verb preceded by a negative particle, as in example (27), implying a strong prohibition.

(25) *rāḍyo↑/ baddi hiyyi ganni↓*
PM radio↑/ badde 3SG/PL sing↓
 '[Having put on the] radio, they *indulge in singing*'

(26) *ādi↑/ baddi tekkīni awiyi↓*
PM sitting↑/ badde talk loud↓
 'Sitting [there], they were *really talking* loud'

(27) *badēn aletli mas badde pūti mahal*
PM then say no more badde enter shop
 'Then they said that I should no more *enter* the shop.'

6 On the Possible Impact of Sinhala

Although closely related (through the circular[7] migration of most of its speakers) to other varieties of AMAP spoken by a cluster of mainly South Asian migrant communities in neighbouring Arab countries, PM proved to be spoken only by the female Sinhala Sri Lankan community based in Lebanon, for reasons debated elsewhere (Bizri 2010 and 2014a). It appears, therefore, as a case where a pidginized variety is produced with only one substrate involved.

The discourse regulating devices developed in PM, quite innovative with regard to both the superstrate and other AMAP varieties, may well be an independent development. However, a look at the Sinhala language from a pragmatic perspective points towards a possible influence from the substrate in the development of PM. Sinhala is itself a special case in Indo-Aryan languages (Gair and

---

[7] Cf. Zapata-Barrero and Sánchez-Montijano 2012 on circular temporary labour migration.

Paolillo 1997), as it is geographically separated from other languages of the same family, and has long been in contact with Dravidian languages, mainly Tamil and Malayalam, which resulted in both internal developments and contact-induced changes.

Sinhala is a highly diglossic language, and Colloquial Sinhala is the form discussed here because it is the native and only language – apart from PM – spoken by the majority of Sri Lankan housemaids in Lebanon. In Colloquial Sinhala, focused constructions are strikingly frequent in discourse, and they are grammatically required in certain contexts such as with Wh-questions (cf. Gair 1971, 1983 and 1986). In fact, focalized structures appear in Sinhala at a much lower threshold than in any of the Indo-Aryan languages to which it is related, or even for that matter than in any of the Dravidian languages that have historically participated in shaping the Sinhala focalizing arsenal (Gair 1997: 162).

In spite of its basic (non-rigid) SOV order, Sinhala shows a cleft-like construction that reserves the postverbal (finally-detached) position for focusing. Assertive marking is achieved through the use of the focalizer *tamā* or *tamay*. Originally, *tamā* is a reflexive pronoun meaning "one's self", "one's own" (Gunasekara 1891, reprinted in 1986) that was used in classics after pronouns to reinforce their meaning (such as in 32). This use was then extended to other parts of speech (28). In verbal predicates, focalization can be achieved by a verbal focalizing particle (here: *–nnē* for present) with final detachment of the focused constituent (compare unfocalized 29 to focalized 30–31). Focalization can also be achieved without necessary final detachment, but simply with *tamay* indicating on what constituent the emphasis falls[8] (32).

(28) *oyā kiyana eka ættæ tamay*
SIN 2SG saying one truth tamay
'What you say is *indeed* true'

(29) *mama pota liya-nawā*
SIN 1SG book write-PRES
'I write the book'

(30) *pota liya-**nnē** mama*
SIN book write-PRES.FOC 1SG
'*It is me* who writes the book'

---

8 It is also possible to achieve focalization simply through a raising intonation, that is without neither *tamay* nor final detachment.

(31) *mama liya-**nnē**   pota*
SIN 1SG   write-PRES.FOC book
'*It is the book* that I write'

(32) *mama tamay pota liya-**nnē***
SIN 1SG   tamay book write-PRES.FOC
'*I* write the book *myself*'

If the focused element is the verb itself, then only *tamay* can achieve such meaning (33), similar to *badde* in PM.

(33) *mama pota liya-nawā   tamay*
SIN 1SG   book write-PRES *tamay*
'What I do is to *actually write* the book'

On the other hand, Colloquial Sinhala not seldom resorts to marking themes also. The theme marker *naŋ* (sometimes transcribed as *nan* or *nam*), shown in the examples (34–35) below, is extremely frequent in spontaneous communication. *naŋ* requires that the theme of its clause immediately precede it, and it also carries an implicit contrastive meaning. However, unlike in PM, no specific intonational contour is attached to this type of constructions in Sinhala. Example (34) is extracted from a conversation where a grocery shop assistant answers his client asking for rice to buy.

(34) *hāl naŋ ada   næhæ*
SIN rice *naŋ* today no
'As for *rice*, well, we don't have any today.'

(35) *oyā kiyana eka ættæ wenna puluwan, ēt mama naŋ ēka*
SIN 2SG saying one truth be   can   but 1SG *naŋ* that
    viśvāsakaranna bæhæ
    believe   unable
'What you say may be true, but, *as for me*, I cannot believe it'

Interestingly, and very much like in PM (such as in PM4, presented under section 3), Sinhala *if*-clauses are expressed through the conditional suffixed particle *naŋ* (sometimes transcribed *nam* or *nan*) such as in (36). Haiman (1978) noted the affinities shown in a number of unrelated languages between themes and conditionals, where the protasis constitutes the framework to which the following predication, the apodosis in the main clause, will refer (cf. Haspelmath

2008 for more). Both the thematic *naŋ* and the conditional *naŋ* in Sinhala are thought to have originated from *namut* or *numut*, meaning "although" (Geiger 1938; Gunasekara [1891] 1986). In PM too, the affinity between the theme marker/conditional correlator intoneme on the one hand, and the contrastive "although" on the other is attested, as in (37).

(36) *ada   yanawā naŋ, kār-ek-en   yanna*
SIN today go   if   car-INDF-INS go.IMP
    '*If* you are going today, *then* go by car'

(37) *ma pi   salli ana↑ hōn pi   pakkare alla↓*
PM   no there is pray 1SG   here there is think Allah
    '*Although* I don't pray, I do think of Allah here [showing the location of her heart]'.

Finally, the discourse regulating strategy achieved in PM through THL seems to map a similar strategy in Sinhala involving the conjunctive participle (CP) followed by an intonation pattern similar to that discussed for PM. The main discourse-regulating function of Sinhala CPs is that of sequencing events in narratives, i.e. not just intraclausally (as in 38), but also interclausally (as in 38–39). Sinhala CPs function, therefore, in a THL manner, where the last verbal predicate of the preceding clause, is repeated at the beginning of the following clause, with a short pause, giving both speaker and addressee a break between two chains, and ensuring a smooth continuity of narration.

(38) *gedara gihilla, bat kālā,   tē   bīwā*
SIN   house go.CP   rice eat.CP tea drink.PAST
    'After having been home, after having eaten rice, (we) drank tea'

(39) *tē   bīlā,   āyet wædæ-ṭa giyā*
SIN   tea drink.CP again work-DAT go.PAST
    'Having drank tea, we went back to work'

Unlike many Indo-Aryan languages, but similarly to Dravidian Tamil for instance, Sinhala CPs do not necessarily require the same subject as the matrix clause, such as in (40). In PM too, example (11h) clearly shows a case of THL with a different subject.

(40) (Gair and Paolillo 1997: 49)
SIN *ammā leḍa welā,   gedara sērama wæḍa karanne api*
    mother sick become.CP house all   work do.FOC 1PL
    'With mother sick, it is we that have to do all the housework'

In sum, it is important to note that the pragmatic innovations which characterize PM are far more frequent in the speech of Sinhala housemaids whose migration to the Arab world (and, therefore, use of pidgin Arabic) is strictly limited to Lebanon[9], than in that of Sinhala housemaids who had travelled across the Middle East. In this context, it is all the more expected that the highly demanding discourse requirements (theme-rheme requirements) in Sinhala trigger some kind of pragmatic innovation in PM. This innovation then develops freely because there is less pressure or competition from different substrates.

7 Summary

A close-up on the information structuring strategies in Pidgin Madam shows how pragmatic motivations foster morphosyntactic developments. Three devices are examined here: First, an intonational pattern creating an IP boundary and delimiting an initially-detached thematised constituent. The theme is not limited to one syntactic role in the utterance, it could be a subject, a verb, an object, a subordinate clause where the intonation acts as a correlator delimiting the protasis of correlative sentences. The same strategy also serves the purpose of co-ordinating narrative sequences through tail-head linkages, whereby the main verbal predicate of the last clause finds itself as an initially-detached theme at the beginning of the new clause. Second, a contrastive device consisting of the double occurrence of the theme delimiting intonation pattern after each element highlights the difference between them. And third, a verum focus device achieved through an assertive marker developed from a Lebanese Arabic pseudo-verb *badde* (originally denoting desire or intention). These three devices happen to have echoes in Sinhala, where the thematic and the rhematic functions are highly salient in spontaneous communication: A Sinhala particle *naŋ*, very frequently used in oral discourse, which is itself a correlator in conditional clauses, delimits the boundary of the initially-detached theme; the use of CPs followed by an intonation pattern similar to the theme marking intoneme in PM

---

[9] Where the linguistic contact with other Asian migrant communities was lacking for reasons discussed elsewhere.

regulates Sinhala narratives in a THL manner; and a specific focalized verbal form, preceding a finally-detached focalized constituent. PM has only developed a VF particle with no signs of final-detachment in the sample used for this study.

A set of sociological parameters distinguishes PM from other Arabic-based pidgins spoken by migrants based in other Arab countries within the same phenomenon of Asian labour migration to the Middle East. Of these parameters: an ethnic and a linguistic bias (only Sinhala-speaking Sri Lankan workers speak PM in Lebanon), a gender bias (only female Sinhala workers are involved), and an extremely confined context (mainly live-in housemaids are concerned) making contact with other migrant communities, as well as exposure to a larger spectrum of Arabic difficult if not impossible. Therefore, female Sinhala-speaking Sri Lankan live-in housemaids who have spent between 3 and 30 years exclusively in Lebanon are more or less bilingual in both PM (not Arabic) and Sinhala. In this bilingualism, the pragmatic importance of focus and detachments by which Sinhala achieves meaning and hierarchizes it into structures pressures PM speakers into investigating new pragmatic devices in the pidgin.

References

Al Azraqi, Munira. 2010. Pidginization in the Eastern region of Saudi Arabia: Media presentation'. In R. Bassiouney (ed.), *Arabic and the Media. Linguistic Analyses and Applications*. Leiden: Brill. 159–174.

Al-Moaily, Mohamad. 2013. *Language Variation in Gulf Pidgin Arabic*. PhD: Newcastle University.

Al-Moaily, Mohamad. 2008. *A data-based description of Urdu Pidgin Arabic*. MA: Newcastle University.

Al-Salman, Abdul Karim. 2013. *Jordanian Pidgin Arabic*. MA thesis: Yarmuk University, Irbid, Jordan.

Avram, Andrei. 2012. On the functions of FI in the verbal system of Arabic pidgins. *Romano-Arabica* 12: 35–57.

Bakir, Murtadha. J. 2010. "Notes on the verbal system of Gulf Pidgin Arabic". *Journal of Pidgin and Creole Languages* 25 (2): 201–228.

Bizri, Fida. 2014a. Maids' Talk: Linguistic Containment and Mobility of Sri Lankan Housemaids in Lebanon. In Victoria Haskins and Claire Lowrie (eds), Colonization and Domestic Service: Historical and Contemporary Perspectives, 164–192. Routledge International Studies of Women and Place.

Bizri, Fida. 2014b. "Unity and Diversity Across Asian Migrant Arabic Pidgins in the Middle East". In Journal of Pidgin and Creole Languages Vol 29.2, Special Issue Arabic-based Pidgins and Creoles edited by Stefano Manfredi and Mauro Tosco, pages 391–415.

Bizri, Fida. 2013. "Pidgin Madam". *Online Encyclopedia of Arabic Language and Linguistics*. Leiden: Brill.

Bizri, Fida. 2010. *Pidgin Madame: Une grammaire de la servitude*. Paris: Geuthner.

Bizri, Fida. 2009. "Sinhala in contact with Arabic: The birth of a new pidgin in the Middle East". *Annual Review of South Asian Languages and Linguistics 2009*, ed. by Rajendra Singh, 135–149. Berlin and New York: Mouton de Gruyter.

Bizri, Fida. 2005. "Le Pidgin Madam: Un nouveau pidgin arabe". *La Linguistique*, vol. 41 Plurilinguismes, fasc. 2/2005: 54–66.

Bizri, Fida. 2004. *Le Pidgin Arabe des Domestiques Singhalaises au Liban*. PhD thesis, Ecole Pratique des Hautes Etudes : Paris.

Chafe, Wallace. 1988. "Linking intonation units in spoken English". In : Haiman J. & Thompson S.A. (eds) *Clause Combining in Grammar and Discourse*. Amsterdam & Philadelphia: John Benjamins Publishing Company, pp. 1–27.

Culioli, Antoine. 2002. "Je veux ! Réflexions sur la force assertive". In : Botella, C. (ed). *Penser les Limites: Ecrits en l'honneur d'André Green*. Neuchatel: Delachaux et Niestlé: p102–108.

Denison, David. 1985. 'The origins of periphrastic *do*: Ellegård and Visser reconsidered'. *Eaton 1985*: 45–60.

De Vries, Lourens. 2005. "Towards a typology of tail-head linkage in Papuan languages". *Studies in Language* 29/ 2: 363–384.

Gair, James W. 1997. La Focalisation en Singhalais. In: Annie Montaut (ed.) 1997. *Faits de Langues: Les Langues d'Asie du Sud*. Ophrys : Paris, 155–162.

Gair, James W. 1986. Sinhala Focused Sentences: Naturalization of a Calque. In Bh. Krishnamurti, et al. éd.: 147–164. Reprinted in Barabara C. Lust (ed) 1998. *Studies in South-Asian Linguistics: Sinhala and Other South-Asian Languages*. Oxford University Press: New York, Oxford.

Gair, James W. 1983. Non-configurationality, Movement, and Sinhala Focus. Study presented at the Linguistics' Association of Great Britain, Newcastle. Reprinted in Barabara C. Lust (ed) 1998. *Studies in South-Asian Linguistics : Sinhala and Other South-Asian Languages*. Oxford University Press: New York, Oxford.

Gair, James W. 1971. Action Involvement Categories in Colloquial Sinhalese. In M.D. Zamora, J. M. Maher and H. Orenstein (eds). *Themes in Culture, Essays in Honor of Morris E. Opler*: 238–256, Quezon City: Kayamanggi. Reprinted in Barabara C. Lust (ed) 1998. *Studies in South-Asian Linguistics: Sinhala and Other South-Asian Languages*. Oxford University Press: New York, Oxford.

Gair, James W., & Paolillo, John C. 1997. *Sinhala*. Languages of the World/ Materials 34. Lincom Europa : München-New Castle

Geiger, Wilhelm. 1938. *A Grammar of the Sinhalese Language*. The Royal Asiatic Society Ceylon Branch: Colombo

Gunasekara, Abraham Mendis. [1891] 1986. *A Comprehensive Grammar of the Sinhalese Language*. Asian Educational Services : New Delhi.

Haiman, John. 1978. Conditionals are Topics. *Language* 54-3: 564–89.

Haspelmath, M. (ed.). 2008. *Language Typology and Language Universals*. Berlin/Amsterdam: de Gruyter.

Höhle, Tilman N. 1988. Vorwort und Nachwort zu Verum-Fokus. In Sprache und Pragmatik 5, 1–7.

Höhle, Tilman N. 1992. "Uber Verum-Fokus im Deutschen". In: Jacobs, Joachim, ed. (1992): Informationsstruktur und Grammatik, 4:112–142.

Næss, Unn Gyda. 2008. *Gulf Pidgin Arabic': Individual strategies or a structured variety? A study of some features of the linguistic behaviour of Asian migrants in the Gulf countries*. M.A. thesis, University of Oslo.

Smart, Jack R. 1990. "Pidginization in Gulf Arabic: A first report". *Anthropological Linguistics* 32.83–118.

Stein, Dieter. 1990. *The Semantics of Syntactic Change. Aspects of the Evolution of 'do' in English*. Berlin: Mouton de Gruyter Traugott, Elizabeth C. 1972. The History of English Syntax. New York: Holt, Rinehart and Winston, Inc.

Van Valin, Robert. 2007. "Recent development in the RRG theory of clause linkage". *Language and Linguistics* 8.1:71–93.

Versteegh, K. 2010. *Pidgin Verbs: Infinitives or Imperatives* Talk at the Non-European lexifier (and/or non-West African substrate) Pidgin and Creole languages Workshop.

Wiswall, Abdul-Qadir. 2002. Gulf Pidgin: An Expanded Analysis. Unpublished pro-seminar paper of June 3, 2002. Ohio State University.

Zapata-Barrero, R., R. F. Garcia and E. Sánchez-Montijano. 2012. Circular Temporary Labour Migration: Reassessing Established Public Policies. International Journal of Population Research, doi: 10.1155/2012/498158.

Peter Slomanson
14 New Information Structuring Processes and Morphosyntactic Change

1 Introduction

This paper concerns the cross-linguistic transfer of information structuring processes involving focus-driven detachment as a pragmatic motivation for the selective transfer of morphosyntactic features in Sri Lankan Malay, a historically un(der)documented contact language.[1] The structures under investigation are clauses, rather than (for example) arguments of verbs, however their pragmatically-marked reordering with respect to root clauses, and the morphology that has developed to highlight the presence of this reordering, represent a phenomenon that I will treat here as a subtype of detachment, although the relevant structures, focused adjunct clauses, are not subcategorized for by a matrix predicate of whatever categorial status.

Investigations of morphosyntactic change in unwritten vernacular languages are hampered by the absence of attestations that can document linguistic form at earlier stages. Without the assistance of corpora of written texts, linguists engaged in reconstruction of developmental trajectories must depend on plausible models. In the spirit of historical linguistic research generally, the uniformitarian principle is observed. According to that principle, the processes we can observe today exercising a particular effect upon linguistic form are the same processes we take to have applied similarly at another period in time. The understanding of linguistic change in radical contact languages is of special scientific value, because just as incremental change across generations can tell us about the range of effects that acquisition can have on linguistic form, so radical contact

---

[1] The ways in which extreme grammatical change takes place in bilingual speech communities as a result of second language acquisition and bilingualism should be treated as a matter of some importance to linguistic science, particularly from a diachronic perspective. The effects of structurally *similar* languages on each other are obviously scientifically compelling as well, yet the cases in which the typological distance been the languages involved was originally profound prior to convergence of one of the two languages on the grammar of the other are of special interest because it is there that we find changes that are most unlikely to have taken place *without* bilingual language contact. Contact itself is only a metaphor, and we need to refer to actual processes if we want to explain the phenomena.

Peter Slomanson, University of Tampere, Finland

languages can tell us about the more rapid and more extreme effects that by-pass the outer limits of conventional change. The term "conventional", as used here, is intended to characterize the majority of cases, in which social, cultural, and demographic contexts are not conducive to interruptions in the transmission of a relatively stable grammatical system. Although a cohort of child acquirers may initiate significant (for example syntactic) changes due to the reanalysis of input containing an increased percentage of an otherwise marked construction, and this may have implicational effects, children nevertheless do not initiate changes across a grammar that are so profound that the resulting grammar must be characterized as belonging to a different typological class. This is why although most grammars are in some sense "new", it is the grammars that owe their creation to a period of collective adult second language acquisition that we think of as new for the sake of linguistic analysis. This is not because they all have grammatical properties in common (they do not), but because their existence as distinct languages is due to this shared experience, and because the resulting grammars typically differ from the grammars of their respective lexical source languages in ways that cannot be considered the product of incremental change nor of first language acquisition alone.

Since morphosyntactic and syntactic change are difficult to reconstruct in the absence of attestations, as stated above, we are dependent on plausible models. What counts as plausible is complicated by any starting point that is not generally agreed upon. For this area of inquiry, I take that starting point to be the extent to which syntax is borrowable. According to one approach, already expressed in discussions of bilingual behavior by Weinreich in the 1950s, syntax is particularly easy to borrow.[2] This means that a bilingual speaker is likely, not just to engage in code-switching, but to contribute to the diffusion of syntactic organization from one of his/her languages to the other. An extension of this is the idea that the language a bilingual or incipient bilingual is most exposed to will determine the ultimate form of a language that

---

[2] For Weinreich (1953), there is a clear hierarchy of borrowability. We can paraphrase Weinreich's position, as stating that "it is easiest to borrow that which is not attached". In the case of Weinreich, it followed that he viewed syntax, in the sense of linear order, overlooking various clitic types, as being necessarily distinct from morphology, yielding the view that syntax is much easier to borrow than morphology. Phonological words and phrase-level units are not attached and their reordering as a result of contact was taken by Weinreich to be easily accomplished in almost the way that the borrowing of specific lexical items is easily accomplished. In broader terms, I am departing from the view that in principle, anything is necessarily borrowable by bilinguals, and syntax and morphosyntax are far less easily borrowable than lexical items, contra Weinreich. Anything is borrowable, but only under specific conditions, and the most conducive conditions are those embodied in the premises that I just presented.

is less frequently used. I know of no controlled study that systematically investigates these claims longitudinally, and I suspect that such a study would be difficult to design. I will adopt the opposing position, based on what is observable, which is that while transient grammatically superficial reorderings may follow fairly easily from frequency of exposure, rapid profound grammatical restructuring that can be characterized as typological shift does not take place easily, and requires exceptional circumstances. Such circumstances typically involve collective adult second language acquisition of the relevant language, by an adult population speaking a typologically unrelated language, in sufficient proportion to overwhelm and replace the existing linguistic model for L1 learners. Changes in information structuring do not require this step and can therefore be expected to precede it, depending on how salient the new information structuring process is in the new discourse culture.

Why would it be that given the "right" sort of acquisition context, the model grammar is not simply replicated in its entirety? The idea that what is replicated is pragmatically-motivated is a response to this question, together with my caveat about relative pragmatic salience in the discourse culture of the model language. Not all structural facts about the model language ("features" in some accounts) are pragmatically salient. If a morphosyntactic or syntactic process is not motivated by a pragmatic process, it may not become part of the new (i.e. contact) grammar, because it will not be pragmatically-motivated to the same extent. In other words, functional changes may lead to formal change, but the formal changes are less likely in the absence of pragmatic motivation. This follows from the uniformitarian principle. When we observe linguistic behavior in bilingual speech communities, we observe considerable pragmatic accommodation generally, but less typological shift. Where we do observe typological shift, it is never in the absence of pragmatic accommodation, so there is an apparent implicational or feeding relationship between the two processes. As an example of the type of implicational relationship referred to above, I will show how the instantiation of a finiteness contrast in a grammar that did not previously contain one can be motivated in the first place by pragmatic accommodation.

Sri Lankan Malay is a contact language spoken by a historically bilingual population (Malay and Shonam, a Muslim Tamil variety sometimes referred to as Moorish Tomil). Sri Lankan Malay has undergone profound typological change due to convergence on (replication of) the grammar of Shonam,[3] its

---

[3] Slomanson (2011) provides morphosyntactic arguments for treating Shonam as the relevant model language, whereas influence from the morphosyntax of the coterritorial majority language Sinhala is not plausibly treated as equally significant in the development of Sri Lankan

model language, however it is grammatically distinct from Shonam, which happens to have several times the number of speakers, now and historically, and which was historically enormously prestigious as in Muslim communities as the primary vehicle for the dissemination of Islamic knowledge in the region (Hussainmiya 1987, 1990, 2008). In some respects, the grammar of Sri Lankan Malay contains a subset of the grammatical phenomena that we find in Shonam. Shonam, like Tamil varieties generally, is unusually rich in aspectual and modal morphology, much of which has not been replicated in Sri Lankan Malay. In Sri Lankan Malay, predicate focusing in sentences containing a temporally ordered sequence of predicate sequences is a plausible trigger for the development of (non-)finiteness morphology. This functional contrast and its associated morphology are motivated by the failure of the older grammar (varieties of Malay lacking this type of clausal asymmetry) to accommodate two (Sri Lankan) information-structuring processes simultaneously. These include (1) strict temporal ordering of predicates in which the last-occurring event must be the root clause and later (non-primary) events typically appear as adjuncts, and (2) detachment as a strategy for focusing temporally non-primary predicates.

Events in complex sentences typically appear as subclauses in the order in which the events occur in time. In many languages, this linear ordering and context are sufficient to convey event sequence, and focusing a temporally secondary event can be accomplished prosodically. In a smaller number of languages, such as those spoken in Sri Lanka, the temporally non-primary events, those that did not occur first, must also appear as non-finite participial adjuncts. There may also be a tendency to detach such constituents, so that they are realized at the sentence periphery with the goal of focusing them in discourse. In Sri Lankan Malay, nominal constituents can be detached in order to focus them, and verbal predicates representing related events in a temporal sequence are subject to a similar detachment process.

In such an information structuring system, contrastive finiteness marking facilitates the interaction of these two structural patterns, i.e. temporal sequencing and focus. Under focus detachment, a finiteness contrast can preserve the temporal sequence, not necessarily recoverable from context. This becomes necessary when a temporally secondary event is in focus. This constitutes a

---

Malay, although it has influenced the language adstratally in other ways, particularly lexically and phonologically, at subsequent stages in its development. This matter was also extensively debated the following year by Sebastian Nordhoff (2012a, 2012b) and Ian Smith (2012a, 2012b) in the Journal of Language Contact. Historical arguments, including a discussion of bilingual cultural practices and frequent ethnolinguistic intermarriage involving Malay and Shonam speakers, are presented in Slomanson (2013).

discourse-pragmatic motivation for a structural accretion, a case of functional complexification reflected in morphosyntax. The addition of new functional morphology has been treated in recent language contact literature as resulting from generalized feature competition, suggesting random functionally unmotivated processes, however such diachronic models appealing to random restructuring processes are not explanatory, but simply involve restatements of events that took place, whereas it is possible to demonstrate how communicative processes can be expected to motivate the same changes.

2 The case of Sri Lankan Malay

I will show that a case of radical morphosyntactic change can plausibly be attributed, at least in part, to the transfer of information-structuring conventions involving detachment, which I will use as a cover term for movement to the sentence periphery, irrespective of the syntactic status of the constituent's canonical position). The contact language is Sri Lankan Malay and its model language is Shonam. I will adopt two starting points, which remain somewhat controversial in discussions of language contact effects and linguistic change generally. The first starting point is that where linguistic change takes place, it is motivated by something that is not simply random. According to an opposing view, properties of natural languages, particularly those that represent conflicting values for some variable such as head-initial and head-final constituent order, simple and complex syllable onsets, overt morphological case marking or its absence, and so on, are either random or the effects of "ecology" meaning of who in one's vicinity is speaking in which way. According to another view, typological shifts over time are necessarily the cumulative effect of economy, since given the option, every speaker will unconsciously look for the most economical possible way of saying the same thing. This economy imperative itself leads to morphological attrition, in particular, but to other structural changes as well.

The view under which something along the lines of random surface feature selection and ecological adaptation can take place is associated with certain creolists and other contact linguists, including but not limited to Mufwene (Mufwene 1996, 2001). The view that economy with respect to parsing is always ready to overtake other forces in the struggle between near-stasis at one extreme of the spectrum, and radical change at the other is one conclusion that we might potentially draw from the results of psycholinguistic experiments in a number of European languages, undertaken in light of Hawkins (2004) et al. on Early

Immediate Constituents, in which parsing efficiency is ultimately the most important factor in sentence form where different options are available. To the extent that a pragmatically-marked sentence type (for example a detachment construction) is less than optimal for the parser, it cannot be expected to be adopted by a contact grammar. This could be regarded as a challenge to the notion of pragmatic motivation. But Sri Lankan Malay, in its morphology and syntax, consistently manifests complexification at the expense of economy, which suggests that economy does not necessarily play a central role in the type of change that has taken place. The applicability of economy arguments is sensitive to (external) contextual factors, including who is acquiring which language and what the discourse requirements of the more influential language in the bilingual speech community happen to be.

My opposition to the random feature selection view stems from the conviction (naturally an empirical matter), that profound structural change in language, and structural change in language in general, will always be motivated by some identifiable process. We could adopt the assumptions of quantitative (variationist) sociolinguistics and say that conscious and unconscious links between linguistic features and social categories to which their users belong are responsible for variation and change. However while this principle has been shown to apply across dialect continua for closely related varieties, there have been to my knowledge no systematic attempts to demonstrate structural diffusion between grossly typologically divergent unrelated languages, particularly where the features in question are profound structural features such as head direction, overt case marking, the presence of absence of a finiteness contrast, and so on. Sri Lankan Malay, once a highly analytic SVO language, has become an agglutinating SOV language, essentially Dravidian, using native Malay morphemes. Malay morphemes, assuming the form of clitics and of actual inflectional material in the modified grammar, have come to encode grammatical contrasts that were absent from the original language. Predictably these are frequently not exact mappings from the model language, primary Shonam, whose effects on the contact language Sri Lankan Malay are nevertheless apparent. The likelihood of these developments in the absence of a South Asian model language is minimal.

I adopt the position here that discourse-pragmatic factors do constitute a motivation. From my perspective, the corollary is actually that discourse-pragmatic factors will be the motivation for radical change in the absence of evidence to the contrary, particularly in those bilingual situations in which contact with the original grammar is not entirely lost. If Malay speakers retained some contact with conservative varieties, what would motivate their replication of

Shonam morphosyntax using Malay lexical material? If we examine a cross-section of language contact situations, we will find that pragmatic accommodation comes easily in stably bilingual speech communities, and profound systemic change in syntax, for example, takes far longer and requires a set of external conditions that are not always met. Foremost among these conditions is second language acquisition with or without language shift, in which the influence of adult acquirers, whether through demography or sociolinguistic prestige becomes so strong that traditional native speakers begin accommodating to the L2 model, which ultimately leads to the absence or rejection of traditional L1 triggering evidence for children.

3 The apparent anomalousness of a "borrowed" finiteness contrast

From a general language contact perspective, finiteness contrasts (plus/minus finite) have been implicitly viewed as a kind of morphosyntactic noise, part of the grammar of a target or model language, but with little communicative salience. Certainly, it is difficult to find genuine infinitives and participles in pidgins and creoles, in which a finiteness contrast in the model language, English, French, Portuguese and so on, tends to be lost in the contact language.[4] But a finiteness contrast can nevertheless develop in a contact variety of a language such as Malay that lacked such a contrast, given an unambiguous information-structuring function in the discourse culture in which the speakers, now bilinguals, must participate. We should bear in mind that it would be inaccurate to treat contrastive finiteness as a unitary phenomenon in a functional and pragmatic sense. Furthermore, in spite of the relative lack of communicative salience associated with finiteness contrasts generally, as opposed to tense and aspect, for example, it does not make sense to treat finiteness contrasts as necessarily a functionally vacuous morphosyntactic property of grammars. This becomes quite clear when we consider the function that a finiteness contrast has assumed in the grammar of Sri Lankan Malay, a matter to which we will return,

---

4 Under the view that contact languages are not likely to develop or redevelop ostensibly non-salient functional contrasts, except in decreolization, an explicit grammaticalized finiteness contrast is unlikely to develop. However if we look at a cross-section of creoles, we do find infinitive markers in a small number of languages, as in Holm & Patrick (2007). We also find that there is a strong tendency for those to be purposive, which constitutes functional content. One exception is Berbice Dutch (Kouwenberg 2007), in which "when following a modal verb, a *fu*-infinitive is non-purposive, and appears to be equivalent to a zero-infinitive".

to see that cross-linguistic pragmatic accommodation can in principle motivate the development of all manner of functional contrasts, although presumably not contrasts lacking a communicative advantage in discourse.

4 The role of information structure in motivating change

In the language development scenario presented here [of Sri Lankan Malay], in which typologically-discordant grammars were in contact, there was a communicative benefit to replicating a cross-clausal finiteness asymmetry in the morphosyntactically-restructured grammar, or in what would become a restructured grammar. The finiteness contrast functions as an information-structuring device. The information in question is the hierarchical status and temporal ordering of predicates (technically of clauses) in an utterance in which a sequence of related events are listed. The discourse-pragmatic function of the finiteness contrast in this context is to formally distinguish the most recent event from subsequent ones. The most recent event can take place prior to the actual utterance or not, but it must be tense-marked. The relationship between the clauses is encoded by expressing the temporally primary event (the last event to take place) last, as a tense-marked verb, and the subsequent events first, and in the order of their occurrence, as participles (1). This could be achieved through linear ordering alone, however the morphological contrast permits the reordering of event clauses, in order to focus a temporally secondary event clause, now to be overtly marked as non-finite. This enables an override of the inherent clausal focus on the most recent event, marked through the use of tense morphology, the only available reflex of finite status. The finiteness contrast in negation morphology is a consequence of this more general development.

SRI LANKAN MALAY
(1) iskuul na a(bbi)s-pi,   mulbar a(bbi)s-blajar, **Miflal attu=nyanyi su-tulis**.
    school P ASP.NFN-go Tamil   ASP.NFN-learn Miflal IND=song   PST-write
    "Having gone to school, (and then) having learned Tamil, Miflal wrote a song (in it)."

In (1), the clause with the enlarged bold font is the temporally-primary matrix clause that is explicitly tense-marked. The preceding clauses are participial adjunct clauses representing temporally secondary events, marked as non-finite. The aspectual/participial and event prefixes are underlined in the example.

This is a sequence of clauses, each within its own intonation phrase, but clearly falling within a single sentence, as the initial clauses are non-finite adjuncts, and obviously dependent. This type of sentence is not required in an analogous context in English, of course, and the English translation provided sounds rather odd or stilted, but it is nonetheless grammatical, and adequately illustrates what is required in languages other than English that are spoken in Sri Lanka. Note that agreement of any type as an additional reflex of finiteness has never developed in Sri Lankan Malay. As we will see, the pragmatic motivation for the finiteness contrast in affirmative contexts in Sri Lankan Malay carries over to negative contexts, in spite of the fact that tense information is obscured in those contexts, yielding finite negation markers (*tərə*, *tuma*) and a single non-finite negation marker (*jang*).

What sort of alternatives are there for a grammar to select to express the sequence of events in (1)? Possible alternatives include *inter alia* the earlier Malay pattern, requiring a chain of clauses of equal status, with the focusing of a temporally non-primary clause signalled prosodically. However the adoption of the Sri Lankan areal pattern in which right-peripheral focus is strongly preferred over prosodic focus (which also exists) creates communicative contexts in which grammaticalization to yield the finiteness contrast is motivated. It is not motivated by some predictable process of morphological convergence, in which a language necessarily adopts even the most marked features of its model language. Such a process does not necessarily occur in language contact. A discourse culture-specific pragmatic motive is more plausible where discourse conventions first shift without morphosyntactic change. How would speakers of Sri Lankan Malay then otherwise reassign focus to a temporally non-primary clause, given the discourse culture in which they had become participants? The answer to this in (1), repeated here below, in which the interclausal finiteness asymmetry is exemplifed, renders the clause sequence in (2) possible.

SRI LANKAN MALAY
(1) *iskuul na a(bbi)s-pi,   mulbar a(bbi)s-blajar,   Miflal attu=nyanyi su-tulis.*
    school P ASP.NFN-go Tamil   ASP.NFN-learn Miflal IND=song   PST-write
    'Having gone to school, (and then) having learned Tamil, Miflal wrote a song (in it).'

SRI LANKAN MALAY
(2) *iskuul na a(bbi)s-pi,   Miflal attu=nyanyi su-tulis,   mulbar abbis-blajar.*
    school P ASP.NFN-go Miflal IND=song   PST-write Tamil ASP.NFN-learn
    'Having gone to school, Miflal wrote a song, having learned Tamil.'

As we will see in section 7, asymmetrical negation morphology follows from this, since for independent reasons, independent morphological reflexes of finiteness and of its absence are suppressed under negation in the Dravidian sprachbund. If in a contact language, in this case Sri Lankan Malay, the finiteness contrast observed in the model language becomes highly salient as a result of a shift in discourse organization, then it becomes increasingly necessary for non-primary clauses to signal non-finiteness overtly. This requirement that non-finite affirmative clauses be marked as such has been extended to negated clauses. In Sri Lankan Malay, reflexes of finiteness are associated with the pre-verbal position, however due to the Functional Stacking Constraint in that language limiting the number of verbal prefixes to one (Slomanson 2006 et al.), no marker of non-finiteness (infinitival or participial) can co-occur with a marker of negation. This is why a specifically non-finite negation marker *jang* became necessary.

5 Discourse-pragmatic accommodation yields new surface configurations only

My position with respect to the necessity of in the first place discourse-pragmatic triggers, and in the second place second language acquisition, is supported by the argumentation of Ellen Prince with respect to the pragmatics of Yiddish. According to Prince's view, much of what looks like major structural change in a language in a bilingual contact situation is only discourse-pragmatic change, whereas given a suitably cataclysmic context, essentially an undetermined but substantial degree of influence from interlanguage speakers, quantal structural change would have taken place. This matter is discussed in Prince (2001), but Prince (1998) is in some ways more explicit on the topic. Quantal morphosyntactic reorganization to a point where we can actually speak of typological shift does not occur in a narrow time frame given unconducive external conditions. What Prince was describing could be characterized as an implicational relationship between pragmatic change and syntactic and morphosyntactic change. In Prince (1998), the author cites one case that is actually similar in certain respects to the Sri Lankan Malay case discussed here, since it also has to do with the temporal marking of verbs relative to each other in sequences of clauses. In brief, this involves a change from the Germanic system in which temporally primary clauses referring to events preceding the time of utterance are expressed as past or perfect, whereas non-primary events are pluperfect. As a result of contact with Slavic, all events preceding the time of utterance are simply expressed as perfect. The decline of the Germanic system eventually led to a dramatic loss of triggering evidence for the original Germanic pluperfect, and this precipitated changes in the grammar. Note that while this is a grammatical change triggered by pragmatic change itself, triggered by language contact, it involves the loss of an existing construction, rather than the addition of an entirely new morphosyntactic contrast such as finiteness. For such an accretion, dramatic events are likely to involve acquisition context and demography, and the acquisition is likely to involve adult learners. Second language acquisition can lead not just to the more familiar situation involving simplification through deflection, not itself a response to pragmatic factors, but it can also lead to morphological complexification, motivated by pragmatics. When the original grammar is destabilized, interlanguage development permits a degree of restructuring that can include the accretion of new functional contrasts and the grammaticalization of supporting morphology.

These outcomes, in which we do not find the same degree of restructuring in Yiddish as in Sri Lankan Malay, stems from the fact that whereas Yiddish speakers became bilingual speakers of Slavic languages, and adapted a range of Slavic discourse conventions, as constrained by their existing Germanic grammar, acquisition of Yiddish by Slavic speakers was negligible. In the case of Sri Lankan Malay, by contrast with the Yiddish case described by Prince, large numbers of native Shonam speakers acquired Malay, with "large" to be understood as relative to the size of the L1 community.

For an example from the literature on interlanguage that seems to confirm Prince's insight, Odlin (2008) discusses a number of issues with respect to focus and L2 speakers, including inaccurate interlingual mappings between L1 and L2 focus constructions and the tendency to transfer the meanings of focus constructions into an L2. The latter phenomenon is relatively well-known from cases in which the new meaning and pragmatic function are maintained as a substrate feature after the L1 is forgotten by the descendants of the L2-speaking population. The Irish to Hiberno-English case may be the best known, since it-clefts in Hiberno-English are more frequent across constituent types than is the case in other varieties of English. The productivity across constituent types suggests structural change, since the original users of these constructions were L2 speakers. Clefting of arguments is of course ordinary in other varieties of English, and generalizing the ability to cleft does not actually involve any profound structural change.[5] What is more significant is that the focal meanings

---

[5] Although tremendous numbers of native Irish speakers acquired English as a second language, and this gave rise to Hiberno-English varieties, the implication is that although the origin of clefting is to be found in the phrase structure of Irish Gaelic, in which non-verbal constituents cannot detach leftwards due to the high structural position of the verb within its clause, the highly salient information structuring function of generalized clefting was borrowable without any need for the phrase structure position of English verbs to change.

assigned to it-clefts in Hiberno-English are based on the meaning found in their Irish (Irish Gaelic) counterparts: they are effective. Odlin cites the following example, among others: *Is é an dream a cuireadh as na Flaithis iad*, which has been translated, somewhat non-idiomatically, as "They were really the crowd that was put out of heaven" with reference to fairies, but this could just as likely have been "It's them that was put out of heaven", with the cleft functioning as an intensifier. An example from Hiberno-English cited by Odlin is "It's me that was afraid o' him", which has been translated as "I assure you that I was very much afraid of him" and the affective meaning, intensification, is quite clear. In practice, new information status and affective status may interact.

6 The function of the finiteness/non-finiteness contrast in Sri Lankan Malay

As we have seen, it is plausible that an initial pragmatic motivation for the development of a finiteness/non-finiteness contrast in Sri Lankan Malay is the fact that the discourse culture associated with the Sri Lankan *sprachbund*, as interpreted by speakers of Sri Lankan Malay, associates the right periphery of a sentence with constituent focus, not just of nominal constituents, but of clauses.

Returning to the example in (1), repeated again below for convenience, note that the first two events are not literally in a temporal sequence, although we should understand that going to school preceded Miflal's learning Tamil.

SRI LANKAN MALAY
(1) iskuul na a(bbi)s-pi,   mulbar a(bbi)s-blajar, Miflal attu=nyanyi su-tulis.
    school P ASP.NFN-go Tamil   ASP.NFN-learn Miflal IND=song PST-write
    'Having gone to school, (and then) having learned Tamil, Miflal wrote a song (in it).'

His going to school was not completed prior to his learning Tamil. The sequence matters with respect to the onset of each activity, but not its completion. It is the non-primary temporal status of the non-finite adjunct clauses that is most salient to speaker and listener, more so than their sequence with respect to each other. In the varieties of Malay originally brought to Sri Lanka, all the verbs in this sequence are likely to have been unmarked for aspectual status, and tense markers, whether free-standing or phonologically-dependent, were unavailable. This means that an L1 Malay speaker in Sri Lanka in the process of accommodating Sri Lankan discourse conventions would be forced to depend on prosody, a disfavored strategy, and on the linear ordering of clauses, which would prevent their reordering for focus.

The Sri Lankan languages, including Sri Lankan Malay, are left-branching SOV languages, and the right periphery is strongly associated with focus. Focus is a highly communicatively salient function in the sprachbund. Non-phonological focus marking, both syntactic and morphological, is preferred over focus marked with prosody. The clause containing the most recent event normally appears in this position as the (tensed) matrix clause. Clauses not representing the most recent event must be explicitly marked as non-finite, so that the status of the most recent event, which will always be tense-marked, will retain its status when a temporally non-primary event is focused through dislocation to the right-peripheral focus position. Note that this is not simply a variant order, but is perceived as a pragmatically-marked order. The cross-linguistic parallel can be seen from the following Shonam examples, that correspond with the Sri Lankan Malay examples in (1) and (2):

(3) iskul-ukku   pee-thə, tamil paadi-cci, Miflal paath-ondu elludi-naan.
    school-ALL go-PRT Tamil learn-PRT Miflal song-DET   write-PST
    'Having gone to school, (and then) having learned Tamil, Miflal wrote a song (in it).'

(4) ıskul-ukku   peethə, Miflul paath-ondu elludi naan, tamul paadi-cci.
    school-ALL go-PRT Miflal song-DET   write-PST   Tamil learn-PRT
    'Having gone to school, Miflal wrote a song, **having learned Tamil**.'

7 Expression of the finiteness contrast under negation

In Sri Lankan Malay, the development of an analogous clausal asymmetry strengthens the marking of temporal hierarchy, particularly in sentences in which a temporally non-primary clause is in focus. Negation elements marking finite predicates in Sri Lankan Malay are variants of the Malay form *tara* (5), or of the form *tuma* (6). *Tuma*, in etymological terms, is a contraction of *tara* (negation) and *mau* (volition). Although their phonological shape signals that they are finite, and tense, in the absence of agreement, is the only morphological exponent of finiteness, these negation elements are essentially unspecified for tense, although *tuma* is interpreted by some speakers as irrealis, and by others as habitual non-past, in the sense of "I never (will) do this". There is no explicit past-present-future contrast under negation, as there is in affirmative contexts. *Tara* and *tuma* only negate verbs that, in affirmative contexts, can be tense-marked. Negation elements marking non-finite verbs in Sri Lankan Malay, whether these are participial or infinitival, are variants of the Malay form *jang* (from *jangan*) (19). This is historically the negative imperative marker in Malay, a function that it also retains in modern Sri Lankan Malay. *Jang* can only precede verbs that cannot be tense-marked in affirmative contexts, including participles, infinitives, and imperatives.

SRI LANKAN MALAY
(5) *Miflal nasi tara-makan.*
    Miflal rice NEG.FIN-eat
    'Miflal did not eat rice.'

SRI LANKAN MALAY
(6) *Miflal nasi tuma-makan.*
    Miflal rice NEG.FIN-eat
    'Miflal does/will not eat rice.'

SRI LANKAN MALAY
(7) *Nasi jang-makan na, Miflal si-hendat.*
    rice NEG.NFN-eat P Miflal PST-tired
    'Not having eaten rice, Miflal became tired.'

The contrast is motivated by the fact that Sri Lankan Malay, like Shonam and other Tamil varieties, suppresses tense morphology and other markers of finiteness status under negation. This may be regarded as a constraint that must be circumvented in some way, if the relevant information structure contrast, salient as we have seen in the discourse culture, is to be maintained in negation contexts. It is necessary for one's interlocutor to know which clause is finite and which ones are not, regardless of whether these are affirmative or negative clauses.

Sri Lankan Malay, in order to accommodate the discourse conventions of Shonam, also affixes non-finite negation morphology to any negated lexical verb, albeit pre-verbally, rather than post-verbally, using the element *jang*, diachronically a regrammaticalized Malay imperative marker (Slomanson 2006, 2009). Sri Lankan Malay has creatively extended the functional scope of *jang* to encompass all non-finite negation contexts, including participles, in adjunct clauses and infinitival complement clauses. This approximates the Dravidian model.

We can see that replication of non-finite negation is not a simple process of calquing from Shonam, since Sri Lankan Malay did not select the literal equivalent of 'without'. It did not even select its equivalent in Sri Lankan Malay, the complex postposition *tra na(ng)*, which is in fact also a creative replication, loosely modelled on Shonam. *Tra na(ng)* was reserved for nominal constituents that are not clausal, as seen in the following examples. In (8), 'without rice' is expressed with the postposition *tra-na*, whereas in (9), an infinitival clause, *nasi makan tra-na* would be ungrammatical. The function of *jang* in examples (9) through (11) and in example (13) is to express negation and the absence of finiteness. The function of *tara* in (10), (11), and (13) is to express negation and finiteness. Based on the Malay lexical source varieties, this is likely to have been the original negation morpheme in all but imperative contexts. As morphological tense prefixation developed, yielding forms such as *si-pi*, (8) and (9) with past tense reference, *a(rə)-pi* with present tense reference, and *a(n)ti-pi* with future tense reference, these contrasts could not be expressed under negation. This is a Dravidian constraint not reflected in the grammar of Sinhala.

NOMINAL CONTEXT (SRI LANKAN MALAY)
(8) *Miflal Kirinde na si-pi,* [*nasi tra-na.*]
Miflal Kirinda P TNS-go rice NEG-DAT
'Miflal went to Kirinda without rice.'

CLAUSAL CONTEXT (SRI LANKAN MALAY)
(9) *Miflal Kirinde na si-pi,* [*nasi jang-makan na.*]
Miflal Kirinda P TNS-go rice NEG.NFN-eat P
'Miflal went to Kirinda, not having eaten rice.'

PARTICIPIAL CLAUSE (SRI LANKAN MALAY)
(10) *jang-tidur, Miflal nasi tara-makang.*
NEG.NFN-sleep Miflal rice NEG.FIN-eat
'Not having slept, Miflal did not eat rice.'

INFINITIVAL CLAUSE (SRI LANKAN MALAY)
(11) *jang-tidur na, Miflal nasi tara-makang.*
NEG.NFN-sleep P Miflal rice NEG.FIN-eat
'To not sleep, Miflal did not eat rice.'

IMPERATIVE CLAUSE (SRI LANKAN MALAY)
(12) *Nasi jang-makang!*
rice NEG.NFN-eat
'Don't eat rice!'

SRI LANKAN MALAY

(13) *iskuul na ja<u>ng</u>-pi na, mulbar <u>jang</u>-blajar na,*
school P NEG.NFN-go P Tamil NEG.NFN-study P

Miflal attu=nyanyi <u>tara</u>-tulis.
Miflal IND=song NEG.FIN-write
'Not having gone to school, (and then) not having studied Tamil, Miflal did not write a song in it.'

Note that (14) is the negated version of (1), repeated again below.

SRI LANKAN MALAY

(1) *iskuul na a(<u>bbi</u>)s-pi, mulbar a(<u>bbi</u>)s-blajar, Miflal attu=nyanyi <u>su</u>-tulis.*
school P NEG.NFN-go Tamil NEG.NFN-learn Miflal IND=song PST-write
'Having gone to school, (and then) having learned Tamil, Miflal wrote a song (in it).'

SRI LANKAN MALAY

(14) *iskul na ja<u>ng</u>-pi na, mulbar <u>jang</u>-blajar na,*
school P NEG.NFN-go P Tamil NEG.NFN-study P

Miflal atu=nyanyi <u>tara</u>-tulis.
Miflal IND=song NEG.FIN-write
'Not having gone to school, (and then) not having studied Tamil, Miflal did not write a song in it.'

The Sri Lankan Malay negation contrast is partly sprachbund-discordant (Slomanson 2010), since the function and distribution of *jang* does not map straightforwardly from Shonam negation morphology. It is reasonable to treat this as a generalization of a morphosyntactic feature of Shonam however, that extends to all non-finite verbal contexts, infinitives, participles, and imperatives, though in Shonam, imperatives are not marked in the same way as other non-finite verb forms.

8 Infinitival contexts

The development of an infinitive, of the form *mə*-V, from the phonological weakening and (re)grammaticalization of the volitive/irrealis element *mau/mo*, is likely to have appeared subsequent to the instantiation of non-finite participial adjuncts, of the type we have seen in (1). While the finiteness contrast arose as a way to displace and focus temporally non-primary clauses, the development of infinitival morphology and its corresponding negation with *jang* is a response to the development of contrastive tense morphology. This enabled tensed verbs in Sri Lankan Malay to take bare VP complements (i.e. INF-V TNS-try, meaning "try to V"), in contexts (15) in which neither a second tense-marked verb nor a participle could appear in the Shonam model grammar.

INFINITIVAL BARE VP COMPLEMENT (SRI LANKAN MALAY)
(15) *Musba waghanam-yang mə-dingar na si-liyat.*
     Musba vehicle-ACC   INF-get   P TNS-see
     'Musba tried to hear the vehicle.'

NEGATED INFINITIVAL BARE VP COMPLEMENT (SRI LANKAN MALAY)
(16) *Musba waghanam-yang jang-dingar   na si-liyat.*
     Musba vehicle-ACC   NEG.NFN-get P TNS-see
     'Musba tried not to hear the vehicle.'

* * *

Schematic restatement of the proposed diachrony of grammaticalized finiteness in SLM

Diachronic sequence:

stacking criterion ⟶ tense-finiteness / right-peripheral focus

In stages:

stage 1
The discourse culture imposes the rigid temporal stacking structure, however tense contrasts need not be morphologized, since clause ordering provides the relevant hierarchy, and this can be highlighted to some extent by prosodic means.

stage 2
The discourse culture expresses focus by displacement to the right, while the focused constituent may become the topic of a subsequent sentence. The focusing of a non-matrix clause can only take place in accordance with stage 1, if finiteness is morphologized. This is because the non-matrix status of the focused constituent must be marked, in order for the chronological order to be recoverable. This motivates finiteness/non-finiteness marking of verbs.

stage 3 (condition)
The organization of tense in the model language imposes a constraint blocking the overt expression of tense and of non-finiteness status in negated contexts. (Only negation is expressed.)

stage 4 (solution)
The conflict is resolved by Sri Lankan Malay, the replica language, with negation markers, which are contrastive with respect to finiteness, and which convey a minimal tense contrast (past/non-past, as opposed to past/present/future).

9 Summary

A series of structural changes was triggered by focus requirements, from stage 2 onwards. If we view stage 1 as a kind of focus requirement, with tense as a predicate focusing device in the sprachbund, and the right periphery as a syntactic device that permits secondary focus in pragmatically-appropriate contexts, then all of the stages can be said to follow from focus requirements. Stages 2 through 4 do not necessarily occur in sequence, but are implicational. (If focus is instantiated, then the other changes are motivated and triggered, given an external context that supports this degree of restructuring.)

We have seen that Sri Lankan Malay features a discourse configuration, the temporal stacking of a sequence of clauses, could serve as a catalyst for morphosyntactic changes, in the first place the introduction of contrastive finiteness morphology. The cross-clausal finiteness contrast in negation marking was replicated in turn in order to circumvent the obscuring of this contrast under negation. This replication was accomplished without borrowing or calquing the analogous Shonam non-finite negation morpheme, the abessive suffix *aamee*. Instead, the functional scope of a candidate in Malay, a negative imperative marker, was expanded, in order to reproduce the function of the Shonam construction. The element *jang* constitutes a reflex in negation contexts of the finiteness contrast in Sri Lankan Malay that has high communicative salience in the discourse culture in which Sri Lankan Malays have participated since their ancestors were brought to Sri Lanka by the Dutch. The contact grammar function of *jang* can therefore be attributed to the need to continue to mark the temporal status of a late-occurring event as secondary, even after it is focused through dislocation to the right (focal) periphery of the sentence.

10 Conclusion

Logically, related non-simultaneous events have a very strong cross-linguistic tendency to be recounted in their temporal sequence, in order for the speaker to effectively communicate the actual sequence of events. In southern South Asian languages, this robust cross-linguistic tendency is accompanied not just by rigid temporal sequencing in the unmarked case, but by morphological and syntactic contrasts between predicates that highlight the contrast between predicates in complex sentences of this type. The form that this takes is a sequence of adjunct clauses containing a participial predicate, and at the right edge of the sentence, a matrix clause in which the predicate is tense-marked and finite. This pattern is highly salient in narratives and is used very frequently. It is therefore not surprising that Malay speakers adhered to this convention in Sri Lanka, likely marking the asymmetry between secondary clauses and the matrix clause by prosodic means.

In the "old" Malay discourse culture, non-matrix clauses were (are) little different from matrix clauses, and a sequence can be reordered using prosody, adverbs, and other indicators of reordering. In the "new" discourse culture in Sri Lanka, any reordering is reflected by participial morphology and the adjunct status of temporally non-finite clauses. That discourse culture shift is a plausible precursor to the association of focus with the right sentence periphery, as it is associated in Sri Lanka. The pragmatic need to focus temporally non-primary clauses, specifically by detaching them through dislocation to the right periphery of the sentence, a region to which nominal constituents can also be dislocated, led to the development of tense morphology and morphological and syntactic markers of non-finiteness in L2-speakers and L2-influenced speakers. Predicate-focusing is a plausible trigger for the development of a grammaticalized finiteness contrast, with non-finite verbal and adjectival predicates supporting the focal status of the tense-marked predicate.

Abbreviations

1S	first person singular	IND	indefinite
3S	third person singular	INF	infinitival
ABE	abessive	NEG	negative
ACC	accusative	NFN	non-finite
ADE	adessive	NMX	non-matrix
ASP	aspect	P	preposition/postposition
AUX	auxiliary	PLU	plural
CMP	complementizer	POS	possessive
COP	copula	PRD	predicate
DAT	dative	PRG	progressive
DET	determiner	PRT	participle
EXS	existential	PST	past tense
FIN	finite	PTV	partitive
GEN	genitive	TNS	tense
ILL	illative		

References

Bakker, Peter. 2000. Rapid language change: Creolization, intertwining, convergence. In C. Renfrew, A. McMahon and L. Trask (Eds.), *Time depth in historical linguistics* (pp. 585–620). Cambridge: McDonald Institute for Archeological Research.

Hawkins, John A. 2004. *Efficiency and Complexity in Grammars*. Oxford: Oxford University Press.

Holm, John & Peter L. Patrick. 2007. *Comparative Creole Syntax*. Plymouth: Battlebridge Publications.

Hussainmiya, B.A. 1987. Lost Cousins: The Malays of Sri Lanka. In *Dunia Melayu Occasional Paper* 2. Bangi: Universiti Kebangsaan Malaysia. Institut Bahasa, Kesusasteraan dan Kebudayaan Melayu.

Hussainmiya, B.A. 1990, 2008. *Orang Rejimen: The Malays of the Ceylon Rifle Regiment*. Bangi: Universiti Kebangsaan Malaysia. Institut Bahasa, Kesusasteraan dan Kebudayaan Melayu.

Hussainmiya, B.A. & Peter Slomanson. Cultural and Linguistic Fusion: the case of south and southeast Asian communities in Sri Lanka. (in preparation)

Kouwenberg, Silvia. 2007. Berbice Dutch (Creole Dutch). In Holm & Patrick.

Mufwene, Salikoko S. 1996. The founder principle in creole genesis. In *Diachronica* 13 (115–168).

Mufwene, Salikoko S. 2001. *The Ecology of Language Evolution*. New York: Cambridge University Press.

Nordhoff, Sebastian. 2012a. Establishing and Dating Sinhala Influence in Sri Lanka Malay. In Robert Nicolaï (ed.) *Journal of Language Contact*, 5:1. (pp. 23–57)

Nordhoff, Sebastian. 2012b. Commentary on Smith's papers. In Robert Nicolaï (ed.) *Journal of Language Contact*, 5:1. (pp. 23–57)

Prince, Ellen F. 1998. The Borrowing of Meaning as a Cause of Internal Syntactic Change. In *Historical Linguistics 1997*. Current issues in linguistic theory. Amsterdam: John Benjamins (339–362).

Prince, Ellen F. 2001. Yiddish as a contact language. In *Creolization and contact*. (N. Smith and T. Veenstra, eds.) Amsterdam: John Benjamins Publishers.

Slomanson, Peter. 2006. Sri Lankan Malay Grammars: Lankan or Malay? In *Structure and Variation in Contact Languages*. (A. Deumert & S. Durrleman, eds.) Amsterdam: John Benjamins Publishers.

Slomanson, Peter. 2007. The perfect construction and complexity drift in Sri Lankan Malay. *Lingua* 118(10). (P. Cole and G. Hermon, eds.)

Slomanson, Peter. 2009. Morphological Finiteness as Increased Complexity in Negation Systems. In *Complex Processes in New Languages*. (E. Aboh and N. Smith, eds). Amsterdam: John Benjamins Publishers.

Slomanson, Peter. 2011. Dravidian Features in the Sri Lankan Malay Verb. In *Creoles, their Substrates, and Language Typology* (C. Lefebvre, ed). Amsterdam: John Benjamins Publishers.

Slomanson, Peter. 2013. Known, Inferable, and Discoverable in Sri Lankan Malay Research. In Sebastian Nordhoff (ed.) *The Genesis of Sri Lanka Malay*. Leiden: Brill. (pp. 85–120)

Smith, Ian R. 2012a. Adstrate Influence in Sri Lanka Malay: Definiteness, Animacy and Number in Accusative Case Marking. In Robert Nicolaï (ed.) *Journal of Language Contact*, 5:1. (pp. 5–22)

Smith, Ian R. 2012b. Comments on Nordhoff's "Establishing and Dating Sinhala Influence in Sri Lanka Malay. In Robert Nicolaï (ed.) *Journal of Language Contact*, 5:1. (pp. 58–72)

Smith, Ian, Scott Paauw, & B.A. Hussainmiya. 2004. Sri Lanka Malay: The state of the art. *Yearbook of South Asian Languages 2004* (R. Singh, ed.). Berlin/New York: Mouton de Gruyter.

Smith, Ian. & Scott Paauw. 2006. Sri Lanka Malay: Creole or Convert? In *Structure and Variation in Contact Languages*. (A. Deumert and S. Durrleman, eds.) Amsterdam: John Benjamins Publishers.

Weinreich, Uriel. 1963. *Languages in Contact: Findings and Problems*. reprint. The Hague: Mouton.

Name index

Abbott, Barbara 44, 98
Abdulaeva, Indira 255
Abdulaev, Arsen K. 253
Abdullaev, Isa K. 253
Abney, Steven Paul 35
Abraham, Werner 280
Aikhenvald, Alexandra 112
Al-Azraqi, Munira 286
Albizu, Pablo 124, 140, 145
Alho, Irja 31
Al-Moaily, Mohamad 286
Al-Salman, Abdul Karim 286
Altube, Severo 122, 145
Amon, Marri 213
Anderson, Gisle 187
Apothéloz, Denis 10, 150
Ariel, Mira 33
Arregi, Karlos 128, 145
Ashby, William 150
Atlas, Jay D. 41
Avram, Andrei 286
Axelsson, Karin 169, 170
Azkue, Resurreción María 122, 145

Bakir, Murtadha 286
Bassene, Mamadou 49
Beaumont, Ronald C. 46
Benincà, Paola 114, 115
Bentley, Delia 2, 79, 80, 95, 101, 105, 111, 113, 117
Benveniste, Emile 8
Berruto, Gaetano 100, 106
Biber, Douglas 19
Birner, Betty 98
Bizri, Fida 3, 285, 286, 290, 293, 296
Boeckx, Cedric 147, 198
Bolinger, Dwight D. 46
Bonnard, Henri 10
Bonnot, Christine 267, 281
Börjars, Kersti 217, 218
Bril, Isabelle 266
Brody, Michael 132, 145
Bross, Fabian 280
Brown, Gillian 63

Büring, Daniel 130, 177, 248, 258
Burykin, Aleksej A. 171

Campbell, Lyle 167, 168, 182
Chafe, Wallace 33, 116, 197, 267, 268, 287
Chao, Wynne 33
Chao, Yuen Ren 191
Cheng, Lisa Lai-Shen 193
Chomsky, Noam 33, 130, 208
Ciconte, Francesco Maria 2, 95, 97, 106, 117
Cinque, Guglielmo 198
Clancy, Patricia M. 57, 67
Cole, Peter 183
Combettes, Bernard 10
Conrad, Susan 19
Corbett, Greville 115
Cote, Sharon 61, 62
Couper-Kuhlen, Elizabeth 150
Croft, William 183
Cruschina, Silvio 2, 95, 96, 98, 106, 111, 112, 114, 117, 145
Culicover, Peter 170
Culioli, Antoine 265, 266, 296

Daneš, Frantisek 10
Dehé, Nicole 175
Denison, David 295
De Rijk, Rudolf 122, 125
De Vries, Lourens 289
Diessel, Holger 214, 217, 229
Diewald, Gabriele 279, 280
Dik, Simon C. 59
Dixon, R.M.W. 81, 83
Donnellan, Keith 48
Downing, Pamela 57, 67
Duranti, Alessandro 150
Dvivedi, Veenita 269

É. Kiss, Katalin 122, 124, 146, 147
Elordieta, Arantzazu 122, 123, 125, 129, 130, 132, 133, 135, 137, 140, 142, 143, 145, 146
Elordieta, Gorka 122, 123, 125, 129, 130, 132, 133, 135, 137, 140, 142, 143, 145, 146

Engdahl, Elisabet 213, 228
Enkvist, Nils-Erik 11, 19, 21
Epstein, Richard 214, 217
Erelt, Mati 228
Erteschik-Shir, Nomi 1, 33, 55, 58, 59, 130, 145, 197, 198, 200
Etxepare, Ricardo 2, 121, 123, 125, 128, 135, 140, 144–146
Everett, Caleb 77, 81, 85–91
Everett, Daniel 77, 81, 85–91

Fernandez-Vest, M.M.Jocelyne 1, 7, 9–15, 17–22, 25, 26, 150, 155, 157, 191, 268
Finegan, Edward 19
Fischer, Kerstin 280
Forker, Diana 3, 122, 239, 253, 254
Francez, Itamar 97, 103
François, Jacques 28, 267
Frascarelli, Mara 114
Fretheim, Thorstein 33
Friedman, Victor 251
Fry, John 59
Fujiwara, Miho 63, 64

Gair, James W. 296, 297, 300
Ganenkov, Dmitry 243–245, 249
Gast, Volker 249
Geiger, Wilhelm 299
Geluykens, Ronald 150
Ghomeshi, Jila 48
Gillon, Carrie 46
Givón, Talmy 60
Gordon, Bryan 49
Görgülü, Emrah 46–48
Greenberg, Joseph H. 217
Grice, H. Paul 37–40
Grohmann, Kleanthes 147
Grosz, Barbara J. 55, 56, 60
Grosz, Patrick 178, 180
Gunasekara, Abraham Mendis 297, 299
Gundel, Jeanette K. 2, 33, 36, 38, 40–42, 44, 46, 47, 49, 50, 211, 214, 267

Haddican, William 125, 135, 136, 140, 141, 146
Hagège, Claude 9, 10
Haiman, John 266, 298
Hakulinen, Auli 25, 31
Halliday, M.A.K. 13
Harris, Alice 167, 168, 182, 185
Haspelmath, Martin 122, 183, 240, 242, 266, 298
Hawkins, John A. 40, 216–218, 220, 230, 233, 309
Hayashi, Makoto 214
Hazout, Ilan 97
Hedberg, Nancy 2, 33, 38, 41, 46–48, 211, 214
Heine, Berndt 77, 167
Heinonen, Tarja-Ritta 31
Helasvuo, Marja-Liisa 149, 152
Herburger, Elena 129, 146
Hergé (Georges Prosper Rémi) 11
Hiietam, Katrin 217, 218
Himmelmann, Nikolaus P. 214, 217, 228
Hinds, John 57
Hinds, Wako 57
Hoffmann, Sebastian 185
Höhle, Tilman N. 294
Holland, Garry B. 29, 145, 146
Holm, John 311
Horlacher, Anne-Sylvie 150, 157, 164
Horn, Laurence R. 38, 39, 41, 42, 50
Hualde, José Ignacio 142, 145–147
Huang, C.T. James 191, 210
Hudson, Richard 175, 185
Humnick, Linda 49
Hussainmiya, Bachamiya Abdul 308

Iida, Masayo 61, 62
Irurtzun, Aritz 121, 135, 143, 145, 146
Iwasaki, Shoichi 57

Jackendoff, Ray 33, 129
Johansson, Stig 19
Joshi, Aravind K. 55, 56, 60

Kalinina, Elena 239, 251
Kalvik, Mari-Liis 213
Karlsson, Fred 25
Kazenin, Konstantin 239
Keenan, Edward 122, 146, 183

Kehler, Andrew 41–45
Kellogg, Rev. S. H. 263
Kerbrat-Orecchioni, Catherine 8
Kern, Barbara 81, 85–87
Khalfaoui, Amel 49
Kibrik, Aleksandr E. 242, 244, 249, 250, 252, 254, 255
König, Ekkehard 249, 256
Koivisto, Vesa 31
Korhonen, Ritta 31
Kouwenberg, Silvia 311
Kresić, Marijana 279, 280
Krifka, Manfred 1, 129, 146, 239
Krug, Manfred 185

Lacher-Dutour, Anne 267
La Fauci, Nunzio 97
Lahiri, Aditi 268
Laka, Itziar 121, 124, 125, 133, 134, 137, 146
Lakshmi, Bai B. 263, 277, 278
Lambrecht, Knud 1, 9, 33, 79, 97–99, 108, 115, 116, 150, 153, 191, 200, 210, 212, 214, 219, 220, 231, 240
Langendoen, Terence 191, 210
LaPolla, Randy J. 55, 56, 78, 80, 96
Laury, Ritva 3, 25, 27, 149, 217
Leech, Geoffrey 19
Lee, Eunhee 73
Leone, Alfonso 111
Leonetti, Manuel 98
Levinson, Stephen C. 40, 41
Li, Charles N. 146, 191, 210
Lindström, Liina 213
Lumsden, Michael 98
Lü, Shuxiang 194, 204
Lyons, Christopher 214, 220

Maiden, Martin 106
Mal'čukov, Andrej L. 169
Mameni, Morgan 46, 47
Manzini, Maria Rita 114
Marten, Lutz 108
Matić, Dejan 3, 13, 167, 168, 188, 239
Matthewson, Lisa 46
Maynard, Senko K. 57
McGregor, Ronald S. 269, 272, 278

McNally, Louise 98
Mihkla, Meelis 213
Miller, Jim 9, 19
Milsark, Gary 98
Mohanan, K. P. 267, 269
Mohanan Tara 267, 269
Montaut, Annie 3, 263, 265, 266, 278
Moro, Andrea 98
Mufwene, Salikoko S. 309
Mulkern, Ann E. 36, 41
Müller, Gabriele M. 150, 157, 164
Musan, Renate 146, 239
Mutalov, Rasul O. 241, 245

Næss, Unn Gyda 286
Napoli, Donna Jo 98
Nespor, Marina 139, 141, 147
Neveu, Franck 10, 149, 150
Newmeyer, Frederick J. 11
Nichols, Johanna 251, 253, 258
Nordhoff, Sebastian 308
Novikova, Klavdija A. 169

Ochs, Elinor 150
Ohala, Manjari 268
Ortiz de Urbina, Jon 121, 126, 128, 129, 131–133, 139, 144–147
Öztürk, Balkız 47

Pajusalu, Renate 213–217
Pan, Victor Junnan 3, 191, 193, 194, 196, 197, 207, 210
Paolillo, John C. 297, 300
Paoli, Sandra 114
Paris, Marie-Claude 7, 191, 193, 210
Parry, Mair 97
Patil, Umesh 268
Patrick, Peter L. 311
Paul, Hermann 33
Paul, Waltraud 191, 193
Peirce, Charles Sanders 10
Pekarek Doehler, Simona 150, 153, 163, 164
Peterson, David A. 251, 253, 258
Pinto, Manuela 97
Polinsky, Maria 250, 252, 258
Portolan, Daniele 130, 131, 147

Postal, Paul 35
Potsdam, Eric 250, 252, 258
Potts, Christopher 214
Prince, Ellen F. 33, 191, 210, 214, 314, 315

Rando, Emily 98
Rebuschi, Georges 146, 147, 266
Reinbold, Julia 77, 81–84
Reinhart, Tanya 123, 147, 191, 208–210
Remberger, Eva 98
Repp, Sophie 252
Rizzi, Luigi 9, 99, 114, 131, 132, 147, 196, 210
Roberts, Craige 33
Rohlfs, Gerard 106
Ross, John R. 128, 147, 192, 210

Saccon, Graziella 116
Sadrai, Mahmoud 47
Sahkai, Heete 211, 213–215, 217–220, 223
Sailor, Craig 170, 171
Salveste, Nele 213
Sánchez-Montijano, E. 296
Savoia, Leonardo 114
Schulze, Wolfgang 250
Schwartz, Anne 1
Schwarz, Florian 214
Selkirk, Elizabeth 139, 147
Selting, Margret 150
Serdobolskaya, Natalia 247
Shapiro, Michael 263, 272, 278
Shimojo, Mitsuaki 55, 57, 73
Shyu, Shu-ing 191, 210
Sidner, Candace L. 60
Siemund, Peter 256
Slomanson, Peter 305, 307, 308, 314, 318, 320
Smart, Jack R. 286
Smith, Ian 308
Sorjonen, Marja-Leena 157
Sornicola, Rosanna 111
Sperber, Dan 36, 111
Stein, Dieter 295
Storto, Luciana 91
Strawson, Peter 33
Sudhoff, Stefan 252
Sumbatova, Nina R. 239, 241, 245, 251
Sweetser, Eve 103

Tael, Kaja 213
Talibov, Bukar B. 246
Tang, C.-C. Jane 145, 196, 210
Tanimura, Midori 57, 62
Tao, Hongyin 152
Teng, Shou-Hsin 193, 210
Testelec, Jakov G. 242, 243, 246, 255
Thompson, Sandra A. 191, 210
Toldova, Svetlana Ju. 255
Tortora, Christina 97
Tottie, Gunnel 185
Tsao, Feng-fu 191, 193, 210
Turner, Ingrid 77, 85, 86

Uriagereka, Juan 121, 146, 147
Uribe-Etxebarria, Myriam 125, 140, 146
Uslar, Petr K. 243, 244

Vallduví, Enric 33, 213, 228, 239
van der Auwera, Johan 249
van der Wal, Jenneke 248
van Dijk, Teun 66
Van Valin, Robert D., Jr. 1, 2, 55, 56, 77, 78, 80, 96, 97, 106, 108, 114, 167, 191, 213, 289
Vilkuna, Maria 31, 153
Vogel, Irene 139, 141, 147
Von Heusinger, Klaus 48
von Prince, Kilu 191, 210

Walker, Marilyn 61, 62
Ward, Gregory 41–45, 98
Wedgwood, Daniel 13, 168, 188, 239
Weinert, Regina 9
Weinreich, Uriel 306
Weinstein, Scott 55, 56, 61
Weydt, Harald 279, 280
Whitman, John 210
Wiese, Heike 212
Williams, Edwin 97
Wilson, Deidre 36, 111
Wilson, Deirdre 36, 111
Winterstein, Grégoire 249
Wiswall, Abdul-Qadir 286
Wlodarczik, André, 267
Wlodarczik, Hélène 267
Wu, Jian-Xin 196, 197, 210

Xajdakov, Said M. 239
Xu, Lie-Jiong 191, 210

Yamura-Takei, Mitsuko 63, 64
Yoon, Kyung-eun 214
Yoshida, Etsuko 57, 62, 63
Yule, George 63

Zacharski, Ron 2, 33, 38, 41, 214
Zamparelli, Roberto 97, 98
Zapata-Barrero, R. 296
Zeevat, Henk 249
Zhang, Ning 194, 210
Zubizarreta, Maria Luisa 129, 147
Zucchi, Alessandro 98

Language index

Agul 244
Akhvakh 255
Arabic (Lebanese, Levantine) 3, 49, 285–287, 290, 292–295, 300, 301
Archi 242, 243, 245, 250, 251, 253
Asian Migrant Pidgin Arabic (AMAP) 286, 287, 296, 300
Avar 239, 242, 251, 254, 256

Bagvalal 242, 244, 249, 253, 255, 256
Banawá 77, 80–84, 88, 91, 92
Basque 2, 121, 122, 124–126, 128–130, 132, 134, 135, 137–147
Bengali 268, 286
Bezhta 251, 254–256
Budukh 246

Chinese 2, 3, 46, 47, 49, 77, 108, 191, 193, 195–198, 200, 202, 206–210

Dargwa (Icari, Khuduts, Shiri, Qunqi) 241, 243, 245–247, 249, 252
Dravidian languages 297

Eegimaa 49
English 9, 14, 19, 35, 44, 46, 47, 49, 50, 63, 78–80, 83, 84, 88, 97, 101, 130, 131, 133, 150, 153, 164, 170–172, 175, 184, 185, 187, 196, 197, 208, 212, 214, 256, 264, 268, 291, 295, 311, 313, 315
Estonian 3, 211–214, 216–221, 224, 231–233
European languages 19, 77, 249, 309
Even 2, 3, 19, 100, 167–175, 177, 178, 180–188, 243, 253, 280
– Bystraja dialect 181, 182, 185
– Lamunkhin dialect 173, 185
– Tompo dialect 167, 171, 172
Evenki 168, 187

Finnish 3, 8, 9, 14, 18, 20, 25, 26, 149–152, 157, 163, 217, 224
French 2, 8–10, 12, 13, 15, 16, 18, 21, 26–28, 150, 153, 164, 170, 268, 296, 311

– Southern ~ 16
– Southwestern ~ 15, 18, 21

Georgian 122, 147, 246
German 90, 170, 180, 210, 212, 279, 294
Godoberi 251, 252
Gulf Arabic Pidgin 286

Hiberno-English 315, 316
Hindi 3, 146, 263, 265–270, 272, 273, 279–281, 286
Hindi-Urdu 122, 147
Hinuq 241, 245, 247, 248, 251, 253, 256
Hungarian 77, 122, 145, 146

Indo-Aryan languages 265, 266, 29–299
Indo-European languages 24, 29, 77
Ingush 239, 242, 254
Irish (Irish Gaelic) 315, 316
Italian 79, 80, 95–102, 106, 108, 114, 150
Italo-Romance 2, 95–97, 100, 106, 117
Italo-Romance (dialect of)
– Acquaro (Calabria) 95, 107, 111, 113
– Anacapri (Campania) 95, 106, 109
– Ascoli Piceno (Marche) 95, 111
– Badalucco (Liguria) 95
– Felino (Emilia) 95, 101, 103–105
– Ferrara (Emilia) 95, 109
– Gallo (Marche) 95, 104–106, 116, 117
– Gambettola (Romagna) 95, 109
– Grosio (Lombardy) 95, 111, 115, 116
– Grosseto (Tuscany) 95, 111
– Guardiagrele (Abruzzo) 95, 109
– Gubbio (Umbria) 95, 109, 113
– Milano (Lombardy) 95
– Modica (Sicily) 95, 111–113
– Polignano a Mare (Apulia) 95, 106, 113
– Premosello Chiovenda (Piedmont) 95, 114
– Santa Croce di Magliano (Molise) 95, 104, 109
– Soleto (Apulia) 95, 106, 109
– Squinzano (Apulia) 95, 111, 113
– Tursi (Basilicata) 95, 109

Japanese 2, 46, 49, 55–57, 59, 61, 63, 72, 73, 77, 79, 147
Jarawara 81
Javanese 286
Jordanian Pidgin Arabic 286

Karitiâna 77, 82, 88, 89, 91, 92
Kashmiri 122, 147
Korean 73
Kumyk 49

Lak 242, 250, 251
Lezgian 239, 240, 242

Malagasy 122, 146
Malay 3, 286, 305, 307–323
Malayalam 297
Mandarin 3, 46, 49, 77, 108, 191, 193, 195–198, 202, 206–208, 210
Marathi 266

Nagh-Daghestanian 2, 3, 239, 240, 242, 243, 248, 250, 251, 253, 254, 256–258
Northern Sami 8, 14, 24

Oceanic and Papuan languages 289
Ojibwe 49

Persian 47–49
Pidgin Madam (PM) 3, 285–301
Prakrit 266

Romance 10, 95, 114
Russian 46, 49, 50, 181, 188, 281

Sami 8, 9, 14, 24
Samic languages 24
Sanskrit 266
Saudi Asian Pidgin 286
Sechelt (Sháshíshálh) 46, 47
Serbo-Croatian 279
Shonam / Moorish Tamil / Sri Lankan Muslim Tamil 307–311, 315, 317–322
Sinhala 285, 286, 296–301, 307, 319
Sinhala (Colloquial, SIN) 285, 286, 297, 298
Spanish 46, 49
Sri Lankan Malay 3, 305, 307–322

Tabasaran 243, 244
Tagalog 286
Tamil 286, 297, 299, 307, 308, 312, 313, 316–318, 320
Tsakhur 242–244, 250, 253, 254
Tsez 250–254, 256
Tunisian 49
Turkish 47, 48, 122, 146, 256

Urdu 146, 286
Urdu Pidgin Arabic 286

Wari' 77, 81, 82, 85–88, 91, 92

Yiddish 314, 315